Cirque Global

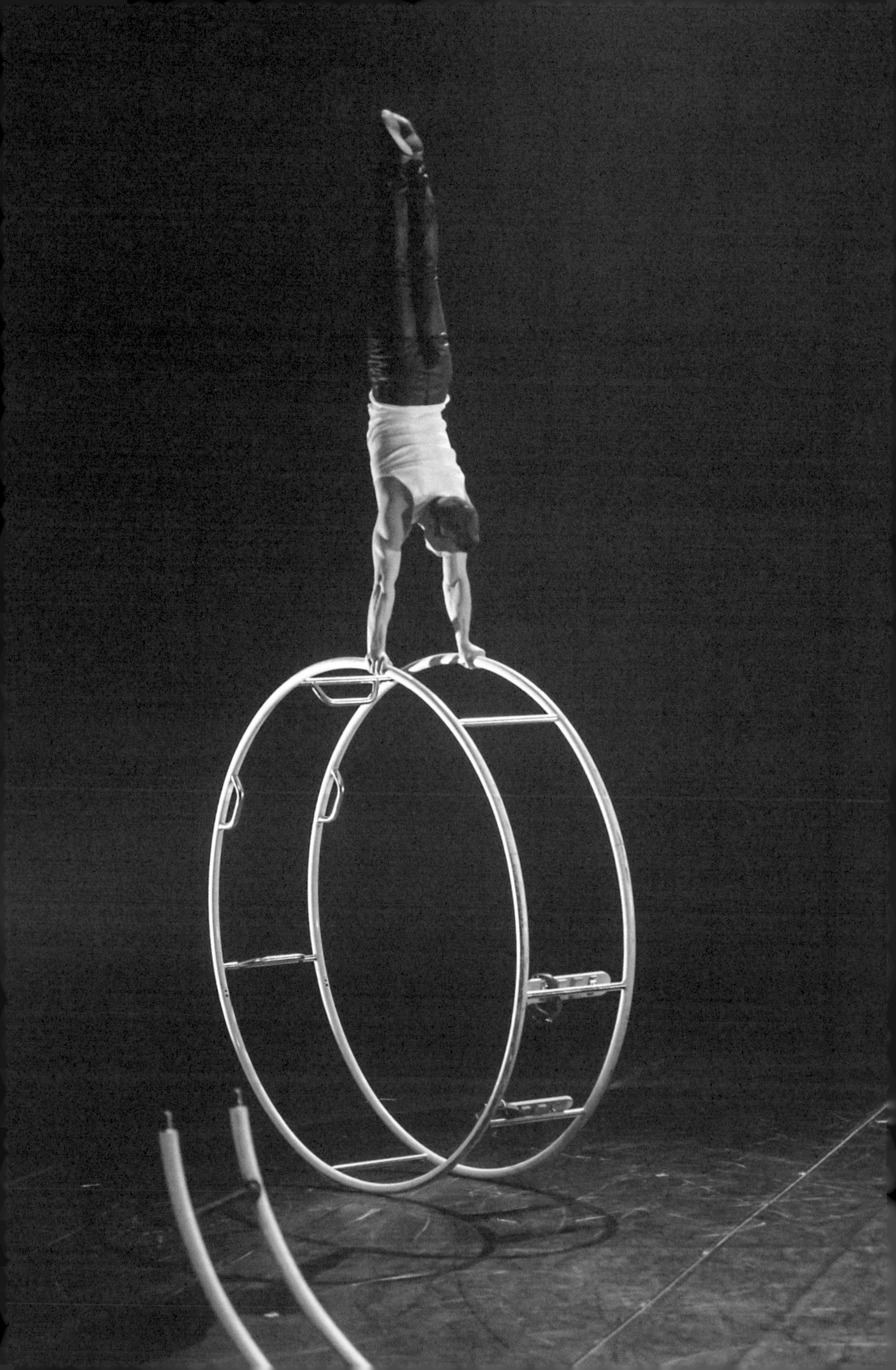

Louis Patrick Leroux and Charles R. Batson, Editors

Cirque Global

Quebec's Expanding Circus Boundaries

McGill-Queen's University Press
Montreal & Kingston • London • Chicago

ISBN 978-0-7735-4672-1 (cloth)
ISBN 978-0-7735-4673-8 (paper)
ISBN 978-0-7735-9870-6 (ePDF)

Legal deposit second quarter 2016
Bibliothèque nationale du Québec

Printed in Canada on acid-free paper

This book has been published with the help of a grant from the Canadian Federation for the Humanities and Social Sciences, through the Awards to Scholarly Publications Program, using funds provided by the Social Sciences and Humanities Research Council of Canada.

Funding has also been provided by the Aid to Research Related Events (ARRE) Program of the Office of the Vice-President, Research and Graduate Studies, Concordia University.

McGill-Queen's University Press acknowledges the support of the Canada Council for the Arts for our publishing program. We also acknowledge the financial support of the Government of Canada through the Canada Book Fund for our publishing activities.

Library and Archives Canada Cataloguing in Publication

Cirque global : Quebec's expanding circus boundaries / Louis Patrick Leroux and Charles R. Batson, editors.

Includes bibliographical references and index.
Issued in print and electronic formats.
ISBN 978-0-7735-4672-1 (cloth).–ISBN 978-0-7735-4673-8 (paperback).
–ISBN 978-0-7735-9870-6 (ePDF)

1. Circus–Québec (Province). 2. Circus–Québec (Province)–History.
3. Cirque du Soleil–History. I. Leroux, Louis Patrick, 1971–, editor
II. Batson, Charles R., editor

GV1805.C3C57 2016 791.309714 C2016-900709-X
C2016-900710-3

Contents

II Cirque Brands

III Dramaturgy and Aesthetics

IV Circus Problematized

Illustrations and Tables

All photos and illustrations used with permission.

Illustrations

Tables

Acknowledgments

This project would not have been possible without the generous support of many individuals, associations, and companies who believed that the time was ripe for such a collection to act as a cornerstone to scholarship both on circus emanating from Quebec and on contemporary circus cultures that this art form has influenced.

Concordia University in Montreal has been a constant support for various stages of the book, from the initial seed-grant for travel to Las Vegas to understand Cirque du Soleil's presence there to its assistance in the translation of French-language articles and further material aid for the publication of this volume. Union College in Schenectady, New York, has offered significant support through its Humanities Faculty Development Funds and its conference travel monies. Montreal's École nationale de cirque has also offered constant moral and logistical support without which this project could never have taken form.

The Canadian Social Sciences and Humanities Research Council offered funding through its Connections Conference and Workshop Grant program for the "State of Circus Research in Quebec Workshop Session on the Models and Conditions of Possibility." This initial event brought together many of the scholars represented in this collection and was held in September 2012 at Concordia University, McGill University, and the École nationale de cirque, with further support offered by the McGill Institute for the Study of Canada.

A number of scholars received research funding or postdoctoral funding from the Social Sciences and Humanities Research Council and the Fonds québécois de la recherche sur la société et la culture specifically for research published in this book. Support from the Natural Sciences and

Engineering Research Council–funded Canada Industrial Research Chair in Colleges in Circus Arts has also been essential to forging new, often unexpected, links and to conducting research at the École nationale de cirque.

This book has been published with the help of a grant from the Federation for the Humanities and Social Sciences, through the Awards to Scholarly Publications Program, using funds provided by the Social Sciences and Humanities Research Council of Canada. This book has also received generous support from Concordia University's Office of the Vice-President, Research and Graduate Studies, through its Aid to Research Related Events, Publication, Exhibition and Dissemination Activities program.

We offer heartwarm thanks to our editorial and research assistants who aided us through this process. Our eagle-eyed and clear-headed editorial assistant, Nicole Nolette, prepared the initial manuscript. Geneviève Robichaud worked as a research assistant to Louis Patrick Leroux and provided invaluable help in organizing the initial conference and preparing the expanded book proposal for submission. Joel Mason and Alisan Funk relieved the strained eyes of this book's editors in their work as research assistants in preparing the volume's final form, and Clara Nencu offered careful assistance in preparing the index.

Thanks go to Professors Debbie Folaron and Danièle Marcoux at Concordia University for having coordinated, supervised, and made possible the translation of the French-language chapters. Thanks also to their translation students – Ann Marie Boulanger, Tania Grant, Caitlin Stall-Paquet, Tiffany Templeton, Aimee Wall, and Michelle Wong – who took the exercise seriously and offered the strong work showcased here. Thank you to Debbie Folaron for her careful revisions of those translations.

We would like to express our gratitude specifically to the École nationale de cirque de Montréal's Anna-Karyna Barlati (librarian), Patrice Aubertin (director of research and teaching training), and Myriam Villeneuve (assistant to the director of research) for their advice and unwavering support throughout the entire process.

Thanks also go to Michele Kaplan, research facilitator for the Faculty of Arts and Science at Concordia, for having had the essential insight, a few years ago, to bring together researchers working on Quebec circus from various fields and disciplines and suggesting that we find ways to work together.

Certain chapters have appeared previously, in part or in whole, as articles, and permission was granted by the following journals to authorize their current publication in original English or in English translation. The book's introduction draws on excerpts from Louis Patrick Leroux's articles "Contemporary Circus Research in Québec: Building and Negotiating an Emerging Interdisciplinary Field," *Theatre Research in Canada* 35, no. 2 (2014), and "Le Québec à Las Vegas: pérégrinations postidentitaires dans l'hyper-Amérique," *L'Annuaire théâtral* 45 (2009). Portions of Leroux's "A Tale of Origins: Deconstructing North American 'Cirque' Where Québécois and American Circus Cultures Meet" were originally published as "North-South Circus Circulations: Where Québécois and American Circus Cultures Meet" in *Québec Studies* 58 (2014). The original article can be accessed at http://liverpool.metapress.com/content/122810. An earlier version of the chapter was also woven into the introduction to a 2014 special issue of *Québec Studies*, "North-South Circus Circulations between Québec and the U.S." We would like to thank the American Council for Quebec Studies and the University of Liverpool Press for their permission to print a reworked version of these articles.

"The Multiple Bodies of Cirque du Soleil" by Erin Hurley is a revised and translated version of "Les corps multiples du cirque du Soleil," *Globe: Revue internationale d'études québécoises* 11, no. 2 (2008). Sylvain Lavoie's chapter, "The Last Man in Quebec: Between Circus and Religion," is a revised and translated version of "Le dernier homme, entre cirque et religion," published in *Spirale* 227 (2009). Simon Harel's "A Las Vegas of the North? The Architectural Brutalism of Cirque du Soleil" is a revised version of an article originally published in French as "Un Las Vegas du Nord? Le brutalisme architectural du Cirque du Soleil" in *L'Annuaire théâtral* 45 (2009). Deborah Leslie and Norma M. Rantisi's "Creativity and Place in the Evolution of a Cultural Industry: The Case of Cirque du Soleil" is a revised version of an article published in *Urban Studies* 48, no. 9 (2011).

Other chapters first appeared as papers or presentations. Erin Hurley's "Performance Services: The Promises of Cirque du Soleil" was originally prepared as a presentation made to the Montreal Working Group on Circus Research on 22 October 2010. Pascal Jacob's "The Québécois Circus in the Concert of Nations: Exchange and Transversality" is a revised and updated version of his keynote address at The State of Circus Research in Quebec conference, held at Concordia University, McGill University, and the National Circus School on 21 September 2012. Jennifer Spiegel's chapter, "Singular Bodies, Collective Dreams: Socially Engaged Circus Arts and the 'Quebec Spring,'" draws upon "Singular Bodies, Collective Dreams and the Making of a Mass Movement: How Street Circus Helped Create the

'Maple Spring,'" a paper presented at the 2012 conference. The chapter by Sylvain Lafortune, Jon Burtt, and Patrice Aubertin, "Introducing Decision Training into an Elite Circus Arts Training Program," synthesizes their 96-page report on the topic – *L'introduction de l'entraînement à la prise de décision dans la formation supérieure en arts du cirque et ses effets sur les strategies d'enseignement sur l'apprentissage et sur la performance* – produced in 2014 under the auspices of the National Circus School.

Quebec circus companies and artists were very generous in allowing us to use their photos. Thanks to École nationale de cirque, Cirque du Soleil, Les 7 doigts de la main, Cirque Éloize, Compagnia Finzi Pasca, Nord Nord Est, Cirque Alfonse, Throw2Catch, and Nadère Arts Vivants.

We would like to offer specific thanks to various individuals, some of whom are mentioned above, who particularly facilitated our quest to document and showcase the art and artists of Quebec's *cirque global*: Anna-Karyna Barlati and Christophe Rousseau of the École nationale de cirque; Stéphane Zummo and Marlène Lemyre of Cirque du Soleil; Marion Bellin and Joanie Leroux-Côté of Les 7 doigts de la main; Sylvie Krauss Baumann, formerly of Cirque Éloize; Geneviève Dupéré and Viviana Cangialosi of Compagnia Finzi Pasca; Anna Ward and Benoît Landry of Nord Nord Est; Andréane Leclerc of Nadère Arts Vivants; Alain Francoeur; the entire Cirque Alfonse company; and Samuel Roy of Throw2Catch. Thanks as well to Jen Reimer for editorial assistance in formatting the images at various stages.

And finally, a huge expression of gratitude goes to McGill-Queen's University Press and editor Jonathan Crago for their support and courage in venturing into a new field of inquiry. Additional thanks to Ellie Barton for her engaged copy editing and proofreading.

PROLOGUE

Reading Quebec's Expanding Circus Boundaries

Charles R. Batson

This book has been organized to offer both a cogent telling and a sharp analysis of the multiple tales of origin, transmission, and disruption marking Quebec's contemporary circus scenes. Presented as they are in dialogue with each other, our authors together point to, explore, and offer a critical gaze on the multiple shapes and expressions of what has, over the course of a few short years, become a globally influential art form. In its overview of the current state of Québécois circus production and the scholarship that has grown to give us vocabularies and ways of seeing, Louis Patrick Leroux's introduction reminds us that this current collection comprises the very first academic book that offers both a deep and a broad look at these particular contemporary circus arts that are influencing performances around the world. As Leroux tells us, "From the first touring productions in Quebec of Ricketts's travelling circus in the late 1790s to Quebec's unexpected place, today, among the circus nations of the world, the story and history of Quebec circus provides fertile ground for research and exploration" (21). Our contributors point us to the rich discoveries, provocative questions, and intriguing analyses sparked by close attention to the *cirque* and *cirques* emanating from Quebec.

Quebec on Planet Circus

This book's first section, Quebec on Planet Circus, opens with a foundational piece by Pascal Jacob that explores what he calls the "exchange and transversality" that have garnered Quebec's cirques their noted and notable dominance on the world's stages. This prominent French circus historian – and jet-setting artistic director of Cirque Phénix and Cirque de

i.1 Gilles Ste-Croix stilt-walking, 1980

demain, talent scout for Franco Dragone, and sometime costume designer for the Barnum and Bailey and Ringling Bros circuses – here declares that, as of the early 2000s, Québécois circus has written a new page in "circus history worldwide" (32). In his historical analysis, after periods of influence on circus aesthetics and practices that were, since the late eighteenth century, led in turns by the English, French, Germans, Americans, and

Soviets, "Quebec [is] the new world of the circus" (30). Pascal points to the "planetary earthquake" (28) that was the 1984 founding of Cirque du Soleil but goes on to note the important maturation and expansion of the Québécois circus scene beyond any one, albeit iconic, company. For Pascal, it was this diversity of expression, supported by a world-class educational institution, the École nationale de cirque de Montréal, that has given to the Québécois circus arts their position of worldwide influence.

Louis Patrick Leroux's "A Tale of Origins: Deconstructing North American 'Cirque' Where Québécois and American Circus Cultures Meet" serves as an important companion piece to Jacob's analysis of the place and influence of Quebec's circuses beyond provincial and national borders. Focusing on the historical relationships between Quebec's circuses and those of the United States, Leroux looks back on periods predating that 1984 watershed year. Working from previously neglected scholarly literature and historical accounts of circus activity, Leroux observes that "Quebec and the United States have had a long shared circus history" (52), with an oft-repeated pattern of Quebec "steering its talent southward and providing northern venues for touring shows" (52). Late nineteenth-century circus artists such as Louis Cyr and Louis Durand find life in Leroux's analysis not only as important artists of their period but also as noteworthy early precursors to the entrepreneurial Québécois *circassiens* that have influenced American circus life since the closing years of the twentieth century. Leroux's analyses further our understanding of the context and content of the Québécois *cirques*, from the Soleil through Cirque Éloize to Cavalia and Les 7 doigts de la main, that distinguish the contemporary North American scene.

"Are Quebec Circuses of Foreign Origin?" pursues this section's examination of cross-border influences, here through a focus on performances by English and American troupes in the province of Quebec. Presenting original archival material tracing these foreign artists' scores of visits to Quebec over the course of one hundred years, Julie Boudreault points to the ever-popular pantomime as having particular staying power in what developed as Québécois art. Her survey closes with a reference to the 1967 visit of the Ringling Bros Barnum and Bailey Circus to Montreal's World Exposition, a signal moment in the period when "American circus's undisputed reign [came] to an end" (61) and post-Expo Montreal became known as a global city, with its arts moving onto the world stage. Boudreault continues the project laid out by Jacob and Leroux to chart the construction of

i.2 From *La Vie*, with Emilie Bonnavaud and Sébastien Soldevila, Les 7 doigts de la main (7 Fingers)

Quebec's contemporary circus scene. With her new research added to theirs, we come to understand more fully the influences of and on a Québécois cirque global.

Cirque Brands

The second section, Cirque Brands, explores several of the particular marks left by these increasingly influential Québécois circus troupes and artists. The three chapters presented here examine products, productions, and images related to the biggest, oldest, and richest of Quebec's *nouveaux cirques*, Cirque du Soleil, and its billion-dollar atlas-straddling enterprises and clear brand orientation. A pioneer in scholarship on Quebec's circus arts, Erin Hurley opens this section with new writing that moves beyond her early focus on "the production side of Cirque du Soleil[:] the ways in which the Cirque's global aesthetic has helped to create its market niche, build its brand, and inform the company's multinational organizational structure" (71). In this short but powerful chapter, Hurley presents what may be seen as a position piece that poses new questions about the "reception side" (72) of Cirque du Soleil's productions and builds on her more recent research on the role of affect in the performing arts (see, for example, Hurley 2010). The question, for example, "What kind of 'experience' is Cirque du Soleil selling?" (76) leads, for Hurley, to an understanding of what she calls a "performance service" (74), a sold-and-bought product that provokes and manages certain feelings and emotions in an economic exchange favourable to the maintenance of Cirque du Soleil as a purveyor of such goods. Hurley leaves us noting that these goods have essentially become an "experience" that contributes to a new economy inflected by brandscaping (see Klingmann 2007), in which consumers seek out not only objects but sensations and lifestyles, and in which producers seek to both stoke and slake such desires.

Sylvain Lavoie's "The Last Man in Quebec: Between Circus and Religion," appearing here in expanded form from its influential 2009 French-language publication in *Spirale*, reminds us of the popular celebration of Cirque du Soleil and Guy Laliberté – Cirque du Soleil's founder and, until its recent sale, CEO – through which the company and the man are granted near-mythical status as the source of the "radiance of our nation" (79). In Lavoie's evocative language, this "divine posture" (84) forms and informs the centrality and importance that Quebecers give to the troupe and that the company, with Laliberté as its "Guide" for some thirty years, has given to itself. Drawing on Nathalie Heinich's (2005) notions of where elitism inflects artistic vocations, Lavoie gives a trenchant analysis of Laliberté's long-standing status and the popularity of the images circulated about the company. Not merely associated with an older "paradigm of the romantic artist" (81), Laliberté, for Lavoie, serves perhaps as a new god in a nominally secular post–Quiet Revolution Quebec: a god of self-determination and self-sufficiency, created in an ethos of flight and individualized accomplishment, reflecting positively onto the collective but not necessarily implicating it.

In her "Circus and Gentrification," the prolific performance studies scholar Susan Bennett joins Lavoie and Hurley in an examination of circus as a cultural product as she explores the role that Cirque du Soleil productions have played in revitalizing neighbourhoods in particular cities. Looking specifically at Portland, Oregon; Vancouver, British Columbia; and Los Angeles, California, Bennett offers cogent analyses linking Cirque

i.3 Guy Laliberté, 1981

du Soleil's performances to the "business of creating and maintaining place identity" (85). In their desire to increase revenue streams, reverse urban blight, and attract tourist dollars, these cities worked to attract the productions of Cirque du Soleil and then sell its products as newly integral aspects of their urban environment. But the success of these products, Bennett suggests in her discussion of the failed venture of *Iris* in downtown Los Angeles, "cannot be understood in isolation, as constructed from the quality of the company's performance work" (96); Cirque's very global brand is, in Bennett's final analysis, dependent on intricate interworkings in the local terrain.

Dramaturgy and Aesthetics

The book's third section, Dramaturgy and Aesthetics, proposes three ways of writing about the circus arts. This section's opening chapter, my own "Les 7 doigts de la main and Their Cirque: Origins, Resistances, Intimacies," offers the first in-depth analysis of the Montreal-based troupe Les 7 doigts de la main (known in English as the 7 Fingers), which has now joined

Cirque du Soleil as a powerful force of the *nouveau cirque québécois*. Much of the existing scholarly literature on Quebec's cirques has focused on the brightly shining Cirque du Soleil; this chapter, in both its length and depth, calls attention to at least one of the influential troupes founded since the early 2000s that has contributed, beyond Cirque du Soleil, to Jacob's notion of "Quebec as the new world of circus" (30). In these pages, I explore the 7 Fingers' "aesthetics of intimacy and authenticity" (100), which resists certain dominating practices of the older Cirque du Soleil. Examining this troupe's principal productions since their 2002 founding, I also look back to the fertile years of the 1980s to suggest that some of the intimist and physical charge of the 7 Fingers' shows draw on "a heightened physical language of performance – the *nouveau bouger montréalais*" (100) – that has thrived in Montreal's streets and on its stages. I close with an analysis of how the writings of Roland Barthes might help us understand the power and function of the tropes of authentic, intimate exchange that this troupe's works engage.

From its initial 2008 French-language publication in *Globe*, Erin Hurley's "The Multiple Bodies of Cirque du Soleil" has influenced and been cited by many circus scholars, including several whose writings are featured in this volume. Appearing here in English for the first time, this chapter presents, in Hurley's characteristically clear language, a certain taxonomy of the extraordinary bodies that populate and form the productions of Cirque du Soleil. Focusing on the big-top show KOOZÄ, Hurley offers analyses that build on David Graver's (2005) notions of "character body," "performer body," and "fleshy body"; she points to the multiple layers of meaning at play on the artists' bodies themselves in an art that, in her analysis, cannot fully escape its history of exhibiting the "freak." As scholarship in circus studies begins to take both more solid form and higher flight, Hurley's chapter adds an important vocabulary describing bodily exceptionalism.

Karen Fricker's "'Somewhere between Science and Legend': Images of Indigeneity in Robert Lepage and Cirque du Soleil's *Totem*" adds new scholarship to her earlier examinations of Robert Lepage's work for the Cirque. Exploring in particular the engagement of his 2010 *Totem* with themes of indigeneity and with indigenous artists, Fricker suggests that, even as Lepage may have wished to join a recognition and "celebration of indigenous cultures" (157) arguably on the rise in North American theatrical productions, his work ultimately "became entangled in representational systems that complicate the productive cultural work he undertakes"

(143). In Fricker's nuanced analysis, Lepage ends up both undercutting and conjuring "Western assumptions and cultural shorthands around questions of evolution and progress" (157). Grounding her analyses in the director's aesthetic and dramatic choices present in the show itself, Fricker joins Hurley and myself in explorations of the meanings created and transmitted from and across these troupes' performance spaces.

Circus Problematized

The three chapters presented here point to wide and fertile fields of inquiry associated with reflections on the ethos and practices of circus cultures and enterprises. Together, the three authors join lines of inquiry already begun in these pages to look critically at what is being communicated through certain choices and customs – and, importantly, to what purpose. These contributors often offer challenging critiques of circus's business decisions both locally and abroad, not shying away from important ethical issues.

Mediation and communication specialist Isabelle Mahy's contribution, "Creativity's Tug-of-War between Artists and Managers: A Mediator's Perspective on the Case of Cirque du Soleil's 'Complexe Cirque,'" examines the actual, day-to-day discussions and decisions marking the development and subsequent abandonment of a Cirque du Soleil project, in the early 2000s, to create Complexe Cirque, a cultural, creative, and intellectual pole in downtown Montreal. Mahy draws on her first-hand exposure to those consultations and conflicts to explore what results when differing cultures from within a creative industry – here, artists and managers – find themselves in necessary, if friction- filled, dialogue with each other. With Mahy, we see that the successes and failures of Cirque's management practices may well be revelatory of the challenges of other large artistic enterprises. We also recover the value of mediation and of mediators in the melding of skills, talents, and goals.

Major Quebec scholar Simon Harel adds his voice to this section's critical gaze on the industry's practices and their public perception through this first English-language publication of his "A Las Vegas of the North? The Architectural Brutalism of Cirque du Soleil." In its placement here, this chapter reflects back on work on circus brands from this book's second section as it examines the presence of Cirque du Soleil "in the urban landscape" (181) of a Montreal desirous of repositioning itself within discourses on architecture, entertainment, and urban development. Focusing on Cirque du Soleil's early- to mid-2000s pursuit of its ultimately failed casino project for the Peel Basin in Montreal's Pointe-Saint-Charles neighbourhood, Harel writes in a tone that echoes that of Lavoie as he suggests that Cirque du Soleil exploited a fantasy image of enterprise and urbanity. Harel's chapter engages in dialogue with such sources as the writings of theorist Robert Venturi and comments in the popular press, closing on a hint of the power of public resistance to officialized and capital-rich projects that adopt what could be seen as a brute language of size, strength, materiality, and functionality.

In her "The Chinese Connection: The Transnational Origins of Québécois Circus Arts," Tracy Zhang continues this book's focus on the border-crossing aspects of Quebec's cirque global, exploring the subtleties and possible para-diplomatic implications of the international nature of this circus. In her analysis, Cirque du Soleil in particular has not only served since the early years as the noted employer of scores of Chinese artists but has also drawn on Chinese circus performance structures to construct its now world-recognized aesthetics. In turn, this Quebec-based company has influenced how Chinese creators wish to conceive of productions sold as made-in-China. As Zhang writes, "few people are aware that the recent recruitment of Quebec artists [to help create these "made-in-China" circus productions] has a historical dimension linked to China's socialist acrobatics and also to the emergence of Québécois circus arts" (202). Offering important insight into the China-Quebec connections, Zhang's chapter draws on information gathered from archival research and from personal interviews with Chinese artists. With Zhang, we get perspective not only on labour practices and institutional governance; we get a glimpse of the drives and choices of real individuals working in a particularly complex field. Her critical gaze on these transnational movements further helps us see the "international, global, hybridized culture of reinvented circus" (11) now operating in and out of Quebec.

Affecting Change

The contributors to this book's fifth section, Affecting Change, examine three areas where circus cultures, enterprises, and practices bring change to their surrounding environments and related institutions. Cultural geographers Deborah Leslie and Norma Rantisi, in this revised version of their 2011 "Creativity and Place in the Evolution of a Cultural Industry: The

Case of Cirque du Soleil" from the influential journal *Urban Studies*, open this section with an examination of how discourses and policies related to space and place may both mark and be marked by impulses and practices of the creative enterprises that engage them. As they (re)tell the story of Cirque du Soleil's stellar rise in global influence, Leslie and Rantisi "argue that the company's evolution has been a *place*-dependent process and has relied on geographically and historically specific resources tied to the Montreal region" (238). Their geographers' voice further calls us to focus on "the purposive action of agents who mobilized change by giving meaning to and enabling nascent synergies" (238). Their analyses respond to their own call for "an acknowledgment of how history and place matter for future prospects, and a view of history as 'made' rather than simply 'inherited'" (239). In doing so, Leslie and Rantisi offer an important way of "explaining why this global firm [Cirque du Soleil] represents a place-based phenomenon" (239).

"Introducing Decision Training into an Elite Circus Arts Training Program" by Sylvain Lafortune, Jon Burtt, and Patrice Aubertin explores the change that comes both to a school and to its students when new pedagogies are deployed. Founded in 1981, the École nationale de cirque de Montréal (National Circus School) offered training originally modelled on Soviet-inspired, high-performance elite programs. Although the school later integrated interdisciplinary pedagogical approaches, some observers have suggested that its early relationships with major industry players remained arguably close. In later years, however, outside scholars have been invited to participate in the creation and development of instructional practices at the school, and this chapter stands as a major contribution to this cross-pollination of research and practice. The authors, all instructors at this school of international renown at the time of their work, introduced, on a trial basis, the sports-training approach known as Decision Training. They document here, for the first time in the scholarly literature, this approach's effect on teaching and learning practices in an elite circus program. Of particular value are the qualitative analyses resulting from interviews with students and coaches, yielding new insight into the challenges and potential rewards of changing pedagogies. In its placement here, this chapter reminds us of the necessary integrations of the physical with the aesthetic and the artistic that lie at the heart of the high-performance circus arts emanating from Quebec.

Jennifer Beth Spiegel, in her "Singular Bodies, Collective Dreams: Socially Engaged Circus Arts and the 'Quebec Spring,'" offers an important

i.4 "Le livre des souhaits," research-creation workshop at l'École nationale de cirque, 2007. Artists: Guillaume Biron, Valerie Cote, Gisle Henriet, and Nael Jammal. Director: Sharon Moore

analysis of the potential to retool and redeploy the circus arts for social change. After tracing the development of what she calls "the interrelated histories of professional, social, and alternative circus initiatives" (267), Spiegel explores how the "Quebec Spring" – the popular protests of early 2012 initiated by students revolting against announced tuition hikes – augmented and rallied "various social currents within the circus community." This event, she argues, marked a distinct moment for the development of socially engaged circus performance. This moment is alive with paradox: Speigel notes that the alternative circus was nourished by government- and industry-supported institutions; for example, various protesters used their government-funded École nationale de cirque de Montréal–trained skills in their demonstrations. Her analysis calls attention to the expansion of socially engaged circus artists, troupes, and movements that both fed, and were fed by, the protests of the Quebec Spring. She concludes by considering the currently active and productive interdependence among the multiple strands within circus scenes in Quebec and beyond.

i.5 From *Fibonacci Project* in Mexico, 7 Fingers

Epilogue

This book has taken as a principal point of departure an explicit engagement with and encouragement of the emerging scholarship on Quebec's circus arts. Even as we reprise particularly influential pieces, including some that originally appeared in French, we worked to give space to research and writing that had, prior to this book's publication, existed only in early stages of development. Indeed, the large majority of our chapters present brand-new research. We saw ourselves acting as midwives of sorts, encouraging our colleagues as they produced their then-nascent work and became even more actively involved in the emerging field of contemporary circus studies, a field that bridges multiple disciplines. The lion's share of the scholarship taking form as we prepared these pages was focused on Cirque du Soleil. Some materials, including my own, gave attention to Les 7 doigts de la main, and some others to the École nationale de cirque. Scholarly writings on Cirque Éloize and other companies had yet to take shape. Other writing, touching on histories of this nouveau cirque québécois, offering perspectives on the art of criticism, and engaging in direct conversation with artists and practitioners, *did* take form as this book was being prepared; these interesting and important pieces, alas, could not be included in this already voluminous tome.

We see this volume as a call for future work and investigation. Quebec circus arts should not be understood as a homogenous environment that gravitates exclusively around Cirque du Soleil, for example, even as one of course cannot understate the company's continued influence as a draw for circus practitioners and a well-versed creative class. Nor can one fully understand this globally influential art form without engaging in dialogue with its artists, producers, and critics. We also see possibilities for immediate application of the research and developments newly examined in this book's pages. Extrapolations from Zhang's work on transnational exchange and hybridity, for example, will allow researchers to explore more fully the stakes at play when Russian authorities employed members of Les 7 doigts' Montreal-based creative team to craft portions of the opening ceremonies of the 2014 Sochi Winter Olympics, which ostensibly showcased Russian culture, history, and art. Theorists and historians can also draw on Spiegel's presentations, to take another example, in reclaiming and resituating the politically engaged aspects of the street arts in which several

i.6 From Daniele Finzi Pasca's *La Verità*, 2013

of the original creators of Cirque du Soleil participated prior to their troupe's founding. Many of these moments that deserve closer attention in light of this new research, including Gilles Ste-Croix's work with the US-based Bread and Puppet Theater,[1] point back to the complexities of the border-crossing, contestatory origins of what has become a powerful, capital-filled institution.

This collection's epilogue highlights some of the key points in the constellation of forces driving Quebec's current and future cirque global. The epilogue also presents some of the younger troupes and artists working and creating in the province and making a name for themselves both in and beyond its borders. It thus echoes the call made throughout these pages for increased attention to the constantly developing arts of Quebec circuses and their presence and influence on the world's stages. As such it underscores the impulses behind the future work of Montreal's growing Working Group on Circus Research, which hopes among other things to document oral histories, analyze Quebec's pre-nouveau circuses, and explore the "others" of circus who lie outside or beyond the mainstream.

We further offer, in the book's closing pages, a glossary of circus terminology, in order to give even more precise and complex vocabulary for research on this art and its creators, producers, and critics – research that we hope most fervently will grow from the foundations presented in this book.

As Louis Patrick Leroux intimates in the introduction, there are multiple paths leading into the study of Quebec's circuses. My own path involved early in-depth focus on the dance and theatre scenes of another particularly vibrant site, the Paris of the early decades of the twentieth century, where multiple disciplines came together to give shape to the art forms that in turn influenced the direction of the avant-garde, of modernism, and of the performing and visual arts for the rest of the century (Batson 2005). In the rich materials presented in this collection's pages, it may be tempting to see, with Pascal Jacob, the Quebec of the early part of the twenty-first century playing a similar role for the circus arts of our own contemporary period. It is, of course, future research and future creative endeavours that will ultimately show us the shapes, forms, limits, porosities, and influences of the currently expanding boundaries of this cirque global.

Cirque Global

0.1 *ID*, Cirque Éloize

INTRODUCTION

Reinventing Tradition, Building a Field: Quebec Circus and Its Scholarship

Louis Patrick Leroux

In thirty short years, circus – in its contemporary narrative-driven, animal-free form – has blossomed in Quebec to the extent that it has become a potent cultural and economic symbol of the successful marriage of creativity and, yes, entrepreneurship. Circus is both performing art and business, fundamentally global and multinational in its traditions and the provenance of its artists and, in the case of Quebec, very much presented as a distinctive hybrid model for creativity emerging from a distinct society. This voluminous book was prepared during the year marking Cirque du Soleil's thirtieth anniversary and Cirque Éloize's twentieth. And it was finished in the weeks following the sale of Cirque du Soleil to two global private investment firms – the American-based TPG, a private equity company based in Texas, and the Shanghai-based Fosun – and to Quebec's own pension fund company, the Caisse de dépôt et placement. These cultural and financial changes will no doubt have an impact on the future development of contemporary circus in Quebec and its international reach.

The National Circus School (École nationale de cirque de Montréal) has offered world-class training for thirty-three years, and the third wave of contemporary circuses in Quebec, starting with Les 7 doigts de la main, which emphasizes the individual and the shedding of stage masks and flashy costumes, is nearing its fifteenth-year mark. There have been articles, master's theses, and PhD dissertations on Quebec circus, yet there has not been an academic book offering a perspective both wide and deep on contemporary circus in Quebec, or indeed North America.

The impact of circus on the Montreal economy reached, at its peak, $1 billion annually in direct revenue, not counting the trickle-down effect and impact on secondary and tertiary industries that rely on circus activity locally and abroad.[1] Cirque du Soleil's annual gross revenues reached their peak in 2012, with over 85 per cent coming from the United States through touring shows, product sales, and – mostly – eight permanent Las Vegas productions, with the remainder coming from ten touring productions throughout the world.[2] Its administrative and creative headquarters are situated in Montreal, as are its costumes, properties, sets, multimedia workshops, production and touring offices, and many of its creative partners such as Sid Lee Marketing (with whom Cirque du Soleil created the joint venture Sid Lee Entertainment but subsequently sold much of its stock to another Chinese investment company) and Geodézik (since bought by one of Cirque du Soleil's subsidiaries, 4U2C). Before the recent wave of job cuts (thirty in the fall of 2012, four hundred in the winter of 2013, and depending on sources, close to a thousand through early 2014 and an additional seventy positions in late 2014),[3] Quebec-based expenses accounted for roughly 85 per cent of Cirque's operating budget. Cirque du Soleil's impact, locally, is phenomenal.

However, in a candid exchange with *Wall Street Journal*'s Alexandra Berzon, Guy Laliberté confirmed in December 2014 what had been rumoured for over a year: Cirque du Soleil was indeed positioning itself to increase its value for an eventual sale of up to 30 per cent of its stock value. While such news resonated with some short-term economic sense, the company's concordant firings and business rationalizations were of little comfort or inspiration to those employees who had remained. For close to eighteen months, Cirque du Soleil restructured the company by creating clear "disciplinary" divisions with focused scopes of activities and autonomous reporting, although many of these divisions collaborate on common projects and are all grouped under the Cirque du Soleil brand. Cirque's archives were reduced to a bare-bones structure, and its once proud research and development division was all but dismantled, save for ongoing collaborations with external partners for a time. It has since refocused in-house research and development on high-impact industrial research with immediate returns on evaluating various aspects of performance. Cirque du Soleil then declared that it wanted to reduce its circus activities and to diversify its activities – and sources of revenue.

In April 2015, Guy Laliberté's much mediatized and scrutinized sale of the majority of his Cirque du Soleil shares (90 per cent) to foreign equity investment firms provoked public concern, political outcry, and general consternation in a province particularly sensitive to and aware of the importance of its culture, emerging economy, and sociopolitical and cultural discourse. Some fought for the company to show moral engagement in keeping its headquarters and artistic decision-making in Montreal. For those closer to Cirque du Soleil and its immediate circles, the news came as an inevitable outcome to a frantic and tense few months in which the company had initially sought partners to revitalize and recapitalize one of the largest, live entertainment companies in the world. The outcome wasn't as dire as many predicted. Investment firms most likely won't try to meddle in creative content, nor will they adversely try to dilute a "winning" brand, one for which they paid a substantial sum to add to their "investment platform." It is interesting to consider that Quebec has produced such an unlikely marriage of art and investment in such a short period.

This corporate Walt-Disneyfication of the bohemian troupe from rural Quebec was, perhaps, inevitable, but fortunately for the circus arts emanating from Quebec, Cirque du Soleil does not stand alone as a force in this art form. Like a locomotive, Cirque du Soleil has pulled the development of large numbers of circus artists and companies. And it continues to do so. Its sale to American and Chinese investment bankers whose business is to ensure their assets are profitable and, to a certain extent, driven by prestigious, recognizable brands, should give leverage to what had become a very large, sprawling corporation to accomplish what it might have lost the will and ability to achieve in the past few years. China had long resisted Cirque du Soleil's charms, even though Franco Dragone's presence in Macau and his new show and theatre space in Wuhan revealed the potential and interest in China for contemporary circus. With Cirque du Soleil focusing on noncircus activities and developing new far-flung markets, creative activity will continue to attract talent to Montreal, perhaps allowing for a home-grown scene to finally and fully emerge from the corporation's shadow and come into its own. (For developments in Cirque du Soleil's post-sale China projects as well as the company's "special projects" offshoot, 45 Degrees, see Bergeron 2015a and 2015b.)

The next category of Montreal-based circus companies, Cirque Éloize (in which Cirque du Soleil once had a 49 per cent stake) and the independently run Les 7 doigts de la main (known in the United States as the 7 Fingers), along with their subsidiary companies, have operating budgets of around $10–12 million each.[4] Most of their revenue comes from international touring. Another forty smaller circus companies account for roughly $1 million in direct economic activity in Montreal. I'm not including the

0.2 *Donka*, Compagnia Finzi Pasca

five circus-for-social-change organizations, the École nationale de cirque de Montréal (the only government-funded elite-level school in North America), the twenty "feeder schools" and studios, Montréal Complètement Cirque (the city's annual international circus festival), or the TOHU, North America's only permanent theatre-in-the-round devoted to contemporary circus, which offers a complete subscription season. Quebec schools now regularly offer circus activities as part of their physical education curricula or extracurricular activities. Finally, the province of Quebec, since 2001, has recognized circus as a legitimate art form and has ensured steady provincial funding for more experimental productions through a program exclusively devoted to circus arts.[5] Contemporary circus with its combination of artistic activity and sports ethos has permeated Quebec society in ways that cannot be ignored by the academy.

Following Cirque du Soleil's quick and phenomenal success worldwide, its spectacular success in the United States and effective infiltration into American pop culture with the resulting economic consequences (witness Cirque's presence twice at the Oscars and twice at the Super Bowl, and the integration of circus arts in the acts of musical stars such as Madonna and

P!nk – on this topic see Batson 2014), the very term *cirque* has come to differentiate the high-value artistic brand from the traditional family-oriented circus. *Cirque* has become a buzzword to the point where many American companies and circuses have sought to distinguish themselves from traditional circus – and perhaps share some of Cirque du Soleil's lexical magic – by integrating the French term into their names. As I explain in my "Tale of Origins" chapter in this collection, Cirque du Soleil sought "ownership" of the word *cirque* by trying to obtain a copyright of the word on American soil after an excessive number of companies copied its style and maintained a certain level of confusion with the Québécois company by using the French moniker. Cirque du Soleil sued Florida-based Cirque Inc. (also known as Cirque Productions) but lost the lawsuit in 2004, after a five-year battle reportedly costing each company up to $4 million (Benston 2004). One company's quest to copyright a generic term caused outrage in the French-speaking cirque community, but it nevertheless illustrates to what extent the very term *cirque* has become totemic and pervasive of a clearly recognized world-beat-inflected and highly aestheticized brand in North American culture. However, circus emerging from and being produced in Quebec is more than a single "brand." It offers multiple perspectives on a popular art form unafraid of blurring the boundaries between low and high cultures.

Planet Circus

French circus scholar Pascal Jacob, in a 2012 keynote address at The State of Circus Research in Quebec, a workshop session held at Concordia, McGill, and the National Circus School (a revised and updated version of the talk is included in this book), spoke of Quebec's place among the circus nations. He identified six "circus eras" that could be associated with different countries. England, with its equestrian and military culture, reintroduced the circus in its modern form (1768–1830), while France had its first heyday in refining equestrian acrobatics and introducing the clown (1830–80). The following period (1880–1930) was polarized between Germany, with its introduction of exotic animals and extreme acrobatics, and the United States, with its freak shows, dime museums, and especially its three-ringed extravaganzas. The Soviet Union (1930–80) introduced elite training and focused on artistic expression; France pursued this artistic project and sought to give social significance to circus from the 1970s to the 2000s with its nouveau cirque. Now Quebec, on the coattails of Cirque du Soleil's globalized success and Les 7 doigts de la main's circus of individualized ethos, has become the Western circus nation to emulate or to react against.

Quebec's brand of theatrical, mostly animal-free, contemporary circus[6] born out of French nouveau cirque, Soviet-inspired elite acrobatic training, and American entrepreneurship and showmanship has emerged from a burgeoning nation preoccupied with its own singularity and distinctiveness. Paradoxically, however, its circus sometimes comes across as blandly "global," without local flavour, to audiences seated in front of its presentations of assumed cultural neutrality or, as Karen Fricker has put it, a "purposeful cultural blankness" (2008, 130).

Cirque + Global

Quebec circus offers a fascinating paradox. It is both athletic and aesthetic. It draws on European circus tradition and *commedia dell'arte* tropes, yet only fully came into its own when it sought to break away from explicit circus codes, drawing on the vocabulary of theatre and dance. It stems from a society much concerned about its distinct culture and linguistic survival, a mainly francophone, lapsed Catholic, and mostly left-leaning nation of 8 million surrounded by a mostly English-speaking and neoliberal North American population of 340 million in a globalized society in which English functions as the lingua franca. Quebec's distinctiveness has traditionally been linguistic, cultural, and political. In a sense, circus is very much an incongruous cultural and economic export for a nation whose very existence reposes on these distinctions and its differences from forces of dominance. Cirque du Soleil's emergence as a dominant power in live entertainment worldwide, the omnipresence of Quebec-based and Quebec-trained circus artists across the continents, and Montreal as a New World circus hub: all of this upsets many of the tenets of Quebec national discourse, unless of course one defines and brands "creativity," "know-how," and "technical excellence" as particularly Québécois. Cirque du Soleil took the United States by storm from its 1987 production in Los Angeles – beginning decades of constant touring with multiple shows – to its ongoing domination of the entertainment offerings on the Las Vegas Strip with eight permanent productions in that one city, albeit one totemic of a post-literate entertainment-savvy hyper-America. Cirque's presence has become pervasive in America, and it has established working relationships with major players in the entertainment industries including, as we have seen, Madonna, the Oscars, the Grammies, the Super Bowl, and now Broadway.

While Cirque du Soleil, to Americans, remains vaguely French, and certainly international, its efficient marketing and substantial means of production marks it as decidedly American to all others. Frédéric Martel (2011), in his study of global cultural industries, *Mainstream*, concludes that America produces a "standardized diversity" that is both pervasive and incredibly efficient in its distribution (536). He refers to this model as "Tex-Mex" culture, neither Texan nor Mexican but a tamed, watered-down version of the original properly formatted for export. In a sense, Cirque du Soleil's global success is the result of its now embedded presence in American popular culture and its uncanny integration of its branding and production strategies.

Yet the presence of Quebec circus on most continents cannot simply be explained by Cirque du Soleil's American form of globalism. What of Cavalia's presence in Abu Dhabi in a much modified and culturally sensitive version of its signature show on the Arabian Peninsula (albeit one in which "brownface" and *arabisant* costumes were imposed on the Western cast by the minister of culture)? What of Cirque Éloize's, Les 7 doigts de la main's, and Cirque Alfonse's constant touring of European and American subsidized performing arts venues? What of Les 7 doigts de la main's opening ceremonies at the Sochi Olympics or Daniele Finzi Pasca and Julie Hamelin's closing ceremonies for the same event? What of the decidedly experimental and uncompromising shows by Nord Nord Est or Andréane Leclerc (Nadère Arts Vivants), which combine performance art, dance, and theatre while working within the circus tradition? While it is true that most circus performers have worked for the Big Three (Cirque du Soleil, Éloize, Les 7 doigts de la main) at one point or another, or have been trained at the École nationale de cirque, a veritable *culture* of interdisciplinary creation exists in Montreal that both integrates and confronts artists. It is also, one must add, a subsidized culture, lending credence to Quebec's discourse of cultural distinction. Interestingly, Montreal draws a number of international circus artists who come to work and study and, in many cases, never leave, or in other cases, take away with them a distinct circus culture drawing from many traditions. They are contaminated (following Dawkins's [1976] meme theory) by a model that places creativity and high-level circus training on the same level.

One might argue that there's a world of distinction between a meme and globalism. Globalism was once referred to more positively as the "global village" (McLuhan) but also, more negatively, as "empire" (Hardt and Negri 2000). Patrick Lonergan (2009) writes that "the dominant value in the global theatre network is mobility. Put simply, this involves the ability to move easily around the world" (216). Yet, as Dan Rebellato (2009) has argued, there is also the danger of homogenization, as was seen with the 1980s and 1990s musicals *Cats*, *The Phantom of the Opera*, and *The Lion King*, where producers sought to standardize the liveness and uniqueness of each performance (40–1). The emergence of what Rebellato refers to as "McTheatre" has allowed for global success with hollowed-out versions of shows that entertain without offending and that titillate with spectacle and otherness without alienating audiences.

Goran Therborn (2000) suggests that there are five discourses of globalism (as paraphrased and contextualized by Patrick Lonergan 2009, 18): (1) global capitalism, (2) social criticism, (3) discussions on the nation state and its future, (4) the spread of international-global culture, and (5) ecology (global warming, pandemics). There is often very little overlap in these discourses and, indeed, perspectives of globalism. Quebec-based circus does,

0.3 Abidjan, March 2001. Social circus models promoted by Cirque du Monde

however, engage with a number of these discourses of globalism, as we will see in this collection. Cirque du Soleil's branding and production models fall within the global capitalism model, allowing for the spread of money across national borders and the implication of branding strategies on local consumption allowing money to flow across borders and branding strategies to influence local consumption. The company also engages in social activism and mediation through well-funded philanthropic projects and social circus (spreading its social circus programs, training, and ethos across borders) and in the ecology discourse through One Drop Foundation (its water-themed foundation). However, under new ownership, in October 2015 Cirque du Soleil substantially reduced Cirque du Monde staff and in-house advocates for the social circus initiatives for which their leadership had become legendary and widespread. It is too early to anticipate how the art-for-social-change sector in the circus world will adjust to this sudden change in Cirque du Soleil's corporate responsibility platform. Governmental, cultural, and media references to Quebec circus abroad have served to swell Quebecers' sense of the nation state being in a perpetual state of becoming. Artists and cultural industries are ambassadors for Québécois creativity, ultimately spreading an international, global, hybridized culture of reinvented circus and a reinvested understanding of how to create art that seeks to entertain and enthrall. And now, apparently, to attract international investors.

Early Scholarship

In spite of Cirque du Soleil's commercial and aesthetic domination of the current circus world, and perhaps because of the sometimes triumphalist reiteration by the local media and the state (on this topic see Harvie and Hurley 1999; Hurley 2011; Lavoie 2009b; Leroux 2009a, 2012), scholarship on circus in Quebec was slow to develop, save for a smattering of articles and a handful of theses and dissertations crafted usually as descriptive appreciations of the world-beat aesthetic and the "reinvention" of circus by Cirque du Soleil, and written by academics very much from a safe distance from the scene they were describing. A few exceptions, including Julie Boudreault's (1996, 1999) master's and PhD theses as well as Isabelle Mahy's (2008a) PhD dissertation and later book were pioneering in the sense that the authors did research from within the structures they were investigating. Recently, however, a gradual legitimizing of circus research – for example, with the creation of a research centre and the funding of an

Industrial Research Chair at the National Circus School; the publication of a few special issues devoted to Quebec's contemporary circus in *L'Annuaire théâtral* (2002a, ed. Julie Boudreault and 2009c, ed. Louis Patrick Leroux), *Spirale* (2009b, ed. Sylvain Lavoie), and *Québec Studies* (2014c, ed. Louis Patrick Leroux); and a growing understanding among circus companies and artists of the nature of research and implications for their own practices – has allowed for more extensive experiential work in which students and researchers have access to their objects of study.

Theatre and dance have long allowed student observers without particular incident, yet circus resisted academic scrutiny for cultural and economic reasons. Circus culture has traditionally relied on hard-earned apprenticeship and oral transmission of its trade secrets. What has tended to distinguish (and to position in terms of marketability) one artist over another is not general aptitude, but rather the specificity of their trade – their "trick," rarely described or broken down to outsiders. Add to this the very secretive nature of a highly successful commercial environment known for poaching audience-drawing acts, and you have the makings of a protective milieu, bent on developing its own research and development capabilities independent of academic outsiders. For years, researchers came through with their preconceptions, briefly gathering data, occasionally misreading signs, and quickly moving on to other topics. Only recently has the contemporary circus world in Quebec produced emerging scholars who have an intimate knowledge of the training, practices, and culture of that world and also possess the analytical tools and broader understanding of research needs and practices.[7]

When I started working on circus a mere seven years ago, I had to address concerns about my goals as a researcher. Before anyone talked, before I was allowed "in," they needed to know whether I was coming in as a tourist or making a long-term commitment. Although concerned with objectivity and appropriate scholarly distance, I quickly understood that I had to truly engage with the milieu, to be *present*. To offer an honest, non-complacent reading of it, I first needed to experience it up close through ongoing conversations, panel discussions, and open forums involving practitioners, scholars, and policy-makers on topics that were of vital interest to the community: contractual ethics (Achard et al. 2013), international recruitment of Chinese artists by Cirque du Soleil (Zhang 2011), managing pain in training and in performance (Leclerc, Holmes, and Aubertin 2013), archiving circus production (Barlati and Zummo 2014), and circus as community-building (Wall 2014). Interestingly, these topics were just beginning to appear in scholars' areas of inquiry. Only by listening was I able to gain the practitioners' respect and confidence and draw them into a discussion of scholarly concerns, which are also their own, from dramaturgy (Leroux 2014d) to circus and its "others."

A number of research projects have bridged academic pursuits, pedagogical concerns, and circus's growing interest in understanding its own processes and impact. These include an in-depth exploration of decision training in a high-performance setting (Lafortune, Burtt, and Aubertin 2014, developed as a chapter in this book), the sociocultural impact of social circus (Spiegel 2012a, 2012b, 2014), physical literacy and high-performance training (Kriellaars 2013), thinking and writing about contemporary circus (Fricker et al. 2013), creativity and urban regeneration (Leslie and Rantisi 2010), and the "political body – embodied protest in contemporary circus" (Lavers 2012, 2014), to name but a few recent talks hosted by Montreal's Working Group on Circus Research. My own research into circus dramaturgy combines a study of the vocabulary of circus disciplines with the aesthetic choices made through the narrativization of contemporary productions (Leroux 2013). My interest in nonverbal, theatrical dramaturgy connects with the École nationale de cirque's commitment to develop a coherent vocabulary and eventual program in circus directing and to pursue research into new interactive and immersive technologies in the circus arts.

Montreal Working Group on Circus Research

The working group began in 2010 as an informal gathering of academics interested in the aesthetics, economics, and ethics of Cirque du Soleil as both a force in renewing circus arts in Quebec and in promoting Québécois creativity and commercial innovation. Erin Hurley, Karen Fricker, and I, after having contributed to a special issue on "Le Québec à Las Vegas" for the scholarly journal *L'Annuaire théâtral* (2009), combined forces with economic geographers Norma Rantisi and Deborah Leslie who were already engaged in Cirque-related research. We soon invited colleagues such as Patrice Aubertin and Anna-Karyna Barlati from the École nationale de cirque to participate in the discussions, and it was the most important decision we would make. They openly discussed the issues, challenges, and outcomes of our ongoing research, which we shared in informal seminars.

By the end of the first year and into the second, the working group began to widen its scope to circus practices in Quebec and abroad. Concordia University and the École nationale de cirque, through the working group, formed a research partnership with three objectives: (1) to develop specialized knowledge retention in circus arts training and practice for performers and pedagogues; (2) to disseminate circus-related knowledge through academic and industry channels; and (3) to widen the scope of scholarship and encourage dynamic academic approaches to studying the circus arts (through research creation, experiential practices, economic geography, sociology, and other complementary disciplines).

To fulfill these objectives, the working group initially focused on three thematic axes that correspond to its ongoing work and anticipated fields of investigation: (1) circus pedagogy; (2) historical traditions and current states of circus practices, including discourse, aesthetics, ethics, and economics; and (3) circus dramaturgy, including a series of hands-on experiential explorations between academics and circus artists.

From five or six scholars sharing emerging research at ad hoc meetings at Concordia University to an active list of over two hundred scholars, students, practitioners, pedagogues, and industry players, the Working Group on Circus Research has grown into something of an essential hub for critical thinking on contemporary circus and cultural discourse, branding, and issues of training and pedagogy in both high-performance programs and applied creativity. Our meetings, held at Concordia University, the École nationale de cirque, and occasionally at McGill, now regularly attract between twenty and forty people every six to eight weeks. These meetings and the research emerging from them have also prompted invitations from European research groups and American universities. As this book goes to press in 2016, we have held fifty events, talks, and panels to share our insights and research methods.

An Emerging Field in an Interdisciplinary Research Landscape

That ad hoc discussion group has grown very quickly, and unexpectedly, into a community of scholars and practitioners building a field that departs from theatre and performance studies, as well as from existing American studies of circus history or European heuristic studies of nouveau and contemporary circus. This new field – North American contemporary circus studies – is arising from the initial impetus of studying and understanding the contemporary circus emerging from Quebec, a hybrid scene that combines European circus aesthetics and ethos with American commercial and industrial creativity and practices. In parallel to the working group's emergence from sideshow to partner, the École nationale de cirque has structured its own research activities under a new research centre, establishing university and industry collaborations. It obtained a five-year Canada Industrial Research Chair for Colleges in Circus Arts.[8] The École nationale de cirque has been involved in training much of the talent hired by the most selective circuses worldwide. It has a high-performance program at the high school and collegial levels, and a professional program that includes instructor and circus trainer programs. Just over half of its students are from Quebec, while 10–15 per cent are from the US, 10–15 per cent from France, and 10–15 per cent from other Canadian provinces. There is a consistent representation of the world's nations, from Australia to Germany, Norway to Chile, Russia to Palestine. In 2012–13, for example, there were 184 students enrolled in six programs.[9] The principal focus at the school has been circus training, pedagogy, and promoting its students through its high-value, end-of-year productions held at TOHU. The creation of the Industrial Research Chair in Circus Arts in 2012–13 and the school's growing and active interest in research and innovation has opened up circus culture to formalized research and has encouraged that very community to ask for agency over the research. The funding structure of the Chair, part governmental, part industry-driven, has allowed for a rapprochement between the National Circus School, the Montreal-based partner industries (Cirque du Soleil, Cirque Éloize, Les 7 doigts de la main, and Geodézik), and university researchers. In-depth, experiential research that was not possible a few years ago is slowly developing – to everyone's advantage.

Circus research requires interdisciplinarity in a way that I haven't seen in theatre or dance research, at least not in the form of ongoing, open discussions between researchers from a wide variety of disciplines and theoretical frameworks. One can always anchor research within the disciplinary confines of a particular analysis or reading, but Quebec circus – as a global phenomenon, as a billion-dollar industry, as an emblematic representation of national know-how and innovation – remains steeped in many converging fields: aesthetics, dramaturgy and creative process, cultural politics, nationhood and paradiplomacy, circus training and pedagogy (from high-performance training to physical literacy), ethics, philanthropy, social circus, engineering (massive structures, complex rigging), sports medicine and injury (epidemiology), branding and commerce, urbanism and social spaces,

0.4 Applied exams at l'École nationale de cirque, 2013. Artist: Kyle Driggs

and hands-on research and development stemming from individual companies and the newly developed research and pedagogy nexus at the École nationale de cirque.

Looking ahead, the working group and other circus researchers face a number of challenges. These include finding the time and resources for extensive, immersive research allowing a multidirectional flow of knowledge – knowledge that can be both published in peer-reviewed journals and made useful, in concrete terms, for the studied milieu. Second, we need to foster a sense of legitimacy among colleagues in disciplinary fields baffled by the study of circus, while maintaining an interdisciplinary spirit of collaboration. Third, we are working toward establishing a clearly defined, inter-institutional research centre through which we can funnel and make available to other researchers and students the incredible amount of research emerging from our individual and collective projects.[10] The scope of the field is so large that it cannot be contained by a single Chair, a single institution, or a single working group, for that matter; we will need to start thinking in terms of a multiplication of relatively specialized research poles and methods that can nevertheless share research, resources, and a commitment to a growing and complex field. Finally, circus researchers must negotiate the complexities of doing research within a multilayered commercial, artistic, and pedagogical context where there is constantly at play a fascinating convergence of ethics issues and nondisclosure agreements, all of which underline the materiality and significance of the process and its understanding.

A portrait of current research on Quebec circus must be more than a list of research projects, papers, and publications.[11] It must be the ongoing tale of an emerging field, pulled in every direction by disciplinary and professional concerns, yet brought together by a fundamental engagement in the interdisciplinary nature of a commercially successful performing art that resonates deeply with Quebec's aspirations and its ever-present sense of its own becoming. To date, the Working Group on Circus Research has touched upon aesthetics, criticism, and dramaturgy; we have investigated practice and pedagogy and examined economy, commerce, and branding; and we have explored ethics, social circus, and community building. In a sense, this current collection acts as both a "contemporary circus reader" and a cornerstone for ongoing and future scholarship in an emerging field in and beyond Quebec to encompass North America more generally.

Methodology and Scope

Yet how does one reconcile such disparate objects and methods of study? How can we bridge the scientific, the artistic, the pedagogical, the curricular, the industrial applications, and the management-driven questions, as well as those stemming from cultural discourse and yet others from marketing? Mostly, by reading our object of study through our individual disciplinary methodologies, their codes, expectations, and traditional dissemination methods and journals. While circus, as an inter- or rather a transdisciplinary field, brings researchers together, we perceive the object of study according to our disciplinary and methodological biases, too numerous to detail here.

For years, research had been conducted in discrete silos, not allowing for transdisciplinary curiosity and scrutiny. The emergence of this new field of research was made possible, in part, by encouraging researchers from various disciplines to meet and share their work on a common object. It was further realized with the understanding, at the École nationale de cirque and its partner institutions, of the very value of such research. It could serve, for example, as a legitimizing discursive tool when considering aesthetics, history, cultural discourse, management practices, or analysis of social circus and philanthropy. Such research could also prove to be economically viable. Industrial research, epistemology studies of accident rates and probabilities, physical efficiency models, applications of engineering to circus rigging, research and development of technological tools for circus artists: all of these streams offer a potent return on investment to companies and artists who have opened themselves up to researchers.

To impose a unifying methodological framework would be to limit the scope and depth of the field, artificially constraining the variety of perspectives and objects of study as well as their anticipated value to the contribution of knowledge. However, I can point to an ethos of engagement in research that the Montreal circus scene has come to embrace. Contrary to circus culture's defining protectiveness of its distinctiveness, the ethos of these researchers' engagement has promoted frank discussion and exchange. The regular meetings, the sharing of ongoing work, the discussion and cross-pollination have contributed to collaborative work, much of it unexpected. Circus research has taken me, for example, to work with an engineer on the creative process and to assistant direct a technology and dramaturgy workshop, and I was for a time engaged in a health equity study into the Quebec social circus model as it exists in Ecuador. Other colleagues have similarly moved outside their disciplinary comfort zones.

I'm reminded of structuralist Tzvetan Todorov's (1968) effort to define the hermeneutic field of "poetics," flirting with semiotics, yet essentially trying to bridge the traditional hiatus between "interpretation" and "science" in literary studies. He felt that a disciplinary approach, one founded on science, was needed to take the object of study into its fundamental scientific domain, yet a rigorous disciplinary reading (for instance, a psychological or linguistic or mathematical reading) would not necessarily be relevant to the larger field of literary studies. In the same spirit, contemporary circus research needs disciplinary frameworks, methods, and peer assessments, but it also needs to be read and considered not as a novelty of our originary fields (forever reprising the same banal introductions), but rather as a complement to the knowledge of both the distinct discipline (history, physical literacy, education, aesthetics, performance studies, etc.) and the larger circus studies field. What has emerged over the past few years has been an actual research community driven by a desire to comprehend and analyze contemporary circus in all its distinctions and asperities.

De facto research clusters are imposing themselves, and so we have decided to promote their distinctive paths by placing them at the heart of the transnational, transdisciplinary research network growing out of the Montreal Working Group and involving many partners. For these clusters to inform each other, we have to ensure a constant exchange of knowledge in order to avoid silo effects, where parallel research streams develop independently from one another and are hindered by their inability to enlighten colleagues in either stream.

How to embark on such a hermeneutic project? By reminding ourselves that contemporary circus defines the field, and by funnelling much of our current research through four fundamental research clusters and points of entry as shown in the diagram: Nation, Globalism, and the Transnational on a philosophical, historical, and discursive plane; Dramaturgy, Directing, and Creativity, the aesthetics and creative process; Ethos, Ethics, and Business, from branding to corporate responsibility; and Applied and Empirical Studies, which include industrial and creative applications as well as measurement-driven research. As a sign of the very transdisciplinarity that marks such an undertaking, we note that a research project led by Karen Fricker, an original member of the working group, and Charles R. Batson, who joined the group in its second year, has already begun to investigate notions of "circus and its others" across lines of gender, ethnicity, class, genre, training, vocation, and sexual orientation and expression by asking questions that touch each of these four fundamental clusters. Another

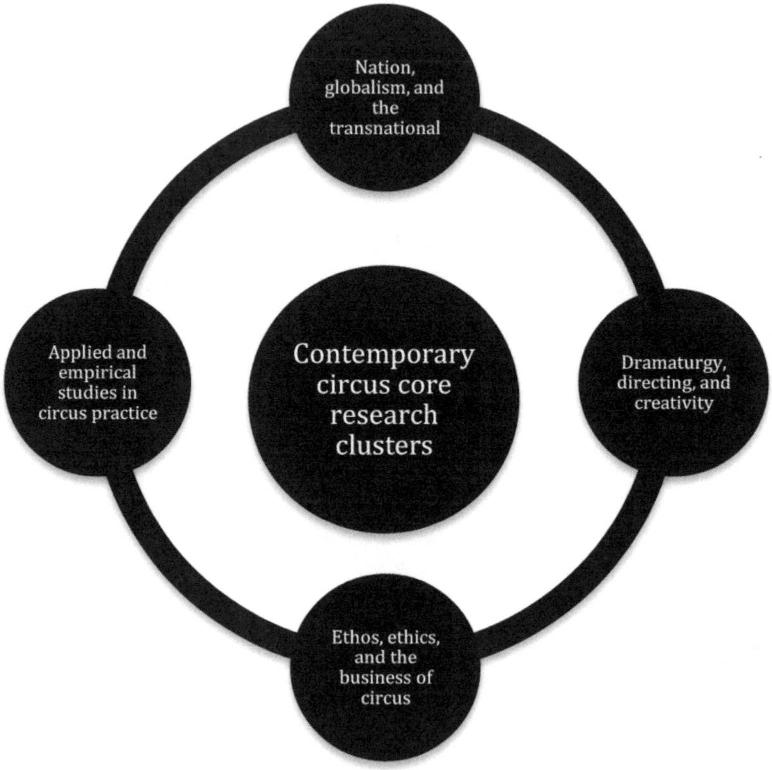

0.5 Contemporary circus core research clusters

study, led by former École nationale director and TOHU cofounder Jan Rok Achard and me, has begun interviewing key players in the transition period from traditional to contemporary circus in order to build an accessible, oral and material archive of early modern circus in Quebec.

Curiosity about one aspect of contemporary circus has led many young researchers into a career-defining research program. They will benefit from a stronger, better defined field, one that has legitimizing, structuring bodies such as associations, peer-reviewed journals, and research chairs; others will welcome the ad hoc vibrancy of working within a field forever on the cusp of being defined in a young nation like Quebec, forever in a state of becoming. Circus has allowed Quebec, a small, self-conscious nation, to have its artists travel the world, to be recognized and applauded for its creativity, know-how, entrepreneurship, and innovation. Circus research, given such a context, could perhaps initially be nothing but self-reflective and auto-ethnographic. It needed to define its parameters from a national perspective that also took into account a postnational artistic and entrepreneurial discourse. From there, it could open up to the world. It has, and it is.

Conclusion

From the first touring productions in Quebec of Ricketts's travelling circus in the late 1790s to Quebec's unexpected place, today, among the circus nations of the world, the story and history of Quebec circus provide fertile ground for research and exploration. Reflecting the current circus scene's resistance to antiquated models of nostalgic, faded-glory circuses of yore, we initially sought to look at what we were calling trends of emergence. It fast became obvious that circus was not suddenly "reinvented" in 1984 by stilt-walkers and fire-throwers from Baie-St-Paul as the global phenomenon we know. Its roots are multiple and complex, and they burrow through many *terroirs* and little-told histories: those of street theatre, clowning, acrobatics, gymnastics, strongmen, burlesque, pantomime, North American touring, assumed exoticism, cultural avatarism, and mobility. Perhaps by recognizing these complex origins and understanding the long-standing relationship with these international scenes and practices, Quebec circus will be able to imagine its way beyond a potentially limiting contentment in having contributed to reinventing an art form that will invariably morph into something new and different within a generation. Already, there is a growing sense among younger companies and artists not wanting to be affiliated with "the Big Three" that circus is less about performative exceptionalism and more about a spirit of athletic and aesthetic actualization. In other words, experimentation and radical departures from circus topoi are set to become the norm for current explorations into contemporary "post-nouveau" cirque. And this exploration will be happening, for the most part, outside a corporate model and in an ongoing exchange transgressing borders and artistic boundaries.

I.

Quebec on Planet Circus

CHAPTER 1

The Québécois Circus in the Concert of Nations: Exchange and Transversality

Pascal Jacob

Translated by Tiffany Templeton

Only plants have roots …
Its landscape: a meandering river.
Its scenery: grass, earth, and dust.
Its props: a horse, a blood-red uniform, a drum, and a fife. A delicate, white, trembling feather to transform soldier into elegant acrobat.
Its seductive power: imbalance and recovery.

The circus is essentially an aggregate of intentions. And emotions. Delicately constructed, it is tried and proven by its rich succession of fragments that privilege the principles of the mosaic in its codes of representation and creating performances. The contemporary circus is a new genre steeped in references, remnants, and differences in a genetic code that can be traced back nearly 250 years. But its history is fragmented – it is tempting to say disjointed, given its powerful relation to body and strength – into multiple parts that incessantly transform themselves even as the circus itself evolves. It is now obvious that there is not just "the" circus, with a sealed and codified aesthetic, but rather multiple performance experiences coloured by equestrian arts, acrobatics, games, and dance. It is not my intention here to denigrate any of the more contemporary models of an art form whose roots are ancient and powerful, even uncompromising, but rather to reevaluate the codes of representation of a genre that began during the Enlightenment and continues to change with perplexing regularity. In fact, the circus draws its strength from these successive mutations over the course of decades, constructing itself with steel, stone, and lumber, and crowning itself with perfumed oilcloth as it becomes a unique and an essential actor in the world of performance art.

The layperson who endeavours to understand the multifaceted mechanisms of the circus is perhaps most intrigued by its extraordinary ability to slip into the slightest social interstice, the tiniest urban crevice, the slimmest spiritual territory, to the point of merging with these aspects of culture – a brutal moment of birth that we might like to imagine as sunlit and radiant. If we push our analysis further, we find that the circus reveals its driving force in unexpected ways. And this circus is divisive; it always has been. Some are drawn to its glitter and to its tireless, voracious energy. For others, the circus has a faded aura. Therein resides its dark side, criticized by its detractors and just as ferociously defended by its admirers. Puerile and potent, agile and elegant, docile and provocative – all these qualifiers can be applied to this unique form vibrating within a circle only thirteen metres wide and dressed in strange rags or princely finery shimmering as falsely as a desert mirage. And yet, in the end, the circus pays no heed to adjectives. Generator of fortunes, catalyst of fate, dream machine, and weapon of mass seduction, it borrows much and gives back little, yet so capably and wholly transcends things, gestures, and people that it cannot but inspire admiration.

Fundamentally, the circus as an art has a simple, tree-like structure: its roots run deep, at times profoundly so, into the symbolic fertile ground of human history. Deeply buried, at a distance of nearly 5,000 years, lie the ancestral roots of acrobatics stemming from the hunt and other rites imitating the behaviour of prey. As time passes, we see the propagation of object manipulation and, eventually, human complicity with the horse, faithful companion in labour and in war. And finally there is laughter, intentionally provoked by gesture, pose, or mimicry, undeniably ageless, imbued with the irony that springs from daily life, whether for *Homo ergaster* or *Homo habilis*. These elements, vital for establishing a circus arts vocabulary, fuse at the base of the trunk and mature from 1768 onward. The adventure of the modern circus began with Philip Astley, Antonio Franconi, Charles Hughes, and John Bill Ricketts. It is they who set the stage, fixed the circle, and shaped the roles.

This is the beginning of the story, the moment when all these practices, autonomous from Antiquity to the Renaissance, suddenly become techniques and proclaimed disciplines of the circus. Circus acts, even. For the next two centuries the modern circus, in semantic opposition to the circus of Antiquity,

1.1 Early Cirque du Soleil big top in the Gaspésie region, 1984

developed without really progressing. And then in 1968, exactly 200 years later, the circus abruptly underwent almost daily metamorphosis. Amid the social, political, and cultural revolutions of the time, the branches reached to the skies, yielding fruit that fell to the ground and fertilized it. This in turn gave birth to myriad possibilities, forms, hybrids, and intensities. This arboreal anatomy illustrates the diversity of forms that emerged, developing into other ways of producing circus. The roots nourished these branches, invigorated them, and combined their nutrients. But most of all, this one and indivisible circus has transmogrified into a space with many centres, and from this abundance have sprung new forms of circus arts.

In 1797 when John Bill Ricketts decided to take the northern route and send a troupe to Montreal, he could not have imagined that this step would be the prelude to a story with enduring ramifications. He could not have known that the seeds he planted – the desire for circus – would flower two centuries later. For this is exactly what happened. In Quebec, circus vocations flourished during the nineteenth century and beautiful artistic experiences developed throughout the twentieth. However, it was during the 1980s and 1990s that the Québécois circus freed itself from the more traditional register to form a new aesthetic, fashioned by a handful of confident visionaries. When Guy Caron decided to create a circus school in Montreal (see Jacob and Vézina 2007 for a more detailed history of this inaugural moment), he anchored the spirit of future artistic developments in a mentality that was both highly cultured and popular. By offering everyone the possibility to "do" circus, he made training accessible in techniques that had hitherto remained secret and mainly transmitted through families and clans. This revolution had begun in Europe some years earlier, but galvanized by his newly acquired experience from the Budapest school, a satellite of the influential Moscow Circus School, Guy Caron subsequently laid the foundation for a new Québécois circus. From this school, new artistic initiatives were forged, destined to make their mark in North America before spreading to Europe and the rest of the world. But no one involved, immersed as they were in the daily training and creation of the early performances, was aware that their work would lead to another cultural revolution on a continental scale.

In 1984, Guy Laliberté and Daniel Gautier created Cirque du Soleil, a "spectacular idea" that would quickly resemble a planetary earthquake. In some twenty-five years, this "reinvented circus" (an allusion to the title of one of its initial performances, *Cirque Réinventé*) would establish itself across the globe. The quarter-century interval is symbolic: in the span of exactly twenty-five years, the modern circus that originated in London in 1768 would find its bearings in Philadelphia in 1793. Between these two milestones, Philip Astley and his followers conquered Europe, Russia, and America. This amusing, astonishing coincidence from the point of view of the evolution in forms is demonstrative of the nascent history of circus.

Cirque du Soleil soon established itself as a powerful enterprise, able to produce several shows at once. This principle of allowing the company to simultaneously manage up to twenty different entities constituted the backbone of its development, and its strategic choices defined early on depended, most notably, on efficient communication. When creating a poster for its American tour, Cirque du Soleil dissociated itself from the American circus through humour: a clown in vibrant colours springing out of a monochromatic grey surface, openly parodying a Barnum & Bailey circus poster. The challenge was clear: its mission was an aesthetic one, deliberate and voluntary. Cirque du Soleil's triumph at the Los Angeles Arts Festival in 1987, and the immediate attention the company garnered, was decisive for what would

1.2 *Varekai,* Cirque du Soleil. Costumes: Elko Ishioka.

follow – the extraordinary ascension that culminated in the installation of a permanent show in Las Vegas. In 1993, the creation of *Mystère*, one of the many shows directed by Franco Dragone since 1984, signalled the start of a new era in the development of the company. Spectators had to wind their way through a casino to access a theatre invisible from the outside. The combination of the meandering magic of the casino and the surprise of a theatre expressly conceived to accommodate unique creations was particularly fitting: it was somewhat like a quotation, a room inserted within a room discovered, as in the Opéra de Versailles, only after one secretly journeys through the passageways of the château. Such unsettling parallels reveal a taste for bending the rules.

The subsequent successes of *O*, *KÀ*, *Zumanity*, *Love*, and *Believe*, and of *La Nouba* and *Zed* abroad, confirmed the extensive influence of Cirque du Soleil and identified Quebec as the new world of the circus. This notion was further confirmed by the creation in 1993 of Cirque Éloize, a company founded by a group from the Magdalen Islands, driven by the energy and fiery will of Jeannot Painchaud, Daniel Cyr, Jeannot Chiasson, Robert Bourgeois, and Sylvette, Damien, and Alain Boudreau. Cirque Éloize embodies yet another facet of a unique circus identity, impregnated with values and a popular culture all its own. Above all, in an ambitious pursuit of artistic perfection, it founded its image on a circus in perpetual motion: one day in Cognac, the next week in Honolulu, a three-day stop in Berlin, the following month in Alaska. The "flying circus" so dear to English-language terminology was never so appropriate as for this enterprise! And while Cirque du Soleil used the big top to make its mark, Éloize chose venues that already existed, from theatres to sports and conference centres, thereby aligning itself with the customs of the early travelling troupes that moved a performance rather than a circus in the material sense of the word. It was obviously an economical and logistical decision, but one implicitly revealing specific artistic ambitions, as evidenced most notably in the performances of the Sky Trilogy: *Nomade – At Night, the Sky Is Endless*; *Rain: Like Rain in Your Eyes*; and *Nebbia*, created in 2002, 2004, and 2007 respectively by Daniele Finzi Pasca. Even if Cirque du Soleil reached tens of millions of spectators, Éloize's eight productions and more than 5,000 performances across the planet were also indicative of the reach of the Québécois circus beyond its borders.

As is always the case in history, there are significant dates. Just as 1984 was the starting point of a global journey by an iconic company, 2002 was equally momentous for the development of circus arts on a territorial scale that was a precursor in the domain. That year, Cirque du Soleil presented *Varekai* in Montreal's Old Port, an important show given the reorganization the company underwent after Daniel Gautier's departure. A little further down in the Old Port, Cirque Eos's big top was raised. Founded in 1998, this company embodied the fragile middle ground between Cirque du Soleil and Éloize. In June 2002, Éloize presented *Nomade* in Trois-Rivières. At the

1.3 From *Psy*, 7 Fingers. Group with Nael Jammal

same time, seven artists had conceived a show and company – Les 7 doigts de la main – and performed their first body of work, *Loft*, for that year's iteration of Montreal's Just for Laughs festival where they won the Prix de la Relève (Prize for Emerging Talent).

The year 2002 was thus a crucial milestone in the recent history of Québécois circus arts. In the space of one month, a dynamic artistic form materialized within the parameters of one tiny area, where all the facets of today's circus – whether neoclassical, new, or contemporary – managed to flourish. Spurred on by the momentum of new companies such as Luna Caballera in 1999, Cheval Théâtre in 2001, Cavalia in 2003, Cirque Alfonse in 2005, and Cirque Akya in 2006, Québécois circus distilled the aesthetic currents running through the circus arts worldwide. Its representatives travelled across North America and to other parts of the globe. The act of reappropriating codes of representation from the original circus, transcended

1.4 From *Nebbia*, Cirque Éloize and Compagnia Finzi Pasca

or revisited by artists and audacious entrepreneurs, was simplified by the absence of a fissure between two worlds that seemed to be ignorant of one another (unlike the fratricidal battles in France in the 1990s between the adherents of a traditional form and the heralds of renewal like Les Arts Sauts). This neutrality facilitated the development of companies that had very different ambitions, and whose artistic projects privileged identity and creative difference over consensus. The strength of what sprang forth contributed to reframing an understanding of the circus arts in Quebec and circus history worldwide.

The renewal of the Quebec circus sprang from a common sense of dispossession, felt throughout the world for nearly half a century, toward the conventional circus. The immediate international success of Cirque du Soleil, its extensive aesthetic influence in countries that hitherto had dominated the domain artistically and technically and that had never thought they might have any serious contenders, along with the regular presence of Quebec's other companies, notably in Europe and North America, all contributed, season after season, to the idea that – after the English, French, German, American, and Soviet epochs – the new circus era belonged to Quebec.

In order to reach this point at such a swift pace, a number of conditions present for about thirty-five years converged. For three decades, a series of principles, structures, and strategies on artistic, technical, and logistical levels prepared the terrain. The birth of Cirque du Soleil, the evolution of circus arts training, and the emergence of multiple companies were all major events that revealed to varying degrees a fundamental choice of Québécois culture. Historically, the circus was a family affair. Parents passed on their knowledge, secrets, and know-how to their children. Little by little, children became familiar with the different disciplines, and they would choose the one that exploited their natural aptitudes. But parents often projected their own visions of the circus onto their children and, slowly but surely, their techniques atrophied and died. A single branch that is never pruned eventually stops bearing fruit or even leaves. From 1968 onward, however, in France and in many Western regions such as Quebec, Australia, the United States, and Scandinavia, the "circus" would progressively transform into the "circus arts," a new generation of forms and disciplines that favoured the development of another kind of circus, a contemporary one that resonated with the world around it.

That influential Tower of Babel, the École nationale de cirque de Montréal, founded so close to the birth of Cirque du Soleil, possessed exceptional wealth in the diversity of its student body, extending far beyond the borders of Quebec. Its extraordinary development and its installation inside an iconic building shaped the world's view of the circus arts in North America, anchoring it within the professional sphere and making it both witness and artistic prescriber for a sector – *le nouveau cirque* – craving points of reference. The creation labs initiated by the school in 2004 allowed young artists to express their abilities by integrating themselves into artistic projects upon graduation, offering another full-scale experience of encountering the audience and preparing for their début. The founding in 2004 of TOHU and the Cité des arts du cirque by three major forces in the Quebec circus world – En Piste (an association promoting the circus arts), Cirque du Soleil, and École nationale de cirque de Montréal – was an astounding cultural, social, and environmental project that gave rise to a vital stakeholder in the promotion of circus arts across the continent. The creation of the Montréal Complètement Cirque festival in 2009 confirmed the city's status as "circus capital," making it an important international benchmark for the performing arts. The fifteenth anniversary of En Piste in 2012 coincided with recognition of the circus arts as an art in its own right, with its own devoted office and funding, by the Conseil des arts et des lettres du

Québec. Indeed, this all seems something resembling the birth of a unique, atypical, and universal "nation."

And so, in an age when globalization continues to seep into the unexpected cracks in our Western societies, it is clear that the circus arts constitute an exceptional creative breeding ground, and that the repertory of ancient forms, acrobatics, balancing, and object manipulation continues to evolve and produce meaning, emotion, and endless fascination with the mysteries of the human body and spirit. For this is what it is really about: the circus is a powerful catalyst for memory, a fantastic conveyer of energy, a spectacular construct, one that is original and intuitive, sensitive and deeply moving.

The immediacy of clearly accomplished natural prowess, inscribed within a dramaturgy of feats and calculated risks, creates a unique and unpredictable experience for both the performers and the audience. It is this fragility, this possibility, that still attracts tens of millions of spectators to circus rings the world over, and incites them to return. They are propelled, perhaps, by an ancestral desire for shared experience and amazement.

The dazzling free fall, the raw and refined virtuosity of object manipulation, the precise elegance of acrobatics in all its forms, and the intensity of rhythms and colours do not belong exclusively to the circus, but are part of a popular fascination that has held sway throughout the ages.

The circus arts of today and yesterday retain traces of their ancient heritage. Those shadows looming in the cave beyond the ring of first fire that generated fantastic stories and served as a primitive threshold for cohesion among clans now find stylistic echo in the flicker of projectors magnifying the silhouettes cast within this playground. The central hearth – here, the circus ring – empty and akin to a small bit of preserved territory, incessantly erupting with new legions of heroes who in turn disappear, is a powerful metaphor of life. Whether running, gliding, or flying, the acrobats – as benevolent giants or as Lilliputians suspended from a bouquet of translucent spheres – reinvent the mystery of humanity's origins with every leap. That moment in time when everything shifted, when human beings discovered that their strength could generate beauty, and when the sacred became intertwined with the profane such that distortion, humour, and balance were lifted to the ranks of performance art. Somewhere between shamanism and magic, the circus arts continue to single out the ultimate quest of humans: the desire to be free of worldly constraints and to find the perfect point of balance, traversing a line like a tightrope walker one step

1.5 *O*, Cirque du Soleil. Costumes: Dominique Lemieux

at a time where only the right choices and tenacity will ensure success. A metaphor for destiny. Far from being a tale of fairies and magic, yes, but not completely dissimilar from it either.

Today, with the presence of Cavalia in Australia, Cirque du Soleil in Europe, Asia, and America, Les 7 doigts de la main simultaneously in Russia, France, and Canada, and Éloize in the United States, the Québécois circus reigns over a symbolic empire. An empire in which the sun – both the star and the company – never sets.

CHAPTER 2

A Tale of Origins: Deconstructing North American "Cirque" Where Québécois and American Circus Cultures Meet

Louis Patrick Leroux

What's in a seemingly generic term? *Cirque*, for instance. The French term for circus when used in English has become shorthand either for Cirque du Soleil–styled circus or, more generally, for theatrical, narrative-based contemporary circus. While researching the origins of both the term and its usage as well as the little-known history of Quebec circus before the mid-1980s, I stumbled upon unsuspected riches of neglected historical records. This chapter will serve as a wanderlust thrust into the history of a term and its impact on both Quebec and North America. After exploring the current usage of the term *cirque* by anglophones, I will examine ongoing and historical peregrinations between the Quebec and US circus scenes, from Ricketts's early touring circus taking Montreal and Quebec City by storm in 1797 to contemporary examples of Quebec-based circuses influencing Americans' embracing of the new possibilities of circus.

While the dominant reading of Quebec's circus history is to link it to the emergence of France's nouveau cirque (see Fagot 2006, all the works of Julie Boudreault, and Pascal Jacob), with other emerging scholars starting to explore the influence of Chinese practice and training (Zhang 2011, 2014), I'm interested in understanding how Quebec circus has evolved in a dialectical relationship with American circus practice and, later, with American audiences who had lost interest in traditional circus. Quebec circus history remains a largely unexplored continent, which does indeed span all of North America. By assessing both the American and Quebec circus scenes in their historical perspective, I hope to give a clear sense of the scope of Quebec circus and the interconnectedness of our shared (and embedded) past.

Cirque in the United States

Following Cirque du Soleil's spectacular success worldwide and effective infiltration into American pop culture, with the resulting economic consequences, it appears that the very term *cirque* has come to differentiate the high-value artistic brand from the traditional family-oriented circus. Cirque has become a buzzword throughout America to the point where many companies and circuses wanting to distinguish themselves from traditional circus – and perhaps wanting to share some of the lexical magic with Cirque du Soleil – have integrated the French term into their names. One only has to think of Cirque School Los Angeles (its slogan "For anybody with any body," quite the antithesis of Montreal's cirque scene populated by some of the most rigorously trained and accomplished artists in the Western world), Cirque USA (with offices in the same cities as Cirque du Soleil and offering corporate shows rather explicitly emulating Cirque's brand), Cirque Mechanics (born in 2004 from the collaboration of Birdhouse Factory and the Circus Center of San Francisco), Cirque Hamptons, and even Cirque d'Art Theatre and School in Portsmouth, Ohio.

Cirque du Soleil, after its initial introduction to America, American pop culture, and celebrity endorsements at its do-or-die performance at the 1987 Los Angeles Arts Festival, has imposed its European-inspired brand of animal-free, *commedia dell'arte*–infused nouveau cirque on a market that was ripe to be conquered. Cirque du Soleil found its niche in Las Vegas, changing and raising the bar for Sin City's entertainment offering. It introduced thrilling artistic and athletic international extravaganzas, set records for production costs for live performance, and tested the market's elasticity (see Fricker 2008; Leroux 2009a). From a single show at Wynn's Treasure Island in 1994, Cirque du Soleil now features eight permanent productions in Las Vegas, most in coproduction with MGM. It also has a permanent production, *La Nouba*, at Disney World in Orlando (ongoing since 1998). Until its recent closure, Cirque du Soleil also had a "permanent" production in Los Angeles, *Iris*, a Hollywood-themed show originally slated to run for ten years (for a closer study of this production, see Leroux 2014b and Bennett's chapter in this volume).

Facing an excessive appropriation of the term *cirque* in the United States, most notably by companies offering rather explicitly imitative shows, Cirque du Soleil filed for trademark infringement, dilution, and unfair competition. It sued Cirque Inc. (also known as Cirque Productions) and its "Cirque Ingénieux" production, citing Florida state and federal trademark laws. Reporting on the ruling that rejected Cirque du Soleil's claim for the cirque name, Liz Benston (2004) noted that the five-year-long lawsuit cost each company between $3 and 4 million. The 2004 judgment clearly established that the generic term *cirque* was free to be used. The Florida-based Cirque Productions continued to present "French [*sic*!]-style" circus, playing on the ambiguity of its name to draw corporate contracts and audiences. Cirque du Soleil and the generic *cirque* have permeated American pop culture and drawn their fair share of admiration, mockery, and attacks. What the emerging new American circus scene was tapping into, however, was more than lexical magic: it was sharing in the "popular high art" aesthetics of this new hybrid form of dance-theatre-circus-spectacle. Having discovered the strong tradition of nouveau cirque not from France but rather through Cirque du Soleil's success in the centres of American pop culture and excess (Los Angeles and Las Vegas), Americans saw echoes of their own native claims to "The Greatest Show on Earth," except this time it was otherwise exotic and summarized in one French word: *cirque*.

The story told in the international circus world was that Cirque du Soleil sought to copyright the French generic word for circus for its own use, which only contributed to widening the gap between its commercial nature and objectives and the artistic ethos of nouveau cirque and contemporary circus in France and Quebec. The company briefly used shark-like intimidation tactics against smaller Quebec-based cirques, but fortunately it dropped the cease-and-desist orders when confronted with the absurdity of the request.[1] In any case, the companies have since grown closer to each other, and Cirque du Soleil has ultimately played a supportive role.

The fact of the matter is that Cirque du Soleil does stand apart as an effective corporation creating art within commercial and branding models. Its attempt to trademark the *cirque* term and brand echoes its previous claim to have reinvented circus in a "circus-less land," a discourse perpetuated by the company and the Quebec circus scene since the 1980s. Indeed, the success of contemporary circus activity over the past thirty years in North America has all but obliterated the memory of previous forms of circus and their transnational networks.

Contemporary Quebec Circus in Relation to the United States

While the bulk of performances and revenues for Les 7 doigts de la main (the 7 Fingers) and Cirque Éloize is generated from tours in Europe, Canada, and South America, and occasional performances in Russia and the Middle

East, both companies have been making inroads into the American market dominated by traditional American circus and Cirque du Soleil. The 7 Fingers was present Off-Broadway for over a year with its high-energy production *Traces*, featuring a mixed cast of Canadians and Americans exploring acrobatics, as well as basketball, skateboarding, and confessional direct-address to the audience. Contrary to Cirque du Soleil, the 7 Fingers' artists perform heightened versions of themselves on stage. They don't hide behind makeup and costumes; they mumble, and in spite of their stunning athletic abilities, they sometimes self-consciously stumble and fumble and this is, precisely, the source of their charm (see Batson, this volume, for an in-depth analysis of their aesthetic choices). *Traces* and *Patinoire,* a daredevil solo piece developed by Patrick Léonard for the 7 Fingers, have toured the United States and achieved what Cirque du Soleil never quite could in New York – that is, generate buzz and become the (nonmediated) talk of the town, attracting national media attention without generating substantial profits. The 7 Fingers did, however, build up esteem and cultural capital by playing New York for a few months, an experience repeated in 2013 with their participation in the Broadway revival of *Pippin* and in 2014 with their production *Queen of the Night* at Hotel Paramount's Diamond Horseshoe.

The slightly older Cirque Éloize has had a regular presence in the United States with touring shows, most recently with *Cirkopolis*, choreographed by Quebec dance "enfant terrible" Dave St-Pierre (from the Jan Fabre and Pina Bausch traditions, but also a contributor to choreographies for Cirque du Soleil's *Love* and *Zumanity*). After touring Europe and Mexico in 2013–14, *Cirkopolis* had a month-long residency in Schenectady, New York, followed by an extensive tour through Texas, Georgia, Kentucky, Virginia, Arizona, and Vermont, before returning for its Montreal "premiere." Indeed, Éloize was the first circus from Quebec to tap into the subsidized Performing Arts Centers network from the mid-nineties until today. Other Quebec companies have followed suit, including the 7 Fingers and Cirque Alfonse. Cirque Éloize has been continually present in America with touring productions meant for theatre spaces and auditoriums, finding a growing niche market in college towns, regional hubs, and eventually larger cities, involved both with subscription-based Performing Arts Centers and occasionally with commercial ventures.

Following in the footsteps of Cirque du Soleil and the American tradition of the "extravaganza," the equestrian company Cavalia (founded by Cirque du Soleil cofounder Normand Latourelle) has been touring the United States for a number of years, first with its eponymous show *Cavalia: A Magical*

2.1 *Cirkopolis*, Cirque Éloize

Encounter between Human and Horse, and currently with *Odysseo*. The new show is presented in what is touted as the "world's largest touring tent" (Kidd 2012), covering a total of 100,000 square feet, with a stage area of 27,000 square feet. The touring show features sixty-one horses (thirty-two on stage at once), forty-nine performers, an 80,000 gallon lake, 15,000 tons of soil, and a large cyclorama requiring twenty projectors.

2.2 *Timber!*, Cirque Alfonse

To complete this survey of contemporary Quebec circus in the United States, we should mention relative newcomers such as the "neo-trad" singing and hirsute axe-wielding performers of Cirque Alfonse, who, after a European tour, brought their lumberjack-themed show *Timber!* to New England in 2013–14 followed by a Manhattan run in the fall of 2014. Quebec troupes have indeed reinvested circus and have been extensively touring in the United States, relying on that market for growth and profitability. In Quebec, contemporary circus has attained a high degree of social, institutional, and cultural capital in a relatively short period. In addition to regular media coverage, special-themed issues in the general media, and articles in academic journals, circus in Quebec – the only North American state to officially recognize circus as an art form and offer subsidies for its production and touring – has been fully integrated into the cultural makeup and has positioned itself as an example of artistic excellence, creativity, and commercial success both locally and internationally. Montreal features a state-subsidized, elite training circus school, a theatre-in-the-round devoted to circus, and an international circus festival. Major productions by Daniele Finzi Pasca and Cirque Éloize have played Montreal's Place des Arts, and the 7 Fingers opened the 2013–14 season of the

Théâtre du Nouveau Monde. The 7 Fingers also worked with international choreographers to develop a dance-circus production, *Triptyque* (2015), which toured important dance venues such as Sadler's Wells in London. This social (and political) acceptance of circus as a legitimate art form (save for the usual resistance from the artistic elite suspicious of popular appeal) is a relatively new phenomenon in Quebec, linked to the international success and recognition of the "Big Three" circuses (Cirque du Soleil, Cirque Éloize, and the 7 Fingers) and their contributions to developing the local economy and enriching the possibilities of cross-pollination within the cultural industries.

Montreal is now home to TOHU, North America's only permanent and institutional circus space with a regular subscription series, and hosts a season of Quebec-based and international contemporary circus plus the Montréal Complètement Cirque festival, which draws leading companies from Europe and Australia. Yet very little contemporary American circus makes it to this new circus capital. From Montreal's perspective, the rest of North America appears to be a blank slate, save for a few imitative cirques. It needn't be this way. There is also a clear sense of hope and potential emerging from various interesting hubs of circus activity, such as San Francisco, Seattle, Los Angeles, New York, Chicago, St Louis, Minneapolis, and rural Maine, where a circus school has been announcing its opening for a few years now.[2] In a panel discussion in July 2013 (see Leroux and Moss 2014), American circus performers and teachers based in Montreal were asked why they had chosen Montreal to train and work, and how this has affected their understanding of circus or their discipline. The vibrant discussion was important for both the panelists and the audience, which included many of the active players in contemporary American circus, many of whom were taking the full measure of the Quebec circus scene for the first time. While contemporary circus in Quebec has relied on its success in the United States, it has nevertheless stood as a beacon for innovation and renewed circus practice in an emerging scene south of the border, where rapid changes are occurring with the foundation of Circus Now, the inauguration of the Chicago Contemporary Circus Festival (which in its first edition in 2014 featured shows from Quebec), and New York's Skirball Center's regular programming of an *intensif* contemporary circus festival at Washington Square under the label "Circus Now."

Early American Circus in Quebec

As we have seen, the commonly accepted historical trope has been that Quebec was a barren land for circus before Cirque du Soleil emerged from street performance – with the backing of then Quebec premier René Lévesque and a million dollar provincial grant in 1984 – to "reinvent circus," as the company boldly claimed with its productions *Cirque Réinventé* and *Nouvelle expérience*. But we might argue that circus was less reinvented than *reinvested* with European artistic sensibility and American business acumen. French circus historian, promoter, consultant, and teacher Pascal Jacob (2006) writes:

> Cirque du Soleil emerges from a virtual ahistorical land in terms of circus, yet a land capable of challenging traditional forms where they had seemed indestructible. Forever affected by the international success of this company, the changing expectations of audiences in America, Europe, and Asia, circus has taken stock. Circus is engaged in movement, it is evolving, shedding its old skin. (223; my translation)

When Quebec is compared to English, French, or American circus traditions, which benefit from rich documentation and historical analysis, Jacob's assessment proves rather accurate. To a certain extent, Quebec's relative inexperience with traditional forms of circus allowed it to transgress accepted forms and traditions, drawing on what various cultures and national traditions had to offer without having to contend with high cultural capital and expectations. That generation of Quebec circus creators were free to invent and innovate, which isn't to say that they did not learn specific lessons from French nouveau cirque, from Swiss and German tent and apparatus rigging, from Soviet circus training practices, or from the American "risk it or lose it" entrepreneurial ethos.

In spite of this oft-repeated and "romantic New World" ahistorical contention, most circus scholars agree that early Quebec circus history is richer than we have been led to believe and that most of it has yet to be written. In a sense, Quebec circus memory mimics the relation of Quebec theatre to its own history. Jean-Marc Larrue (1988–89) writes convincingly about a 140-year-old discourse in Quebec theatrical history of constant "births" of an authentic form of national theatre. Forgetfulness and ignorance were justified given the nature of a society preoccupied with building and becoming.

> It's just that (historians) engaged in a present they were busy projecting onto a future that they needed to build found the past rather cumbersome. An empty past, made up of nothingness, is an airy, practical past, an uncompromising past that can only flatter the present. In short, the past these historians needed was not constructed on History (but on the history of their object of study). (69; my translation)

While Quebec theatre historians have begun to address these issues, circus history research lags behind. There have been efforts to make sense of the archive that remains to be compiled. Notably, in articles, a thesis, and a dissertation, Julie Boudreault (1996, 1999, 2002b, 2002c) builds on previous scholarship by theatre historians Baudoin Burger (1974) and André-Gilles Bourassa (2004), and cultural historians Yvan Lamonde and Raymond Montpetit (1986). Others, over the years, have focused on early visits by Ricketts's travelling circus and on the historical recollections of John Durang's tour to Canada (F. Boudreault 2009; Durang 1966; Moy 1980). Louis Cyr and his Cirque Cyr-Barré have been of constant interest (see Clairoux 1988, 1993, 2009; Beauchamp and Lavoie 2003). Studies by historians have also demonstrated the importance of acrobatic performance and the pervasiveness of various forms of circus in Montreal throughout the nineteenth and twentieth centuries in private leisure gardens such as Jardin Guilbault (1833–69; Gaudet 2009; Massicotte 1923–24, 1937), Sohmer Park (1889–1919; Lamonde and Montpetit 1986), and Belmont Park (1923–83; Proulx 2005). These gardens and parks attracted strongmen and trained local acrobats, and regularly featured touring circus productions or acts. All of the aforementioned historians have drawn on articles from various dailies and weeklies, from works on historical place names, and from the detailed *fiches* (descriptive character sketches) prepared by early twentieth-century archivist and historian Édouard-Zotique Massicotte. His painstaking collation of personalities, events, venues, and practices linked to popular arts and entertainment is a trove of riches.

James S. Moy (1980) traces the historical narrative of American circus back to the late eighteenth century, writing that "John B. Ricketts introduced the first large scale circus to America" and that during his "brief eight year American career Ricketts managed to 'materially interfere with the profits [...]' of the established theatres of the day." In 1792, Ricketts opened a riding school in Philadelphia and by the next year was performing equestrian circus acts inspired by Charles Hughes of London's Royal Circus. By 1796, he had added acting, juggling, and tumbling to the equestrian acts. In 1797 Ricketts brought his company to Montreal, where it remained for a year, performing its entire repertoire in French, English, and German. After a lengthy and successful run in Quebec City, the company returned to Montreal for the remainder of 1798. For the next decade or so, theatre in Quebec appealed to the broader public by integrating circus elements.

Yet if we look closely at Ricketts's foundational circus presence and the regular tours of British and American circus companies on Quebec soil, we find a number of French-Canadian circus artists embedded in the American circus economy and tradition. These local artists often disappear from the narrative because of exotic *othering*; that is, they lose their cultural specificity by adopting Italian, Russian, or English personas. Interestingly, strongmen from Quebec succeeded in imposing their strength and their names, most notably Louis Cyr and Horace Barré. The latter toured the United States with The Flying Jordans in 1895 and the Sheridan City Sports Burlesque Company in 1896 before joining Louis Cyr, the "Strongest Man in the World," to found the Quebec-based Cirque Cyr-Barré, which toured from 1899 to 1904.

Cyr's popularity was as astounding as his feats. He was a rare headliner in a circus world that otherwise gave strongmen little credence. Biographer Paul Ohl (2013, 269–91) writes that Cyr reportedly earned $2,000 a week in 1897–98 from John Robinson's Circus at a time when weekly salaries in Lowell's cotton mills, where Cyr had worked as a young man, were about $5 a week (Lebergott 1960, 449–500). However, discussions with incredulous archivists at Ringling's Circus led me to suspect that this amount must have been inflated, perhaps as much as tenfold, to create the myth of Cyr's success abroad. In any case, his experience as a well-paid curiosity – first with John Robinson, then with Ringling Brothers for a yearlong American tour in 1898 – challenged his dignity and convinced him that a life in the circus was not for him, at least not in someone else's circus. Ringling made Cyr lead the town parade, lift excessive amounts, and allow himself to be challenged for a $25,000 prize offered to anyone who could surpass his strength. Cyr built a considerable fortune with the circus, in both Ringling's and his own Cyr Brothers Specialty Company (1892–96, touring mostly in New England), but it is his collaboration with Horace Barré (whom Ringling Brothers insisted on calling "Horace Barré of France") that established him as the founder of the first fully Quebec-run circus. During his American tours, Quebec judged Cyr a sellout who transformed himself into a "bête de cirque" (Ohl 2013, 283–5). Longing to return to family life in Quebec and for recognition at home, Cyr founded the Cirque Cyr-Barré in early 1899, using lessons learned from his friend Joseph Ringling. The company drew on a mix of international and local talent (the Chaput brothers, the Bédard family, his nephew Francis Cyr, and his daughter Émilienne), toured mostly in Quebec and Ontario travelling by train, and performed under a big top that could accommodate 3,000 spectators. It featured thirty-five horses and twenty-five performers, with a working crew of seventy-five men and thirty musicians. Cyr's health began to decline in 1902, and Cirque Cyr-Barré folded in 1904 after 600 shows. Cyr and Barré brought experience and an entrepreneurial circus culture from the United States and laid the foundations on which later Quebec circuses would build.

"Reconquering Our Heritage of Strength"

The trope of the strongman has historically been associated with French-Canadian resilience in the face of difficult circumstances. Indeed, tales of mythic strongmen usually involve conquering nature (Olivier Tourangeau and Louis Dubois wrestled with bears), conquering English or Irish rivals (Jos Montferrand faced Orangemen in Ottawa and Louis Cyr took on Irish workers in Lowell), and sometimes even conquering nature and souls (François Archambault explored the American West and Siberia, and proselytized native peoples). These examples are from archivist and naturalist Édouard-Zotique Massicotte's 1909 book, *Athlètes canadiens-français: Recueil des exploits de force, d'endurance, d'agilité des athlètes et des sportsmen de notre race, depuis le XVIIIe siècle.*[3] In addition to documenting the past, Massicotte strove for a moral "reconquering of our heritage of strength," symbolically undoing the British Conquest of 1759 (7). Employing myth-making rhetoric, making giants and heroes of men of the golden era of French rule, he writes of generations of settlers who needed to be multitalented, strong, and resourceful in order to survive. And those who did survive left a legacy of strength and athleticism. Equating sport, performance, and nation are nothing new, but in this case, Massicotte used his work to advocate for "physical literacy" through the regular practice of gymnastics and sports in order to redress the national character and build self-confidence (15) at a time when tensions between francophones and anglophones ran high in Canada. Whereas physical exploits and performance are often celebrated as individual achievements, Massicotte's narrative is a social reading of exceptional performance that reflects collectively on French Canadian aspirations. In the recent biopic *Louis Cyr* (Roby 2013), based on Paul Ohl's (2013) biography and owing much to an earlier work by Weider and Massicotte (1999), the French Canadian strongman tells his acolyte and friend Horace Barré that he is carrying both the weight and the honour of his fellow French Canadians and that he is always acutely aware of his vulnerable position: "What separates me from poverty and the life I now lead is this weight of this dumbbell I need to lift" (Roby 2013).[4]

Interestingly, the tradition of the strongman coincided with the early development and popularization of acrobatics in Quebec, the building of interdisciplinary gymnasiums in Montreal, the increase in American touring circuses in Quebec, and the emergence of private leisure gardens and amusement grounds such as Dominion Park (1906–37) where (mostly American, but also a number of local) athletes and acrobats regularly performed.

Gymnasiums and Public Parks

In order to understand where French Canadian talent developed, we must look to gymnastics schools – sometimes integrated into general athletics gymnasiums, sometimes specialized – that emerged in Montreal during the nineteenth century. Early schools where performers trained before moving on to Jardin Guilbault, Sohmer Park, or American circus companies included former British soldier Frederick S. Barnjum's gymnastics school, which became the Montreal Gymnastic Club in 1858, and the Montreal Gymnasium, founded in 1868 and later taken over by the Montreal Amateur Athletic Association. Guilbault's circus school, founded in 1862, was integrated into his subscription-funded Glaciarum, a monumental building that included both an ice rink and a gymnasium with high wire, trapezes, and other apparatuses that attracted year-round audiences to his vast private gardens (Gaudet 2009, 27–8).

Lamonde and Montpetit's (1986) history of European-inspired private parks in Montreal – notably Sohmer Park – establishes that these parks played a major role in offering an alternative space for leisure and art, commodifying public space in an early example of "brandscaping" or an "experience economy" that featured classical music, skating, acrobatics, vaudeville, animal circuses, freak exhibitions, botanical curiosities, and much more. The authors emphasize the regular presence of acrobats and circus displays in the park: "Feats of daring and acrobatics of all kinds were constantly in vogue at Sohmer Park from its opening season to its eventual closure. Consequently, over thirty years, a steady stream of jugglers, tightrope walkers, jumpers, divers, acrobats, contortionists, ventriloquists, swimmers, speed and figure skaters, cyclists, and gymnasts performed in the grand pavilion" (140; my translation). While Quebec may have little memory of its circus heritage, it nevertheless has had an ongoing tradition of circus performance and an enthusiasm for the meeting of sport and art.

Louis Durand, the Adventurer

In contrast to Louis Cyr's well-known and often politicized performances abroad, there were a number of active circus professionals simply making a living, travelling internationally, and quietly integrating themselves into the American circus industry. In a sense, these lesser-known performers disappeared as individuals, their place of origin and ethnicity obscured by foreign or English-sounding stage names.

Montreal-born Louis Durand had a long international career as a contortionist, tumbler, clown, juggler, tightrope walker, pantomime, actor, and equestrian acrobat. His career is bookended by performances at Montreal's private parks: as a nine-year-old acrobat at the Jardin Guilbault in 1859, and with his daughter in a balancing act at Sohmer Park in 1894. Between those two dates, however, Durand trained in the United States and worked extensively with American-based circuses (Massicotte 1909, 169–72). The record indicates that he won first prize in acrobatics at Montreal's Dominion Theatre (which confirms an existing competitive athletics and acrobatic culture), after which he began his long US career working for Barnum, Forepaugh Circus; as a clown for the Chiarini Royal Italian Circus; Dan Costello Circus; Denby Continental Circus; Morosco's Royal Russian Circus; as an equestrian acrobat for Fryer's; as a pantomime and tightrope walker for the Ideal Company; and for the Marvels of Peru, a contortion quartet. The French Canadian acrobat was a chameleon, claiming various ethnicities (Italian, Russian, Peruvian) and performing different disciplines to suit his producers.

In 1884, after performing with his American wife at San Francisco's Woodward's Gardens, Louis Durand joined Fryer & Co. New United Shows for a Pacific tour, which took him to Hawaii, Australia, New South Wales, and India. On the subcontinent, he joined Abel Klaer and Olyman's Circus before founding his own company, the Mme Durand Ideal Comedy Co., which combined sketch humour, pantomime, and acrobatics. With this company, according to Massicotte (1909), Durand toured India, China, Japan, the Caribbean, and Mexico, before returning to the United States. Durand's story is all but unknown in Quebec and warrants further documentation in order to understand his impact on other French Canadian performers and his relative lack of fame in Quebec. Durand's international travels and entrepreneurial endeavours in India and Asia distinguished him from his peers. The Pacific, Asian, and Australian circuit had been established in the 1850s by Joseph Andrew Rowe, an American who employed a diverse mix of international circus performers, according to Matthew Wittmann (2012) in his chapter on the "Transnational History of the Early American Circus" (74). Interestingly, Durand's life and career were seamlessly woven into the fabric of the American circus, which drew on international talent and toured tirelessly around the world. Durand seems like an explorer, an adventurer following different disciplinary and commercial paths until returning to relative anonymity in Montreal after a rich life abroad. The pattern of Durand's life in the circus, while extraordinary at the time, set the model for Quebec artists working for large American circuses.

Quebec-Based Circuses

Although Quebec did not produce many local circus companies until relatively recently, there are some that can be rescued from historical obscurity. Following the two-month visit of James West's Circus in 1821 (West had been one of the stars of Charles Hughes's Royal Circus in London), James's brother William stayed behind and joined forces with a local businessman to create Cirque West et Blanchard, which produced shows in Quebec City from 1824 to 1826 (Boudreault 2002a; Burger 1974; Cyr 2003; Roy 1936). Various buildings were erected, notably the equestrian Cirque Royal in Quebec City in 1824 (transformed into a traditional theatre two years later by innkeeper Nicholas-François Mailhot). As we have seen, there followed a long gap before Cirque Cyr-Barré was founded at the turn of the twentieth century. Closer to us, Cirque Gatini was founded by Michel Gatien in 1977 and toured extensively until 1979, running two simultaneous big-top touring shows.[5] It was a traditional circus that emulated the American-based Circus Vargas, which at the time was enjoying success in Quebec with its 5,000-seat big top (Bordez and Iuliani 2002, 18–19).

American Circus and Quebec's "Cirque"

Julie Boudreault, in this volume, identifies seventy-two touring shows of American circuses in Quebec between 1846 and 1967, the year of Montreal's International Exposition. Contrary to the earlier circuses of Ricketts and West, which performed for long periods in the same cities to recoup the costs of their buildings, American circuses preferred big tops that gave them mobility and meant they could easily include Quebec in North American circuits. While Barnum & Bailey performed under its famous big top during that period and the Shriners and Cirque Gatini also used *chapiteaux*, other travelling circuses have since taken up performing in hockey rinks and auditoriums. Today, the American circus presence in Quebec has slowed to a trickle and what does remain, sporadically during the summer season in suburban parking lots, is mostly traditional, like the Shrine Circus, and features animals. In a sense, the phenomenal success of Cirque du Soleil took circus out of most of the province by presenting lavish productions in larger cities.

After continuous activity in the first half of the twentieth century, with Belmont Park picking up where Sohmer Park and Dominion Park left off and circuses touring throughout the province, the 1960s and early 1970s saw a gradual decline in the number and variety of circuses and circus acts presented.[6] That decline, in addition to the collective memory lapse about earlier circus practices, gymnasiums, and cross-border activity, created the conditions in 1970s Quebec for that oft-mentioned "rebirth" or reconceptualization of circus in a province aspiring to cultural autonomy and statehood. Contemporary Quebec circus may well have been influenced by the aesthetic and collectivist ethos of the French nouveau cirque, but it also grew out of the athletic high-performance training practices of Soviet circus schools and gymnastics[7] and the province's own tradition of public displays of acrobatics on stages and in gymnasiums.

As Jacob and Vézina (2007) write in their history of the National Circus School, *Désir(s) de vertige*, part of the momentum behind the creation of a hybrid arts-sports training centre in 1981, then named Centre Immaculée-Conception after the old school in which it was housed, came from fortuitous circumstances that brought together people from the alternative street-theatre scene (such as Michel G. Barrette who became Cirque du Soleil's first ringmaster and Gilles Maheu who went on to found the dance-theatre company Carbone 14), the burgeoning clown scene (with people like

Rodrigue "Chocolat" Tremblay), and the first-class gymnastics world (trainer André Simard and gymnast Pierre Leclerc). There had been a strong clowning presence on Radio-Canada television in the 1960s and 1970s with household favourites Bim, Sol, and Gobelet, and Paul Buissoneau's mobile theatre and television show *La boîte à surprises*. These shows had established a playful working method and an environment focused on audience interaction in which many of the founding members of the Quebec contemporary circus scene had their formative and performative experiences. Traditional American-style circus activity in Quebec from the 1950s through the 1970s does not figure at all in their narrative and, in many ways, contemporary circus in Quebec developed alongside it.

Interestingly, one of the first contemporary touring circus companies to emerge from this new hub of circus training and activity would be called Circus, a Latinate name it would share with the school for a few years. Considering how the term *cirque* would come to permeate the American imagination, it is ironic that the cirque brand started out in Quebec with the foreign-sounding name of Circus. Its links ran East-West, with collaborations with Chinese acrobats and an early 1980s European tour that established connections with Annie Fratellini, Cirque Aligre, and the German Cirque Roncalli. With the 1984 founding of Cirque du Soleil and a formal break between Circus la compagnie and Circus l'école (Jacob and Vézina 2007, 40), the performing company became DynamO Théâtre, finding a subsidized niche in the legitimate theatre world. The company sought to renew circus through a theatre of "acrobatic movement" with a particular focus on imagination-based spectacle for children (DynamO Théâtre 2012, 4–5 and 14; see also Beauchamp and Lavoie 2003, 12). Circus's and, later, DynamO's focus on theatricality and the dramaturgy of acrobatic movement proved to be thirty years ahead of the current resurgence of interest in circus dramaturgy (Cruz 2014; Leclerc 2012; Leroux 2013; Métais-Chastanier 2012). For a few years, before the commercial and cultural success of the province's circuses, the Quebec theatre, dance, and circus scenes were interwoven. Theatre artists, clowns, acrobats, and dancers trained alongside each other. Gilles Maheu (1978), in a manifesto for his company Les Enfants du Paradis, wrote that he sought to "recreate a theatre where dynamic movement and form would trump literary codes." He advocated "a theatre of mimes, acrobats, and jugglers where action would dominate traditional dialogues" (81; my translation). Unexpectedly in a theatrical milieu then dominated by speech and cultural affirmation, Maheu

2.3 Early Cirque du Soleil "Fête foraine" parade down a street, 1983

believed that "only through the world of sports can we really access the world of theatre" (79). Hélène Beauchamp and Bernard Lavoie (2003), in their history of DynamO Théâtre, closely examine the theatrical descendants of those early contacts between theatre and circus, following Circus la compagnie into its contemporary iterations.

As we know, Circus l'école joined institutional ranks as the soon-to-be state-funded École nationale de cirque de Montréal and came to train players in (and define) the emerging nouveau cirque scene, including early companies such as Cirque du Soleil, Cirque du Tonerre (1990–92), Cirque Éloize, the 7 Fingers, and generations of performers and directors since, working internationally.

While Quebec and the United States have had a long shared circus history, with Quebec playing a supporting role until the 1990s, steering its talent southward and providing northern venues for touring shows, what is clearly new in recent history is the strong European influence on the aesthetic, moral, pedagogical, and organizational makeup of circus training and practice. What has made Quebec circus so compelling to North American audiences is its hybrid nature: American showmanship and commercial acumen, European artistic sophistication, Eastern European elite circus-training technique, and Quebec's particularly rich creativity.

North-South Circulations and the Cult of Performance

Cirque du Soleil's early and obstinate obsession with "making it" in the United States eventually inversed the north-south circus relationship, with Quebec steadily imposing its aesthetics and challenging American circus on its own soil. Cirque du Soleil's international success has been consolidated by its integration into American pop culture through its two entertainment centres, Hollywood and Las Vegas, yet its difficulty in breaking into the New York cultural scene has nagged at the company's pride. We should also note that although Los Angeles served as Cirque du Soleil's entry point into the American market and imagination (with the city's animal-free-vaguely-international-and-highly-artistic-circus-for-all market desegmentation), the city's large market proved rather resistant to Cirque's offering beyond attendance at touring shows. Cirque du Soleil found its niche and also cultural and economic growth in Las Vegas, where it tested the market's ability to support eight permanent shows in a single destination.

The Frenchman Sylvain Fagot (2006), assessing the situation with bemused European disdain when faced with the American ethos of placing absolute value on success and physical exploits, clearheadedly describes the threefold nature of the cult of performance at stake in Quebec circus:

> Culturally ensconced in a society which is both "entrepreneurial and athletic," a society which values physical achievement and glorifies social success, circus in Quebec appears to be the paradigm of three socially relevant obsessions: 1) the overvalued status of executives and triumphant entrepreneurs, 2) the celebration of a consumer product, which, in spite of its broad marketing, is seen as an object of distinction, and, finally, 3) the reinvestment of the circus artist's physical qualities as a symbol of "social distinction." Because, in circus as in society as a whole, performance remains the perfect achievement, the mother of all actions. (241–2; my translation)

Performance as the mother of all actions indeed situates performative exceptionalism as the cornerstone of socioeconomic legitimization by placing value on pushing one's limits physically, creatively, and commercially. In that sense, Quebec's "Big Three" (Cirque du Soleil, Cirque Éloize, and the 7 Fingers) have opted for a resolutely American business within the "experience economy," one that is aligned with brandscaping, brand cross-pollination, and for better or worse, a triumphalist cultural and political discourse in Quebec (see Leroux 2009a). Commerce, art, and recuperative national mythmaking have never been so clearly interconnected. Perhaps this is where Quebec circus has most effectively "reinvented" circus, or rather reconfigured it, and brought it most convincingly to the forefront of both cultural and entertainment industries. Quebec's imaginative stamp has been seen repeatedly in American popular culture, as Charles Batson (2014) argues when he refers to the "québécisation" of the entertainment industry in deconstructing pop artist P!nk's normative use of Cirque-style silks during high-impact performances, including the Grammies.

The success and recognition of Quebec circus abroad, and specifically in the United States, have profound implications on the nation's sense of self. This success abroad has strong resonance in Quebec, a nation forever trying to live up to its own expectations and fantasies and acutely aware of the other's gaze upon it.

As Jean Beaunoyer (2004) writes in his opening sentence of *Dans les coulisses du Cirque du Soleil*: "To fully understand Cirque du Soleil's story, we must link it to Quebec's evolution and understand that one's destiny is intertwined with the other's. To share Cirque du Soleil's story is not only to tell the tale of the reinvention of circus in Quebec, but also, and perhaps mostly, to describe a nation condemned to survival through creativity" (15; my translation). *Condemned to survive and to create*. In this context, what is created needs to be essential, magnificent, transformative; it needs to travel, amaze, and appeal to the largest number of people while giving them the sense that they have touched upon something different, something exceptional, something distinct, something that could never have become so big, or so significant, without America's fascination with our version of cirque.

CHAPTER 3

Are Quebec Circuses of Foreign Origin?

Julie Boudreault
Translated by Tania Grant

At the turn of the nineteenth century, Lower Canada was the northernmost destination of the troupes of travelling performers that criss-crossed the continent. These entertainers – comedians, animal trainers, acrobats of all kinds – usually set out from Philadelphia and made stops in a few large cities, such as Boston and New York, before reaching Montreal and Quebec City. Most of them were anglophones of British or American origin. Therefore, from its very beginning, the world of entertainment in Quebec was influenced by British and American cultures.

Given this fact, should we ask ourselves if our circuses today are not simply the successors of the circuses that came from elsewhere? Are there particular links, filiations? If so, can they be traced all the way up to and including Cirque du Soleil? These questions call for some reflection; to offer insight into possible answers, this chapter will revisit the first two main periods of circus history in Quebec. Because the story began with the arrival of a British company in 1797, let us start by looking back at what I refer to as the Grand Era of the British Circus.

The Grand Era of the British Circus

In England, historians generally agree that the creation of the so-called modern circus can be attributed to Philip Astley. However, Astley did not use the term *circus* to describe either his establishments or the shows he presented within them. The first person to use the term *circus* to designate the place as well as the show was Astley's main rival and former employee, Charles Hughes.

Indeed, in 1782, while Astley was introducing his new concept of entertainment in France, Hughes took advantage of his absence to open the Royal

Circus in a location close to his former employer's London establishment. To achieve this, he associated himself with Charles Dibdin, a theatre artist and poet who had authored several pantomimes. Thanks to Dibdin, the Royal Circus was equipped with both a stage and a ring, a concept that was quickly reproduced by others. Astley himself adopted the formula when he realized that his rival was favoured by the public. Consequently, when the Royal Grove, Astley's early performance establishment, burned down in 1794, Astley had it rebuilt according to the Royal Circus design. When that new building was also lost to fire, he once again integrated the stage and the ring into the construction of his new Royal Amphitheatre of Arts. However, that was not the end of the story: the Royal Amphitheatre of Arts also burned down. William Batty, the owner of the property upon which it was built, had it rebuilt once more incorporating the double formula of stage and ring. In fact, the concept was so well suited to the theatre that in 1861, when Batty filed for bankruptcy, the building was able to accommodate plays.

As for Hughes, it is not accurate to credit him with importing the circus to America;[1] rather, it was his student, John Bill Ricketts, who did so. Ricketts started out by directing a riding school in Philadelphia in 1792, and he opened a circus a year later. At first it was a temporary establishment at the corner of Market and 12th Streets; it later moved to its permanent location at the corner of Chestnut and 6th Streets. This first permanent circus in North America was named the Art Pantheon, and its interior design was not unlike that of the Royal Circus in London, as Dominique Jando (n.d.) explains: "In the manner of European circuses, the Art Pantheon was equipped with a ring for equestrian displays and a stage for the performance of pantomimes and some acrobatic acts – a concept developed by Charles Dibdin, a prolific author of pantomimes, who had been the partner of Ricketts' mentor, Charles Hughes." In 1797, Ricketts founded a new troupe that set out for Montreal to open another circus. The production was received with such enthusiasm that the temporary wooden structure built for the occasion was replaced by a permanent stone building. Soon afterwards, in 1798, Ricketts sent his troupe to Quebec City where, once again, a permanent circus building soon followed. It was located outside the Saint-Louis Gate.

In 1821, James West's Circus came to Lower Canada from the United States. It remained in Montreal for two months, at the corner of Craig and McGill Streets. It is interesting to note that James West, the British owner, had been one of the stars of Charles Hughes's Royal Circus in London. There are thus several links between the Royal Circus in England, which intermingled circus arts with theatrical performances, and the emergence of circuses in Quebec.

James West eventually left Quebec, leaving behind his brother William West, who developed a business relationship with William Blanchard, whose nationality is undetermined. This relationship resulted in the creation of the West and Blanchard Circus in 1823.[2] For many years, their circus travelled between Montreal and Quebec City, putting on shows in both cities. West and Blanchard also established two permanent circuses. The first, built in Quebec City in 1824, was alternatively called the Cirque Royal (a translation of Royal Circus) and the Théâtre Royal. According to Baudoin Burger (1974), the author of an in-depth study of the performing arts in Quebec between 1765 and 1825, this establishment "remained for several years the capital's only public place of entertainment where theatre productions alternated with equestrian exercises" (306).

On 10 July 1824, the following appeared in the *Québec Mercury* on the subject of the Royal Circus:

> West and Blanchard, whose equestrian exercises have been given with such eclat in Montreal, are about to establish a Circus and Theatre in this city; having received every encouragement, and the sanction of the civil authorities, to their undertaking. They have purchased, as we understand, the lease of a vacant lot in rear of Malhiot's Hotel, where they propose to erect a suitable building. The plan will comprise a Circus for horsemanship, and a Stage for Dramatic Representations, upon a plan similar to that of the Equestrian Theatres in London.

West and Blanchard's second circus was built in Montreal in 1825. Along with the circus ring, it included a small stage for alternating plays and equestrian exercises, according to an advertisement taken out by the two men in the *Montreal Herald* on 5 May 1824, in which they informed the ladies and gentlemen of the time that "in addition to the circus, they have erected an elegant stage, with new scenery, dresses, etc."

In summary, the double formula of stage and ring became the standard during the Grand Era of the British Circus. The ring was used for equestrian numbers whereas the stage was employed for acrobatic displays and pantomimes. More precisely, the circuses of the time presented a varied program that included equestrian performances, acrobatic exercises, dance, comedy acts, songs, and more. And although the programs shared some elements with today's circuses, a particular emphasis was placed on pantomimes. For example, the newspapers used large capital letters for the titles of pantomimes. Advertisements for Ricketts's Circus announced pantomimes such as *The Death of Captain Cook* or *The Voyageurs* or *Harlequin in Montreal*.[3] I am highlighting this because pantomimes have an important place in Quebec's circus history.

In the theatre, the term *pantomime* can generally be defined three ways: as the physical movements and gestures of an actor, as the pantomime actor him- or herself, or as a stage production in which only body language is used. In other words, in the context of the theatre, a pantomime is a silent performance. However, in the circus, this was not necessarily the case. In the circus, pantomimes were performed on stage or in the ring and could be spoken, danced, sung, played out on horseback, and even swum in establishments equipped with a pool for aquatic acrobatics. They served to link performances. They sometimes involved several characters and often incorporated elements of set design. The stories could be quite simple, of course, but more elaborate narratives were sometimes presented. In particular, some farcical pantomimes with complex stories required performances by the clowns and sometimes included other artists in the troupe. In Lower Canada, the equestrian melodramas and comic pantomimes were the main attractions. They sometimes starred career actors such as the American John Durang, who referred to the circus in Lower Canada in his memoirs, providing us with additional insight (Durang 1966).

Circus and theatre blended so smoothly during the Grand Era of British Circus that Burger (1974) concluded that "circuses were a component of the theatre of the time" (114).[4] So, if we fast-forward to today, can we see a link between the British circuses of the eighteenth and nineteenth centuries and Cirque du Soleil? Can't we say that Cirque du Soleil favours hybrid spaces and produces shows that are entirely pantomimes? I will put these questions aside for now in order to focus on the next period of circus history in Quebec, which I call the Grand Era of the American Circus.

The Grand Era of the American Circus

To date, I have been able to trace no fewer than seventy-two tours of North American circuses in the province of Quebec between 1846 and 1967 (see Table 3.1 at the end of this chapter), and all but one troupe originated in the

United States. The sole non-American troupe was the Cirque Cyr-Barré (1899), which was directed by Quebec strongmen Horace Barré and Louis Cyr. My research is ongoing and I may yet come across others, but one thing is nevertheless certain: the years 1846 and 1967 mark the beginning and the end of the Grand Era of the American Circus. During that period, young and old people from all walks of life flocked to events marking the arrival in their city of one of the American mega-circuses. No one wanted to miss that moment. "From high society down to the lowliest urchin, everyone [wanted to] see them," as *La Revue canadienne* of 1846 explains (Robert-Macaire 1846, 215).[5] The infatuation was so strong that people were willing to cut back on vital expenses in order to see the show. The *Gazette des campagnes* of 10 August 1876 gives the following account:

> It is unfortunate that this troupe [in this case, the circus of John H. Murray] has come during such tight times, when money is scarce and people can barely make ends meet. It is incredible that in Montreal and Quebec, where so many are living in such misery, no fewer than 40 000 people attended the four recent performances of the circus.[6] ("Le Cirque" 1876, 311)

An amusing anecdote from 1883 points to the popularity of American circuses in Quebec. According to the story, when the Barnum & London Circus passed through town, everyone was expected to have the memorable experience of seeing Jumbo the elephant. Barnum himself was astonished to find out that one of Montreal's notable citizens had not caught even a glimpse of the famous pachyderm. The citizen in question was the editor of a major newspaper who had refused to announce the arrival of the circus and had turned up his nose at the idea of attending the show. This was all it took to prompt Barnum, "the master of the bluff," to start spreading the rumour that he would lash that particular editor to Jumbo's side. He even "went so far as to offer him three thousand dollars a year to perform the role of curious beast" ("Causerie" 1883).[7] The editor, whose identity was never revealed, apparently refused, but rumours being what they are, Barnum succeeded in having his circus mentioned in the newspaper.

The American circuses that toured Quebec from 1846 to 1956 all performed their shows under the big top. These were set up in vacant lots or in public places, markets, and parks such as Guilbault's Botanic and Zoological Garden in Montreal. The travelling circuses did not always follow the same route, but all those that stopped in Montreal stayed for one to six days. Generally, they stayed only one day in each of the other cities they visited. All of these circuses put on two performances a day.

The arrival of the circus was often announced with a parade through the streets of the city. The parade served to draw onlookers toward the location of the performances where, amid the fanfare of the band, a number of acts would unfurl in succession: equestrian numbers, animal-taming performances, various acrobatic acts, clown tricks, and so on. The program – somewhat similar to what we find today in traditional circuses – also included pantomimes; however, the pantomimes did not seem to play the important role that they had in the time of the British circus. The American circuses placed more emphasis on exotic animals, particularly rhinoceroses and elephants, which could be viewed even more closely in the sideshows. Before or after the main show, spectators were invited to tour the menagerie and to visit the tents where they could view the freaks, museum shows, and other curiosities.

One last feature of the American circuses was the increase in the number of rings. It is a well-known fact that, in the American tradition developed over time, circus shows took place in three rings encircled by an oval arena. This innovation was credited, in 1880, to Phineas Taylor Barnum and his associate, James Antony Bailey. However, although the three-ring concept became the most common, it was not systematically used by the troupes that came through during the Grand Era of American Circus. For example, an advertisement in *La Minerve* on 14 July 1883 for the Barnum & London Circus announced that the troupe would be performing its show in three rings, a large oval arena, and a 60 x 80 ft stage (approximately 18 x 24 m). On 13 July 1905, in *La Patrie*, the Ringling Bros Circus boasted that its latest production would be presented in six rings. On 29 June 1907, in *La Patrie*, the Adam Forepaugh and Sells Bros Circus took it even further, with eight rings and eight stages. It is clear that the dimensions of the space, as well as the size of the menagerie, were objects of rivalry between the American companies, who all claimed to offer more than their competitors.

In the pivotal year of 1956, the Ringling Bros Barnum & Bailey Circus stopped their big top shows. When they returned eleven years later, it was to the Autostade at the 1967 World Fair in Montreal. On that occasion, dozens of exotic animals strolled down Craig Street to the Expo, where they put on twenty-six shows. By that time, the American circus had already undergone a transformation and was no longer what it had been in the past.

In the years that followed, the people of Quebec became accustomed to seeing smaller American circuses whose shows were performed in arenas or in venues such as the Vélodrome, the Forum, the Colisée, and the Centre Bell (formerly the Centre Molson). Sometimes in the summer, the performances took place under big tops that were erected in shopping-centre parking lots. The American circus's undisputed reign had come to an end. However, starting in 1967, Quebec became more and more open to the world and went through a turbulent period that preceded the creation of several Quebec circuses, notably Cirque du Soleil (see, for example, Leroux's contribution to this volume or Babinski 2004), which, in my analysis, was created as a response to the American circus.

Conclusion

The principal intent of this chapter was to discuss the circus arts in Quebec up to Cirque du Soleil. On the basis of this survey of the first two significant periods in our circus history, can we without question affirm that Quebec's circuses are the descendants of British and American circuses? In my opinion, the fact that certain parallels can be identified in the performance content of foreign circuses of the past and Quebec's circuses of today indicates that there indeed are some filiations between them. For example, the British circuses passing through Quebec in the 1880s and Cirque du Soleil both propose hybrid spaces (ring and stage, multiple stages with ring, etc.) and emphasize the role of pantomimes. Both also mix theatrical and acrobatic performances.

The filiations with American circuses may be less apparent, but they are present. It is important to note that Cirque du Soleil was created, at least in part, to offer a more intimate show centred on acrobatic performances in response to the mega American circuses – even if it itself can be considered a "mega circus" now. In fact, some segments of Cirque du Soleil shows can be interpreted as comments or winks on past (American) circuses. Therefore, a form of dialogue exists between past and present circuses.[8]

However, these filiations tell us only part of the story. To really understand Quebec's new generation of circuses and the birth of Cirque du Soleil, we need to look at the cultural movements growing in Quebec when the American circus was experiencing its decline. It was during this unique time of collective brainstorming that the "nouveau" became possible. It was precisely from

1967 onward that it began to be conceivable to experiment, break conventions, reinterpret traditions, and blur the distinctions between different styles and genres.

Despite a certain number of features shared by past and present circuses, we must ultimately say that Quebec's circuses are not simply successors to the foreign circuses that visited throughout the years. Cirque du Soleil and the new generation of like-minded companies in Quebec are the products of the twentieth century and Quebec's distinct culture. And this is precisely what the other chapters of this collection will demonstrate.

Table 3.1
Some American circuses that toured Quebec between 1846 and 1967 (and their French promotional names)

Mammoth Circus Rockwell & Stone's New York Circus (Cirque Mammoth – propriétaires Rockwell & Stone)	1846
Howes & Co. Circus (Grand cirque des États-Unis de Howes & Co.)	1848
Spalding & Rogers Circus #2 The #1 travelled on water and was called Spalding & Rogers's Floating Palace Circus. (Cirque Colossal dramatique et équestre de l'Amérique de Nord de Spalding et Rogers)	1853
Nixon & Kemp Circus Kemps's Mammoth English Circus and J.M. Nixon's Great American Circus (Grand cirque américain de J.M. Nixon et Kemp's Mammoth English Circus) (Cirque Nixon)	1858
Levi J. North National Circus (Cirque de J. North ou Cirque Levi J. North)	1860
Whitby & Co's	1861

Table 3.1 (*continued*)
Some American circuses that toured Quebec between 1846 and 1967 (and their French promotional names)

G.F. Bailey & Co. (Grand cirque français et américain de G.F. Bailey & Cie)	1861
L.B. Lents' Hippozoonomadon (L'Hippozoonomadon)	1862
Le Grand Mastodonte : Nouveau et grand Equescurriculum This troupe includes the Cirque Olympique de Tom King, the Cirque de Jos Pentland, and the Cirque national de Lent.	1863
S.O. Wheeler's International Circus and Hatch & Hitchcock's Royal Hippodrome Combined (Cirque et Hippodrome Royal de Wheeler, Hatch & Hitchcock)	1864
S.B. Howes' Great European Circus This circus was in fact American. It was made up of a combination of Forshay's Sands & Co. Circus and a collection of European wagons that Howes had brought back from England in 1863. (Cirque européen de S.B. Howe)	1866
Geo. W. De Haven's Imperial Circus (Cirque Impérial de G.W. de Haven)	1867
Howes Trans-Atlantic Circus and Risbeck's Menagerie (Le Grand Cirque Transatlantique de Howe & Gregory)	1868
P.T. Barnum New and Greatest Show on Earth (Cirque Barnum)	1874
John H. Murray's Circus (Cirque de John H. Murray)	1876
P.T. Barnum New and Greatest Show on Earth (Le Grand Cirque de Barnum)	1877

Table 3.1 (*continued*)
Some American circuses that toured Quebec between 1846 and 1967 (and their French promotional names)

Adam Forepaugh's Circus (Cirque Forepaugh)	1880
P.T. Barnum's Greatest Show on Earth & Howes' Great London Circus & Sanger's Royal British Menagerie (Barnum & London)	1883
Adam Forepaugh's Circus (Cirque de Forepaugh)	1884
P.T. Barnum's Greatest Show on Earth & Howes' Great London Circus & Sanger's Royal British Menagerie (P.T. Barnum et Grand Cirque de Londres)	1885
Adam Forepaugh Circus (Nouvelle et colossale exhibition de variétés de Adam Forepaugh)	1886
P.T. Barnum's Greatest Show on Earth & Howes' Great London Circus & Sanger's Royal British Menagerie (Le Cirque de P.T. Barnum)	1887
Barnum & Bailey's Greatest Show on Earth (Le Cirque P.T. Barnum)	1889
Cook & Whitby	1894
Barnum & Bailey's Greatest Show on Earth (Le Cirque Barnum et Bailey)	1895
Buffalo Bill	1885
Buffalo Bill	1897
Cirque Walter L. Main	1898

Table 3.1 (*continued*)
Some American circuses that toured Quebec between 1846 and 1967 (and their French promotional names)

Forepaugh-Sells Adam Forepaugh and Sells Brothers Enormous Shows United (Adam Forepaugh and Sells Brothers)	1899
Ringling Bros World's Greatest Shows (Cirque Ringling Bros)	1901
Adam Forepaugh and Sells Brothers Enormous Shows United (Les Grands Cirques de Adam Forepaugh and Sells Bros)	1902
Ringling Bros World's Greatest Shows	1903
Great Pan-American Shows (Le Grand Cirque Pan-Americain)	1903
Ringling Bros World's Greatest Shows (Cirque Ringling Bros)	1904
Adam Forepaugh and Sells Brothers Enormous Shows United (Le Grand Cirque Adam Forepaugh and Sells Brothers)	1904
Ringling Bros World's Greatest Shows (Cirque Ringling Bros)	1905
Barnum & Bailey's Greatest Show on Earth (Barnum & Bailey, Le Plus Grand Cirque du Monde Entier)	1906
Adam Forepaugh and Sells Brothers Biggest Show on Earth (Les Grands Cirques de Adam Forepaugh & Sells Bros)	1907
The Greater Norris & Rowe Circus	1907
Cole Bros Greatest World Toured Shows	1908
The Greater Norris & Rowe Circus	1909

Table 3.1 (*continued*)
Some American circuses that toured Quebec between 1846 and 1967 (and their French promotional names)

Buffalo Bill's Wild West combined with Pawnee Bill's Great Far East (Buffalo Bill)	1909
Barnum & Bailey's Greatest Show on Earth	1913
Sells Floto Circus	1913
Robinson Famous Shows	1914
Sparks World Famous Shows (Sparks Circus)	1919
Sells Floto Circus (Sells-Floto Super Circus)	1920
Carl Hagenbeck & Great Wallace Circus (Hagenbeck-Wallace Circus)	1920
Ringling Bros and Barnum & Bailey Circus (Cirque Ringling Bros et Barnum & Bailey)	1922
Ringling Bros and Barnum & Bailey Circus (Cirque Ringling Brothers & Barnum & Bailey)	1925
Ringling Bros and Barnum & Bailey Circus (Cirque Ringling Bros et Barnum & Bailey)	1926
Sparks Circus (Cirque Sparks)	1926
Sparks Circus (Cirque Sparks)	1927

Table 3.1 (*continued*)
Some American circuses that toured Quebec between 1846 and 1967 (and their French promotional names)

John Robinson Circus (Cirque John Robinson)	1928
Ringling Bros and Barnum & Bailey Circus (Barnum-Bailey et Ringling Brothers)	1929
Sparks Circus (Cirque Sparks)	1929
Hagenbeck – Wallace Circus	1929
Ringling Bros and Barnum & Bailey Circus (Cirque Ringling Bros et Barnum & Bailey)	1931
Sparks Circus (Cirque Sparks)	1931
Ringling Bros and Barnum & Bailey Circus (Cirque Ringling Bros et Barnum & Bailey)	1933
Cole Bro's Circus, Greatest World Toured Shows	1937
Robbins Bros Circus	1938
Cole Bros Circus (Cirque Cole Brothers) (Le Cirque Cole)	1938
Ringling Bros and Barnum & Bailey Circus	1939
Cirque Hamid-Morton	1945
Ringling Bros and Barnum & Bailey Circus	1950
Ringling Bros and Barnum & Bailey Circus	1953

Table 3.1 (*continued*)
Some American circuses that toured Quebec between 1846 and 1967 (and their French promotional names)

King Bros and Christiani combined Circus	1953
Ringling Bros and Barnum & Bailey Circus 1953	1955
Ringling Bros and Barnum & Bailey Circus	1956
Cirque des Shriners	1958
Ringling Bros and Barnum & Bailey Circus	1967

Source: The archives of the Circus Historical Society, which has been collecting documents on the history of the circus in North America since 1939, and the digital collection of eighteenth-, nineteenth-, and twentieth-century newspapers at the Bibliothèque et Archives nationales du Québec (BANQ). The newspapers consulted at the BANQ are listed in the references.

Note: The table lists the names of circuses, with the original capitalization and spelling, as found in the American archives and, in parentheses, in the Quebec newspapers. Because the business names of American circuses were often loosely translated from English to French when a troupe arrived in Quebec, I decided to list all the designations I came across, whenever possible. I would also like to mention that it was not always easy to establish the nationality of a circus. What criteria should be used to determine the nationality of a circus? Should it be based on the nationality of its founder? On the country in which it originated? On the location of the headquarters? I decided to base it on common use. As an example, common use dictates that the Hagenbeck-Wallace Circus and the Cook & Whitby Circus were American even though one of each of their respective founders was German or British.

II.

Cirque Brands

CHAPTER 4

Performance Services: The Promises of Cirque du Soleil

Erin Hurley

In my past work, I have focused mostly on the production side of Cirque du Soleil. The ways in which Cirque's global aesthetic has helped to create its market niche, build its brand, and inform the company's multinational organizational structure and funding have been of particular interest. By global aesthetic I am referring to Cirque's international casts costumed in otherworldly garb moving to world-beat music and sacrificing individual recognition to the greater importance of "the show." As such, and in combination with an opportunistic relation to place (where Quebec is often depicted as a kind of creative tabula rasa in terms of circus and as a small market that demands innovation), Cirque du Soleil generates its own geographically, ideologically, and aesthetically coherent space, which is conceived as being beyond or above national boundaries. Jen Harvie and I have called this space Cirque du Soleil's land of "imagi-nation," where the image and imaginaries of unimpeded movement and self-discovery prevail over national codes or collective priorities (Harvie and Hurley 1999).

In this way, Cirque du Soleil's shows offer happy representations of globalization and its effects. As Karen Fricker (2004) and Patrick Lonergan (2009) have argued in other contexts, global performances like those of Cirque du Soleil (or, in Fricker's example, Robert Lepage) give audiences a sense or experience of globalization in miniature, if you will. They offer spectators the chance to see juxtaposed in front of them simultaneous representations from East and West, North and South. We watch the world shrink in front of us; we see its populations mingle, its representational codes switch. These performances also offer the chance to watch and identify with transnational travellers like KOOZÅ's "L'Innocent" or *Quidam*'s little girl, characters who enter Cirque's world of imagi-nation (without need of passport or any other identification papers) where they are transformed – generally into extraordinary beings – by its potentialities. Thus, L'Innocent becomes the master magician (or, maybe, the ringmaster of old) with power over the whole spectacle of *KOOZÄ*; it is he who, in the end, turns out the lights (Hurley 2008). Their world-beat aesthetic and narrative of free movement is a fantasy about globalization.

In addition to my focus on the production aspects of Cirque du Soleil, another unifying feature of my previous work is my critical stance – somewhat chastising – toward the company. It should be noted that this is not at all an unusual stance among Québécois academics and intellectuals. Take, for instance, the 2009 dossier "Rayonnement du cirque québécois" in the Quebec cultural review *Spirale*, curated and edited by Sylvain Lavoie (2009b). In its pages Cirque is compared to the Catholic Church of the *grande noirceur* (Lavoie 2009c), a siren song to "real" theatre directors (David 2009), an absurd universe in which a machine is the protagonist (Tardif 2009), a dramaturgically thin production machine (Leroux 2009a), and a force for normalization in an environment that had formerly valued durable differences in the form of freakery (Hurley 2009).

So, to take another perspective on Cirque du Soleil, and one that is consistent with my more recent research into theatre and feeling, I wonder what looking at Cirque from the reception side might reveal. What is its appeal, an appeal that is manifestly widespread? Indeed, theatre historian and reception theorist Susan Bennett (2005, 422) writes: "Cirque du Soleil shows may well have been seen by more people around the world than any other (more than forty million in Cirque's twenty-year history)." What is it offering to, for instance, the Montreal-based spectators who go to the new Cirque show every spring – a population that is more generationally and ethnically mixed than what we are accustomed to seeing at the theatre, as Patrick Leroux (2009a) points out in his *Spirale* piece? What is the promise that draws Las Vegas visitors into the theatre to take in *Mystère*, Cirque's longest-running show? It is notable that on 18 October 2010, *Mystère* celebrated its 8,000th performance, at which point it had been at the Treasure Island hotel and casino for seventeen years and had played for over 12 million people.[1] This kind of longevity, these kinds of numbers force us to ask after the needs and desires to which such a product responds so effectively. I propose that what is on offer in an evening with Cirque du Soleil is a quality and type of affective address from which late-capitalist subjects are increasingly alienated

4.1 *Amaluna*, Cirque du Soleil. Costumes: Mérédith Caron

(or, at the very least, to which they are increasingly unaccustomed). Cirque du Soleil's sought-after "product," then, is a form of emotional labour where its aesthetic elements and narrative through-lines provoke, organize, and authenticate affective experience. Let's call this product a "performance service."

Performance service is an attempt to express the junction of immaterial labour and the efficacy imperative at which Cirque du Soleil – and much expressly commercial performance – operates so successfully. As Michael Hardt and Antonio Negri (2000) have persuasively argued in *Empire*, their analysis of the new political order of globalization, immaterial labour "has assumed the dominant position with respect to other forms of labor in the global capitalist economy" (Hardt 1999, 90). It is not simply the dominant form but the signal form of labour in our "information economy," a postmodern economic structure in which we have passed from the industrial economic model of modernity to a postindustrial informational economy fuelled by services. In an article that anticipated *Empire*, Hardt defines service as follows: "The term *service* here covers a large range of activities from health care, education, and finance to transportation, entertainment, and advertising. The jobs, for the most part, are highly mobile and involve flexible skills. More importantly they are characterized in general by the central role played by knowledge, communication, and affect" (91). The performing arts – which draw on the knowledge, communication, and affective skills of a mobile and flexible (and often unemployed) workforce of artists and technicians – are embedded within this service or tertiary economy. We see this enmeshment most clearly when considering urban tourism. In "Theatre/Tourism," Susan Bennett (2005) assesses performance's role in urban tourist economies as follows:

> For tourism, theatre's importance may not be the artistic product per se but what it contributes literally and symbolically to the contextual commercial environment [...]. The presence of a flourishing theatre district contributes to a city's signification – urbanity, a rich cultural capital, a public life of art and pleasure – an economics that spreads easily beyond the literal box office to encompass other activities (pre- and post-theatre dining and drinking, bookstores and other retail outlets, taxis, and so on). (412)

So, in this service economy that runs on tourist dollars, performance forms like nouveau cirque are valued not merely for their aesthetics but for their "rich signification" – their contribution to creating image – and also for their pleasure, their selling of experience. If, under modern industrial conditions, one might buy a widget or cultivate a respectable image with a string of pearls worn around the neck, with one's ticket to *Wintuk* (New York City,

2007–11) one purchases instead a good time and a feeling of middlebrow cultural respectability.

Following the usage of feminist sociologist Arlie Hochschild (1983) in her book *The Managed Heart: Commercialization of Human Feeling*, I have called this type of transaction "feeling-labour"; by this, I intend to capture the work that theatrical performance does in making, managing, and moving feeling in all its types (affect, emotions, moods, sensations) in a publicly observable display that is sold to an audience for a wage (Hurley 2010). Cirque du Soleil boasts a vibrant stage picture animated with colour and pattern, made sonorous by a live band, and filled with action engrossing on both the narrative and performative levels transpiring simultaneously on multiple levels. In its simultaneous offerings to eyes, ears, and body, it offers a fulsome aesthetic experience that appeals to our full and complex organism.

Number two: the efficacy imperative. Theatrical performance in the service economy is additionally valued for "performance" of another kind; performance studies scholar Jon McKenzie in *Perform, Or Else* calls this second kind of performance "organizational performance." Performance services "serve" in the service economy by being *performant* (successful) in the business-world sense of performance/performing – meeting productivity goals and expectations, operating at maximum capacity, delivering the deliverables. For entertainment products, being *performant* is to ensure bums in seats and satisfied consumers at show's end. With O still selling at 95 per cent capacity every night at the Bellagio in Vegas, for instance, many of Cirque du Soleil's shows have been superior organizational performers. In fact, theatrical performance like Cirque du Soleil's in Las Vegas has been taken up as a model of "new economy" production. In their book *The Experience Economy: Work Is Theatre and Every Business Is a Stage,* Joseph Pine and James H. Gilmore have evocatively called Las Vegas's an "experience economy." Pine and Gilmore (1999) advance a new mode of economic production in which companies script, cast, and stage their goods and services in memorable and transformative "experiences" for their customers. They write, "When [the customer] buys an experience, he [*sic*] pays to spend time enjoying a series of memorable events that a company stages – as in a theatrical play – to engage him [*sic*] in a personal way" (2). That the sensations of experience are felt personally, intimately, is the major selling point. According to Pine and Gilmore, "No two people can have the same experience – period. Each experience derives from the interaction between the staged event and the individual's prior state of mind and being" (12). In short, no two customers buy the same product, even if they are present at the same event; rather, each has a product tailored precisely to their soma. According to industry analysts, selling experience – something the circus has done since time immemorial – is the new growth frontier: "In a survey by Shaw and Ivens, 85% of business leaders said that differentiation by price, product and service is no longer a sustainable business strategy. 71% of these leaders also stated that they believed that 'customer experience' is the new battleground. The same survey found that customers found 44% of customer experiences to be bland and uneventful" (Millard 2006, 12). Theatrical performance of the kind provided by Cirque du Soleil is a superior mechanism for the transmission and delivery of affective experience that, as it happens, is also "successful" in economic terms.

So what kind of "experience" is Cirque du Soleil selling? One promise Cirque du Soleil shows may hold out in their multisensorial attractions is that of being engaged as a complex individual. Optimally, the Cirque du Soleil "experience" produces what famed psychologist of happiness and creativity, Mihaly Csikszentmihalyi (1990), has termed "flow." Measures of flow experiences include (1) losing track of time, (2) having a high level of concentration, (3) forgetting personal problems, and (4) feeling fully involved (Chen et al. 2010, 305). Psychologist Kiyoshi Asakawa (2004) sums up flow nicely as "the optimal state of mind in which an individual feels cognitively efficient, deeply involved, highly motivated, and experiences a high level of enjoyment" (124). In flow, you are both fully differentiated from others and fully integrated with the social group. This is Csikszentmihalyi's definition of a complex organism. You are differentiated or individualized in as much as your own cognitive and physiological systems are working at the top of their game; you are completely engaged in the experience (think here of the multisensorial tracks of Cirque performance tapping both affective and cognitive hardware). At the same time, you are fully integrated with the social group as you experience those heightened sensations as part of a collective; indeed, that collective may serve to heighten the sensations even more (as when audiences collectively gasp and then realize they've taken breath in at the same moment).

Moreover, flow is a fundamental component of creativity and invention – that is, it is both a catalyst to creativity and a product of the same; it is, then, another value of "performance services" and a precondition to

4.2 *Dralion*, Cirque du Soleil. Costumes: François Barbeau

their optimal "organizational performance." Significantly, although Csikszentmihalyi first developed this psychological model of flow in relation to challenging leisure or sporting activities such as rock climbing, business gurus have since taken it up as a management strategy for optimizing employee performance – which brings us full circle to "organizational performance" in the service economy … and back to Cirque du Soleil. Leisure researchers in Taiwan studied the relation between the experience of flow and overall psychological well-being and life satisfaction. Sampling 434 audience members attending a performance of *Alegría* in Taiwan in 2009, they demonstrated that this particular leisure experience, in producing an experience of flow in the spectators, positively affected the sample group's overall life satisfaction (Chen et al. 2010).

The state of flow is difficult to attain as a worker in a service economy, as the abundance of tracts offering strategies to managers for cultivating environments in which flow might happen indicate. Might Cirque du Soleil's "experiences" of happy globalization also be proffering a kind of balm to globalization's precarities? In *Cruel Optimism*, Lauren Berlant (2011) names clearly what Hardt called mobile labour with flexible skills – these are drudges in the grey economy, temporary and contract workers, and unemployed youth. The dominant working conditions of contractual labour in postindustrial societies are shared by artists at Cirque du Soleil. These more precarious positions are some of the societal and, importantly, affective outcomes of globalization and its common travelling companion, neoliberalism, which refers to the deregulation of industry, the corporatization of the public sector, and a social safety net in which the net is rather more loosely knotted than it might be and has been. The "organizational performance" at which Cirque du Soleil excels surges to the fore in a present moment most strongly characterized by a rhetoric of crisis – particularly of economic or financial crisis with the 2008 crash and subsequent recession – that has both crystallized and catalyzed what Lauren Berlant deems the increased insecurity of labour in late-capitalist economies. That is to say, many are living in conditions of precarity, especially with respect to labour. But so does "feeling labour" – at which Cirque also excels – surge to the fore under these conditions. Indeed, it may be that the latter compensates for or somehow makes more palatable the former. The appeal of a fulsome and compelling affective address that raises goosebumps and tickles your fancy, that excites the imagination of better (even transcendent) possibilities and satisfies a need for sensation, is hard to deny. Particularly in conditions that regularly deny (or defer in bad faith) such an address to one's complex organism in the name of that organism's instrumentality and efficiency.

CHAPTER 5

The Last Man in Quebec: Between Circus and Religion

Sylvain Lavoie
Translated by Caitlin Stall-Paquet

Whether our freaks, bohemians, and other street entertainers who came before like it or not, cultural discourse is responsible for reminding us that our circus began in 1984 with the creation of Cirque du Soleil in Baie-Saint-Paul. While Cirque du Soleil focuses on themes as old as time (magic, earthly elements, figures of duality, etc.), and the art form in which it partakes is a thousand years old, the company effects, through its form and genre, an act of inauguration attributable to Guy Laliberté. Consequently, in such a logic, it is to him that we owe the brilliance, the very radiance of our nation, thanks to an art form that would seem to have existed forever.

Not only must we point out the insistence with which we recreate this shining genesis when we discuss the Québécois circus – as if this short chronology could serve as an explanation and would suffice to explain the phenomenon.[1] We must also stress the pervasiveness of the idea of innovation as a sign of a desire for *dissociation* and *rejection* of a questionably glorious past, as the circus was often seen as a grossly popular art form. Thus, on the one hand, there is the circus that "[does] not have a beginning in narrative" and therefore, according to François Paré (1992, 33), comes to pass, as if *sui generis*, as the dominant discourse, while on the other hand, here is a circus company that is so innovative that its art form, apparently, is "never really fully born" (34).

Often polarized between celebration and mutism, discourses on the circus in Quebec usually claim that this art form has difficulty engaging in real dialogue with its observers. These meanderings of language – even as they should not surprise us much (it is not unusual in these lands for critical tools to fail) – seem to be based on many factors. The question of the circus is further complicated when placed within the Québécois context, notably because the circus phenomenon revolves around a brilliantly staged entity that acts as both the starting point and the inevitable reference for a new manifestation of the "national." It is also made more problematic because the Québécois circus (but, we also ask, is this inherently an exclusively Québécois reality?) evolves in a fragile, *small* culture and stems from a genre considered as minor.

Interrogating Cirque du Soleil would not simply mean criticizing its shows, but would rather challenge the identity, the brilliance of a culture that, when success emerges, carries such an epithet as both practical and highly inclusive. This cultural value is rarely scrutinized, this problematic sense of belonging rarely questioned. It's just that this *small* culture truly needs such recognized values, probably to celebrate its identity while freeing itself of several inferiority complexes.

The difficulty is clear when we look at the phenomenon in a global context. In the rare studies devoted to it in Quebec, the circus is most often considered as an artistic product and rarely as a social and/or political form of expression. Beyond the often-explored semantic preoccupations, we ask ourselves little about the conditions of its existence, the mechanisms that shape it, or even the propaganda in which it participates. Indeed, what can we find that is truly Québécois, with the exception of a few names, of course, in this vision and in this aesthetic? The almightiness of the new genre suffices for us. Rid of the animals (ethics and good taste require it) whose odours were replaced by the smell of cash, it profits from the work of sociologists and anthropologists thanks to whom we now speak of a "cultural grab bag" that can include anything from true prowess to a swift kick in the ass, from a synchronized swimming number to insects juggling with giant kiwis. Hybrid mixing will be evoked, the glorious value of which our country is loudly proud. However, does openness to others here not, rather, hide an unspoken fantasy to throw a dart on the great map of the world and say, "We've been there"?

But anyhow, what kind of fool would dare question the qualities of this *Gesamtkunstwerk*? Isn't the success of Cirque du Soleil, the richest ambassador in the field, the guarantor of its value, of its raison d'être and superior qualities? Because – what a supreme honour – it is in comparison to and alongside our national Cirque that many companies from around the world continually position themselves.

Aristocracy and Bourgeoisie

The diversity of Cirque du Soleil is not just characterized by a mix of styles. Cirque du Soleil represents, at least for the land of its birth, an artistic super-elite that somewhat transcends the sociological category of *l'élite artiste* identified by Nathalie Heinich. Indeed, when we take up the subject of Cirque, it is no longer only a matter of excellence and singularity in a democratic regime, meaning the "shift of the professional paradigm [...] to the vocational paradigm" (Heinich 2005, 20) that underlies this artistic activity, but rather a discursive and ideological balancing act perfectly orchestrated between the various axiological incarnations of the old and the new guards. Laliberté's company has built its image as much on bourgeois principles that, as we know, rhyme with power and money, as on an aristocratic system that remains synonymous with prestige even when it has fallen or been displaced by what may henceforth be deemed the star system.

The paradigm of the romantic artist that defines the vocational system described by Heinich is notably based on *singularity* – a paradoxical singularity, as it requires the association of marginal actors in order to be represented. Except that here marginality is no longer considered as a means, that is, the price to pay to deserve one status or another (and if so, it is insidious), but as an end unto itself that characterizes our new circus, one that is always accompanied by the words *innovation*, *risk,* and *audacity*. This idea continues to be a gain for the company, while performers also embrace the notion of romanticism. The company does not hesitate to showcase this sacrifice in the television series it produced, *Sans filet*: a reality show where the performers, those bohemians, testify about the difficulties of exiling themselves to be a part of one of the largest entertainment enterprises in the world. Marginality, which we must recall is no longer the business of freaks, manifests itself in the isolation of these artists who, for once, emerge from anonymity only to claim the sacrifice inherent in success for which Cirque takes home all the fame. Let us also note the consequent disappearance of the projection of an "artistic temporality [...] in the future" (Heinich 2005, 19) because Cirque's overwhelming success is registered in an immediacy that already guarantees posterity. For according to Laliberté, the "Guide," "Every show must be one of a kind" (Collins 2009).

Valorization is bestowed upon the creators – usually Québécois – to whom unlimited resources are granted to bring their wildest dreams to life.

5.1 *Varekai*, Cirque du Soleil. Costumes: Elko Ishioka

They are the ones who possess a (natural) gift, while the talent of the performers, acquired through training in circus schools paired with practice and use of the body, is the work of artisans. From an economic standpoint, there is no need to remind ourselves that all of this is inseparable from a resounding financial success – the highest tribute in a capitalistic era. Along with making us forget about the negative image of the artist with little talent for business or numbers in general (meaning, in such a view, out of touch with "reality"), this glory guarantees to simplistic observers that the company offers a higher-quality product.

It's all there. First, there is work, which breaks with the image of the idle artist completely disconnected from normal life. This work entails long and arduous training that in the end is rewarded with financial success. Second, there is creativity, which is routinely contextualized within nationhood and identity (Cirque du Soleil is *made* in Quebec), even though this sense of cultural belonging is quite problematic and is combined with a claim of continuous innovation on which many similar enterprises base their own productions – indeed, there is even talk of spying! There is also prestige, an amalgamation of all these factors that allows Cirque du Soleil to shine almost everywhere around the planet. Therefore, as Heinich (2005, 350) writes, "Everything happens as if the artist was now collectively responsible for making a fantasy of all-powerfulness come true."

Inscribed as Religion

And lastly, there is the power of an empire that spans from sea to sea and has conquered the hearts of many millions of spectators for the last quarter century. But beyond the artistic dream there is the social and spiritual dream: there is Guy Laliberté, the Guide we have deemed "rich, philanthropic and environmentally-conscious" (Cardinal 2009),[2] the self-made man to whom we have granted honorary doctorates, who purchases ski resorts to "reinvent tourism offerings" (Brousseau-Pouliot 2009), whose name was invoked one day to save a Formula One circuit, who provides water to children of poor countries, to whom we owe allegiance for discovering the rich vestiges of African art, who revitalizes impoverished neighbourhoods, who can make crowds proliferate in cities in decline. His Cirque du Soleil, which "is also our circus," Cassivi (2009) affirmed in *La Presse,* is ranked "in the triple A" of entertainment. The business that "could care less about the financial crisis" (Cloutier 2009) has offered to "reinvent Moulin Rouge" (Brousseau-Pouliot 2009) and have Elvis move to Vegas,

5.2 *Criss Angel Believe*, Cirque du Soleil. Costumes: Mérédith Caron

thereby continuing to be "Montreal's greatest cultural ambassador" as well as its "most prestigious brand" (Cassivi 2009).

These quotations taken from newspapers over the space of only a few weeks show the degree of praise that Cirque enjoys. Quebec is not atheistic. And if it ever was, it was for a short period: artistic expression has become a religion, with figures such as Laliberté granted a servitude reminiscent of that manifested by our good old French Canadians toward a religion that, while often serving them, held them in disconcerting submission.

In taking up an ancient art form and continuously "renewing" it, Cirque du Soleil expands into practically infinite temporality. Likewise, space is invested to a point of ubiquity: not only does the Guide have the gift of spiritually being in two different universities at the same time,[3] but his company, in 2008 alone, took form in 271 cities in thirty-two countries and attracted 11 million spectators (Collins 2009). The creator's fortune climbed to approximately $2.5 billion according to *Forbes*. Power, money, prestige ...

This divine posture is made possible by placing the different affects onto either the group or the individuals that make it up. It is truly a question of the poetics of diversity where, thanks to this art form invested with such diversity, we can dip into all discourses and regimes. This is how Cirque du Soleil has erected itself as religion in one of the most pious lands on the planet.

CHAPTER 6

Circus and Gentrification

Susan Bennett

There can be little doubt about the value of Cirque du Soleil, at least in economic terms. Company spokeswoman Renée-Claude Ménard reported that in 2012 Cirque du Soleil generated almost $1 billion in revenue from 14.2 million tickets sold across nineteen productions running in that twelve-month period.[1] And a "fact sheet" posted on the company's website boasts that since 1984 (its first year, as a group of street performers) "Cirque du Soleil has brought wonder and delight to more than 100 million spectators in more than 300 cities in over forty countries on six continents" (Cirque du Soleil 2013). The breadth of geography and the size of attendance comprise persuasive evidence for this worldwide popularity, as well as demonstrate that an extraordinary number of consumers seize the opportunity to see one or more shows. It is this kind of success, surely, that led *Maclean's* business writer Benoit Aubin (2006) to brand Cirque du Soleil "The Disney of the New Age."

My examination here, however, turns to value neither in a direct economic sense nor in a more typical analysis of intrinsic merit in a particular performance or production and its attractiveness to spectators. Rather, I look to assess the instrumental value of circus in the context of urban gentrification. I want to illustrate how Cirque du Soleil shows have contributed to the revitalization of particular city neighbourhoods, and how, in this way, the performances are implicated in the business of creating and maintaining place identity. While cities have seen the expansion of cultural activity as inherent to an aspirational agenda for particular localities, I argue that this model poses both advantages and risks for Cirque du Soleil's ongoing success. To explore this relationship between circus and urban gentrification, I will look at three North American venues that have hosted Cirque du Soleil shows: Portland, Oregon; Vancouver, Canada; and Los Angeles. In each case, the neighbourhood where Cirque du Soleil has staged its work has been the site of expansive – and expensive – redevelopment plans.

Inner-city regeneration in the last decades of the twentieth century has often relied upon the presence of artist communities to stimulate the adaptive reuse of postindustrial neighbourhoods and usher in new businesses and inhabitants. This phenomenon first drew public attention by way of Richard Florida's (2002) promotion of the "creative city." He suggested that artists living and working in a particular area were a precursor to, or even a trigger for, revitalization of urban locales, and that the development of a "creative ecosystem" (298) was essential for a city to flourish socially and economically in the twenty-first century. Certainly, urban redevelopment has been understood as driven by what Canadian geographer David Ley (1996) has usefully described as the provision of urban amenities. He argues that the presence of these amenities (including – among others – art galleries, restaurants, and environmental quality) is usually indicative of "the incidence of gentrification" in a prescribed area (117). In other words, artists themselves, along with cultural amenities in general, are key stimuli that provoke the return of middle-class populations to inner-city neighbourhoods where previous industrial activity has ceased and where a new service economy is anticipated. The goal, simply put, is to reverse the identity of urban areas that citizens (and visitors) actively avoid, ignore, or do not even know, so those neighbourhoods become, instead, sought-after destinations for stakeholder populations.

As city branding has become more and more commonplace and a site of increased investment from government at all levels (municipal, regional, and even national) as well as from corporate sources, the importance placed on the contributions of culture, both as infrastructure and as content, has exponentially developed. Sometimes cultural content is understood only as instrumental – what Can-Seng Ooi (2002, 98) describes as cultural "baiting," places and events specifically designed to make both local and visitor populations consume in the city. In this analysis, culture, in whatever form, is what draws people to a particular location where they then spend money on all kinds of things and at a level that typically exceeds by substantial factors the cash invested in whatever functions as the bait cultural attraction; thus, if a consumer spends $100 on a ticket to a performance, he or she will likely also spend on restaurants, transportation, merchandise, and in some cases accommodation. These cultural baits may even inspire

6.1 Iconic blue and yellow big top (*grand chapiteau*)

consumers to make their home in the area or suggest to businesses that they will benefit from proximity to such cultural vibrancy. Consumer behaviour created in this way, then, increases benefits to the local economy far beyond the event that served to initiate a specific interaction with place.

It is in this context, I suggest, that Cirque du Soleil has been pursued as an effective contributor to the branding of cities generally and in the rebranding of neighbourhoods specifically. The popularity of *grand chapiteau* performances has been harnessed to the realization of municipal and corporate development agendas; bringing spectators to a particular area has "trained" them to think in new ways about that place. Commensurately, the appeal and attractiveness of those city brands add to – indeed, compose – the company's global reputation: for example, Cirque can advertise how the best of North America's "creative cities" want the company to perform there year after year. In short, circus and gentrification are explicitly linked.

Portland, Oregon, is a city of about 619,360 people (United States Census Bureau 2015), internationally recognized (and often studied and imitated) for its innovative, socially responsible, and green-committed planning policies. It has also been a regular stopping point for Cirque du Soleil's touring shows: when *Totem* played there in the spring of 2014, it became the eleventh production to visit the city (Butler 2013). Cirque du Soleil's grand chapiteau first set up in Portland for *Saltimbanco* in 2000; this and subsequent stopovers (typically six to eight weeks in length) were situated on an empty site just southwest of the downtown area, adjacent to the Willamette River and part of a neighbourhood subject to the city's "River

Renaissance Project." This plan had been devised to reclaim and beautify the bankside extending from the downtown core toward the Marquam Bridge, beginning with the removal of the Harbor Drive Freeway in the mid-1970s (City of Portland 2004, v). The city's earlier *Downtown Waterfront Urban Renewal Plan* (Portland Development Commission 1977)[2] had outlined strategies that would revitalize and improve the river's environs – hotels, restaurants, and retail units – but acknowledged the lack of destination use by locals and visitors, given that this had been a car-only throughway linking downtown to Interstate Highway 5. After the freeway was torn down, the area was, for some time, left empty, which no doubt increased the lack of appeal and of safety. The residence, even temporarily, of a prestige cultural product like Cirque du Soleil reintroduced city inhabitants to this otherwise desolate locale that was still very much in the shadow of other elevated highways leading to the Marquam Bridge.

RiverPlace, a development adjacent to the site where the grand chapiteau was raised for the first time in 2000, had broken ground in 1985 with plans for a hotel and restaurant complex. When the project was finally completed, it had added 480 homes as well as 26,000 square feet of retail and 42,000 square feet of office space to the area – an outcome that illustrates Ley's (1996) assertion that "the orientation of cities toward an office-based service economy is of cardinal importance for the production of gentrifiers" (119). *Saltimbanco* was a huge success for the city in its run from 11 May to 25 June 2000, and between 2002 and 2011 seven further Cirque du Soleil productions visited the city on the same site.[3] Over the same time period, Tom McCall Waterfront Park, designated "an optimum, pedestrian oriented environment for downtown," was successfully established by the city to span the area between RiverPlace and the downtown core, and today is a well-used part of the city that offers easy pedestrian and cycle-path access and is home to many annual festivals. Perhaps not surprisingly, then, with RiverPlace "complete" and footfall well established, the grand chapiteau circus has moved on from the waterfront neighbourhood to a second Portland development site.[4]

When *Ovo* visited Portland in 2012 (5 April to 20 May), the performance site was moved to the north end, an area that was attracting renewed attention after the rejuvenation of the metropolitan Expo Center and the addition of new urban amenities in the Center's environs. A long-standing but tired facility that had originally been built as a livestock exhibition hall in the first years of the twentieth century, Expo Center had been refreshed by the construction of new convention centre buildings as well as a terminus station for one of the lines in Portland's rapid transit network (Portland Expo Center 2012). Cirque set up *Ovo* for a seven-week run on the Expo Center's fifty-three-acre campus, and performances of *Totem* were also staged there in March and April 2014. In addition to its new link to downtown and other neighbourhoods through the rapid transit system, the Expo Center benefits from proximity to the Portland International Airport and a dedicated exit from Interstate 5. In tandem with the convention centre development, there are two thousand nearby hotel rooms, allowing both Center and circus to draw on local, regional, and even more distant visitor populations – a strategy that would boost marketing opportunities and, hopefully, audience numbers for Cirque performances. In this way, the city's tourism draws direct benefit from this particular cultural bait. Whether as part of the repurposing of the RiverPlace area or the reinvigoration of the Expo Center, the history of Cirque du Soleil performances in Portland is significantly one with instrumental benefits to the host environment and the city at large.

Portland is not the only West Coast city that has looked to Cirque du Soleil shows as part of a strategy to upgrade urban neighbourhoods and enhance the attractiveness of its brand for visitors. Indeed, Vancouver had been one of the first cities outside Quebec to see a Cirque show when *La Magie Continue* premiered there in conjunction with Expo '86 (five stops in Quebec along with Ottawa and Toronto followed), but it was not until 2003 that a grand chapiteau tour included the city. *Alegría* (July–August 2003) and then the following year *Quidam* (May–June 2004) visited, setting up in the area of Vancouver known as "Concord Pacific Place." Despite the fancy nomenclature, this is no more than a piece of open ground close to a waterfront and beside a network of elevated roads that lead to and from that city's Cambie Bridge – remarkably similar, then, to the first of the Portland sites. Importantly, Concord Pacific Place is not far away from Vancouver's major sports venues, Rogers Arena and BC Place, and it has been long tagged, at least since Expo '86, to extend opportunities for downtown living and to enhance the destination potential of this part of the city. But development did not pick up in the first years of the twenty-first century, and Vancouver settled as only biennial stop on the company's West Coast grand chapiteau tour – *Varekai* in 2006, *Corteo* in 2008, KOOZÄ in 2010, *Amaluna* in 2012–13 (dates ran from December to January), and *Totem* in 2014.[5]

Nonetheless, Cirque's effect in bringing people to Concord Pacific Place contributed significantly to keeping this neighbourhood in the public eye as well as advertising ongoing ambitions to extend the city's entertainment district beyond its sports facilities. BC Place, built originally for Expo '86, had had a massive upgrade and refurbishment in 2010, and the city was keen to add yet more appeal to the neighbourhood. The announcement, then, of a "massive new Vancouver development" (Griffin and Robinson 2013) in the local press only days after tickets went on sale for performances of Cirque du Soleil's next Vancouver show (*Totem*) hardly seems like sheer coincidence. The landowner, Concord Pacific, detailed plans for eight new condominium buildings (1,300 units) to be constructed on this site with marketing for the first building, One Pacific, to start the following month. In fact, this impending construction was very much in evidence by way of hoardings around the building site and a sales trailer situated in the parking area surrounding the grand chapiteau that was designated for use by Cirque audiences. The development, according to planner Michael Geller, will be one of the city's largest and will turn the surrounding neighbourhood, known as False Creek Central, into "downtown's new sports and entertainment district" (Griffin and Robinson 2013). Not surprisingly, frequency of visits accelerated somewhat with the 2014 tour of *Totem* on site from 15 May to 6 July, directly after the show's run in Portland and only fifteen months after *Amaluna*'s visit.

The robust history of Cirque du Soleil performances in Portland, as well as the company's appearances in Vancouver, evinces an instrumentality to its work in these cities. The stakes, after all, are high. As Michael Beyard et al. (2001, 26) have pointed out, successful revitalization efforts increase property values, taxes, and sales tax revenues; stem crime; generate employment in the construction industry and in the new development itself; improve the city's image; and attract tourists. Even through Cirque du Soleil's temporary occupation of a designated development locale, cities and commercial developers can exploit a tangible potential for stimulating and enacting a larger and longer gentrification plan.

Destination development has also benefited from permanent locations of Cirque du Soleil shows. Las Vegas is, of course, a familiar case study in this context since the company's expansive profile in that city has been at the heart of its transformation from gambling outpost to the largest tourism economy in the United States. But I want to turn here to a permanent show project that demonstrates the risks and challenges of neighbourhood gen-

6.2 Hollywood & Highland Center, Los Angeles

trification. *Iris: A Journey through the World of Cinema*, the show that occupied the 3,000-plus-seat Kodak/Dolby Theater at the Hollywood and Highland Center in Los Angeles from July 2011 to January 2013,[6] was supposed to be the answer for what to do with the venue over the 364 days the Oscars were not being presented. Commissioned on a contract that anticipated at least ten years of performances, *Iris* was intended to be the anchor tenant of a retail destination development that epitomized what Beyard et al. (2001) have called "the trinity of synergy" – entertainment, restaurants, and retail – "within a pedestrian-oriented and multi-use environment" (28). The kind of development, then, that would reduce what Barbara Kirschenblatt-Gimblett (1998) has called the "down time and dead space between high points" in any visitor experience (7). If Hollywood was the prompt to come to this part of Los Angeles, then the gentrification of this iconic spot through development of the Hollywood and Highland Center, with *Iris* the jewel in its crown, aimed to ensure that a variety of activities would keep tourists there, occupied – and spending – 24/7.

The Hollywood and Highland intersection had previously been best known for Grauman's Chinese Theatre,[7] opened in 1927 at the then eye-watering cost of $2 million, and the legendary "walk of stars" along its frontage and down Hollywood Boulevard. But in recent times, the area was commonly recognized by locals and tourists alike as a particularly unattractive part of the city that provided little reason to linger and, indeed, was often seen only from the window of a tour bus because of perceived lack of personal safety at street level. Panhandlers populated the busy intersection, and retail outlets comprised mostly cheap souvenir and snack shops and carts. The neighbourhood was palpably "low end" but nonetheless the destination, albeit briefly, of 18 million tourists each year (Johnson 2011). Not unlike the neighbourhoods in Portland and Vancouver, Hollywood and Highland was an area identified as in need of revitalization and stabilization.

Cornerstones to an expanded tourism market were the newly built commercial development adjacent to the Chinese Theater and, across the street, the revitalization of another Grauman movie theatre, El Capitan, for the Disney Corporation. The El Capitan is used for exclusive prerelease screenings of Disney movies and as a recording studio for the Jimmy Kimmel show. Trizec Hahn's development, soon known as the Hollywood & Highland Center, was given a vaguely ancient Egyptian styling and heavily advertised as the home of the Oscars (and *Iris*). The site was rounded out by the exemplary – one might say, predictable – "trinity of synergy" (shops, restaurants, and entertainment venues, including a multiscreen movie theatre known as the Chinese 6 and a bowling alley) as well as a hotel. Anna Klingmann (2007) has astutely observed that the combination of interests in this urban entertainment development at Hollywood and Highland "markets the fictional context of Hollywood as a 'real place'" (93). In other words, the Center was designed to function as a surrogate for a fantasized Hollywood that tourists cannot hope to locate. Thus, infrastructural changes to the local environment planned to trade on the exclusiveness of Oscar night as a year-round attraction, and to this end Cirque du Soleil was asked to design a show that exploited the world's most-watched entertainment event. The budget for *Iris* was reported at close to $100 million (covering both production costs and theatre renovations), a price tag that included a $30 million loan from the City of Los Angeles's Community Development Department (Ng and Zahniser 2012). The crossover between place, city planning, corporate interests, and entertainment was perhaps never more explicit than the inclusion of scenes from *Iris* performed live at the 2012 Academy Awards, a show that is seen on television in more than 225 countries worldwide – premium advertising to say the least.

While the components for development replicated what has been in many locales and different cities a sure-fire formula for increased tourism (Times Square in New York remains the "textbook" example), the chief problem faced by the Hollywood and Highland neighbourhood was (and is) that it remained a place that people visit almost exclusively in the daylight hours. By night, the area continues to register as "unsafe" in the opinions of many visitors, domestic and international alike. In other words, the Dolby Theater presented location inhibitions that the El Capitan across the street largely avoids since audiences for Disney theatres mainly attend matinees or early evening performances and Jimmy Kimmel records his "late night" show at four thirty in the afternoon.

Iris, by general critical review and equally in my own estimation, was one of Cirque's best shows in years. Subtitled "A Journey through the World of Cinema," it combined the usual range of top-tier circus acts with a smart

6.3 Dolby Theater, Hollywood & Highland Center

and engaging media-dense narrative about the genre from its beginnings in silent film through to today's vivified 3-D technologies, and grounded this story in beautiful imagery and imaginative choreography. Kelly Nestruck (2012), in his review for the *Globe and Mail*, cleverly called it a "site specific" performance. Indeed, *Iris* located audiences in their immediate, contextual geography, both literal and psychic, of Hollywood and all its mythic glamour, at the same time as it referenced their presence in the space of the theatre's "other" site-specific show, the Academy Awards.

But the creativity of *Iris*, which it had in abundance, could not compete with difficult and costly parking for travel-in Californian spectators, already stumping up for tickets with a top price of more than $250. The fact that so many southern Californians travel regularly to Las Vegas for its attractions might have been expected to translate into a more local appetite for a Cirque du Soleil show, but even if that had been the case, the state itself surely was unable to provide a large enough audience to fill the theatre eleven times a week over the anticipated ten-year run. At the same time, *Iris* wasn't bringing in the tourist public who, as suggested already, largely stayed away from a neighbourhood still considered undesirable after dark. David Ng (2013), writing in the *Los Angeles Times*, reported that the show was running as low as 25 per cent capacity, far far below the number needed to meet operating costs, and quoted an anonymous "*Iris* staff member" that "the show's location at the Hollywood & Highland complex was a turn-off." While six- to eight-week stays in a particular city neighbourhood have consistently proven successfully for Cirque du Soleil and, as the case studies of Portland and Vancouver illustrate, successful for cities' gentrification agendas, a permanent show did not work in Los Angeles in the ways that the city-business-circus partnership had imagined. Moreover, this is a salutary reminder for those of us who tend to assess intrinsic merit of performances as the most significant component of success or otherwise.

The failure of *Iris* notwithstanding, my various examples illustrate a variety of ways in which Cirque du Soleil shows have been useful in the provision of the experiential content crucial to the business of place-making and place-marketing. And as specific locations, neighbourhoods, and even entire cities benefit from circus presence, so the company has reaped the rewards of ever-larger markets and healthy growth in spectatorship. Over the last couple of decades, this model has been not just viable but extraordinarily successful. Yet with such tremendous success comes risk, especially as Cirque du Soleil (and perhaps circus in general) begins to register with developers, cities, and even audiences as a standardized component of city/neighbourhood branding. We might usefully remember that some of the projects so sought after for city gentrification in the early 1990s have dropped off the infrastructural map; for example, an aquarium, it seems to me, is no longer a "must build, must have" attraction. There may be a danger, too, that Cirque du Soleil shows have become too familiar to audiences.

Cirque du Soleil appears to have made a smart move in what might be called a repurposing of some of its longest-running shows so as to extend the capacity for revenue generation. Redesigning its shows into a format that can fit sports arenas in much smaller markets has given the company access to very many more cities, and even towns, in the world – places that can now claim the prestige of being on the company's circuit. It is also true that these scaled-back versions circulating to places that have never before seen one of the company's shows live might serve to market the Cirque du Soleil brand more generally and particularly its premium Las Vegas products. The arena shows extend their value in advertising to spectators who might be tempted to see more of the company's work away from home. *Dralion*, for example, premiered in 1999 and spent eleven years on tour as a grand chapiteau show, but has had its lifespan long extended by the production's adaptation to arena performance in 2010. Since this time, *Dralion* has travelled to North American venues including Trenton, Youngstown, Mobile, Fargo, Saskatoon, Tupelo, and Boise as well as international stops across the Middle East. In 2014, the show was seen in the Russian Federation, Belarus, and other European towns and in 2015 travelled to Alaska. If these newer venues are not necessarily tied to explicit gentrification planning, no doubt many of the places see important cultural capital in welcoming a Cirque du Soleil show.

Arguably, the history of Cirque du Soleil's success – and failures – since 1986 is one that has forever changed circus from popular entertainment to premium product. The company's work has consistently demonstrated appeal not just for its content, I argue, but for its significant instrumental value to neighbourhood gentrification and city branding. Cirque du Soleil may well have a particular challenge in staying relevant to the aspirational agendas of cities, rather than finding itself consigned to a list of attributes that no longer provides the cultural or more literal equity that these places are looking for as other entertainment brands become better bait for the sought-after urban demographic. Certainly the fate of *Iris* should sound a note of caution for all present and future city-circus partnerships even as Cirque continues to pursue reciprocally important relationships in the development of new markets globally.

In conclusion, then, Cirque du Soleil has traded effectively on its abilities to bring value to specific places, often a value that endures and develops long after the grand chapiteau has moved on. As the examples of Portland and Vancouver indicate, this continues to work effectively to showcase a neighbourhood undergoing gentrification. Yet the formula is not foolproof as the Hollywood & Highland Center demonstrates: the Cirque du Soleil model is not infinitely adaptable. In this way, its global brand cannot be understood in isolation, as constructed from the quality of the company's performance work, but rather this brand belongs to, and is dependent on, an intricate series of connections with those places where circus has value, in different kinds of ways, as part of the local scene.

III.

Dramaturgy and Aesthetics

CHAPTER 7

Les 7 doigts de la main and Their Cirque: Origins, Resistances, Intimacies

Charles R. Batson

In 1999, three years before the founding of the circus troupe Les 7 doigts de la main (known in English as the 7 Fingers), Jennifer Harvie and Erin Hurley published their seminal "States of Play: Locating Québec in the Performances of Robert Lepage, Ex Machina, and the Cirque du Soleil," one of the first important pieces of scholarship devoted to Québécois circus studies. Their careful and cogent arguments present ambiguities at play as the dominant artistic forces named in the article's title reach out beyond Quebec's borders to position themselves as companies with noteworthy international presence and prestige. In their analysis, even as institutions such as the Quebec government see the prestige of the province itself enhanced by such international productions, the actual "relationship between production and a Québec location" (300) for these companies is, at best, tenuous; in fact, Cirque du Soleil's productions may well be predicated on "that link's demise" (300), since the only "'nation' to which the Cirque du Soleil claims allegiance is the one it produces – its non-territorial 'realm of imagination'" (309).

With such a presentation, Harvie and Hurley explicitly call for a critical gaze on the postures taken by the celebrated Cirque du Soleil and on the very celebration of that troupe, which was named in a 2011 *Les Affaires* poll as the enterprise the Québécois population most admires (Turenne 2011). Sylvain Lavoie's introduction to a series of essays on Quebec circus published in *Spirale* in 2009, some ten years after Harvie and Hurley's article, echoes those calls. Speaking of the "Radiance of Québécois Circus" of his essay's title, Lavoie (2009b) remarks that the brightly shining "Cirque du Soleil of course occupies a central space, but its very standing gets in the way of a full portrait of the situation" (11).[1]

This chapter works to respond to Lavoie's lament and to Harvie and Hurley's call by offering a close look at the 7 Fingers, a circus troupe founded in 2002 that has since garnered significant international recognition even as they take on strikingly anti-Soleil postures. Through an examination of the troupe's history and their pieces, we uncover an aesthetics of intimacy and authenticity that not only governs artistic choices but also resists dominant practices of the older and bigger Cirque. As their shows work to create a sense of identification with their audience members, they provoke a delight in performance as an experience of shared realities both through and beyond the language choices that Françoise Boudreault has cogently and insightfully explored in her 2012 article "Le cirque parlant des 7 doigts de la main." In my analysis, these intimist spectacles take some of their charge from the physicalities at play on Quebec's stages and in city streets since the fervently creative cauldron of the 1980s and the development of a heightened physical language of performance – the *nouveau bouger montréalais* – with such companies as Carbone 14 and Lalala Human Steps. Ultimately drawing on the writings of Roland Barthes to help us conceive of these intimacies even as the troupe now joins Cirque du Soleil as a powerful force of the nouveau cirque québécois, I explore how the sense of authentic exchange may remain alive in the 7 Fingers' richly layered works.

Intimacies and *Grandeur d'homme*: Traces of the Human

In language repeated in official press releases and show programs, the 7 Fingers declare that their troupe was founded with the goal to "apporter au cirque une nouvelle saveur" (bring a new flavour to circus) with the creation of "spectacles à grandeur d'homme" (human-sized shows).[2] With such language, they claim a newness and set themselves up as a contrasting force to what Harvie and Hurley remind us had been the established reference in nouveau cirque québécois, the Cirque du Soleil; such language also serves to position their work as having a "human scale," to use another phrase reiterated throughout the company's textual material including the program for their 2012 creation *Séquence 8*. It is this human scale, if we follow the rhetorical gesture, that stands as their new flavour, their new texture, their new posture, one that is necessarily different from the offerings of the dominant Cirque. Harvie and Hurley (1999) were among the first to remind us that Cirque du Soleil's productions end up erasing specificities of any one particular space and, even, of any one particular performer. From their "fantastical costumes, masked or heavily made-up performers, [...] world-beat music written in an Esperanto-like language, and the gibberish of the Cirque's 'speaking' clown characters" (312) to the "effacement of performers' ideological, cultural and national placements" (313), Cirque creations are of a scale that removes traces of any specific originary space or any originary human.

A study of Cirque du Soleil's history suggests, however, that such artistic choices stand at a remove from the energies present at that troupe's creation.[3] As buskers, stilt-walkers, and clowns who had performed in the province's streets and festivals in the 1970s and 1980s, Cirque's founders had used their street skills to garner provincial funding in 1982 for a *fête foraine*, a sort of fun fair in which several nascent troupes participated including the musical group La Fanfafonie, the physical theatre-dance troupe Carbone 14, and the circus group Le Cirque du trottoir. It is from this early rough-around-the-edges atmosphere, where artists from multiple disciplines could juggle and toss their talents together, that Cirque du Soleil took shape and, with this fête-honed creation, ultimately embarked on a tour of the province in celebration of the 450th anniversary of Cartier's discovery of what would become Quebec. In those early moments of the troupe, provincial origins and specific provenances seemed all but fêted themselves in these festivals that grew from the street arts of the performers and founders. It is with *Alegría*, a show developed some ten years after the company's founding, that Cirque programs began to represent "the acts in photographs without captions" (Harvie and Hurley 1999, 313), with the attendant effacement of the particulars of the human performing the act, an anonymity that remains integral to the company's standard working procedures.

As we know, the Cirque shows and, importantly, their particular practices grew in visibility through increasing numbers of touring productions and the establishment of fixed-theatre creations in Las Vegas and Orlando that exposed their specific forms of nouveau cirque to ever-swelling numbers of spectators. It is in such a context that the 7 Fingers formed to create their *nouvelle saveur*, with its particularly human flavour. In 2002, seven circus artists from various national origins (France, Quebec, USA), training regimens (the École nationale de cirque, elite sport, family circus exposure), and performance histories (Cirque du Soleil, San Francisco's Pickle Family Circus, Quebec's Cirque Éloize) created a collaborative collective to feed their first performance project that would, as a 2010 press release would have it, "move away from the standards of a circus of the fantastic."[4]

In a 2011 *New York Times* article, Shana Carroll, founding member of the 7 Fingers, makes reference to the experience of performing with Cirque that all seven of the founding Fingers shared and wished to step beyond: "We owe them our careers. But when you've been at Cirque so long, and you're hidden in costumes and makeup, there was this desire to break all that down" (qtd in Pincus-Roth 2011). For her and her cofounders, the effacing practices of a cirque had to disappear to make way for its *matière première*, its primary matter of human performers, human artists.

Now more than a decade after their founding, the troupe considers their first performance piece, the 2002 *Loft*, to be "our first baby, through which our collective's work took on all its meaning": it is "how we first presented Les 7 doigts to the public, and how we first revealed our artistic language and vision of circus on a human scale."[5] This performance thus carries signal importance for understanding their origins and the particular flavours of their resistance to the dominant Cirque. Produced in the context of the Juste pour rire festival that for some twenty-five years took place in the sometimes gritty streets around Montreal's Quartier Latin, the show's very setting recalls the origins of the nouveau cirque québécois and the street performers who busked, stilt-walked, and juggled on their way to create their Cirque du Soleil. Rejecting the shades and textures of the fantastic that they see inflecting the shows of that originary troupe, the 7 Fingers created their "Loft" to present "seven close friends" who "strip down layer by layer to their own idiosyncratic cores"[6]; such psychological revelations are both mirrored and informed by the exposure of these friends' bodies in minimalist costumes of white t-shirts and briefs. The 2011 *New York Times* article notes that Gypsy Snider, another of the founders, calls this work "kind of the 'Friends' of circus," in reference to that popular television show that followed the daily lives of a group of friends in Manhattan. Instead of talking about the varying successes and failures of their love lives, however, these circus-performing friends reach for the eclectic objects found in their shared loft – "apples, shoes, bathtubs, flashlights, knives, lampshades, Barbie dolls – to entertain themselves in the monotony of their daily lives."[7]

It is instructive to note that by the time of production, the seven close friends, the real 7 doigts performers and not just their staged characters, had ended up living in their own loft together in Montreal, often using their shared living areas as rehearsal or creation spaces. Gypsy Snider's rhetorical analogy thus suggests that, as the friend-performers refer to each other by their real names as they toss their apples, shoes, and dolls around their

7.1 From *Loft*, with Faon Shane, 7 Fingers

loft, the Phoebes, Joeys, and Rachels of the circus stage – Isabelle, Sébastien, and Shana, for example – somehow reveal something about themselves as individuals, with their own idiosyncrasies, as they perform their personas. When Patrick throws himself forcefully onto his foam steps, or as Shana languidly ascends on her trapeze for an oneirical sequence; when Faon twists and twirls in her aerial chains, offering a contrast between the harsh sounds of the metallic apparatus and her lyrical movements, or as Gypsy shows an intimacy with the knife she spins and thrusts: in these moments, the audience senses that it gets a glimpse into the human complexities nourishing the performers' actions.

A key element of the production that encourages this kind of identification occurs prior to the show's beginning, when some audience members enter the hall through a stage door designed to look like the door to the loft's kitchen refrigerator. As these audience members enter, the artists introduce themselves and each other as they guide their public to their seats, a gesture that solidifies the recognition of the human scale of their creation. Welcome to our loft, they seem to say; make yourselves at home. At the reprise of this work at Montreal's TOHU in 2004, as the inaugural show for this unique circular performance space designed specifically to showcase the circus arts, several late-arriving audience members were shown to their seats through this stage door as Patrick went on wrestling with his stairs mere inches away from where they were walking, thus continuing to blur distinctions between the public and the performers. Both audience and artists trace steps on the floor of this space.

In an interview with the UK's *Guardian* in the context of a review of the 2010 tour of the troupe's second creation, *Traces*, Snider offers strikingly similar language to that used by Carroll in the 2011 *Times* article: "We weren't so much escapees from Cirque du Soleil as graduates. But we wanted to be creators, not just performers – making circus on a human scale" (Gardner 2010). She goes on to note that this choice was not merely one of reaction or resistance to the dominant aesthetics and practices of Cirque; the founders saw in it an artistic tool. "We discovered that the wow factor is magnified when you establish an intimate relationship with the audience. Watching someone diving through a hoop is more jaw-dropping when you feel you know them" (Gardner 2010). As we, the audience, make ourselves at home in this space where people walk around their lofts in their underwear, introducing themselves to us, we feel we know, or at least recognize, the Sébastiens and the Isabelles of their *Loft*. Snider's argument suggests that such an identification enhances our response to the art these Sébastiens and Isabelles create. We are more touched, affected, troubled when we see them in an intense hand-to-hand sequence or twisting in an aerial feat, as they literally move beyond any other Sébastiens or Isabelles that we know in our own quotidian spaces. These humans whom we feel we know, who walk, talk, and wrestle with boredom, are suddenly doing things that partake of the extraordinary. Since what we thought we knew about them is troubled, so too may what we think we know about ourselves be troubled.

In her important text "Intolerable Ambiguity," the theorist Elizabeth Grosz has argued that such extraordinary beings "traverse the very boundaries that secure the 'normal' subject in its given identity" (1996, 64).[8] While Grosz's article traces reactions provoked by what is frequently called the "freak," her arguments on the extraordinary body also speak to what Snider calls the power of the "wow factor" nourished by our sense of identification with these humans who are noted by and in their difference: such a being, for Grosz, "confirms the viewer as bounded, belonging to a 'proper' social category" (65), while provoking a recognition that the exceptional being is our differently shaped mirror-image. Being one of us yet escaping from what we think we know about ourselves, this remarkable being threatens the understood "limits of our own identities" (65) while occasioning in us a "narcissistic delight" (65) at considering our own possibilities through identification with these different images of ourselves.

The Sébastien and Isabelle we "know" to be like us are now shown to be wowingly extraordinary, provoking questions about our own ordinary nature: with Grosz, we can apprehend the valences of our delight at seeing limit-exploding, exceptional versions of ourselves in underwear, hanging from chains and twirling knives. Such delight may well be less present, less provoked, when, to revisit Shana Carroll's terms, the humanity of the exceptional human is hidden in costumes and makeup. With its glitz and shine, Cirque du Soleil may offer "glamour," as Erin Hurley (2009, 25) has suggested in her review article "Le cirque: de la différence à la ressemblance"; the 7 Fingers, with their troubling intimacies, offer frissons. In a 2011 review of the New York version of *Traces* that names it among the year's top ten plays and musicals, the American newsmagazine *Time* summarizes this very distinction: "At Cirque you sit in awe. Here [with the 7 Fingers] you're on the edge of your seat" (Zoglin 2011).

In early 2006, the 7 Fingers produced a first version of *Traces* to sold-out houses at Montreal's Théâtre Corona, with five new artists performing under the direction of two of the original Fingers, Carroll and Snider. In this troupe's path toward creating for their audiences the feeling that we understand these strangely knowable, thrilling strangers – these circus artists who may be like us but who do things that we cannot do – this production offers a significant paving stone. Here, the intimacies are shared even more explicitly with audiences through spoken words that are presented as autobiographical texts uttered by the performers as they go about creating their traces, those things that might be left behind in a world that may disappear tomorrow or even tonight. In a shared disaster shelter, the artists offer their names; they reveal, through both gesture and word, their anxieties and their hopes; they speak of what feeds them and of what they would like to feed others both in the shelter and beyond. Such an artistic choice to include significant and meaning-filled speech as the artists move about the stage, a

choice that indeed nourishes our perceived closeness to them, is also decidedly a non-Cirque choice, where texts, if they exist, are declaimed in that no-man's language noted by Harvie and Hurley (1999), uttered at a significant distance from any recognizable human production.

In an interview in the green room of the TOHU in November 2012, as the troupe was preparing for that evening's show of their creation *Séquence 8*, Shana Carroll recalled the creative process behind *Traces*'s first iteration. Noting that it was a "conscious choice to present the characters as real people," she and her fellow creators wanted to work to have "*that* as the emotional experience," the charge of recognizing real people doing real things on stage. The virtuosic circus numbers, such as the Cyr wheel, double Chinese poles, and increasing numbers of stacked Chinese hoops, are constructed to arise out of ordinary actions like playing basketball, playing the piano, and riding a skateboard. During the creation process, Carroll notes, the performers crafted their "texts built on their own lives," ultimately "creating their characters out of their *own* character," a process aided, perhaps, by the directors' previous relationships with the performers.[9] Carroll and Snider knew them from well before the show took shape, having frequented their performances in San Francisco prior to their enrolling in Montreal's École nationale de cirque.

The creators encouraged them to "use their skills that *we* knew they had," emphasizing the multivalences of their talents in order to include the musical numbers and parkour-inflected sequences, for example, that set them apart from other, more classically trained circus performers who might be highly skilled in only one particular discipline. These particular artists, Carroll noted, possessed a "rebellious energy" that further distinguished them from their more traditionally trained peers, an energy that the creators knew from early on that they wished to showcase on stage. The show thus offers the artists to us, the audience, in multiple layers: their lives inform the texts they declaim and the characters they embody, their specific performance and training histories give shape to the structure of the show, and importantly, their particular nonconventionality underlies the entire enterprise from its very inception.

7.2 Opposite From *Traces*, with Francisco Cruz and Gisle Henriet, 7 Fingers

After *Traces*, the troupe produced the first shows of its *Fibonacci Project*, a series of intensive collaborative experiences created in conjunction with international circus troupes designed both to showcase artists from differing cultures and to model practices of collaboration with creators from significantly different experiences and expectations. The troupe's engagement with this long-term project, first with the Cirko De Mente of Mexico City in 2007 and then with the Artcirq of the Nunavut Amerindian communities in 2008, stands arguably as a gesture that mirrors the troupe's foundational moment of forming a *collectif*: from out of their multiplicities, their differences, and their individualities comes their eponymous hand, crafted to work in both strength and flexibility.

The *Fibonacci Project* will continue through 2017, its collaborations with practitioners of multiple arts, including digital media, shepherded by founding member Samuel Tétreault. This reaching out to other forms of performing arts continues to guide the company's artistic directions. Gypsy Snider, for example, worked with the noted theatre director Diane Paulus as choreographer of the circus sequences for the award-winning 2013 Broadway revival of *Pippin* at New York's Music Box Theatre. *Le Murmure du coquelicot* (The Murmur of the Poppy), a 7 Fingers creation for Montreal's Théâtre du Nouveau Monde in the fall of 2013, unites quite explicitly the theatrical and circus arts in a play created by another founding Finger, Sébastien Soldevila. In that creation, Tétreault joins award-winning Québécois actors Rémy Girard and Pascale Montpetit in a marriage of the physical and the theatrical, the choreographed and the declaimed. Furthermore, *Cuisine & Confessions*,[10] which premiered in Montreal's TOHU in October 2014, builds on themes and structures developed for the company's *Queen of the Night* that was conceived for New York's Paramount Hotel as an interactive "fusion of performance, music, circus, cuisine, and design."[11] Collaboration among the arts thus continues to mark this troupe's artistic directions.[12]

In 2007, the 7 Fingers were invited for a residency at Lower Manhattan's Spiegelworld, where they created *La Vie*, an exploration of the sensations and meanings of death and life set in a kind of purgatory where a master of ceremonies, played by Sébastien Soldevila, stands to judge any eventual salvation. True to their originary story of distinguishing themselves from dominant aesthetic practices, Soldevila reports in a *La Presse* interview that Spiegelworld wanted "a 'late-night show' somewhat along the lines of the film *Moulin Rouge*, with big, flamboyant, titillating costumes." His next phrase is perhaps particularly revelatory: "But that's not us, big flamboyant costumes, so we fought to be able to tell a story [...] to show that it's not necessary to be naked to be sexy" (Blais 2008).[13]

Indeed, in costumes that mimic the everyday wear of denizens of the waking world (three-piece suit, négligée, lab coat), the artists – all seven of the original Fingers – use their circus-trained skills to evoke a senses-filled life-after-life as they spin diabolos, balance on blocks, twist in aerial chains, and cavort in hand-to-hand exchanges. Even as the artists themselves remain arguably accessible to their public, not hiding behind flamboyant costumes and revealing through word and gesture essential pieces of their characters' lives and deaths, *La Vie* presents these characters (an airplane pilot or a patient in a psychiatric ward, for example) principally as fictional ones, not autobiographical or, even, autofictional. The very conceit of the show – purgatory cloaked in the trappings of a cabaret in which artists and spectators are all dead – speaks little to the lived realities of the public.

It is with *Psy*, created by Shana Carroll with assistance from Isabelle Chassé, that the troupe reestablishes a clear link with that other element of their originary story: not only do they reject dominant aesthetics, they do so through offering shared intimacies that suggest the revelation of the human in the artist. The program notes from the work's February 2010 premiere at the TOHU point to such a process: the creators remark that as the show, which stages "the dense and surreal depths of the human psyche,"[14] was taking form, "on top of their role as interpreters, [...] the artists gave of themselves, down to their soul."[15] On stage, the show's eleven artists confront and perform neuroses that seem fully to live in their skins, in their bodies. Even as they take on names that differ markedly from their own – Guillaume Biron portrays the schizophrenic Michel Michel, for example, and Danica Gagnon-Plamondon plays Lily the agoraphobe – the performers take on postures that recall those of *Traces* in their declamations of who they are and how they walk, spin, and climb through the world. Constructed around sessions of group therapy, one-on-one conversations with a psychiatrist, and communal moments of exorcising psychological demons, the structure of the show demands such staged revelations.

As the show moves along, the artist-characters' actions take on meaning that informs and is informed by such revelations: "a man hears voices ordering him to hang from a trapeze by his toes in the peaceful office of his psychologist ... An obsessive-compulsive patient caught in a crowd tries to escape through a series of acrobatic movements across the human mass; a woman overcomes her agoraphobia by swinging in the air; a man looks for his identity in a balancing crowd of masked faces."[16] As with *Traces*, these characters both move and talk, with the second act staging a lengthy group therapy session where there is little action (the artists stand in a sort of static semicircle) but many words. The language here is immediately recognizable to anyone having attended any therapy session – and at the show's Montreal 2010 premiere, the artists used their bilingual city's two principal languages, French and English. These are people we, the audience, are meant to understand: they speak our language(s).

The troupe's vaunted grandeur d'homme comes across in these artists' soul-filled offerings, or so several reviewers would suggest, including a review of a highly successful tour in Stockholm in which the reviewer notes that this piece "comes out of our human fragility," the artists' "bodies telling the story, and turning their bodies and souls inside out" ("Dansant" 2009). It is perhaps instructive to remember Harvie and Hurley's (1999) comments on Cirque du Soleil and the no-man's-land created in their shows; here the 7 Fingers work to showcase "the dense and surreal depths of the human psyche," the troubled lands of the mind.[17] Indeed, as the show moves along in its explorations of these very human obsessions and compulsions, presented, as that Stockholm review would have it, with "every number begin[ning] in an everyday situation," we audience members find ourselves thinking that we may know some other people from our quotidian lives who, without their Prozac or their Lexapro, could well be climbing Chinese poles, swinging from ropes, and throwing knives.

Séquence 8: Intimacies and Resistances a Decade Later

In a morning-after review of the company's 2012 creation, *Séquence 8*, following its July premiere at the TOHU as the inaugural show of the annual Montréal Complètement Cirque festival, *La Presse* notes that "since *Loft*, their first show, the 7 Fingers have invested in closeness with the audience, letting their members' personalities show themselves" (Lapointe 2012).[18] This language of authenticity, of shared intimacies, of revelation, begun some ten years earlier, thus continues to circulate in this production directed and conceived by Shana Carroll and Sébastien Soldevila for eight recent graduates of the École nationale de cirque. But instead of getting to "know" the 2012 versions of the Isabelles and Patricks in their underwear-baring, trace-revealing intimacies, *Sequénce 8* offers the premise, if not the illu-

7.3 From *Séquence 8*, with Colin Davis, 7 Fingers

sion, of experiencing them as their performative selves. As the show progresses through virtuosic cigar-box, Korean plank, and Russian bar numbers, for example, the artists sometimes pause – often at the prodding of Colin Davis who, in a role intimating that of an emcee, animates a kind of faux radio show – to tell us what is going on and how they are doing what they are doing. They thus reveal, if not their psyches, then their training, their past, their present. In their reviews, journalists remark on the effect of such revelations. A feature article in Montreal's *Voir* magazine notes, for example, "Through interaction with the audience and a few ironic moments, *Séquence 8* yet again gives power to the spectator's emotions" (Pépin 2012);[19] *Stage Magazine* remarks, in a review of the show's touring engagement for the Merriam Theater in Philadelphia that began shortly after the Montreal opening, that "7 Fingers creates a personal mood of charm, intimacy, and camaraderie" (Miller 2012).

Some ten years after *Loft*, as these journalists emphasize that language of shared authenticities, they note this troupe's differences from the bigger and older nouveau cirque québécois, Cirque du Soleil. Pépin (2012), for example, observes the 7 Fingers' focus on avoiding the dominant "watered-down versions" of circus language to "create an intimacy with the public."[20] *The Arts Fuse*, in a review of *Séquence 8*'s fall 2012 Boston engagements, insists on laying out "the difference between Les 7 doigts and Montreal's better-known nouveau cirque export, Cirque du Soleil" (Thai 2012). For this reviewer, the distinctions are noted and notable in the aesthetics of the show itself: "While the latter's shows also feature a thematic or narrative through line, the virtuoso displays have only a tenuous relationship to the larger story. Les 7 doigts, by contrast, treats acrobatics as a form of acting, not as interludes between the more character-based pieces." And the whole, in *Séquence 8*, is "all at the service of exploring the process of the work the performers do, the role that jealousy, camaraderie, love, and admiration play in the act of creation, the relationship the troupe members have with the audience, and how their performances are interpreted." The reviewer's next line is particularly revelatory in terms of the shared authenticities these journalists sense and then share with their readers: "Indeed, it should be noted that a number of the cast members studied and performed together as duos prior to joining Les 7 doigts" (Thai 2012).

That "indeed" suggests, of course, a slippage between the characters perform*ed* on stage, taking shape through gesture, word, and acrobatics, and the artists perform*ing* on stage, whose own creative processes and relationships with their art and each other inform those very shapes. The show's simple backdrop of several frames, some oval, some rectangular, may contribute to this understanding of a slippage: these frames suggest a *jeu*, a play or set as the French language would have it, of hanging mirrors or portraits capturing or reflecting the shapes of the performers – as well as their movements, as the frames shift and move in the air currents caused by the performers' actions. These performers' "thing done" is always thus a "doing," to borrow language from the performance theorist Elin Diamond (1996, 1), pointing to the liv*ed* experiences that their audience senses as liv*ing*.

Near the show's opening and again near its close, Colin Davis remarks, in an aside to the audience, that he and his fellow artists will have offered, "ici" (here), "un peu de nous, pour vous" (a little of us, for you), "ensemble" (together) in a rhetorical gesture that renders explicit the troupe's proposed aesthetics of shared intimacies since *Loft*. It should be noted that Davis, an anglophone, spoke in French at the performances in Montreal. In this city alive to meanings of language use, such a choice is particularly rich. As Françoise Boudreault (2012) suggests at the close of her article on what she calls the 7 Fingers' "talking circus," "language can lead the spectator to modify the stereotypical image of the superhuman acrobat" because the words point to the artist as a human who is "both performer and author of a text" (133, my translation). Davis, with his accent, reveals his own real and human history as an American who has had to study to learn French. Furthermore, this talented artist who has mastered his physical languages shares them with us in a linguistic idiom that for him is less strong, hinting at an approachable weakness even in his strength; his language of sharing, although not native to him, is the one native to most of his audience, and is thus the one in which emotions, linguists tell us, are more richly experienced.

La Presse's review closes with a reference to Davis's very words in language that suggests that an emotional charge has indeed been passed on: it praises the show as it "weaves a thread between itself and the audience"[21] in its explicit and implicit propositions of shared and reflected intimacies. The result, for the author, is "a successful communion" (Lapointe 2012).[22] If we follow this reviewer, some ten years after *Loft*, the aesthetics of shared intimacies, springing out of resistance to dominant Cirque practices, continues to delight audiences who see themselves in communion with their own images as reflected in the exceptional humans on stage.[23]

Conceiving Intimacies

In the fall of 2003, approximately one year after the 7 Fingers produced their first intimist show, Cirque du Soleil opened *Zumanity* in Las Vegas in an explicit attempt to exhibit an intimacy, an authenticity, through an erotic cabaret with real bodies on display, where an emcee from the world of theatre exploits the power of real words, and where the energies of a real, not watered-down, rough-and-tumble world of seedy performance may be felt. Louis Patrick Leroux's (2009d) important "*Zumanity*: la spectacularisation de l'intime" explores in depth the stakes of such an engagement with what the creators, who proclaimed "We have tried to be real" (71),[24] conceive of as authentic, as real. In his convincing analysis, Cirque du Soleil's presentation of authenticity and intimacy, in this one show that supposedly breaks from the mould of its spectacle-creating machine to give us bodies and souls, remains precisely that, a presentation. "The show prides itself to be one about the intimate – the intimacy of sex, the unveiling of one's desires, of one's perversions and of one's preferences. In fact, it's Cirque that exposes itself" (86).[25]

In such a presentation, instead of real desires pursued by real people, the audience gets a show on how Cirque conceives a show about desire, ultimately serving only to affirm "the will and the capacity of the Cirque du Soleil to reveal its assets without embarrassment or shame" (86).[26] This distance from a human *matière première*, to revisit the language of the impulses that drove the 7 Fingers in their first production, is perhaps most clearly seen in *Zumanity*'s companion piece in what Leroux calls a mutually informing "dyptique" (83), the film of the show's making entited *Lovesick*. It is in the documentary film that we glimpse some intimacy: "The documentary lets one glimpse individuals worthy of interest and empathy instead of types drawn from a sexual bestiary, as they are presented in the cabaret" (84).[27] This intimacy stems, at least in part, from "the full confidence that the filmmaker, Lewis Cohen, succeeds in establishing between his subjects and himself" (84).[28] It is important to remember, however, that our access to Cohen's subjects – *Zumanity*'s performers – is filtered through multiple lenses: the camera is following them because there will be a stage for them, because the enterprise of Cirque is there to exploit, to stage, to mount an "authenticity." This particular intimacy is decidedly a mediated one.

It is instructive to recall here the provocative line in the *Guardian*'s 2010 review of 7 Fingers' *Traces*, which was then touring the United Kingdom: "This is circus for the Facebook generation" (Gardner 2010). The reviewer goes on to explain her comment: "The performers don't just dazzle by flying between poles; they offer up snippets of personal information as they irritate, bond and flirt with each other. They are so human, it feels all the more astonishing when they hurl themselves off poles." Given the reviewer's thrust to emphasize the game-changing intimacy of the 7 Fingers – her very first paragraph mentions their intention "to create a new, intimate kind of circus" – we are asked, it would appear, to explore this new Facebook-ness of the 7 Fingers, particularly as it is *not* what we understand about the nonintimate, not-new Cirque du Soleil. As perhaps on Facebook, the 7 Fingers' performers do offer those snippets. When we look at the stakes suggested by this reviewer's comments, however, we might ask ourselves a question that may be valid for Facebook's revelations as well: what do we end up knowing through these snippets? The analyses of the preceding pages have suggested that we have access to real humans, real emotions; we get a form of intimacy. But is it authentic? The 7 Fingers' show is, after all, a performance; their intimacies are, after all, decidedly mediated. Ian Thai's 2012 review of the Boston run of *Séquence 8* and its shared intimacies includes praise for Colin Davis's role as an emcee who "quizzes the audience, makes quips about the acts that came before," and who, in a striking reminder of the mediation of their art, "draws attention to the irony of a show that has been rehearsed to appear improvised at times." In the face of such mediation, where intimacies are rehearsed and practiced, how might we conceive, feel, touch the authentic?

It is important here to recall the other pluridisciplinary artistic creations taking shape in the 1980s at the same time as Quebec's nouveau cirque. As Erin Hurley (2008) describes it, the theatre of that decade "seems to step back from the dominant model of *québécité* and insists, rather, on the visual image" (18).[29] Placing this shift as a part of the reactions to the failure of the independence referendum of 1980, Hurley writes that "the performing arts kind of abandon their socio-critical gaze and a realistic mode to embrace new forms of expression and to renew the language of the stage" (18).[30]

Among the new groups was Carbone 14, the highly successful theatre-dance troupe that participated in that early fête foraine from which evolved the Cirque du Soleil. In the stimulating cauldron of 1980s Quebec, several troupes influenced each other in the development of a highly physical theatre. It is, after all, a certain physicality and not mere "visual image" that marks these developing Québécois creations. Several theoreticians of this moment of what might be called a postmodern dance theatre refer to a "theatre of the image,"[31] a phrase that seems crafted to point to a diminution, in these works, of the primacy of the text, of the story. Videos of such productions as *Oranges* of 1981, from another dance/movement troupe founded in the early 1980s, Lalala Human Steps, remind us that this image is particularly physical: the dancing, theatricalizing body is shown to be a working body. Indeed, in the physicality that is rendered evident and not hidden behind something called "grace" or "throughlines" or "elegance," we are reminded – for Lalala, for Carbone 14, for the fête foraine – that there are real bodies at work and at play, bodies that not only get up with creaks in the morning but that can do things that might be dance, might be gymnastics, might be embodied vocalizations. The early nouveau cirque, the nouvelle danse, the nouveau théâtre speak – or rather use, move, and perform – similar, or at least mutually influential, languages. As Iro Tembeck (1994) tells us in her *Dancing in Montreal: Seeds of a Choreographic History*, certain critics have termed the resultant "inventive and intensely personal" movement idiom "le nouveau bouger montréalais" (95), an expression whose use of the familiar term *bouger*, "ways of moving," suggests that these were seen to be intimately new ways of showing physicality.

The 7 Fingers, with their staging of intimist physicalities that draw on these new vocabularies from theatre, dance, and circus, point back to those particular origins. Indeed, one of the artists for *Séquence 8*, Ugo Dario, said in an interview for a television station in France that one of the "brand images" of the troupe is its focus on "dance and theatricality,"[32] hallmarks of the Québécois version of the nouveau cirque's origins in the heated cauldrons of local artistic venues. One review of the 2011 Parisian run of *Psy* remarks, too, that this is a spectacle that "gives much space to dance and to the choreographies between the different acrobatic numbers" (Beaudet 2011).[33] This dance, which marks significant portions of both *Psy* and *Séquence 8*, carries striking similarities to the nouveau bouger montréalais as practiced by Lalala Human Steps.

In a December 2012 interview, William Smith, who danced with Lalala in such productions as *Amélie* and *Nouvelle création*, remarked on the similarities he had sensed from having seen *Séquence 8* approximately a month earlier at the TOHU. Drawing on similar corporeal language in their high velocity movements as performers "release into each other, creating a powerful outward impulse" toward a flip or some other "near-gravity-defying" movement, with sequences that intimate a close relationship between "spinning horizontally and spinning vertically,"[34] the 7 Fingers may offer an early twenty-first-century echo of Lalala's practices from the 1980s. To be sure, Shana Carroll and Sébastien Soldevila, creators of *Séquence 8*, were not yet in Montreal in the early 1980s to have participated in those foundational creative moments. In the program notes, however, they comment specifically on the role of their adopted city: "Thank you to Montreal, this warm and cosmopolitan city for having influenced us, the collective."[35] Still alive in many of the corners and venues of this city where physical theatre has had pride of place since the early days of Carbone 14 and Lalala, the nouveau bouger montréalais continues to influence the creations of this nouveau cirque collective.

We do well to remember the intimacies present in these obvious physicalities as we note that the 7 Fingers has become, some ten years after their founding, one of the big players in the Quebec circus world. Yohann Floch, then coordinator of the European circus arts network Circostrada and international relations director at the Paris-based Hors Les Murs, presented a paper at Montpellier's 2011 "A Week of Circus" conference that included some of the specifics of the new Québécois circus context, in which three companies – Cirque du Soleil, the 7 Fingers, and Cirque Éloize – receive more than "the lion's share" of public and private monies and attention, and where new companies "have difficulty breaking through."[36] This overwhelming presence, if we were to extrapolate from Floch's comments, exists in spite of the summer festival Montréal Complètement Cirque, which has given voice and venue to, for example, the new troupes Cirque Alfonse and FlipFabriQue noted in this collection's epilogue: the announcement of the line-up for the 2012 festival included, to great fanfare, the revelation that the 7 Fingers would offer their latest creation at its opening.

7.4 Opposite From *Séquence 8*, group with Camille Legris, 7 Fingers

The 7 Fingers have thus become one of "the references, if not *the* reference, in the eyes of the graduates of the (National Circus) School,"[37] in the words of Marie-Josée Gauthier, an instructor at the school. The 7 Fingers now tour versions of their shows throughout the Americas and Europe, with promised future tour dates in Asia. *Traces* has its own website for US shows, was named among the top plays and musicals by *Time* magazine, and has been featured on US national television, including twice on *America's Got Talent*. A recent show in Mexico, *A Muse*, was conceived for a grandiose performance hall and 5,000 audience members.

Given their growing presence, we should perhaps ask if they have become like the first-generation nouveau cirque québécois, Cirque du Soleil, and have moved star-like into their own kind of Great White Way, leaving the streets and the people and their vaunted intimacy and authenticity to some *third* generation. After all, Quebec's provincial government now remarks on their movements in both local and international communiqués and, in July 2013, confirmed it would grant some $9 million to fund the transformation of Montreal's Musée Juste pour rire into a creation and production centre for the company. Although the venue is known locally as a site of creative activity, the building's moniker as a "museum" may well cause pause for this company that prides itself on not being static or caught in any sterile, fixed language. Furthermore, some of its particularly skilful performers are moving on to create troupes themselves or to join recently formed companies. For example, Maxim Laurin and Ugo Dario, 2011 graduates of the École nationale de cirque and the award-winning duo that created the noteworthy Korean board number in *Séquence 8*, announced in December 2014 that they would join forces with Quebec-based Machine de cirque, itself founded only some two years earlier.

In an early 2012 conversation with members of Montreal's Working Group on Circus Research, Nassib el-Husseini, the 7 Fingers' CEO, promised continued vibrancy for his company.[38] For him, the multiple versions of *Traces* are not the same show, for example: new artists come in, altering the moves made and the tales told, in a decided counter-example to the Cirque du Soleil model in which new artists are trained to be parachuted into already-created roles and numbers. Shana Carroll, in her November 2012 interview, articulated a similar position vis-à-vis the touring versions of *Traces*, that show formed with "texts built on [the artists'] own lives": while certain elements of the show remain to offer a recognizable core structure, new artists, with new combinations of talents, come in to give new texts, new gestures, new energies, new skills.

7.5 From *Traces* in Moscow with Renaldo Williams, 7 Fingers

It behooves us to keep a critical eye open. In his conversation, el-Husseini noted that the company "of course has to deliver the merchandise," namely, a show that was sold to producers in its previous versions, with the texts, gestures, energies, and skills of previous performers. And we should remain critical of even the definition of "new" not only in el-Husseini's celebration of a "new" show but also in Carroll's description of "new" skills, when the 7 Fingers appear to be influencing young artists to train and to perform like them. In an interview for the *Orange County Register* for an early 2012 run of *Traces*, Shana Carroll states: "One of the acrobats in the show now saw it in Berlin in 2006 and it influenced his approach to the circus. He told me he started to train himself for 'Traces' without even realizing it. Five years later we hired him. The girl in this production, her boyfriend was in the original cast. She would visit us when she was in school; she watched the show for years. She was subconsiously training herself for the show too" (Hodgins 2012). Our gaze must be critical, and yet we are also called to recognize that the intimacy of those originary shows, designed to be à grandeur d'homme, remains, even as the company itself becomes one of the *grands*. The *Time* magazine review of *Traces*, for example, points to that very concept, the intimate, to note why their show is powerful as it remarks on the "streetwise intimacy of their presentation (the youthful acrobats, dressed in ordinary street clothes, even give us snippets of autobiography)" (Zoglin 2011).

It is here that I would like to propose a way to understand how the intimacies remain, even in the face of multiplicity, even in the threats to authenticity in the bright lights of the city. It is, in fact, to the city that I turn. Theorists of the modern global city have pointed to the particular presence and power of bodies that mark the city and its creative productions. Roland Barthes (1997), in his landmark essay "Semiology and the Urban," was among the first to suggest that "the city is a discourse, and this discourse is truly a language" (168). He writes of the city centre as "the place of exchange of social activities and I would almost say erotic activities in the broad sense of the word. Better still, the city centre is always felt as the space where subversive forces, forces of rupture, ludic forces act and meet" (171).[39] For Barthes, multiple encounters are not empty encounters: even as bodies and stories change in the ever-mutating city, the frictions of the city mark those bodies and those stories, grounding them, giving them presence, pointing to intimacies that we other denizens of the city may have access to.

Did I, for example, see Patrick Léonard, one of the 7 Fingers' founding members, juggling his poutine as he was trying to open a door to a corner shop on these Montreal streets in the fall of 2012? Could I recognize him and know him as being in and of these streets, having previously seen him only *in performance*, and *on stage*? The "yes" I must give as answer contrasts largely with, for example, the equally forceful "no" most Montrealers would give if they were asked if they could recognize, on the streets, the exceedingly talented native Québécois performers featured as the Spandex-clad and gel-coiffed lovebirds on the trapeze in the 2010 Cirque du Soleil show *Totem*, never mind that the local press wrote numerous image-laden feature articles about them, constantly speaking of them as being from home territory. The intimate, accessible trappings of the city, including those youths in "ordinary street clothes" that *Time* praises, are at home in productions of the 7 Fingers and foreign to the latter-day Cirque; not mere aesthetic choices, they give us knowable bodies and friction-filled stories.

Roland Barthes may have more to tell us in yet another text that suggests how to access authenticity even in a highly mediated, Facebooked age, where intimacy may not be as clear as the words or pixels in which it is rendered. Barthes, whose writings have recently received a new wave of attention due to publication of some of his intimate journals,[40] kept returning to a desire to find a way to talk about bodies, to give words and theories to their power and their charge. In one highly influential essay, he speaks of the "grain of the voice," the grain of the body, in terms of performances – particularly musical ones, but also writerly ones – in which one can sense the body of the performer in the performance itself, in which the perfoming body is not effaced by that which is being performed (Barthes 1997).

As we have seen, the mega-spectacles of the current Cirque du Soleil seem to erase the particulars of the performing body, even as they depend on them. Erin Hurley theorizes this Cirque practice as marked by the primacy of the "character body" (see Hurley's "Multiple Bodies" in this collection), in which the through-line, the thing acted/performed, sublimates the "performer body" that creates it. The performances of the 7 Fingers, to the contrary, seem to let bodies, the performing ones, live and be significantly present as they hurl themselves off and between poles, in the language of the *Guardian*'s reviewer. As such, Roland Barthes's notion of the grain may be particularly relevant here: even if or as the performers' gestures, including those of the verbal text, may create personifying autofictions, the materiality of the gesture, the body that gives it, remains present.

Having looked intently at the traces of intimacy and authenticity alive in the spectacles of the 7 Fingers, this chapter now closes on the idea that it is grainy bodies that remain to resonate, to speak to viewers, even in the face of multiplicities and threats to authenticity. Offering us access to those bodies in a counter-example to the aesthetic and performance practices of the dominant Cirque, the 7 Fingers point to the possibility of exchange – in Barthesian terms, erotic, subversive, ludic – while reminding us of the origins, the resistances, and the power of seeking to be of a grandeur d'homme.

CHAPTER 8

The Multiple Bodies of Cirque du Soleil

Erin Hurley

Two men balance on a high wire approximately twelve metres above the bare stage floor. One crouches down, a long balance-pole in his hands, and tucks his head to his knees, initiating a game of leapfrog. The second prepares, his arms outstretched, takes three quick steps toward his partner and leaps over the crouched form. His knees are pulled up into his body, his back straight, and his head up. But he loses his footing upon landing – actually, it appeared as though he never gained his footing – and careens wildly over the side of the wire, grasping it with one hand only at the last minute. As the jumper holds on for dear life, swaying back and forth, his partner struggles to maintain his precarious balance on the now undulating wire. After everyone audibly exhales – performers and audience alike – the jumper pulls himself back up onto the high wire and walks across it to join his fellow aerialists on their perch. They seem to consult with one another. Then they restart the game of leapfrog, this time completing the leap successfully, and are greeted by a spontaneous, thunderous standing ovation.

This moment from Cirque du Soleil's 2007 touring tent show, *KOOZÄ*, exhibits a recurrent tension around the extraordinary bodies that populate its shows and ground its aesthetic. One the one hand, the tightrope walker's near fall and fantastic recovery crystallizes the grand narrative of Cirque du Soleil – surpassing limits. Cirque du Soleil's performance codes emphasize otherworldliness. Shows are populated by fantastically costumed creatures that perform "superhuman" feats of strength, flexibility, and skill (see Harvie and Hurley 1999). Here too, by walking on air, *KOOZÄ*'s equilibrist exceeds the body's natural limits; he tests psychological limits as well in reattempting an element he had just missed.

On the other hand, the wire-walker's narrow escape from serious injury or even death is rather more resistant to metaphor and narrative than is usually the case in Cirque's aerial acts. Cirque du Soleil's routines are generally pressed more into the service of narrative or thematic continuity than into that of thrilling an audience with their death-defying feats. Its acts emphasize story and character over display and demonstration. Securing narrative progression is the required use of safety apparatuses "when the technique in a number is advanced and when danger exists" (J. Boudreault 1999, 55).[1] With technique supported by the safety device, the performer is freer to focus on the act's artistic content, its conveyance of meaning as well as its visual pleasures. Safeties also advance technique in as much as they allow performers to take larger leaps and more precipitous falls than they could otherwise. In this way, performers augment the sense of the extraordinary without risking the most radical narrative discontinuity of all – injury or death. For their part, members of the audience, relieved of the concern for performer safety, can focus on the act's story element and the beauty of the form. According to Marc Gagnon, former vice-president of human resources (and subsequently vice-president of organization and culture), performers in "Cirque du Soleil are not death-defiers ... Cirque du Soleil exploits the public's imaginary, its taste for dreaming ... not a morbid attraction to danger" (qtd in J. Boudreault 1999, 55).[2] In an oeuvre that has joyously embraced consistently successful execution, the aerialist's near fall in KOOZÄ refocuses attention not only on performance's potential (and potentially tragic) failure. It also refocuses attention on the unique, individual body running that risk in an organizational structure that has resolutely privileged a corporate, and with its expansion to multiple, simultaneous shows, a replaceable body. Of this working condition, journalist Jean Beaunoyer (2004) writes, "With the phenomenal growth of the Cirque, it was necessary very early on to plan for replacements and successors ... they require quality artists to meet the need or also to replace sick, wounded, retired, or non-renewed performers" (178).[3]

In this chapter, I follow this high-wire act's invitation to pay attention to the bodies populating Cirque du Soleil shows in their brute physicality and their uniqueness to discern their impact on and contribution to the much-vaunted Cirque aesthetic. I isolate the most salient characteristics of the Cirque body by drawing on examples from across the troupe's twenty-year history and with particular attention to KOOZÄ. The body *in extremis* is the foundation of Cirque du Soleil's aesthetic, providing its major component, its visual vocabulary, and its most abundant canvas. In a ring largely devoid of "scenery," it is the *circassiens* – their movements, costumes, and talents – who provide the action, the colour, and to some extent, the architecture of the circus.[4] I contend that close attention to these exceptional bodies is rewarded with a glimpse of the political unconscious of this most exemplary "new circus" aesthetic. Cirque du Soleil's unifying aesthetic might be well understood as a concerted effort to regularize these unruly, outstanding bodies. This effort, I believe, belies these bodies' fundamental exceptionalism – a weirdness with deep and fraught, if now often obscured, roots in circus culture.

Character Body: Fictional Uniformity

To date, most scholarship on Cirque du Soleil, when it engages with the bodies in the ring, has focused on what David Graver would call the circus performer's "character body." The character body is the sum of the "gestures and expressions of the actor that signify the life and experience of a fictional character within a fictional world" (Graver 2005, 159). This body has been useful to scholars interested in distinguishing Cirque du Soleil's "new circus" style from "traditional" circus. Briefly, new circus was developed in Europe and North America during the 1970s and 1980s by artists not born to the circus arts, and came into its own in the 1990s. Its single-ring performance emphasizes professionalism (the artists are often trained at circus schools), artistry aimed at an adult audience, and theatricality. Peta Tait (2005) summarizes, "New circus remains closer to theatre in its aesthetic and thematic purpose and unity, and because performers work in relationship with others" (120). Traditional circus refers to the one-ring and three-ring travelling forms featuring distinct animal, clown, and acrobatic acts, generally introduced by a ringmaster, and which developed in a family-based apprentice structure out of eighteenth-century equestrian performance. Traditional circus also often brought a midway with games, rides, and side-show entertainments to town with it, a practice jettisoned by new circus practitioners who concentrate on the circus arts in one ring.

Cirque du Soleil's advancements are generally discovered in its indisputable theatricality, by which most intend the unified production aesthetic, the narrative (or at least thematic) coherence, and crucially, the performers' presentations of fictional selves.[5] All of the company's performers portray a character – from the musicians to the house crew to the specialists. In *Le*

Cirque du Soleil: La création d'un spectacle: Saltimbanco, Julie Boudreault (1996) documents that in the 1992 touring production, *Saltimbanco*, characters were built on the performers' particularities as spied during improvisation sessions, and then elaborated in subsequent sessions under the tutelage of the director, Franco Dragone (73–81). Much as actors do, these circus performers grafted a fictional body to their concrete, physical body, using the latter as a means to enact the former. Isabelle Chassé's aerial contortion act with two lengths of red silk is overlaid with character and story essential to *Quidam*'s (1996) narrative arc. In fact, her expression of an identifiable character's inner conflicts provided *Quidam*'s emotional climax. Using "the body's expressiveness, voice (sighs and shouts) and facial expressions," Chassé played a woman's repressed emotional life (F. Boudreault 2002, 84).[6]

Character bodies are supported by theatrical elements that knit them into the fabric of the show, prompting comparisons of Cirque du Soleil's aesthetic integrity with Wagner's ideal of a "total work of art." All aspects of Cirque productions are governed by a concept – urbanity for *Saltimbanco*, nomadism for *Varekai* (2002), humanity's clownish spirit for *Corteo* (2005). Each boasts a distinct musical score, composed largely before rehearsals such that it might drive the arc of the show and influence the sequencing of individual acts. And Cirque du Soleil has become known and rewarded for its fantastical costumes that imprint on the spectator's mind the fictional nature of the beings in the ring.

A house crew of acrobats also serves to unify the production. They literally paper over discontinuities in performance by dancing or tumbling during scene changes, assembling and disassembling stage equipment. But they also model cohesion across bodies in their performance as a collective as well as in their concerted execution of numbers "entirely created by the Cirque du Soleil, which selects the artists, hires the trainers and oversees all stages of their elaboration" (J. Boudreault 1996, 51).[7] Working as an ensemble, they perform a combination of tumbling (often on trampolines or tracks set into the stage floor, as in KOOZÄ and *Alegría* [1994]), balancing, stilt-walking, Chinese pole work, and teeterboard routines that highlight collective endeavour over individual talent. Unidentified in performance and uniformly dressed, the corps move and react in synchrony. As if to bring this point home, *Le Cirque Réinventé* (1987) featured a chorus of penguins, referencing in their costumes and gait the bird but also corporate America's suited businessman (Skidmore 2002, 251).[8] Drawn from disparate domains and backgrounds – including the circus arts but also synchronized swimming, gymnastics, theatre, and street performance – the corps are trained as a unit as well. Some are graduates of L'École nationale de cirque de Montréal, whose curriculum privileges polyvalence and communication as the goals of circus training. Founded by Guy Caron, who would become the artistic director of Cirque du Soleil in 1985, the school has enjoyed a close historical connection with the Cirque, though it operates independently and is now a less-common "feeder" for Cirque du Soleil shows. The two institutions nonetheless share a similar vision for contemporary circus as a privileged site for innovation where the techniques of the circus arts, dance, and acting "become tools and means of communication" (Lachance and Venne 2004, 248).[9] They follow similar creative processes, beginning with a theme or concept and ending in striking images. Cirque du Soleil has its own four-month training program at its Montreal headquarters (Beaunoyer 2004, 179). Regardless of their provenance, those engaged in a Cirque show undergo a formation at the hands of Cirque show staff and selected mentors for anywhere from three to twenty months (J. Boudreault 1996, 54).

The company's emphasis on "character bodies" serves Cirque du Soleil's unified aesthetic in two ways. First, it curtails individual performers' celebrity; characters displace "stars" so that the show as a whole might be the biggest attraction. As publicity materials trumpet, "La vedette, c'est le spectacle." Second, and more importantly, the character body elevates the circus out of the realm of craft and into that of art. The perceived separation of self from performance entailed by "character" presumes that the performer deploys her skills not to produce a commodity, as a craftsperson might, but instead to represent something else.[10] In other words, performing in character abstracts the performer's labour and rescues the skilled performance from instrumentality: it is not Isabelle Chassé[11] performing an aerial fabric act but a character telling a story; she does not contort herself into a head-seat position to show how it is done, but to represent a difficult time in her character's mental journey. The character body, then, is a crucial proof of Cirque's art, an art upon which Ernest Albrecht's (2002) influential definition of "New American circus" reposes: "By 'new American circus' I mean a current made up of a group of young troupes with the common mission of reinventing the circus in order to reimagine it as a true art form at the same level as music, dance, and theatre" (37).[12] Cirque du Soleil's mission harmonizes with Albrecht's definition: "Since its foundation, [Cirque du Soleil] has wished that its acrobats ... be seen as exceptional artists" (J. Boudreault 1999, 69).[13]

The artistry of Cirque du Soleil performers is cultivated in their training as well as in performance. House troupe members receive an artistic formation that takes as long as their technical training; for *Saltimbanco*, house crew members had apprenticeships in Taiko drumming, Latin dance, flamenco, theatre, acting, mask work, and voice for a period of eight months (J. Boudreault 1996, 72). As to performance, aerialist and academic Françoise Boudreault (2002) explains that in "new circus" aerial acts, "one is looking to touch the public as much by the beauty of the movements, the theatricality, and the staging as by the acrobatic feats" (79).[14] As other scholars have noted, this stepping back from technique and record-breaking feats in the name of "art" and "character" marks Cirque's difference from its predecessors, in which these elements formed the cornerstone. As crucially, however, it also underscores the circus body's scene-stealing potential, its enticement to get lost in the exquisite workings of a prodigious body. In other words, this turn to character reveals what it must suppress for the sake of narrative consistency and aesthetic unity.

Performer Body: Cultivated Exceptionalism

Circus has long featured two overlapping kinds of physical prodigality that Cirque du Soleil alternately capitalizes on and contains for the elaboration of its aesthetic: a trained or cultivated exceptionalism most strongly associated with aerialists, and a "natural" or "born" specialness generally delivered by those differently formed bodies identified as "freaks" in circus discourse. In its invitation to look frankly and apprehensively at physical prowess, *KOOZÄ*'s high-wire act relies on corporeal presences that precede "character," and ones that are more strongly associated with traditional circus than with new circus. In Graver's schema, these are the "performer body" and the "fleshy body," categories that roughly correspond to those of cultivated exceptionalism and natural exceptionalism. It is the engagement of the performer in a technically challenging display (a display that requires intense concentration for its successful execution) that gives the performer body its authority (this, along with that performer body's technical mastery). Graver (2005) explains: "Its authority springs from its skills at commanding attention and serving as a focus of theatrical expressivity as well as from the license to be an object of attention that the cultural institution of theater accords the performer. Its engagement is constituted by its concentrated involvement in the activity of performance" (160). The performer body's exceptionalism resides in what it can do that others cannot, and its exceptional talents are the consequence of training and rehearsal.

The chair-balancing act performed by Zhang Gongli that closes KOOZÄ provides us with an example of an entire act that pivots on the technical adeptness of a performer body completely engrossed in its own performance. Entering the ring slowly and deliberately, his full attention is focused on the four-foot-tall base upon which he will build and then dismantle a tower of eight wooden chairs. As each new chair is added, he executes static holds emphasizing upper-body and abdominal strength, similar to those seen in men's rings gymnastic competitions. When the tower reaches four chairs high, Zhang inserts a balancing pole, balances on one hand and moves into an extreme back bend; his torso remains horizontal over the supporting hand while his feet reach over his back to almost meet his head. At eight chairs high, Zhang leans the back of the eighth chair against the back of the seventh, creating an even more precarious perch secured only by two of the eighth chair's legs. He effects a handstand – one hand on the back and the other on the upturned seat of the eighth chair; then he threads his straight legs between his arms to end in an "L-seat." The exquisite tension between strength and balance entailed by this act mesmerizes. The act's structure builds suspense by calling for ever more daring positions in ever more precarious circumstances, a structure that does not release one's gaze. His is a sublime display of bodily control; the movements are unfailingly slow and smooth and the positions are held seemingly interminably and practically without flinching. His performer body captivates by virtue of its skill. Moreover, the performer's attention directs the audience's attention. Zhang appears completely absorbed by his task. In the whole of KOOZÄ, Zhang is the sole performer to never look at the audience; rather, he looks skyward or turns his focus inward during his act. Even at act's end after descending from the tower, he arises slowly from a crouched position, as if waking from a dream; he takes a single, slow, low bow still avoiding the audience's eager eyes, then turns abruptly and runs off stage.

Zhang's act seems an invitation to marvel at a skilled body's demonstrations of what it can do. Dressed in a naked suit with white briefs, Zhang's performer body – the workings of the musculature, the stretching of the ligaments – is on full display. Significantly, he climbs higher and

8.1 The performer body of Zhang: Chinese chairs. Costumes: Marie-Chantale Vaillancourt

higher, farther and farther away from the audience, thereby reinforcing his body's difference vis-à-vis the presumed "normals" in the audience. In his cool performative demeanour, his revealing costume, and his ascent into the air, Zhang stages an aspirational body. Helen Stoddart's (2000) comments concerning aerialists' aspirational performer body might be as persuasively applied to Zhang's: "The body of the aerialist is weighed down by no regulation and is governed only by its singular self-discipline and strength." This body that may, by virtue of training and technology, defy external laws anchors the circus's "public fantasy of itself as a space of exceptionalism, escape and danger in which the rules which seem to govern the world outside have no currency" (7).

Where Zhang's cultivated exceptionalism is conveyed in his performance of self-control, the tightrope walker's exceptionalism is, paradoxically, most forcefully brought home in his temporary loss of control. Vicente Quiros Dominguez, *KOOZÄ*'s leap-frogging funambule, spotlights his performer body not via revealing costumes but by revealing the operations of the performance itself. I saw *KOOZÄ* twice;[15] both times Vicente Quiros Dominguez missed his landing. This could have been a fluke, of course; leap-frogging on a high wire is complicated, to say the least. And yet, the performers in Los Quiros – the name of Vicente and his two brothers' fifth-generation, Spanish circus act – are known for their ability to jump over *two* crouched forms at a time. The more likely explanation for his near-miss is the time-honoured circus tradition of faking a mistake. This is when a consummate performer misses an element of the routine expressly, which deceives the audience into believing that they have witnessed something unique, thereby increasing the reality-effect of the act. Duping the audience in this way also serves to remind them of the difficulty of the act, of its very real risks, even in the hands of professionals who execute the feats with poise and seeming ease. Circus semiotician Hugues Hotier affirms, "The pseudo-event … communicates a piece of information that the public did not necessarily perceive in the habitual routine of the number: the difficulty that makes the exercise a feat" (qtd in F. Boudreault 2002, 82). Purposefully missing an element further spotlights the extraordinary performer body by reminding the audience of its cultivation, of its training. Hotier continues:

> Faking a mistake allows the number to quit the strict domain of technique to take on a human dimension. The artist himself or herself indicates his or her own limit and testifies to his or her own uncer-

> tainty about his or her success ... We stop admiring the mechanism in, for an instant, rediscovering the weakness of the human being that the performer never ceased being, despite all appearances. (qtd in J. Boudreault 1999, 190)[16]

Giving way to its foibles and then once again overcoming them to leapfrog successfully, this performer body recapitulates in miniature the road travelled to arrive at the summit of his art. In other words, the near miss charts his rise from ordinary (human) to extraordinary (superhuman) body. It also offers us a glimpse of another aspect of that performer body's training – its training for failure. One trains in order to successfully execute all the elements of one's act, certainly. But a high-wire artist is also drilled on how to fall without breaking his neck, on how to recover a missed landing, on how to reestablish lost balance (Hoh and Rough 1990, 172–3). Saving himself, *in extremis*, attests to this frequently hidden training.

We can see in this example the meta-narrative pitting freedom against constraint that Paul Bouissac (1976) ascribes to aerialist performer bodies in *Circus and Culture*. Indeed, Vicente Quiros Dominguez gambles his very life in this battle against the constraints of banality, conformity, regularity, not to mention gravity. And yet, one glimpses that meta-narrative post hoc. In the moment of execution, the performer body captivates or absorbs attention into itself and as itself. The performer body is inherently interesting; it is interesting for itself, independent of its potential meanings. Its virtuosity – its irreconcilable singularity – arrests narrative. The visual and aural cues surrounding Los Quiros's act encouraged a story about conquering heroes. Music – all blaring horns and percussion – thundered forth from a three-story, intricately decorated tower upstage-centre housing the band. From behind the curtain shrouding the tower's stage-level elevation emerged the three men attired in white turbans and flowing red capes over sashed white-and-gold tunics and fitted military-style leggings stitched in such a way as to create the impression of a tall boot's outline.[17] However, once the miss happens, one is struck by the image of the fall, caught up in the fear for his life, restrained by the tightening of the chest. Breathless, the audience just waits, fixed on Vicente's now falling form, now windmilling arms, now dangling legs. In the language of Roland Barthes (1980), the performer body is the *punctum* to the *studium* of the mise-en-scène.

This show-stopping effect is only heightened by the fact that Los Quiros eschew all safety apparatuses; they employ neither harness nor net. If faking

8.2 Los Quiros: Double tightrope. Costumes: Marie-Chantale Vaillancourt

a mistake buttresses the act's reality-effect, an unbroken fall shatters any pretense in its undeniable reality. Its real, felt, physical impact would irrevocably rupture KOOZÄ's continuity. As we saw above, the spectre of the all-too-real unbroken fall has, until KOOZÄ, kept all dangerous or especially challenging aerial acts connected to effectively invisible safety lines. To my knowledge, none of Cirque du Soleil travelling shows have erected a net or used a mattress or cushion as safeguards against aerialist missteps.[18] Although the mattress and the safety line have the same goal – to save the aerialist – their differences are important to keep in mind. The former is situated in the middle of the ring; it presents itself to the spectator as much as a promise of a fall (or at least of real physical danger) as potential saviour. In other words, the net, mattress, or cushion anticipate the equilibrist's fall and project themselves forward to the end of the story. Thus, Cirque du Soleil's tent is usually denuded of this explicit and visible reminder of the precarious conditions in which funambulists work.

Fleshy Body: Natural Exceptionalism

Perhaps most destabilizing to Cirque du Soleil's realm of imagination, however, is what Graver identifies as the "fleshy body." Where "character" bodies are a fictional identity, and performer bodies are skill on display, the "fleshy body" is the nonsemiotic, self-identical corporeal envelope of skin, hair, flesh, blood, fat, and muscle. Graver (2005) writes, "The fleshy body is the aspect of animate life free from volition. One can see it when contemplation reaches an absolute zero where the eye gazes without a purpose beyond the simple joy of seeing, and the object displayed has no purpose or plan beyond being seen" (168). This fleshy body emerges most forcefully when the performer body of the aerialist fails, when the fake is real and leads to the injury or death of a performer. In the universe of Cirque du Soleil, it is the contortionists who most consistently approach the fleshy body's level of corporeal presence.

Fleshy bodies are differentiated from character and performer bodies by what they put on display and by the organization of that display. The fleshy bodies of the contortionists display their bodies qua bodies; the interest of a contortionist is her/his body's strangeness vis-à-vis norms of physical flexibility and extension and with respect to the arrangement or position of body parts. By contrast, performer bodies exude technical mastery that points to the body's cultivation, a cultivation that distances the performer body from its fleshy compatriot. The character body puts even more distance between its fictional self and the fleshy (and performer) body by means of which it signifies.

Where aerialists challenge the external natural law of gravity, contortionists defy laws of anatomy whose impact on the body's construction and capacities are much more intimate. Not only does contortionism display the unusual body's extreme pliability in leg shouldering, for instance, which is a standing split where the leg touches the shoulder. Contortionism also exaggerates the body's prodigality by seemingly dismembering and reconstituting the body in unexpected ways. Body parts are displaced or distorted – the head appears between the performer's legs, or knee joints bend back on themselves, for instance. Sensation associated with such physical distortions is likewise displaced in contortionism. In a discussion of erotic contortionism more strongly associated with nightclubs and music hall than with the circus, Karl Toepfer (1999) argues that contortionism is "the pleasure of a body that has evaded or transcended the violence to which a 'normal' or 'natural' body is vulnerable" (131). Moreover, unlike aerialists, contortionists do not require any supporting technology to perform their act. Their act *is* their body (see Leclerc 2012).

It may be argued that all circus bodies are tainted with the residue of the sideshow freak body. Until about the mid-twentieth century, these bodies shared living quarters and performance spaces in North American travelling circus (Hoh and Rough 1990, 155–7). Both circus and freak bodies push physical and conceptual limits. In the circus, aerialists soar like birds (or gods); the acrobatic corps act as machines, using their arms and hands as trampolines and springboards to send human projectiles into the air; clowns are "trained" by animals. In the sideshow, born freaks' existence "imperils categories and oppositions dominant in social life" (Grosz 1996, 57); the dog-faced boy muddles human and animal while the bearded lady mixes male and female attributes. Yet with the contortionist, the connection to freaks, particularly "born freaks," intensifies. Indeed, contortionists were found more frequently in the circus sideshow under the nicknames of "Rubber Man" or "Snake Woman" than they were in the ring. In the context of circus sideshows, "born freaks" were people with atypical physiques whose "monstrosity" was often the result of a congenital defect (resulting in malformed limbs, for instance), a rare condition (like elephantitis, with which John Merrick, "the Elephant Man," lived), or a hormonal imbalance (as in some instances of dwarfism or gigantism). By contrast, "made freaks" were those performers who modified their bodies to render them exceptional; the Tattooed Man is one example. And "gaffed freaks" were faked freaks, performers who use combinations of costume, *mise en scène*, and makeup to trick audiences into believing they are freaks, as in the illusion of the headless man.

The contortionist too is naturally physically prodigious, even if this prodigality is not quite so immediately visible as the born freak's. Further, in the case of both freakery and contortionism, the body qua body is spectacle (and spectacularized). In the sideshow and nightclub tradition of contortionism, male contortionists usually performed in briefs and female contortionists in bikinis and *cache-sexe*, allowing a glimpse of "the blushing of the skin, the sweat, the sense of strain on the body" (Toepfer 1999, 106). In addition, contortionism's signature positions resonate strongly with the natural freak's singular bodies. Jamie Skidmore convincingly connects Cirque's contortion acts to their sideshow precursors, linking the contortionist's "working act" to the "born" freaks like "human torsos" (those born without arms or legs) and conjoined (or "Siamese") twins, both of which were major sideshow attractions. Positions like the "human knot," in which ankles are placed behind the head, create an illusion of leglessness. Or when two or more contortionists combine to build a new, grotesque form, they harken back to the "born" prodigious bodies of multi-limbed entertainers (those born with a doubled body part – four feet, for instance) or conjoined twins (Skidmore 2002, 202).

8.3 The fleshy body of the contortionists, KOOZÄ, Cirque du Soleil. Costumes: Marie-Chantale Vaillancourt

KOOZÄ's contortionists perform what is called a "living statue act," which consists of a series of balances and acrobatic poses that appear as snapshots, held for several seconds, before slowly moving into the next pose. Significantly, many of their poses conjured images of arachnids (scorpions when individuals executed elbow-stands, spiders when the contortionists worked together), the multi-limbed Hindu god, Shiva, and mythical beasts – each of which implies a "freakish" cross-species mix. In its (predominantly) static display of prodigality, the contortionism act again flirts with its sideshow kin. Freak show acts were generally static. Theirs was not an act of skill but a display of nature's immutable mistakes or eccentricities. In freak-show logic, explains Rachel Adams (2001), "the freak's stasis on the sideshow platform mirrors the enduring and irreversible quality of her condition. Freak shows are guided by the assumption that *freak* is an essence" (6). In contrast, curious onlookers were mobile, able to circle the sideshow platform so as to see the freak on display as completely as possible, thereby encapsulating in more pernicious form circus's meta-narrative of constraint and freedom.

KOOZÄ's contortionists, if more mobile than some, were nonetheless contained by the 360-degree perspective available to their viewers. They were presented on a raised, rotating platform centre stage, which would turn regularly to exhibit to the audience all of the angles of the performers' formations. This exhibitionary practice is significant in the world of Cirque du Soleil for two reasons. First, unlike the traditional European single-ring circus, Cirque du Soleil does not generally make available a full 360-degree perspective on its shows.[19] In 1990, designer Michel Crête inaugurated Cirque du Soleil's signature *piste-public* arrangement: the combination stage-and-ring configuration that results in something closer to the perspective enabled by a three-quarter-round performance space than an in-the-round configuration. The circus ring's return in miniature as the contortionists' revolve singles out this act for a particular kind of attention, one that stems from "the desire to stare" that Adams (2001) identifies as the "primary impulse behind the freak show" (68); a stare, I should add, focused on the fleshy body, on the body as (distorted, fantastically imperfect) flesh. Second, no other acts in KOOZÄ avail themselves of a similar device. The juggler, Anthony Gatto, for instance, presents every angle of his act to view by turning around in a circle while juggling to face different quarters of the house. But his rotation generates the opposite effect to that of the contortionists'; his turn happens not only by his own volition, it also increases the difficulty of the juggling, thereby underscoring his talent. The contortionists' turning is effected externally and, while it requires them to hold their position for longer than they might otherwise, it paradoxically fixes them further into a kind of music-box image. Moreover, their placement on a platform borrows from sideshow staging techniques to enhance their difference from the audience by establishing "distance as well as literal hierarchies between the group of spectators and the lone spectacle on the elevated platform or in the sunken pit" (Thomson 1992, 10). Gatto, on the other hand, moves toward and away from the audience during his act, controlling relations of distance and intimacy with his viewers. The contortionists are more or less fixed on the platform; even when they descend from the platform during their transitions between poses (the transitions are largely composed of mudras and walkovers), they remain grouped fairly tightly around its circumference.

Of course, contortionists are not necessarily limited to the display of fleshy bodies; they may also have performer bodies, or even character bodies. They train to shape and extend their natural pliability, thereby constructing a performer body, and develop characters through a combination of attitude, costume, and narrative encasement provided by the *mise en scène*. For instance, Ame Wilson (2002) understands *Saltimbanco*'s contortion act as a "moving tribute to family, composed of father, mother, and child figures whose togetherness is literalized in their entwining forms" (84). Indeed, contortionism's inclusion in Cirque du Soleil shows has seemed to require its fleshy body's rather complete envelopment. Throughout their history, Cirque's contortion acts have been costumed in full body-stockings (covering even their heads, though not their faces) that obscure the fleshy body. While one may dimly perceive muscles moving, the costume's uniform and complete coverage of the contortionist's body disallows seeing muscle groups as such, never mind sweat or blushes. KOOZÄ's three young female contortionists wore reflective spandex bodysuits in a patchwork of gold and silver. On the one hand, the costumes draw the spectator's eye to the sparkling forms, moving brightly and weirdly on the centre-stage raised platform. On the other hand, the costumes reflected the light, preventing the eye from homing in on any particular part of the body. Rather, the reflections reorient the eye to the physical line of the contortionist and the surprising geometry of the group pose. The contortionists' fleshy bodies are abstracted into form.

And yet, as we have seen, the contortionist's freakishness asserts itself again and again in performance. How to incorporate it into Cirque's universe of aspirational exceptionalism? One answer is to reconsider the meta-narrative according to which Cirque operates. In circus freak shows, freak bodies' abnormalities serve to secure the superiority of the "normal" or ordinary body. Rosemarie Garland Thomson (1992) explains, "A freak show's cultural work is to make the physical particularity of the freak into a hyper-visible text against which the viewer's indistinguishable body fades into a seemingly neutral, tractable, and invulnerable instrument of the autonomous will" (10). Cirque du Soleil shows likewise depend on the amazing contrast between the presumably ordinary bodies of the spectators and the exceptional bodies of the performers. Many Cirque shows incorporate ordinary-bodied audience substitutes or representatives into their frame. The entry of these "normal" characters into Cirque's magical world catalyzes the action of the show. *Quidam* for instance opens with a young girl and her conformist parents who have lost their sense of wonder. A headless character with an umbrella and a bowler hat, who looks like something out of Magritte, inducts the family into his alternate universe, composed largely of transcendent aerial acts. *KOOZÄ* similarly opens with a young child, this time a boy whom the program identifies as "L'Innocent," struggling to fly his kite and let his dreams take wing. For its part, *Saltimbanco* presents itself as the dream-product of its central character, "the Sleeper." However, in significant contrast to circus freak shows, Cirque du Soleil's "ordinary" characters – the audience substitutes – are transformed by the shows' marvels. Thus, *KOOZÄ* closes with L'Innocent wielding the magic wand, giving him a central role in its fantastical world. *Quidam*'s purpose-built grid system, the *téléférique*, lifts the family into the skies, transporting and transforming them in an instant.

In the end, it is difficult to determine which performer body is paramount in Cirque du Soleil productions. The character body seems preferred on the whole, perhaps for the distance it places between Cirque du Soleil and traditional circus's somewhat tawdry image. This image is one legacy of circus sideshow attractions, now curtailed, that debased ethnic others and people with disabilities for profit (the circus's and the performer's, though not in equal portions). But circus's tarnished image derives as well from the form's itinerancy and its performers' overwhelmingly working-class roots. As we have seen, the character body separates the performer from the persona, thereby facilitating a kind of performance of upward mobility when working-class and/or socially marginal performers assume roles of royalty, mythical creatures, and even suited businessmen. As importantly, the character body abstracts what is at base the manual labour of the performer body into a professionalized symbolic labour. That said, the more highly individuated and nonassimilable performer and fleshy bodies mount a significant and sustained challenge to such a preference. And if the opening and closing of most shows returns the spectator to the "surpassing limits" narrative carried by the show's characters, what comes between is regularly punctuated by, and even relies upon, the show-stopping feats of discernably "freaky" bodies.

CHAPTER 9

"Somewhere between Science and Legend": Images of Indigeneity in Robert Lepage and Cirque du Soleil's *Totem*

Karen Fricker

Totem is the second production for Cirque du Soleil directed by Robert Lepage. It premiered in 2010 and has been touring internationally ever since.[1] In keeping with Cirque du Soleil's creative protocols, the production is a series of acts by highly skilled performers across the range of circus skills – acrobatics, object manipulation, balance, aerial, and clown – tied together via an overall concept or theme. That theme, in the case of *Totem*, is the relationship of humankind to other species and natural phenomena: situated, its promotional literature declares, "somewhere between science and legend,"[2] it is billed as "a fascinating journey into the evolution of mankind."[3] Evolution is a complex, historically contested term, and as this chapter explores, *Totem* takes a position in these debates. In an interview about the production, Lepage explained the basis of his approach: "We have in our bodies the memory of what we were: monkeys, mammals, amphibians, fish, a chain of being that circus artists have the subtlety, the muscle, the lightness to show" (qtd in Nightingale 2011). In another interview Lepage positioned the production as a riposte to a contemporary resurgence of anti-Darwinist thinking in the United States: "I find it amazing that a country like the US allows creationism to be taught. I think that's setting them back. I was thinking about that when I made the show," he said, adding "How right Darwin was!" (qtd in Lesage 2010).[4]

In the production, some performers play humans, but others are costumed to represent various animal species, and circus acts are reframed as representations of animal behaviour. In one number, for example, a male-female fixed trapeze duo are figured as "two lovebirds" who "tease, play and sulk in an innocent game of seduction."[5] In Charles Batson's (2012a) reading, *Totem* is "maker and reminder or the message that the human is

9.1 *Totem*, with Nakotah Larance (left) and Christian Laveau (right). Costumes: Kym Barrett

animal, that the animal marks the human, and that the human animal shows us singular possibilities in and through the workings of the animal-like body" (618). As such, the production marks a particular moment in the history of a company that made its name in the 1980s as a circus without animals: with *Totem*, the world of fauna appears on Cirque du Soleil's stages – but as representation, in ways that still align with the company's values, which Lepage says he shares: "Peace and love, let's work collaboratively, everybody's equal, and no harm to any animals" (qtd in Nightingale 2011). In its focus on human-animal links, the production participates in the growing early twenty-first-century interest in species boundary, which has led to the birth of the academic field of critical animal studies and, in theatre and performance research specifically, an engagement with what Una Chaudhuri has classed "zooësis": "the way culture makes art and meaning with the figure and body of the animal" (Chaudhuri and Enelow 2006, 2).

In order to fully appreciate the production's meanings, however, another key element of its content and visual vocabulary must be taken on board: its relationship to indigeneity. The costuming and scenography of several of the production's acts suggest connections with indigenous peoples and cultures, particularly those of North America, and the production's title and the choice of an oversized turtle shell as its main scenographic feature offer further such associations. As such it forms part of a series of contemporary productions in which Lepage explores the culture and history of Quebec's First Nations.[6] Beyond these more overt references to native cultures, *Totem* reveals an investment in Aboriginal ways of knowing the world via its depiction of not only animals and humans, but all aspects of nature, as being interconnected and interdependent. This reflects a belief shared by many native peoples: that there is a "unique living force ... present in all kingdoms of existence extend[ing] to inanimate as well as animate objects and indeed to concepts and forms of knowledge" (Stewart-Harawira 2005, 39). Such a "relational worldview," assuming "relationships between all life forms that exist within the natural world" (Kovach 2009, 34), is a central tenet of an "incorporeal knowledge paradigm that might be termed aboriginal epistemology" (Ermine 1995, 103).

Some of the production's representations and imagery could, if viewed as representative of a Western world view, be seen as endorsing a progress-based understanding of evolution, in which indigenous cultures are figured as less developed and of less value than Western ones. Reading the production with Aboriginal ways of knowing in mind allows us to see these images as largely positive, inclusive, and celebratory. There is one element of the production, however, that remains incommensurable with a positive depiction of indigeneity: somewhat paradoxically, this is the presentation of two indigenous performers, dancer Nakotah Larance and musician Christian Laveau, who are offered as literal evidence of the traditions and virtues of their culture. While the production is clearly attempting to present Larance and Laveau – the first indigenous performers ever to appear in a Cirque du Soleil production representing their own cultures (see Donnelly 2010) – respectfully, even reverently, it does so while shifting the representational codes by which it frames its performers' bodies, and in so doing instrumentalizes that which it intends to enshrine. The presentation of Larance and Laveau invites what Jane R. Goodall (2002) classes an "ethnological gaze, which lingers on people as exhibited bodies," in contrast to the "theatrical gaze, which follows a sequence of action and registers bodies as communicators rather than as sights in themselves" (83). As such, the production extends the discredited tradition of the display of native bodies in popular entertainments, which reached its heyday in late nineteenth- and early twentieth-century ethnological displays and Wild West shows. In her remarkable book

9.2 *Totem*, with Nakotah Larance. Costumes: Kym Barrett

Performance and Evolution in the Age of Darwin, Goodall links this boom in entertainments showcasing ethnic otherness to the publication of Darwin's *Origin of Species*, which provoked massive public interest in "throwbacks, missing links, freak taxonomies, and exotic races" (i). Displays, exhibitions, and performances became an important means to meet this interest (and further feed it). *Totem* emerges at another cultural moment in which the relationship between human and animal is under considerable pressure and scrutiny, and when the recognition and celebration of native cultures is on the increase in the North American mainstream and in the work of Lepage and other artists of European descent. Lepage attempted to capture and respond to this sociocultural moment by channelling native wisdom in an exploration of evolution, but became entangled in representational systems that complicate the productive cultural work he undertakes.

Evolution and Progress

In order to explore *Totem*'s representations and the competing world views they evoke, we need to first establish the larger discourses around evolution and progress that inform them, as well as the central tenets of Aboriginal epistemology. From the eighteenth century to the present day, evolution has been broadly understood in the popular Western imagination to mean a process of ongoing, forward-moving progress. In biological terms, such an understanding figures the history of animal development as one of increasing complexity and sophistication, with homo sapiens at the top of the evolutionary heap. This understanding extended into theorization of the social: in the mid-nineteenth-century burst of scientific engagement with natural and social phenomena that included the publication of Charles Darwin's *Origin of Species*, social evolutionists espoused a vision that "tended towards the optimistic view that human societies were evolving from an inferior to a superior condition" (Johnson and Earle 2000, 2). Implicit in such theories, Allen W. Johnson and Timothy Earle argue, was a "deeply ethnocentric belief" in a "culture-bound concept of progress – that history is a sequence of changes leading inevitably in the general direction of the lifestyle and values of the intellectual elites of Europe and Euroamerica" (3). Such was the "obsessional modernity" of the late nineteenth century, Goodall (2002) explains, that "industrialized nations began to see themselves in Darwinian terms as highly evolved, and their sense of themselves as modern was demonstrated as a capacity to supervise the evolutionary development of peoples whom they took to represent lower stages of advancement" (46). The "progressionist" (Ruse 1997, 31) view of evolution thus helped create the circumstances for the denigration, suppression, and colonization of non-Europeans.

These questions about evolution – its relationship to progress; the relationship of progress-based understandings of evolution to the social-historical context in which they were developed; the implications of the "racist assumption [that]… [i]nferior races could not aspire to the higher levels of achievement because they were incapable of it" (Johnson and Earle 2000, 3); and the value and nature of progress itself – have been debated ever since. A number of important scientific thinkers have argued that there is no necessary connection between biological and social progress, and have offered a variety of hypotheses as to why such links were made and have persisted. Michael Ruse (1997, 526) underlines the point made by Goodall: that biological evolutionary theory arose in the context of an overriding investment in the virtues of Progress (the capital P indicating a social and cultural understanding of the term, rather than scientific) and that this rendered the relationship between them particularly difficult to disentangle. Though the equation of biological evolution and social progress has since been "discredited" (Human 2006, 6) in scientific circles, Ruse (1997) argues that at the popular level, "Progress continues to ride high. I have yet to find a museum or a display or a chart of a book which is not overtly progressionist" (526).

Aboriginal Epistemology

Establishing a working understanding of Aboriginal ways of knowing inevitably, in a study of this short length, requires some generalization; but it is also the case, in the words of Leroy Little Bear (2000), that "there is enough similarity among North American Indian philosophies to apply concepts generally" (79). Makere Stewart-Harawira (2005) agrees that there are "broad groupings of beliefs and values" that "comprise what might be called an indigenous ontology of being" (35). The concept of indigenous epistemology was first substantively identified as such in the Western academic literature in a 1995 article by the Cree scholar Willie Ermine. He portrays the moment of first contact between European settlers and natives of North America as "the meeting of two disparate worldviews" on very different trajectories: Europeans were "bound for an uncharted destination in outer space, the physical," while native peoples were "on a delicate path into inner space, the metaphysical" (101). While schematic, Ermine's formulation offers a useful entrée into some of the central aspects of a native world view (as well as a useful framework in which to consider *Totem*'s climactic depiction of space travel, as we will see). As Ermine explains, knowledge acquisition in an Aboriginal context is inherently subjective, in that all experience is processed internally and personally: in an Aboriginal world view, individuals honour the "inner space that is the universe of being within each person that is synonymous with the soul, the spirit, the self, or the being" and in so doing come to appreciate that "all existence [is] connected" (103). As Stewart-Harawira (2005) further states, in systems of traditional knowledge it is the concept of "life force" that provides this connection:

> Life force's presence in all kingdoms of existence extends to inanimate as well as animate objects and indeed to concepts and forms of knowledge. Within the natural world, each individual rock and stone, each individual animal and plant, as well as every body of land and water, is recognised is having its own unique Life Force. (38)

Stewart-Harawira also notes that exchanges with supernaturals are the "bedrock of native spirituality" (ibid).

Totem's Evolutionary Story

Totem's depiction of evolution is complex, and not always easy to discern. At first blush, the production seems to communicate an investment in progressionism, via the fact that it frames itself as a story of human evolution (rather than evolution more generally), and in its being figured as tracing "the fascinating journey of the human species from its original amphibian state to its ultimate desire to fly."[7] A forward-moving, developmental narrative is signalled, with air and space travel figured as crowning evidence of human achievement and progress. Its strong gesturing in its title, thematics, and scenography to the belief system of totemism also sends a different message. Totemism is an investment in the existence of "a natural object or animal that is believed by a particular society to have spiritual significance and that is adopted by it as an emblem."[8] It forms part of the "animistic philosophy" (Kovach 2009, 34) that characterizes many Aboriginal societies; the English-language word *totem* is derived from the Ojibwe *nintotem*, meaning "mark of my family" (Colman 2012). The turtle is *Totem*'s "totemic animal":[9] the playing area is oval-shaped, and the action happens under, around, and on a large turtle shell that raises and lowers onto the stage. The turtle is in many cultures associated with creation myths, including those of the Huron First Nation, which understands that life on earth began with a woman dropping from the heavens and landing on a turtle shell, which became Turtle Island – otherwise known as North America (Conrad, Finkel, and Jaenen 1998, 17).

The concept of totemism has a particular, benighted history in modern Western thought that forms part of the larger conceptual struggle about the relationship between evolution and progress. As part of the early twentieth century boom in social evolutionist thinking, a number of important thinkers, among them Émile Durkheim, Sigmund Freud, and James Frazier, fixed on totemism as a "possibly universal institution in 'primitive' societies"; they used belief in the totem as evidence in the construction of progress-based concepts of human development that understood non-Western cultures as "fossils of cultural conditions that 'advanced' societies had outgrown" (Von Hendy 2006, 521) and therefore of lesser value. As Harriet Lyons (2008) argues, "Totemism in the Victorian imaginary was a moral, spiritual, and intellectual zero point at the opposite end of a continuum from the beliefs and practices that the Victorian middle class upheld as desirable. Speculations about the origin of totemism were thus speculations about the origin of society itself" (484). This flurry of interest in totemism was relatively short-lived, and since the advent of postcolonial thought has largely been discredited because of its racist and colonialist implications. Viewed in this context, the totem theme could be read as an anachronistic nod in the direction of progressivist evolutionary thinking. Taken as a whole, however, the production reads largely as a reappropriation of the concept of totemism, and a demonstration of how it functions in the context of Aboriginal belief systems.

Take, for example, its opening moment: an acrobat, in a costume covered in 4,500 tiny mirrors, spirals down from the flies, with a gesture of his arms sets the production's action in motion, and spirals back heavenwards. Called the "Crystal Man,"[10] he is "the light that sparks human evolution on earth."[11] He returns at the end of the show and dives into a lagoon, indicating a return to origins in keeping with the circular nature of indigenous knowledge systems (see Stewart-Harawira 2005, 41). The Crystal Man is a supernatural presence that is both embodiment and giver of the life force, and the world that he sparks into being is one in which humans, animals, and nature share the planet in harmony. In the act immediately following the Crystal Man's appearance, acrobats dressed as fish and reptiles are discovered sitting in the long, narrow space underneath the latticework turtle shell, which is filled with mist and lit with a reddish glow; they drum and chant before breaking out into a parallel bars number. The image, as the Montreal *Gazette* critic Pat Donnelly (2010) notes, evokes a First Nations or Native American "sweat lodge, wherein reptilian-clad performers are holding a revival meeting." Clearly, native peoples are being likened to animal species that, in progressionist understandings of evolution, are at the lower end of the developmental spectrum. This is therefore, viewed from a Western perspective, a scene that demeans native peoples. But in the context of an Aboriginal world view, it is celebratory and joyous, an affirmation of the shared kinship between the human and nonhuman without necessarily implying hierarchy or value judgments between species.

Beyond animism, several of the production's acts celebrate the existence of life force in aspects of the natural and material world. A troupe of young female unicyclists flip metal bowls onto their heads, representing "the bustle of the planting season."[12] Here, as throughout the production, Kym Barrett's costume designs play a key role in communicating meaning. Barrett treated fabrics by printing patterns on them, and attaching objects "to recreate ... a broad range of textures, colours, and markings found in nature." Seed pods, shells, leaves, and feathers are attached to the unicyclists' costumes and headdresses to suggest "a time of harvest and the abundance of fall."[13] In another number, two Crystal Ladies wearing sparkle-encrusted leotards juggle equally sparkly squares of fabric on their feet and hands, "evok[ing] the creation of the world and the beauty of minerals"; their appearance echoes that of the Crystal Man, directly linking life force to the "fiery bowels of the earth."[14]

Alongside this spectacular presentation of humans, animals, and the natural world as equally and vibrantly full of life, *Totem* lightly pokes fun at Western, science-led approaches to evolution, which, viewed from an Aboriginal perspective, are limited by their understanding of knowledge as "separate from ourselves" (Ermine 1995, 102) and atomized – broken down into fragments and cut off from the contexts and histories that give it meaning. At the end of the first act, a contemporary businessman with a cellphone pressed to his ear walks around the stage perimeter, followed by performers costumed as Cro-Magnon man, Homo Erectus, and several other iterations of the primate order ending with an ape. This visual quotation of the image frequently used to illustrate the forward progress of evolution provoked knowing laughter the three times I saw *Totem*. An image known well as shorthand for the production's subject matter was being both quoted and, by turning it into an embodied performance, defamiliarized – hence the laughter. Having presented the audience with a familiar image that implicitly buys into a progressionist value system, with contemporary Western man as the consummation of the evolutionary process, the production subsequently underlines its own take on evolution. Stripping off his suit, the businessman reveals a tiger-striped unitard underneath, and joins a troupe of similarly-clad acrobats in a perches number. Contemporary human subjects, we are reminded, are part of the animal world; acknowledging this lineage opens up the possibility of extraordinary feats of physical prowess such as those displayed by the tiger-striped acrobats.

Totem even features a Charles Darwin–like character, a white-haired, bearded, bespectacled Scientist who appears onstage with a monkey sidekick (played, of course, by a costumed human performer). The Scientist "represents reason and the quest to understand the universe in way that can be quantified, measured, and put into boxes."[15] He is presented as comically preoccupied with strategies of categorization and containment: he carries preposterously high stacks of cardboard boxes, and his juggling of illuminated balls inside a transparent plastic cone evokes science experiments. At the end of his act, he symbolically renounces Western science by leaving the contained environment of the cone, and is rewarded by being

9.3 Opposite *Totem.* Costumes: Kym Barrett

transformed into a much younger man: embracing the production's dominant Aboriginal world view, it is implied, allows him to reverse the forward motion of time. The production's remaining references to developed Western society are all delivered via its clowns, who are presented as foolishly preoccupied by and inept at simple tasks (such as cooking an egg while on a fishing boat) and engaging in superficial masculinist displays of prowess (hotdogging on water skis). When he litters, one of the clowns comes into conflict with a character called the Tracker, who is positioned as the production's environmental conscience: the Tracker transforms into a toreador and the clown clumsily imitates a bull, his inability to fully embody animal behaviour revealing the limitations of those with Western-led world views.[16]

The production's final act, as previously mentioned, evokes space travel: a troupe of Russian bars performers march onstage in two lines, wearing cosmonauts' helmets and spectacular unitards whose intricate patterning was inspired by "Mayan drawings."[17] The act, in which acrobats bounce on pliable planks propped on the shoulders of their sturdier colleagues, spinning and twisting high in the air, is framed as an expression – and perhaps brief realization – of the yearning to fly, which Lepage feels is a shared human desire[18] and evidence of our animal roots. Batson (2012a) reads the act as an expression of "some utopic completeness, in which barriers are elided in a joining of past and future, human and animal" (620). The reference to indigeneity in the performers' costumes adds a further layer to this reading: these space travellers are at once evidence of Western technological ingenuity and Aboriginal belief systems. By acknowledging the importance of "inner space, the metaphysical" (Ermine 1995, 101), humankind finds its way to outer space. Two world views, utopically, merge, as critic Christian Saint-Pierre (2010) observed in his review: "The production helps us believe that it may be possible for Earthlings and all the kingdoms (human, animal, vegetable, and mineral) to live one day in harmony, all colours united, in one and the same world."[19]

9.4 Opposite top *Totem*, with Greg Kennedy (left) and Joe Putignano. Costumes: Kym Barrett

9.5 Opposite bottom *Totem*, with Eric Hernandez (foreground) and Christian Laveau. Costumes: Kym Barrett

Totem's Aboriginal Performers

Overall, then, in *Totem*'s scenography, costuming, acts, and *mise en scène*, we are presented with a representational universe embodying a holistic, non-hierarchical, life force–imbued epistemology. Where this representational system snags, in my view, is in those acts that present North American indigenous cultures literally, in particular the acts performed by the Hopi Tewa hoop dancer Nakotah Larance.[20] This young performer – aged twenty at the time of *Totem*'s premiere – learned his dances, as is Aboriginal tradition, from Elders in his community; Cirque du Soleil discovered him via videos of him dancing that his father had put on YouTube (see Donnelly 2010). In keeping with the production's themes, these hoop dances evoke animals and plants (see Berkery 2013): an image of Larance with the hoops looped over and spread along his arms, representing an eagle, appears on the splash page of the show's website and on posters and other promotional materials. This is the central image with which the production wishes to be associated. The other indigenous performer in *Totem* is drummer and vocalist Christian Laveau, a Huron from the Wendake reserve near Quebec City, whom Lepage invited to participate.[21] Laveau plays his own drum and sings, in his native Huron, in *Totem*'s house band, and comes forward out of the band to accompany Larance's dances (see Nadeau 2009). My concern has to do with the fact that Larance (and to a lesser extent Laveau) play themselves, or characters who very much resemble themselves, and whose value in this representational system derives from the culture and traditions they embody.

In order to elaborate this concern, it is necessary to briefly introduce the taxonomy of circus bodies proposed by David Graver (1997) and expanded on by Erin Hurley in this volume. Cirque du Soleil tends to privilege performers' character bodies, which are the sum of the "gestures and expressions of the actor that signify the life and experience of a fictional character within a fictional world" (Graver 1997, 223). Presenting circuses filled with character bodies is part of what sets Cirque du Soleil and other nouveau circus companies apart from traditional circuses. As Hurley argues, the "character body elevates the circus out of the realm of craft and into that of art ... Performing in character abstracts the performer's labour and rescues the skilled performance from instrumentality" (126). Foregrounding character bodies renders performers anonymous and "replaceable"; the show – and in the case of Cirque du Soleil, the company's brand – becomes the "star" (ibid.).

The two other types of bodies in Graver's taxonomy are the performer body and the fleshy body, "categories that roughly correspond to those of cultivated exceptionalism and natural exceptionalism" (Hurley, this volume, 127). The performer body is "typified by an authority that comes from technical mastery and by an engagement required of challenging technical display" (ibid.); it is the body that we see when a circus performer reveals her extraordinary skills honed through training and discipline. When the audience gazes at *Totem*'s fixed trapeze duo as they engage in their risky series of holds, drops, and poses, it is their performer bodies that are on display. While they are costumed and in character as the "lovebirds," the interest in them at that moment is not these character identities, but the amazing things their bodies are doing. Performer bodies "[arrest] narrative" (ibid.); they are part of what makes it very hard to tell a story through circus – the performer body will always pop out of the narrative frame. The final circus body is the fleshy body, the "nonsemiotic, self-identical corporeal envelope of skin, hair, flesh, blood, fat, and muscle" (133). Fleshy bodies appear in Cirque du Soleil productions when performers cannot or do not complete their attempted manoeuvre; they also appear in contortionist acts, where the interest lies in the "contortionist's body's strangeness vis-à-vis norms of physical flexibility and extension and with respect to the arrangement or position of body parts" (ibid.). Fleshy bodies are those most closely associated with the traditional circus sideshow, in which humans born with exceptional bodies – the dog-faced boy, the so-called elephant man, giants, and dwarves – were identified as freaks and put on display, alongside self-made freaks such the tattooed lady (see Batson 2012a; Hurley, this volume).

Totem does not have a contortionist act, but it does have an act in which the performers' primary appeal resides in the special qualities they were born with. Unlike all the other performers in the show, there is very little distinction between who Laveau and Larance are, and what they are meant to represent. Indeed, Larance is one of only four figures in the production given character names, and his is "Amerindian Dancer":[22] his personal identity matches his character identity. Larance was hired because of his exceptional skill in hoop dancing, which he demonstrates. But showcasing this skill, which is more aesthetic than physical, is unusal in this production and in Cirque du Soleil's work overall. While, to be sure, hoop dancing is an athletic form of dance that requires excellent fitness, and has some kinship with the circus skill of object manipulation, the value it is afforded in the production resides in its capacity to evoke images and convey symbolism, and in its status as a living extension of a cultural legacy and tradition. Similarly, Laveau is the only musician in *Totem* whose costuming and performance directly reference a specific culture – his own. As such their performances function differently from the other act in the production that is costumed and staged to suggest North American indigeneity – the roller-skating duo Denise Garcia-Sorta, who is Spanish, and Massimiliano Medini, who is Italian. They wear white costumes with sewn-in beads, long beaded tassels, and fur trim; are transported on and offstage in a canoe; and perform their duet – which is meant to evoke a wedding – on a small round surface resembling an oversize drum. In this instance, the act involves the high levels of risk and training associated with circus and, given that it is performed on roller skates, seems unlikely to be intended to convince audience members that it is an extension of an Aboriginal tradition. Its presentation of an ersatz, decorative Indianness falls outside, and weakens, *Totem*'s evocation of a holistic indigenous world view – but the problems around the presentation of Larance and Laveau are graver still. It is hard to escape the conclusion that these two performers were cast to provide authenticity; their presence literalizes the values associated with indigenous cultures suggested elsewhere in the production.

Batson (2012a) argues that *Totem*'s unique appeal lies in its presentation of "disturbed categories"; images of the "co-mingled human/animal" (performers dressed as animals) and the thematic presentation of "explicit human/animal connection[s]" confront audiences with figures who are at once like and not like them, creating a provocative situation of near-identification that Batson likens to the appeal of the circus freak (610, 619). Freaks simultaneously fascinate, repel, and reassure, in Elizabeth Grosz's (1996) influential formulation, because they "traverse the very boundaries that secure the 'normal' subject in its given identity" and at the same time confirm "the viewer as bounded, belonging to a 'proper' social category" (65). The disturbed categories of human and animal in *Totem*, Batson argues, offer a related sense of titillating "recognition that the exceptional being is our differently shaped mirror-image … [we] delight at seeing limit-exploding, exceptional versions of ourselves" (622). Batson celebrates *Totem* for its presentation of human/animal hybridity – and, by implication, of difference more generally – as something marvellous, rather than threatening: the production "model[s] the posture of the nonanxious celebrant in front of dissolving bounds and boundaries, when monkeys fly on Russian bars and lovebirds are nubile Quebeckers" (621).

Such a reading, however, cannot take account of the representational work that Laveau and Larance are called upon to do in *Totem*, because the way their bodies are treated resists metaphor. They are not presented as suggesting blurred boundaries between human and animal; rather, they are unequivocally presented not just as human, but as a specific sort of human – as Aboriginal – and of value in the production's representational system as such. Their presence onstage recalls the ways in which native peoples were displayed in ethnological exhibitions that were a highly popular form of entertainment in Victorian England. As Goodall (2002) charts, such entertainments responded to public curiosity about evolution and were intended to offer evidence of the veracity of the research of Darwin and others, the "draw-card" being that "no one would believe human beings could differ so immeasurably if it were not for the immediate availability of the evidence" (82). Entrepreneurs including Charles Darwin's contemporary P.T. Barnum and the painter George Catlin played a key role in such activities, their careers "continually cross[ing] between the worlds of show business and scientific natural history" (7). Tapping into the emerging (now discredited) science of ethnology – the study of human races – Barnum and other showmen took a particular interest in locating putative evidence of the close relationship between what they understood as lower orders of humans and other species – that is, the mythic missing link – via displays of humans with unusual physical qualities such as the "man-monkeys" Hervey Leech and William Henry Johnson, and little people including Tom Thumb and the "Aztec Lilliputians" Maximo and Bartola, who were displayed as evidence of the existence of "a race of Pigmies" (53, 56, 66). As ethnography grew in influence in the 1870s, the emphasis shifted from the display of physiological to cultural differences, providing "a new and respectable pretext for the exhibition of indigenous people from various parts of the globe" (82). Displays of "savagery" by Bushmen, Zulus, and Kafirs were notable successes at London's Egyptian Hall and St George's Hall in the 1840s and 1850s, prompting Catlin, who had lived among Native Americans, to transport Ojibwe Indians to his Indian Gallery at the Egyptian Hall and have them perform in staged dramas displaying their culture and ways (91).

These performance traditions extended through the end of the nineteenth century and into the twentieth via the development of ethnological congresses at World Fairs – assemblages of exemplars of different races attempting to offer a comprehensive panorama of humankind – and Wild West shows, outdoor spectacles enacting the violent clash of Western and indigenous cultures. While these latter productions doubtless objectified Native American performers and called upon them to efface their specific tribal and personal identities, scholars differ as to whether the native performers lacked all agency in their relationship to Buffalo Bill Cody and other entrepreneurs. In *Wild West Shows and the Images of American Indians, 1883–1933*, L.G. Moses (1996) argues that the "Show Indians" who participated in Cody's spectaculars were part of a "transitional generation, one that encountered for the first time the full weight of comprehensive government programs to eradicate native life" (7). Wild West shows gave them gainful employment and allowed them to simulate their disappearing culture, much to the consternation of the Bureau of Indian Affairs, which was in charge of settling and westernizing Native Americans: "'Playing' Indian could also be viewed as defiance" (Moses 1996, 277). Norman K. Denzin (2013) contests this revisionism, likening Wild West shows to "minstrel productions" and arguing that "Indians, Aboriginals, savages, the Wild West, and the frontier have been essential preconditions for a global whiteness, for a racialised social order in which whites dominate. The Wild West show modeled this racial order" (30). As Moses notes, while the era of the Show Indian ended with the Great Depression, portrayals of Native Americans continue in contemporary culture, and "the success of films such as *Dances with Wolves*, *Pow Wow Highway*, *Thunderheart*, *The Last of the Mohicans* and *Geronimo* suggested renewed interest by the general public in sympathetic and largely positive portrayals of American Indians" (277). At the same time, the emergence of First Nations and Native American performing arts companies such as the Montreal-based Ondinnok (founded in 1985) provide training for First Nations performers (including Christian Laveau, who studied in a special program for indigenous people at the National Theatre School of Canada, run by Ondinnok) and create productions reviving and celebrating native North American cultures.[23]

Totem does not overtly reference the dark history of the relationship between European settlers and Aboriginal peoples in North America, or ongoing concerns about land and energy rights, the historic abuse of native children in care, unemployment and underemployment, education provision and achievement, and addiction on First Nations and Native American reserves (see Attleo 2013; Keel 2013; National Aboriginal Health Organization 2010). Nor does it directly celebrate the many advances and achievements made by native peoples in the late twentieth and early twenty-first centuries to raise standards of living, education, and employment and to make their voices heard in government and culture (see Attleo 2013; Keel 2013). Its celebration of indigenous cultures rather comes through its evocation of native ways of knowing and its sly undercutting of Western assumptions and cultural shorthands around questions of evolution and progress. Christian Laveau underlines in interviews that he feels *Totem* respects and celebrates his culture:

> Guy Laliberté [founder of Cirque de Soleil] said, "You are a *real* culture, you are alive, so you will sing in your mother language." For me it's really an honour. Every night I use my own drums and other personal items. (qtd in Wright 2012)

Singing in one's own language, however, and using instruments from one's culture – and indeed representing any specific culture – falls outside of Cirque du Soleil's usual representational codes, in which language is invented and the performative world of each production largely fanciful and imagined (Harvie and Hurley 1999, 312). Larance and Laveau are clearly being put forward to showcase the integrity and value of North American Aboriginal cultures, rather than, as in nineteenth and early twentieth century performances, as evidence of the very existence of ethnicities and traditions unfamiliar to audiences. But being used as a reference point nonetheless objectifies Larance and Laveau: the literalism of their onstage presence clashes with the otherwise metaphorical, lateral, and sometimes satirical nature of the production's representations. In attempting to construct a twenty-first-century popular entertainment that captures and responds to its cultural moment by celebrating indigeneity, Lepage ends up conjuring a previous, benighted tradition of the instrumentalization and objectification of indigenous people.

IV.

Circus Problematized

CHAPTER 10

Creativity's Tug-of-War between Artists and Managers: A Mediator's Perspective on the Case of Cirque du Soleil's "Complexe Cirque"

Isabelle Mahy

Introducing Creativity

Creativity is spontaneously, if reductively, associated with the arts, even as it is first and foremost a human competency essential to survival and to development. Mihaly Csikszentmihalyi (1996) tells us that the most creative phase of problem solving exists in an obscure and mysterious space that challenges conscious processes, in a "groan zone" of idleness when nothing seems to be going the way it should. This highly creative moment is one of ongoing tension between the actual mastery of a certain body of knowledge and the ability of the mind to step back and connect ideas coming from multiple horizons within that body of knowledge. Csikszentmihalyi reminds us that, to understand these moments of creativity, it is not sufficient to focus on a single person who is often identified as solely responsible for new ideas or products. In the pages that follow, I propose to illustrate this essential concept by pointing to the communal contributions of Cirque du Soleil's artists and managers, as the company's achievements are not simply the result of the work of founder, principal owner, and self-styled "Guide" Guy Laliberté,[1] even if he is obviously a major link in the creative chain.

Even now that creativity – along with its siblings, creation and co-creation – has become fashionable in entrepreneurial discourse, it is nevertheless often showcased only as a managed part of the corporate image of large organizations that are or want to be seen as avant-garde in their industry. But even if it is a leitmotif in large VIP business gatherings,[2] the sometimes messy notion of creativity is quickly discarded by stakeholders eager to get back to their habitual practice of being in control. It is easily considered a distraction from the principal goals of the business, and in times of crisis, creativity is easily confused with nonessential arts and seen as too costly, too risky, and too insubstantial to confront the complexity of corporate and cultural demands. Csikszentmihalyi considers these conservative reactions as signs of a serious lack of insight into the creative process in circumstances for which solutions from the past simply do not apply. He suggests that, in such moments, it becomes a necessity to think outside the box, in other words, to think and act creatively and mindfully.

This chapter explores the tug-of-war between artists and managers as they seek, with varying degrees of mindfulness, to bridge the gap between their two horizons in the creative process. My analysis is informed by my own experience of doing research at Cirque du Soleil and having found myself between these two subcultures. In this position, I was able to draw upon the concept of mediation to examine a little-known, if daring, attempt by Cirque du Soleil to drive the company to a new era.

The Case

Cirque du Soleil is the world's largest circus comprising, prior to the recent downsizing, 4,000 employees (1,300 artists) of fifty nationalities, speaking twenty-five languages in a hundred occupational categories. Its shows have had 100 million spectators since 1984, and it has not received a public grant since 1992. What Cirque now describes as "other activities" – beyond those of its original circus mandate – represent a variety of competencies that have slowly emerged in the periphery of its productions and are not that well known. Apart from its touring and resident shows, Cirque is active in seven different sectors: (1) hospitality, designing bars and lounges like the Revolution lounge in Las Vegas associated with the Beatles show; (2) exhibitions, designing buildings like the Canadian pavilion at the Shanghai 2010 exhibition; (3) art galleries, where they support visual artists in presenting work related to Cirque; (4) fashion and apparel, where Cirque inspires designers, as in Desigual's special collection; (5) fitness programs, in partnership with companies like Reebok; (6) special events, like large public productions, corporate events, private affairs, and prestigious appearances, for example at the 2012 Oscars ceremony or at the 2004 Montreal Jazz Festival; and (7) motion pictures like the 3D film *Worlds Away* directed by James Cameron, released in 2012. Professionals from various trades are behind these activities, including architects, leisure specialists, sports experts, broadcast media professionals, design teams, and supporting production experts.

Cirque promotes itself and manages its image by presenting a strong discourse on creativity: "Cirque du Soleil places creativity at the core of all its endeavours so as to ensure limitless possibilities. This is why the creative challenge is of the utmost importance with each new business opportunity, whether it is a show or any other creative activity."[3] If artistic integrity is stressed by this statement, the business focus is also very clear. These two streams represent a fundamental tension in this organization, the tension between art and management. At Cirque, this tug-of-war became evident to me during a study on the organization's Complexe Cirque 2001–02 project, which aimed at building in Montreal the prototype of what could nowadays be designated as a living lab. After a period of exclusively producing shows, from its beginnings in 1984 to 1996, the traditionally nomadic company sought to create stable headquarters for its employees and clients, constructing a space named "the Studio" in Montreal's St-Michel district. After small, arguably unfocused projects undertaken elsewhere with other businesses from the entertainment industry, for example in London and in New York, the idea of an urban oasis in Montreal emerged, soon taking shape as a "Complexe Cirque" that was to become a prototype of a laboratory where all concepts useful to the company's projects would be developed. This time, the goal was clear and ambitious. Cirque du Soleil, with private and public investment, would build an entertainment complex and artistic creation centre, the first of a series, where ideas and concepts would be sparked and then spread to the various Cirque locations worldwide. The Complexe Cirque prototype would encompass a hotel, spa, multimedia theatre, restaurants, art galleries, and more, all of which would help Montreal to be recognized as one of the coolest international tourist destinations and the best place to "live an experience," as Guy Laliberté would describe it.[4] At the time, this now quite common marketing idea of going beyond the product to actually provide the context and setting of a client experience was audacious.

The Montreal Complexe Cirque project lasted one-and-a-half years and employed forty to fifty people. Among them were artists, architects, designers, project and finance managers, consultants, partners, and myself. For their work, the creators embraced a large spectrum of influences, like pataphysics, surrealism, and the history of the Tcherkessy territory,[5] which were revealed through the concepts constituting the Complexe Cirque design.

These foundations were influenced by Laliberté's vision, in which the building that was about to be erected would play an ecumenical role. Inside the main building, the artists planned a chapel for weddings and baptisms. They designed ritual baths as part of the services a spa would offer. A philanthropic spirit also supported the vision, as the Complexe Cirque would have partnered with a soup kitchen run by a nearby church. The Complexe hotel would eventually have given free access to a few rooms for homeless people, and it would have been among the first green buildings to be constructed in Montreal.

This project's creative aspects can also be seen in the artists' ability to work with several streams of influences mainly stemming from the visual arts, architecture, and ecology. To give life to the Complexe Cirque, the artists developed a specific architectural language, with structures and details related to ritual celebrations that would take place in the building according to the sun's movements on the walls over the year's calendar. They created a story to support and convey a narrative that became a contextual evocation with characters, a plot, and several cross-references to the city's history and Cirque culture. For instance, the central piazza was to be named after a famous period in Quebec's arts history, the publication of "Refus global." Two of the most fruitful influences that were directly applied to the architecture were nomadism, with caravanserai type of living, and the labyrinth, translated into blueprints shaping the walkways inside the building.

This ambitious and creative project was, however, cancelled mere weeks before construction began. The project's vision and scope had been defined in appealing ways to attract private and public investors, but the task was enormous, and the political and economic climate was already deteriorating, with the whole landscape shifting further after the events of 11 September 2001.

During the intense period of the Complexe's planning and creation, artists and managers formed separate communities with different cultures and perspectives. Both, nevertheless, contributed to create this audacious project. Working on different dimensions of the project, they found themselves regularly opposing each other as they expressed their views. The two communities had very different profiles with regard to their work process, their interaction modes, the tools they used to communicate, their key focuses and concerns, and the "golden rules" they applied to various decision-making processes. In table 10.1, I present a typology of their respective modes of working.

Table 10.1
Artist and manager profiles

Artists' modes of working	*Profile comprising*	*Managers' modes of working*
Creation (research, design, production)	*Process*	Management (strategy, project, finance, risks, clients, human resources)
Encounter and conversation, preferably informal and organic	*Interaction modes*	Business relations and partnerships, preferably structured and formal
Create models, mock-ups, images, video documents, architectural blueprints	*Tools they use and/or create*	Develop business, strategic, and project plans. Elaborate forecasts, budgets, and contracts. Use financial statements and refer to organization charts
Vision Concept Imagining Feeling	*Main focus / concern they have*	Vision Wealth Place in industry Strategic decisions
Establish and maintain artistic integrity. The creation is always collective; no one is a star, everyone is a star when the artwork is a success	*Their absolute Golden Rule*	The goal is always to work at increasing value creation. The organization must nurture clients' desire for the brand by keeping Cirque the top priority in their purchase intentions

As we see, the artists and the managers shared the project but contributed to it differently, and their respective cultures were also very different. Most of the artists were recruited from within Guy Laliberté's close circle of friends and acquaintances. They already shared a certain way of life with the owner, whereas the managers came from different professional backgrounds (accounting, project management, finance, human resources, etc.) and business sectors relevant for the project, like hospitality. Most of the managers were hired based on those specific skills. It is important to note that most of the artists and managers hired for this project were not yet Cirque employees. They elaborated a certain vision of what a permanent place dedicated to circus and other arts could be, in synchronicity with the owner's vision of his Complexe Cirque. As such, they all contributed by bringing in ideas that the Cirque organization was not yet developing or exploring. In 2000, Guy Laliberté invited more than fifty people with different perspectives to participate in an international summit on the Complexe Cirque concept. People shared their views on a different way of living that was emerging at the time from within social circles often referred to as the "Happy Few," a class of the privileged, wealthy international jet set to which Laliberté belonged. At the time, that way of living was seen as mostly innovative,[6] and was particularly typical of the group of artists invited to join the project, who used their own ways of living and working as inspiration, feeding them back into the design of the Complexe Cirque.

Despite the increasingly difficult international context, over the course of 2002 numerous meetings were held with the managers, artists, and potential investors, and the project materialized in the form of construction project and business plans, along with related images. At the last minute, however, a few weeks before starting construction, Laliberté decided to end the project because it didn't appear likely to be profitable. The events of 11 September 2001 had impacted the travel and hospitality industries, among others, and global political and economic contexts were dominated by a dark and gloomy outlook. The decision froze all development, and the team was quickly dissolved.

Even if it is not considered among the organization's successes, however, the long-term legacy of this innovative project is impressive. Its creative gall has been extremely fruitful for the company, which has recycled many concepts created in the process into other shows. It has fed numerous of the "other activities" seen above and other projects produced in various locations outside its initial camp. For example, in 2005, Cirque partnered with

Loto-Québec to plan a cultural centre at the Peel Basin in Montreal (see Harel, this volume), and in 2013, Cirque, MGM Resports International, and Cadillac Fairview partnered to construct a casino in Toronto. This practice of recycling concepts points to continued interest in the creative ideas produced in the context of the 2000–01 Complexe Cirque project. It also speaks of the firm's creativity and know-how in keeping "old" ideas from being discarded.

Back in 2000–01, artists and managers were gathered around Guy Laliberté to realize the Complexe Cirque prototype. To do so, they had to work together, which meant communicating on a daily basis. The two communities communicated in distinct ways: their intent or raison d'être was distinctly different, as were the languages they used, the styles and registers of communication they chose, and the aspects of the product they contributed toward. Again we see how their respective profiles and communication styles diverged (table 10.2).

Where the artists had to attract external investors with a seductive aesthetics made of images and stories created to arouse emotions, the managers had to convince them with a robust business plan. Where the artists would "evoke, invoke and provoke," as the Cirque's creative mission statement puts it (Cirque du Soleil 2011), the managers had to demonstrate the economic benefits of the project. Hence their two distinctive communication tools to prepare and share their strategies.

Although their collective work practices differed, artists and managers met each other halfway by sharing some practices that were distinct from their usual community-specific practices. In table 10.3, I present another simple typology that sets out the respective and shared practices of both communities. This typology illustrates each practice by referring to various thematic images, idioms, or metaphors. Each practice of the typology is bipolar, comprised of a positive and a negative pole corresponding with behaviours that I observed during fieldwork.

I offer the notion of a tribe as the initial metaphor describing the project participants, as the practices observed during fieldwork were distinctively tribal. The central figure, Guy Laliberté, the founder of Cirque, called himself "The Guide." An entourage of privileged persons were attracted to the founder for the advantages this relationship offered. Both groups – artists and managers – shared, enjoyed, and wanted to maintain this way of life and belong to the Happy Few, the ones who had access to the owner and his top team. These artists and managers were aware that they were part

Table 10.2
Artists' and managers' communication strategies, by profile

Artists' main communication strategy	*Dimension of communication*	Managers' main communication strategy
Present the artistic vision Arouse the senses, create an emotion Touch, move the audience	*Underlying intent*	Present the project benefits Obtain buy-in by convincing
Create and share a good story that evokes the project Create and use powerful images to support the dream	*Language used to communicate*	Create and share through a structured discourse Create and use facts and figures that confirm the robustness of the project and the reasons to support it
Evoke key aspects of the vision Translate into illustrations key examples of situations, practices, and behaviours comprised in the vision	*Stylistic means*	Identify and share robust facts and support all goals and rationale by strong figures and numbers
Rely on poetic discourse, blend reality with imaginary, keep the audience dreaming, keep the audience inferring aspects of the vision that would be translated into services, rely on induction	*Register of communication*	Stay inside the borders of rational discourse, present all facts and unfold all project dimensions in a deductive discourse
A work of art comprising all of the above	*Product they create and show the audience to get attention, support, buy-in, and emotional bond*	A rich decision tool that enables the audience to engage in the project, based on all of the above

of an elite, and that many people were trying to get access to and enter this gated community but were not invited. The Happy Few could participate in special events accessible only to an inner circle and touch Cirque's grand narrative about its emergence and genealogy (Mahy 2008b).

The typology in table 10.3 illustrates the tensions that arose between the artists and the managers as this complex project unfolded. These dynamics are marked by seven groups of practices, each of which classifies the artists' and the managers' respective and shared practices. The tensions between the two groups, as well as the inner group tensions, are manifested by a positive versus negative polarity within each practice. For some practices, I observed a constant oscillation between the positive and the negative poles. In others, there was a clear polarization on the negative pole. For example, the practice of dialogue was shared between artists and managers, but it wasn't smooth or easy. Between the poles of misunderstanding and encountering, misunderstanding often prevailed. The positive encounter pole, leading to trust and sharing, was not a daily experience. In the same way, the shared practice of action turned into working in silos instead of benefiting from interdisciplinarity, and the practice of inter- and intragroup rapport manifested itself in endogamy instead of cross-breeding.

This mapping of the practices, documented through data collected during the Complexe Cirque project and forming a grid of the various ways of working in the artist and manager groups, is described in more detail in my 2008 article (Mahy 2008b). As the aim of this chapter is to study the tensions between the two groups through mediation, however, I restrict my current description of that practice landscape to focus only on specific practices that best illustrate the tug-of-war between the two groups. My analysis here focuses on the role I played as mediator in these creative battles, on what was actually mediated, and on the insights gained through these struggles.

The Researcher as Ethnographer

I had encountered the Cirque du Soleil artists in charge of Complexe Cirque a few months before I joined the project, having worked with them on a short assignment and shared my interest in their new challenge. My regular presence with carte blanche access to the organization offered opportunities for questioning the process underway and catalyzing discussions around it. I occupied a somewhat ambiguous position, standing close to the

Table 10.3
Map of artists' and managers' practices

Metaphor describing a series of practices	*Artists' specific practices*	*Practices shared, presented according to their positive and negative polarity (positive vs negative)*	*Managers' specific practices*
Tribe	No specific practice observed	Happy Few vs Plebeians Ancient Wisdom vs Orphans	No specific practice observed
Dialogue		Encountering vs Misunderstanding	
Storytelling	Good Stories vs Noise	Forum vs Closed Doors	Enlightenment vs Dialogue of the Deaf
Innovation	Creative Presence vs Black Hole	Research vs Routine	Art of the Long View vs Blindness

Action	Quartet vs Rope Party	Interdisciplinarity vs Silo Sport vs Fission	Midwife vs Don Quixote
Rapport	No specific practice observed	Cross-breeding vs Endogamy	No specific practice observed
Memory	Through the Looking Glass vs Narrowness of Reality Art of Resetting the Third Eye	No shared practice observed	Knowledge Management vs Reinventing the Wheel

artists, but also offering the possibility of being a bridge between the two groups. This emerging role of mediator became possible due to my knowledge of both of these group's cultures, the business and the artistic. I was not a Cirque employee, but I attended project meetings, events, and daily activities, and followed all the steps of this initial phase of the project. Through participative observation, multiple conversations, and in-depth interviews with all the key participants, I organized the various practices I had identified during fieldwork into units of knowledge, hence of meaning, that could then be shared between groups. That is, I converted my observations into narrative form and shared it with the Complexe Cirque participants after the project ended.[7] I chose to report on the project by writing *un récit*, a story based on ethnographic reporting, using my fictionalized pages to invite the Cirque organization's own collaboration through feedback and potential validation of my interpretation. In this sense, the narrative that I elaborated about each group's experience, competencies, and practices could be seen as a potential mediation tool for opening a dialogue inside the organization and between its members.

Mediation and the Researcher as Mediator

The term mediation comes from the Latin *mediare*, which means to be between two entities, to stand in the middle. Typically, it means a practice that aims at defining the intervention of a third person, the intermediary – the mediator – to facilitate communication and information sharing. According to de Briant and Palau (1999), what is called traditional mediation did not even need naming, as it was performed by such institutions as the church or trade unions that intended to encompass both the individual and the universal, promoting shared values and beliefs. New forms of mediation do not convey any such universality. The modern mediator is neutral and independent of the parties involved. Legal mediation, for example, activates a relationality based on rules and means accepted by both parties, to prevent conflict or solve issues in a social relation. Similarly, current practices of social mediation aim to develope the relationality between two parties to foster a social link or prevent eventual conflicts (de Briant and Palau 1999).

More specifically related to culture and arts is the concept of cultural mediation and, as a subset, artistic mediation, which concentrates on mediating between the arts and its audiences. Cultural mediation can concern all practices and cultural expressions of a population in relation to diversity and the individuation of ways of living, values, and identities. Cultural mediation is part of the larger field of informal education, and its goals are educational, civic, and recreational (Joli-Cœur 2007). As I further examine the findings of my initial study (Mahy 2008a), I see that there is another dimension to mediation in the relationality between organizational cultures and work practices: the mediator can act as a liaison between communities, translating and conversing, softening relationships and keeping the dialogue going. Furthermore, my observations point to another practice that acted as a reflective mediation tool inside the artists' group, namely, the artistic practice of the "Third Eye," which I describe as an example of creative mediation practice later on in this chapter.

Mediating at Cirque du Soleil

The common denominator of all these contexts is the mediator's place: in-between. He/she acts between two cultural universes to raise awareness, facilitate, sometimes even negotiate and invite the groups to converge and share. Being an outsider at Cirque du Soleil, I found myself at the crossroads of different goals, languages, practices, and competencies. My main work consisted of trying to understand as much as possible the work of each community and ultimately to identify the various social practices at work. My mediator's role emerged out of my initial presence in the group of artists who had invited me to participate.

I was sometimes consulted by the artists' team when they did not understand ideas or decisions coming from the management team. I was invited to *translate* the request and explain the tool and expected outcomes, mediating between two world views and providing information to help the team respond to the demand. For example, when the owner asked the artists' team to provide their organizational chart for the next phase of the project,[8] the artists didn't understand the implications and turned to me for clarification. For most of them, working in the context of such a large company and on such a large project, with the pressure and complexity implied, was a new situation. Furthermore, the framework they were asked to use – an organization chart – was a management tool. They had never "created" an organization on paper before, and their ultimately surprising way of sketching out the organizational chart as a process rather than a hierarchy was misunderstood by the managers and seen as an example of the artists' lack of ability to "manage." Consequently, the management team decided that, based on what they had seen, they would provide the organizational chart for every aspect of the project, including the creative team's structure. This reaction triggered yet another moment of frustration and chaos for the artists who were then confronted with orders coming from management; new people came on board, and the artists were forced to let go of their own team managerial leadership and self-organization practices. With their occasional internal fights related to practices presented in table 10.3, the artists hadn't been able to take a step back to fully understand the overall issues at stake and the related leadership and organizational implications. They never regained ownership of their own organization after that.

The occasional, informal mediation involving me had no real impact on the project decision-making processes. Even if there had been an official space for mediation, the outcome might not have changed given the darkening of the world's political and economic outlook. But mediation could have softened the relational dynamics. Having reflected on this project for several years, I now believe that this tug-of-war period could have been a critical moment in which to embed official organizational mediation. Taking the opportunity to define and bring in competencies capable of bridging organizational cultures would have constituted a creative response to an intergroup issue. But at the time, Cirque's management dealt with the situation by restricting one team's autonomy, that of the artists, rather than loosening the constraints and thus letting the artists solve the problem on their own or in partnership with the managers.

The Tug-of-War as a Place for Mediation

The practice of dialogue, on a continuum from misunderstanding to encountering, points to the potential for gifted people to meet each other in a privileged organizational context. The importance given to encounters at Cirque du Soleil helps explain the feeling of entering a tribe, a group of people surrounding the founder who were all co-opted by him or by his close entourage. Membership in the tribe was a fierce competition, a race for privileges; courtship behaviours were therefore common. From my position near the artists, I observed the tensions and conflicts among them and between artists and managers, often triggered by misunderstandings, even failed courtships, as exemplified in discussions concerning the hotel design. At first, the artists considered the hotel as a unique and exquisite place, where each room would have its own aesthetics. They had imagined that the corporate, social responsibility of Cirque would be made tangible by the offer of free rooms for homeless people. In one long meeting of both teams, the artists started to explain that the entire concept for the rooms, and the particularly attractive elements of design, had been inspired by free rooms for the homeless. The leader of the management team, also president and CEO of the company, abruptly interrupted them. He said that such a model would not meet the business goals and that everything they had designed needed to be reconsidered. A member of the artists' team tried to restart the explanation by agreeing with the management leader, and came back to the aesthetics of the rooms. Once again, he was interrupted, this time by Cirque's founder, who said that he wanted to hear something about the room design that took into account the star-rating by square foot that each type of room would have, and nothing else. When an artist tried to address this topic a third time, she was stopped by the founder who said that they should go back to their design boards and that he would listen to them once they had integrated his view.

Such conflicted encounters were frequent, and resolving such communication issues was complex. Over the course of the project, the artists realized that their process was not understood and that they needed to be able to convince the management team of the relevance of their ideas, but they felt that they were being forced to justify ideas that were emerging, still fragile, and therefore easy to discount. Their discomfort was palpable. They also felt that, as they were not employees of Cirque, they were not supported in their creative work. Meanwhile, management started worrying when the economic and political context grew tense, and they increased the pressure on the artists' team. Negative perceptions were legion, and each team felt communication was difficult, even impossible. The way out of such dead ends was to turn to the only person considered credible by both groups – namely the founder – who mediated and finally, in early December 2001, decided to stop the project.

Why did everyone recognize him? The easy answer would be that he owns the company, and that he could hence exercise control. But there is another answer that is less obvious: his skills as mediator. Inside Cirque du Soleil, the person who is universally recognized as the ultimate mediator is Guy Laliberté, whose profile is a successful mix of street artist and gambling businessman. His actions go beyond any actual dialogue between cultures. Involved in decision-making of both the creative and the business aspects of all critical productions, he not only mediates between teams but also decides on the outcome. His interdisciplinarity – his ability to address the project issues from both artistic and business considerations – is well known. This all-encompassing perspective enables him to gather around him a diverse entourage of skilful people. When conflicts arise, his mediation can take unusual forms, as when during some tense times he invited leaders from both the artist and management groups to play hockey. Their games became symbolic battles, where fighting physically helped to dissolve anger by moving the stakes of this high-risk, multi-million dollar project to an ice rink.

An Example of Artistic Mediating Practice

As described above, intergroup mediation in the Complexe Cirque project was either informal or nonexistent unless the founder participated in the meetings. But intragroup mediation, of a different nature and form, did occur among the artists. They integrated a video practice, which they called "the Third Eye," into their project by inviting a young visual artist to film any moment she wanted of the project's unfolding, be it meetings or parties. Initially modelled on the practice of artists who document their own creative process through video journalling or diaries, the Third Eye process had a distinctive feature: it was based only on images. The soundtrack consisted of music that the team listened to from time to time. Integrated into the creative process loop, these sensorial memory clips acted as a mirror into the collective experience, triggering conversations and creating a reflective space, thus quickly proving its relevance as a visual ethnographic tool. This process enabled a recursivity, offering a look back at the team's activities and behaviours. As such, I see it as a relevant, creative mediating tool that translates the group experience into an image-based story, an aesthetic narrative.

After the end of the Complexe Cirque project, I integrated the Third Eye into my own research process to document collective learning experiences and practice-based innovation processes, taking a similar aesthetic stance.[9] In my professional work on organizational change through collaborative practices, my own integration of this creative mediating practice into several action-research and creation-research activities has confirmed the pertinence of the Third Eye as a powerful, visual ethnographic mediating tool.

Lessons Learned: The Complexe Cirque and Beyond

To summarize the main messages of what Cirque du Soleil's artists and managers learned – or in some cases could have learned – from their participation in the Complexe Cirque project (Mahy 2008a, 270), I created a table showing my mediator's understanding of the different experience-based lessons (see table 10.4). In-depth interviews with key participants of the Complexe Cirque project brought to light several insights that could prove useful to artists and managers working in other organizations, as well as to newcomers at Cirque. In initiatives involving arts and business, these insights from the field may become valuable, as the participants confirmed. The table comprises four types of actors: artists from Cirque du Soleil, artists who do not work at Cirque, Cirque managers, and managers who do not work at Cirque. The insights are presented as short messages in clear and simple language – messages that they may share with each other as a mentor, coach, or friend would do.

Managers can learn from Cirque du Soleil's artists (A) to live in a symbiosis, without separating their work from the rest of their life. The artists perceive and experience life like a porous organic whole in which everything is intertwined. There is no hermetic boundary between the self and the others or between the self and the world. Neither is there a boundary between the different dimensions of the self. Such a perspective of life as a whole gives birth to a great capacity to feel, to vibrate, and to express, but this expression – the artistic creative process – is fragile and sometimes confused, difficult for the artists to explain when the work is still in gestation, and difficult for the managers to grasp.

Managers can learn from Cirque du Soleil's managers (C) to exercise their leadership without trying to hide or dissociate their own emotions. They should not lose sight of the fact that the aim of their work is to support creation. They should cherish and protect creation because it is from creation that new voices emerge and re-enchant life.

Artists can learn from Cirque du Soleil's artists (B) to take into account the business context they work in by being aware that their artworks are also a product or a service. Artists can also learn to take their place in the community of nonartists, to defend their creation and value it, as entrepreneurs would do to promote their products or services.

Artists can learn from Cirque du Soleil's managers (D) to deal with the business reality, to contribute by their art in ways that have business potential,

Table 10.4
Lessons learned, insights to share

You are working at Cirque du Soleil as ...	You are working in any organization as *a manager*	 *an artist*
an artist	(A) What managers can learn from Cirque du Soleil artists	(B) What artists can learn from Cirque du Soleil artists
	Borders between work and private life are blurred Festivities, moments of rest, and idle time are intrinsic to the creative process. It is part of the work Creative practices are not necessarily structuring or structured recipes, rather they are states of being To create implies a great sensitivity, a quality that has to be accepted and dealt with carefully The creative process and artwork are difficult to describe when still in emergence	To create in a private business context means to deal with market realities, complex projects, interdisciplinarity, and internal and external forces not always aligned to support creation In such a context, artists do not create an artwork but an artistic product Applicability and feasibility of concepts need to be pursued It is necessary to interpret market tendencies and audience expectations Develop a strong leadership, be convincing, and take into account business issues

Table 10.4
Lessons learned, insights to share

You are working at Cirque du Soleil as …	You are working in any organization as	
	a manager	*an artist*
a manager	(C) What managers can learn from Cirque du Soleil managers	(D) What artists can learn from Cirque du Soleil managers
	Learn to respect the fact that ideas are fragile; refrain from castrating creation, arouse it instead To manage is to create conditions to facilitate creative work and protect creators Resist the need to take control over the creators' ideas	In a business context, a creative team must be managed To create in a very competitive context implies that you – understand and take into account the business issues – are understood by the managers – accept to work under economic conditions that can limit creation – are able to work in an interdisciplnary mode – understand the utility of management tools

and to navigate in a milieu where strategy, revenues, investment, and profitability are key, all without losing their soul.

In summary, even if Cirque's senior executives and Complexe Cirque's artists and managers ultimately consider the project to be a failure due to its sudden cancellation before construction, the knowledge created during the eighteen-month Montreal project has contributed to developing concepts that have been recycled in other settings. In the same way, the experience summarized above could be useful, cycled and recycled, for anyone involved in a creative industry or in a business that is looking to become more creative.

Creativity as defined by Csikszentmihalyi (1996, 8) is a process by which a symbolic domain of culture is changed. And this change, for Csikszentmihalyi, implies learning and mindfulness, and only those who are mindful can be identified as creative. Such learning becomes possible, of course, when we imagine ourselves in another person's shoes long enough to start feeling what that person actually experienced. As Csikszentmihalyi tells us, it requires activating one's own openness and curiosity. As such, this basic mindshifting exercise is an opportunity to perceive reality from a different perspective and to develop one's abilities to intervene, even in the highly complex, interdisciplinary organizational context of multinational corporations like Cirque du Soleil.

In these pages, I identified the need for organizational and artistic mediation to improve project dynamics. It may be that artists, as professional creators, become natural levers to revealing the unseen, complex, or difficult-to-grasp ideas or emotions through metaphors, artworks, stories, and other poetic means. Their involvement in organizations is still rare, as they usually do not have the training to fully grasp the depth of these entities' issues and dynamics. But artists who are willing to develop such an understanding may function as mediators, as unsuspected avenues to help solve organizations' most complex issues.

CHAPTER 11

A Las Vegas of the North? The Architectural Brutalism of Cirque du Soleil

Simon Harel
Translated by Michelle Wong

Cirque du Soleil is an economic and cultural source of pride in contemporary Quebec. It has been a symbol of undeniable success since the early 1990s, championing the notion that Quebec society is neither headed toward inevitable decline nor disposed to obsolete forms rooted in native territory. Cirque du Soleil is a testament to the value of an industry that exports "cultural content," a *brand image* of Quebec as viewed on the international stage. Indeed, it has fostered the rise of a large-scale theatrical art form, one that has broadened the definition of circus art to a world beyond simply the predilections of experimental theatre specialists. Its achievements are all the more compelling given that Cirque du Soleil began its journey on the fringes of the great fairs of popular show culture once exhibited in arenas and other venues across North America.

Cirque du Soleil thus presents us with a fascinating reality. As a source of breath-taking cultural content, it exemplifies a cultural industry often cited for its proverbial productivity, bringing its shows to audiences across several continents. In this context, does the planetary success by Cirque du Soleil escape the bounds of the local forms and flavours of the Montreal landscape? This chapter will focus on the company's plans in the early to mid 2000s to build an integrated complex at the Peel Basin in Montreal's Pointe-Saint-Charles neighbourhood. This project differed from the Complexe Cirque planned for downtown Montreal in 2001–02 (examined by Isabelle Mahy in this volume), but both projects participated in the impulses explored in this chapter.

I investigate Cirque du Soleil's dramatic forms of represention not in performances beneath the big top but through its presence in the urban landscape and its seemingly flawless brand image. *Brand image* is not an arbitrary choice of words: as we know (see Batson 2012a), Cirque du Soleil is an admired business model among Quebec residents. In the same manner as the iconic Jean Coutu and Alimentation Couche-Tard, it is connected to the identity-nourishing ethos of Quebec society, which has left its marginalized past behind as it creates multinational companies in both the manufacturing and services industries. Cirque du Soleil is thus representative of this contemporary Quebec. As will be seen over the course of this chapter, the valorization of such virtues as festivity, ingenuity, and creativity is at the forefront. Cirque du Soleil single-handedly evokes a wealth of complex meaning: our small Quebec appears to have become a place of sophisticated creativity.

Cirque du Soleil deftly operates a global expansion strategy that leaves little doubt as to the economic value of this brand image: the company occupies a prime position in the global media, conquers market shares, and ultimately represents a dollar figure. Indeed, Cirque du Soleil, alongside SNC-Lavalin and Bombardier, is among the companies or designers most commonly associated with the globalized brand image of either Canada or Quebec.

Cirque du Soleil is taking to the stage in Macau, Shanghai, and Singapore: the company favours an international deployment strategy that pays little heed to the former global and cultural metropolises of Paris, London, and New York. It makes no claims of authority in the agora of experimental theatre or performance art. Naturally, Europe and North America remain prime locations; such was the case for the winter show titled *Wintuk*, which premiered in November 2007 at Madison Square Garden. The same could be said of the prominence of Cirque du Soleil in Las Vegas, a gambling mecca that has undergone profound changes over the past several years.

How strange it was, the complicity that brought the Cirque to Las Vegas! In the view of those who specialize in forms of urban settlements, Las Vegas is symptomatic of a violent peri-urbanization that is sweeping through the deserts of Nevada. This Moloch among cities seems to reflect a decaying space representative of a world without a soul. But novel shifts in the urban imagination cannot be attributed to fear or prospect of debauchery. The spread of recreational tourism, which has become a common good, has given us a sense of entitlement to certain pleasures: gambling, losing bets, feigned indifference to our losses.

It was with an iconoclastic eye that architect Robert Venturi took in the vernacular architecture of Las Vegas during the 1960s. For our part, we need look no further than the Montreal landscape for an opportunity to better understand the singular nature of Las Vegas. Gambling and festivity emerged as the new objects of worship in the recent debate over Cirque du Soleil's plans to build a permanent centre at the Peel Basin – a monumental entertainment complex that would be constructed as part of a real estate project managed by Loto-Québec. The controversy made headlines in the media and drew substantial reaction from community-based organizations, citizen advocacy groups, and heritage protection associations. Set to cost more than $1 billion, the bid was poised to transform the urban fabric of a neglected neighbourhood. It was a promise of urban renewal that had been similarly hailed by mayors of large American cities wishing to mitigate the negative image of soulless cities and deserted places. The project would revitalize a city searching for inspiration. Montreal, having been burned by an ambitious surge of real estate and cultural projects in the 1960s and 1970s in the wake of Expo 67 and the Summer Olympics of 1976, was badly in need of a new ideal. It seemed the plans for the Peel Basin casino could not have come at a better time.

But those plans never made it off the ground. The casino remained a fantasy in the minds of designers, architects, and urban developers – those who envisage the layout of the city, ponder its direction. Others would say that the project put forward by Cirque du Soleil and Loto-Québec was a white elephant, unless it served some nostalgic purpose: Cirque du Soleil once epitomized unfathomable creative potential, possibilities that now condemn Montreal to a soul-searching existence. This chapter focuses on the platitudes that shaped the discourse about Montreal, the identity-related tensions that stirred within the city, the validity of this urban project and its integration into the urban scene – namely at Pointe-Saint-Charles, the neighbourhood adjacent to this mammoth real estate undertaking. I will argue that the renunciation of Cirque du Soleil's project constituted a real benefit. Working with Loto-Québec, a Crown corporation, Cirque du Soleil appears to have fabricated an entire urban simulacrum of a large-scale development for recreational tourism, not a trace of which remains today. Aside from many press releases and letters from citizens that were published in the Montreal dailies, the Peel Basin casino project remained pure fiction – a form of fiction, however, that would provoke antagonism and awaken hope.

The urban fiction behind the Cirque du Soleil project allows us to understand the place Montreal occupies in the narratives of architectural postmodernism, a plurality of forms perceived today in the context of fierce metropolitan competition as an obligatory rite of passage. Proceeding from this standpoint, it is possible to address the "à la Vegas" theme that drives the portrayal of Cirque du Soleil in the Montreal landscape. In keeping with the idea that tensions are integral to the signs and meanings of discourse, I believe that the misfortunes that accompanied the Cirque du Soleil project actually represent bold expressions of architectural thought. This mindset purports to create a place conducive to the happiness of its inhabitants, facilitating harmonious relationships among those who have chosen to live in that space. The assertions of architects and developers, therefore, can always be evaluated against their certainty of being right, so effectively do the spaces they propose inspire happiness and accentuate the growing interactions between citizens who demand an agora and the right to be heard.

An Urban Simulacrum

The plans envisioned by Cirque du Soleil conveyed a certain paradox. The casino, a symbol of exploitation and suffering to notable scholars from Richard Florida to Paul Samuelson, was to become a dynamic meeting place of performance and experimentation in the realm of visual arts and theatre. Through this project, Cirque du Soleil was to breathe new life into the abandoned neighbourhood of Pointe-Saint-Charles: the sons and daughters of a blue-collar generation would be transformed into a new wave of artists and acrobats in Montreal's thriving circus! This urban simulacrum, moulded by architects and developers, coincided with a neoliberal political and economic discourse that sought to impose limits on progress, leisure, and the common good. In the specific case of Cirque du Soleil, the blunder that doomed the Peel Basin project should come as a surprise, given the respected brand image maintained by the multinational corporation in Quebec. There was talk of an error in management, a clumsy attempt to weave the global activity of the Cirque into the urban Montreal landscape from which it came. Some would interpret Guy Laliberté's sudden change of heart, which signalled the end of fun and games and the collapse of the project, as a sign of responsibility, definitive proof of the jet-setting businessman's shrewd instincts. Regardless, Cirque du Soleil now serves as a leading example, in the metropolitan context, of the pitfalls that accompany any major cultural or economic development plans. The news stories that emerged from the controversy were enough to indicate that Cirque du Soleil's ambitions for Pointe-Saint-Charles would quickly become legendary.

What glorious future did we let slip through our fingers? What potential for growth did we foolishly ignore? The Peel Basin casino project brings to light a potent antagonism residing within the metropolitan universe of Montreal. While the construction of Place Ville Marie in the late 1950s marked the very birth of modern Montreal, Cirque du Soleil's aborted project suggests oversight and careless error, so fully does it appear to portend the failure of any large-scale endeavour.

This narrative of opportunity lost is nothing new. In fact, it figures systematically in the portrayal of marginal metropolitan cities, too often accused of clinging to a wavering identity in the face of economic decline. Elitist discourse is liberal in its emphasis on the slow death of any city no longer able to call itself a metropolis. From this perspective, Montreal is an urban entity whose core must be revitalized. Despite the evident urban density of the downtown centre, many developers prefer to fill this vibrant landscape with stretches of vacant lots, industrial wastelands, areas without soul. It is as though Montreal is suffering from a chronic attention deficit, and only those developers nostalgic for an industrial colonization of territory have been asked to rebuild a downtown core that lies in pieces.

This line of discourse partly explains the expeditious attitude of both Cirque du Soleil and Loto-Québec with regard to the colossal urban overhaul that the Peel Basin project entailed. It would require recolonizing the land from within, giving a heart and a body to a city in hardship, and ultimately infusing Montreal with a creative exuberance modelled after Las Vegas. The supreme irony of the circumstances was that much like the occasionally tense coexistence of the "upper class" alongside the "lower class" ("gentrified" populations of factory workers in Saint-Henri and other "working-class" neighbourhoods), the Montreal that was alive and well, nourished by the genuine cultural diversity of its eclectic neighbourhoods, would have to give way to the directive of a city rising up from its ashes.

Beneath the "urban legend" that resulted from the planned development of the Peel Basin, we uncover the desire to take possession of an amorphous space in order to better take on the task of bringing it back to life. In this case, the siege consisted in forcing "refractory populations" to adopt certain norms of urban development, namely, those adhering to the triumphant postmodernist movement that is represented today on a global scale by multinational entertainment companies. The proposed casino was not a matter of rebuilding damaged urban infrastructure. Cirque du Soleil's project had no designs on the costly renovation of extensive urban highways, as is the case today with the Turcot Interchange or the Ville-Marie Expressway. Nor did it intend to establish new channels of communication, as envisioned for the Lachine Canal in the nineteenth century, or the less fondly remembered Mirabel airport in the early 1970s. At best, Cirque du Soleil was putting the spotlight on a convivial and transnational means of communication for which Montreal would serve as the launch pad.

The bright future that Cirque du Soleil offered Montreal hinged on a "surface" notion of cultural mobility, relying as well upon showcasing the virtuality of gambling and profits, which when capitalized within the framework of a casino became very real. In this virtual age, it was important to create a new district. Such aspirations, of course, have been voiced before. Every urban development project seeks to improve – to replace crumbling infrastructure, create new parks, urban boulevards, bicycle paths. The underlying discourse in the science of development is one of reform, focusing attention on the common good. Public spaces exist to accommodate citizens. Standards are raised in health and hygiene. The urban miasma must be eliminated. Natural light and pure air are thus the pillars of an environment that enhances the quality of life of citizens.

Throughout Montreal's recent history, several metamorphoses have shaped this reformative discourse, the backbone of urban development. From the construction of the Habitations Jeanne-Mance and the establishment of Place Ville Marie during the 1950s, to the creation of the Quartier international and today's Quartier des spectacles, social discourse has encouraged a spirit of goodwill that promises peaceful interaction between citizens. Urban discourse promotes the virtue of this reformative development, maintaining that the world is on the mend, that buildings align with a set of values that are a precise indicator of how the city's inhabitants are living. How, then, do we explain the systematic battle that took shape in the media during the deliberations that should have culminated in the development of the Peel Basin?

Through assertions of its symbolic relevance to urban planning, we have seen how the siege may be an apt metaphor for our present subject. It is odd, in this context, that this virtual siege (for the Cirque du Soleil project was abandoned overnight) made no mention of concrete forms of urban development at a specified site (the Peel Basin) and that it was blind to the tangible consequences this project would bring about for Pointe-Saint-Charles. In other words, nothing concerning the future of this working-class neighbourhood was ever made clear.

Compared to Pointe-Saint-Charles, the world of Las Vegas was certainly more befitting. From Cirque du Soleil to Celine Dion, this urban space has attained a mythical reputation. Vegas has taken over from the outdated and tacky locations of French-Canadian Florida, of Fort Lauderdale, and of Miami Beach; the popularity of these sites has waned as they have evolved into the highly caricatured universe of the "snowbirds" spending time in the south to establish another "Little Canada." Las Vegas carries very different connotations. The image of Vegas as a city made of glitz, immoderate buildings, and outrageous kitsch is ingrained in our cultural encyclopedia. So which Las Vegas is our current focus? The fanciful universe reflected in the casinos built over the course of the 1940s and 1950s – that is to say, the universe associated with the famous "Rat Pack" of the 1960s? Or is our concern the role of Cirque du Soleil's extravagant performances in Las Vegas? In other words, does the Las Vegas alluded to in light of the rebirth of Montreal at Pointe-Saint-Charles belong to the exotic universe of a kind and patrimonial America once defended by the architect Venturi? Not if Las Vegas may, in fact, be equated to Macau, Singapore, or Dubai; these are the new empires of transnationalism in the era of service economy, electronic commerce, and online games.

My working hypothesis contends that the tourist endeavour promoted by Cirque du Soleil claimed to be a self-created universe, an urban space that showed no interest in any expression of vernacular Montreal architecture. Indeed, from what may be seen in the rare visual evidence available, the Cirque du Soleil project would have destroyed Montreal's urban framework and replaced it with a blank space, devoid of both charm and soul. The failure of the Peel Basin casino project may be attributed, in part, to the manifestation of an architectural monumentality that would have reduced Montreal's urban landscape to a tabula rasa. Cirque du Soleil developers perceived Pointe-Saint-Charles as an unrefined area whose sheer proximity to the Peel Basin made it impossible to avoid. They saw only two options for the basin, where industrial activity has since come to an end: either timely and outright demolition or, as was customary, restoration of a few of the brownfields created by industrial activity on the site. It is this narrow point of view that seems to have sparked the conflict that would bring proponents of aggressive industrial development (chambers of commerce, economic decision-makers, supporters of a Montreal in tune with the American market) into opposition with advocates of the community dynamic and investment in people-centred neighbourhoods.

Formalism and Architecture

Venturi's insight into these themes remains relevant today. *Learning from Las Vegas*, published in 1972,[1] proved to be a kind of iconoclastic architectural manifesto. In a key passage, Venturi describes what he calls vernacular architecture, stating that ornament and symbolism serve a conative function dependent upon referential language (Venturi, Brown, and Izenour 1977, 139). Venturi admonishes architects for building pointlessly complicated structures in which distortion and overarticulation produce oddities. In the end, Venturi criticizes modern architects for having forsaken the understanding of space as place. Modern architects have neglected the sacred nature of place, he argues, in the singular act of creating a structure in the midst of space.

Venturi's arguments can seem contradictory: on one hand, the architect calls for a revaluation of ornament and symbolism, concepts indicative of the vernacular and popular expression he finds in the Las Vegas of the 1960s. On the other hand, he concedes that the symbolic act present in every architectural endeavour is unquestionably obsolete. Venturi underlines the fact that the perceptive fatigue of urban residents, who must contend with various sensory expressions, does not give them the calm required to better appreciate the architectural detail and complexity of past eras. It is in this context that Venturi studies the architecture of Las Vegas, too often scorned, even ignored by the fellowship of architects who see in it a reflection of stagnant kitsch.

What cannot be overlooked is Venturi's view that commercial architecture, exemplified by 1960s Las Vegas, ultimately redeems the simple gesture of constructing within a unique symbolic space.

Indeed, the absolute value of a symbol cannot be determined using a simple scale between commonplace and sacred. Venturi maintains that contemporary architecture promotes the idea of cultural mobility. In his view, architects too often make the mistake of creating an outline, a *templum*, that becomes a permanent scale by which they perceive the world. According to this belief, architecture is the creation of still life, of fixed space – or, as described by Michel de Certeau (1990) in *L'invention du quotidien* (*The Practice of Everyday Life*), of blank space. This notion of cultural mobility conflicts with the discourse upheld during Cirque du Soleil's development project at the Peel Basin. The establishment of a casino, an immense urban enterprise that would boast the name of Cirque du Soleil, was in essence a fixed space, architectural brutalism within an environment that needed to be denied. Let us consider the extent of the paradox: though Venturi continued throughout the sixties to assert the need for architects to be wary of hybrid forms (he compared the piazza of Rome to the Strip in Vegas), the reasoning presented by advocates of the destruction of the Peel Basin underlined the worthlessness of a site that deserved to be obliterated. In the same manner as those who belabour the point of healthiness in the modern city (Baron Haussmann comes to mind), the refrain of social discourse concerning the renovation of the Peel Basin served to justify a tabula rasa, followed eventually by the construction of a palace that would be both pretentious and monumental.

Did there not appear to be, at the heart of this notion of building a gambling mecca "à la Vegas" in Montreal, the makings of a grand deception? In a different context, Venturi (1977, 8–9) further recognizes that certain architects drew upon the industrial language of the time, as demonstrated by aerospace-inspired architecture. The fact remains that commercial art was neglected, reduced to coarse iconology despite being a rich source of eclectic symbols holding deep value. Finally, Venturi interrogates the silence of architects with regard to forms of popular symbolization. If we put aside the contributing role of the Pop Art movement, made famous by Andy Warhol, all commercial references were scorned. Naturally, like Pop Art, Venturi's (1977, 18) comments betray his age, as seen in the following passage:

> Las Vegas is the apotheosis of the desert town. Visiting Las Vegas in the mid-1960s was like visiting Rome in the late 1940s. For young Americans in the 1940s, familiar only with the auto-scaled, gridiron city and the antiurban theories of the previous architectural generation, the traditional urban spaces, the pedestrian scale, and the mixtures, yet continuities, of styles of the Italian piazzas were a significant revelation. They rediscovered the piazza. Two decades later architects are perhaps ready for similar lessons about large open space, big scale, and high speed. Las Vegas is to the Strip what Rome is to the Piazza.

Venturi observes the complementary relationship between movement and immobility in Las Vegas. The gradual aging of the built environment, the construction of new hotels and signs, the addition of parking spaces, all that comprises the commanding nature of commercial architecture, suggest that the world is in motion, that ornamentation is not merely abstract discourse reserved for particular users (i.e., the architect crowd). Conversely, this movement is a driving force that is transforming the city, bringing to life a space in which the confrontation of styles and references takes centre stage.

The Moving Eye

This blend of seemingly incongruous styles is the manifestation of what Venturi (1977, 53) calls "the moving eye in the moving body." An emphasis on motion aims to capture what Venturi further describes as "a variety of changing, juxtaposed orders, like the shifting configurations of a Victor Vasarely painting" (53). The tone of Las Vegas architecture derives from these formal areas of tension, whose apparent eclecticism contains basic anthropological concerns. Venturi tells us that we must protect the Las Vegas of the 1960s. In his eyes, the collison of outwardly disparate architectural references, controlled by an explicit commercial discourse (consisting in selling the gambling empire), was profoundly coherent. Venturi mentions that architects liked the backs of railroad stations insofar as their formalist quality served as an abstract, harmless vocabulary. He asks that we put an end to this deep-rooted contempt for commercial architecture and that we take seriously the world of the façade, which encompasses elements of the piazza and the Strip, not to mention the famous Route 66.

Culture and Location

In this regard, it is surprising that the Peel Basin project, which took shape nearly thirty years after the publication of *Learning from Las Vegas*, would dismiss the collective cultural memory of its location. I will examine this subject through several examples of the journalistic discourse that accompanied the public debate.

Alexandre Shields, writing in the 11 March 2006 edition of *Le Devoir*, accentuates the signature, character, and remarkable creativity of the project. He quotes Alain Cousineau, the president of Loto-Québec: "The very essence of our project stemmed from the dynamic presence of Cirque du Soleil, its distinct signature, the unique character it would impart to every aspect of the complex, its remarkable creativity, and its ability to attract partners in the private sector" (A1).[2] Further on, the Loto-Québec president is quoted as alluding to "an extraordinary tool for development."[3] Cirque du Soleil is thus abundantly praised as a multimillion-dollar company responsible for the artistic direction of the project. Cousineau extols the creativity of Cirque du Soleil and emphasizes "the asset of its international appeal."[4] In this context, opponents of the project, namely, certain community-based groups in southwest Montreal, were seen to be willfully preventing a tremendous opportunity for economic development.

An article by Philippe Mercure entitled "Le Cirque du Soleil mise sur Singapour" (Cirque du Soleil betting on Singapore), which appeared in *La Presse* on 16 March 2006 (and thus after the project's abandonment), assumes that the standard in recreational tourism is no longer Las Vegas, but Southeast Asia:

> Montreal, no. But Asia, maybe. Several days after announcing its withdrawal from the Peel Basin casino project, Cirque du Soleil is partnering with MGM Mirage to make a bid for a lucrative casino contract in Singapore. Four teams are contending for the construction of an immense complex at Marina Bay, Singapore. The project, whose estimated value is US$3 billion, will include a casino, a hotel, several restaurants, one or two night clubs, and a convention centre ... Cirque du Soleil currently has four shows running in hotels operated by MGM Mirage: *KÀ* at the Grand in Las Vegas, *O* at the Bellagio, *Zumanity* at New York-New York, and *Mystère* at Treasure Island. A fifth, featuring the music of the Beatles, will premiere this summer at the Mirage Resort, also in Las Vegas.[5] (A1)

One subheading in Mercure's article reads "A Question of Identity."[6] Has Las Vegas therefore become a stale point of reference, a myth that we pursue out of habit while the true challenges of touristic globalism are settled elsewhere? There is no shame in thinking so. As seen with the incontrovertible success of Celine Dion in Las Vegas, our inferior sense of identity with respect to our American neighbours undoubtedly leads us to glorify a world that, as Venturi pointed out, had already begun its inevitable decline in the 1960s. In this sense, Las Vegas symbolizes an artificial universalism, an empire of "local" entertainment. In the 23 December 2006 issue of the magazine *Les Affaires*, Pierre Théroux writes:

> Daring projects may be nothing new for admirers of Cirque du Soleil, but in 2006, the company led by Guy Laliberté reached new heights. From the début of *Love*, a show inspired by the Beatles – a rare

> collaboration with a band that oversees its legacy with great care – to successful touring shows and new projects in New York, Asia, and South America, the stars have aligned to make this a record year for Cirque du Soleil ... The vision of Guy Laliberté, who still considers himself the "creative guide" of Cirque du Soleil, is garnering admiration across the entire planet.[7] (4)

What is the meaning behind such praise for Cirque du Soleil in a magazine that has little patience for cultural matters? Like the aforementioned cultural industries (from the Quartier des spectacles to Parc des festivals), Cirque du Soleil is not the product of artisans of form, the rare example of a scenographic or theatrical marginality, the exaltation of a poaching brand of creativity that recycles scraps, shoestrings, and rags. No, Cirque du Soleil is the new and monumental face of recreational tourism complexes, briefly epitomized by the Peel Basin in Montreal. At the time, Cirque du Soleil exemplified a modern, globalized fantasy world of large-scale celebration.

Daniel Lamarre shares similar thoughts in an article devoted to Guy Laliberté:

> Guy hasn't forgotten that it was Quebec that got Cirque du Soleil started, and he's doing what he can to return the favour. One of his great contributions has been helping Quebec natives shine all across the globe ... He has likewise had a hand in turning Montreal into an international capital of the circus arts and inspired the creation of companies like Cirque Éloize and the 7 Fingers.[8] (qtd in Théroux 2006, 4)

These remarks hold true. There is clear evidence that Montreal plays an important role in the creation of new networks in recreational tourism. From the multimedia industry to the world of video games (right from Ubisoft to Electronic Arts), Montreal has certainly taken determined strides into the sophisticated universe of the advanced service industry. Théroux (2006) mentions that "the Cirque, [which] receives over 50,000 resumés every year, is also feeling the squeeze at its head offices, which are currently paying the price after a major expansion – its third since first opening its doors in the Saint-Michel neighbourhood in 1997" (4).[9]

Does this mean that the future of Las Vegas is being played out in Montreal? The debate surrounding the Peel Basin becoming a permanent home for

Cirque du Soleil provides varying answers to this question. Nicolas Bérubé (2005) argued in *La Presse* that Montreal should invest in entertainment:

> According to calculations from the Board of Trade of Metropolitan Montreal, the Toronto region encompasses more than three million square feet of exhibition centres, whereas the Montreal region is limited to some 600,000 square feet. "Ottawa needs to understand that Montreal has to up its offer," states Ms. Hudon. The realm of entertainment is the right context for making that happen.[10]

On the other hand, Lysiane Gagnon (2005), also in *La Presse*, maintains that any attempt to model a Montreal landscape on Marina Bay is condemned to failure.

> There you have it – the wheels are in motion and the Casino is in tow. So it is that a project which will associate the image of Montreal with gambling, which will give us a potentially redundant exhibition and performance centre in light of existing facilities, and which no one can promise won't turn out to be as ruinous a venture as the Olympic Stadium, Mirabel, or the Laval subway, has just been given the blessing of our leaders, and the people have only to get on board.[11] (A28)

It would thus seem appropriate to reject the grandiloquent discourse that eyes the creation of a new Montreal aligned with postmodernism. Gagnon deems such discourse a hackneyed form of urban kitsch. As always, it is the financial argument that prevails.

A Grandiloquent Façade

Build, develop, and destroy if need be an urban "zone" whose worthlessness is brought up continually by socioeconomic decision makers – that is the objective. The Las Vegas of the North must become reality. This project would correspond with the new values of globalization in the cultural sphere, values affirmed with conviction by Cirque du Soleil. It would also serve as a place of expression for a necessary pride in the climate of unease that Montreal embodied under the circumstances. And yet, Gagnon (2005, A28) writes:

> It cannot be overstated that any metropolis worth visiting does not have a casino. You won't find any in New York, Paris, or even Toronto. They are tolerated only in small and discreet establishments that have no bearing on their city's image. As a general rule, casinos are housed in small tourist locations, not in large cities that have other things to offer. Do we really want Montreal to become the Vegas of the North?[12]

The implication is clear: developing a neighbourhood (i.e., the Peel Basin) is a matter of real estate. Indeed, a space that would have spearheaded a new tourist hub for Montreal, in partnership with Cirque du Soleil, had been presented to the hotel and tourist industry on a silver platter.

Let us take stock of the breadth of the project. Claude Turcotte notes in the 29 September 2005 edition of *Le Devoir*:

> Loto-Québec would prefer not to sit back, with a $1.175-billion integrated complex at the Peel Basin that includes a 300-room hotel, a stunning spa, a 2,500-seat performance hall, a 10,000-capacity outdoor stage, a marina, both above- and underground parking, and, of course, a casino. Lastly, "the soul of this complex will be Cirque du Soleil," Cousineau explains.[13] (B1)

It is clear that gigantism is on the order of business and that the vernacular architecture advocated by Venturi is woefully out of place. Everything must be new! Excess is in vogue, and Cirque du Soleil is less a developer than a retailer selling a brand image in the form of merchandise. Alain Cousineau takes up this theme in *Le Devoir*, this time on 22 June 2006:

> The Cirque hasn't invested in a performance hall anywhere else in the world. Why should Montreal have been any different? The rights to use the logo, signature, and trademarks of Cirque du Soleil amount to significant costs that are difficult to quantify, but whose value is nonetheless substantial and merits as much consideration as the bricks and mortar. By taking on the role of designer and artistic director for this project, the Cirque would have instilled it with an exceptional magnetism and therefore an opportunity to stand out.[14] (A7)

In short, the emphasis on *brand strategy* at the heart of the Peel Basin casino project was much more important than the bricks and mortar. Partnering with Cirque du Soleil accentuated this image of triumphant festivity upon which Guy Laliberté's company has built its success. As such, Vegas was no longer a credible urban prototype even in this new "festiscape," whereas the rising economic powers of Macau, Shanghai, and Dubai were gathering strength. It is therefore necessary to reexamine the role played by the image of Vegas throughout this entire enterprise, which carried unquestionable and evocative potential. Did this Las Vegas of the North not express a late-blooming discourse that sang the praises of novelty, of architectural triumphalism, while Venturi bitterly noted the gradual destruction of the unabashed, unbridled vernacular architecture of Las Vegas at the hands of the city's developers? Need we mention that urban developers and architects are the least suited to build and dream? Have we no choice but to conclude that these allusions to Las Vegas acknowledge a faltering brand strategy that Cirque du Soleil does not even attempt to maintain, so greatly do its ambitious plans demand its presence in Southeast Asia and in the Near East?

Based on these observations, it is easy to arrive at the conclusion that Cirque du Soleil's Peel Basin project was destined to fail. In February 2006, the Direction de la santé publique du Québec (public health branch of Quebec) stated that a boost in casino clientele, as targeted by Loto-Québec, would directly affect the neighbourhoods of Pointe-Saint-Charles, Petite-Bourgogne, Verdun, and Saint-Henri. It also revealed that the Casino de Montréal, since its creation, had never managed to raise its proportion of foreign visitors above 12 percent. Though many proponents of bringing Cirque du Soleil to the Peel Basin voiced aims for an "international" client base of 25 percent, the Direction de la santé publique du Québec stressed the unrealistic nature of such an increase. Richard Lessard, a doctor associated with the Direction de la santé publique, had this to say:

> Becoming associated with the casino is meant to increase marketing for the project. Increasing marketing for the project is meant to attract more visitors. And attracting more visitors will lead to more gambling problems. This partnership with Cirque du Soleil, which seeks to garner greater visibility and greater social acceptance, will lead to more problems. In other words, this would be a terrific project if there were no casino.[15] (qtd in Lévesque 2006b, A1)

The Direction de la santé publique provided an unequivocal analysis. What were Cirque du Soleil's goals regarding this project with Loto-Québec? Was it not making a serious mistake, given how much its brand image – which happened to be in excellent standing – was losing credibility? A survey conducted by the firm CROP found that out of 12,000 respondents in approximately thirty countries, 90 percent indicated having a positive impression of Cirque du Soleil. This would certainly constitute a remarkable achievement in the world of business and marketing. By the same token, Cirque du Soleil has an excellent reputation in Quebec. The company can thus count on a strong level of public affection that comes with the image of a multinational founded by an eccentric individual, a college dropout who transformed himself into a brilliant manager who rubs shoulders with the international jet set.

The purpose of this chapter is not to deliver a definitive editorial judgment with respect to the relevance of Cirque du Soleil and the validity of this brand image. Nevertheless, the reader will have observed a profound skepticism with regard to the Peel Basin affair, which I believe to have been a serious error in the shaping of this brand image in Montreal. If we consider Cirque du Soleil's architectural successes in the Saint-Michel complex, the surprise is greater still. Was it not Dan Hanganu who established the company's first international head offices near the Metropolitan Autoroute? Was it not Éric Gauthier who, following in the footsteps of Hanganu, envisioned the expansion of these headquarters in 2005, as well as the new annex inaugurated in 2007 comprising 115 studio apartments for young artists in training and an eight-storey tower? This latter feature, visible from the Metropolitan Autoroute, is an impressive sight, as described by Stéphane Baillargeon (2007) in *Le Devoir*:

> A new wing with eight floors, at the heart of which lies a rainwater collection basin the size of a swimming pool. It is as though some gallivanting giant set down an enormous glass of champagne through the roof of the building. Only this crystal vessel is not meant to hold liquids: it empties them toward a drain located at the base of the immense transparent cone – approximately seven metres high, six metres wide, and several tons in heft. Combining ethics with aesthetics, the collector will gather enough rainwater and melted snow to independently power a section of Cirque du Soleil's Montreal complex, the workplace of 1,700 employees.[16] (B6)

Baillargeon adds that the "heated glass, enhanced by lighting effects, adorns the entirety of the two most recent, joint components of the expanded complex, with an ethanol fireplace to evoke winter evenings, a large projection screen, and multiple kitchens"[17] (B6).

Upon reading Baillargeon's account in *Le Devoir* and looking back at the architectural plans and completed projects of Hanganu and Gauthier, both of whom worked at the firm FABG (Faucher, Aubertin, Brodeur, Gauthier), it is easy to fall into a daydream. What if the Peel Basin project had been of the same calibre? What if rejecting the vast recreational tourism complex had been the dismissal of such great potential? A certain Moshe Safdie was able to design and see through the construction of Habitat 67. Modernist architecture, a conspicuous presence in Montreal following the World's Fair of 1967, is often of exceptional quality. From this perspective, financial resources are always the spearhead for architectural projects of a certain magnitude. Are we then to suggest, as many commentators already have, that Montreal has become a feeble metropolis that shies from any major economic or touristic development? Have we lost, in the wake of the Quiet Revolution, all sense of ambition? I find this discourse to be simplistic. Several interpretive criteria demand consideration when addressing the issues raised by the development of the Peel Basin in Montreal.

The concept of a Las Vegas of the North, a term coined by Gagnon, implied that Cirque du Soleil was ready to sell itself according to the needs of a Crown corporation, in this case Loto-Québec, in order to better exploit (there is still something to be said for the gambling allusion) the Montreal landscape from which it arose. Cirque du Soleil's proposition was thin: it came down to the exploitation (thanks to generous public funding) of a captive audience that believed in the integrity of Cirque du Soleil, that admired the creative capacity of this multinational company of the circus arts. How, in this case, was it possible to reconcile the kindly image of Cirque du Soleil, this newly venturesome group exporting "Québécois" and "globalized" cultural content, with the commercial character of a deal that associated Cirque du Soleil with Loto-Québec through public funds? Cirque du Soleil appeared to be lending itself to a form of blackmail, which was in fact the case when it came into association with Loto-Québec and once more when the project was abruptly discarded by Guy Laliberté, who criticized Montreal residents for their lack of ambition.

A Tarnished Brand Image

In any event, the undertaking was ill-conceived. It goes without saying that Cirque du Soleil has learned its lesson from this misdeed. Let us put it this way: Montrealers are appreciative of the enterprising aspect of Cirque du Soleil that conquers market shares in Asia, in the Middle East, and in Europe. They are less appreciative of Cirque du Soleil engaging in an act of immoderation, settling down in Montreal and imposing a "creative" dream upon the city in the form of an immense casino! It will surprise no one to discover that, following this defeat, Lamarre and Laliberté decided to authoritatively "reposition" Montreal's role as an international creative headquarters, as day-to-day business and the development of new projects took place in different parts of the world. In other words, Las Vegas and Macau need not be the identity-driven theatres that Montreal requires of Cirque du Soleil.

I have emphasized that Cirque du Soleil represents a brand image reflective of the new cornerstones of identity in Quebec, putting the labels of local and global to use in the same manner as SNC-Lavalin. So how does Las Vegas fit into all of this? Have we reason to believe that the people of Montreal demonstrated their good sense by refusing a colossal project that would have indelibly changed the face of their city? Could they have spurned the false triumphalism of a pompous and doubtless mediocre architecture that Cirque du Soleil would have introduced to the Peel Basin in its pursuit of higher profits?

If these questions may be answered in the affirmative, as I believe they can, Montreal will have averted a circus à la Vegas that would have replicated, in the form of a high-tech monstrosity, the notorious gated communities that are surfacing in the United States and in other countries. RESO, the community-based organization Regroupement économique et social du Sud-Ouest, rightly objected that the Peel Basin project would have imposed sweeping urban and social restructuring. The title of an article in *Le Devoir* by Kathleen Lévesque (2006a) speaks for itself: "Le RESO émet des réserves au sujet du projet de casino" (RESO expresses reservations concerning the casino project). She writes,

> The developer touts the accessibility of the site and its connection with downtown while declaring that it will be isolated, a feature

> meant to limit negative influences on the surrounding population. The project is either focused inward and aimed at self-sufficiency, offering "visitors a unique experience that will keep them in place for as long as possible and which, in a way, turns its back on the city," or integrated into both the neighbourhood and the city as a whole. Moreover, some insist that "the architectural design, which resembles a spaceship ... has nothing to do with the historical context of the location and its environment."[18] (A2)

RESO's objections are valid. It is impossible to enclose a location in order to limit the effects of a casino on nearby working-class neighbourhoods while at the same time claiming to incorporate this extensive project into the urban framework! What about this idea of a casino that turns its back on the city? Was this not the same ardent criticism expressed by Venturi in the architectural field concerning the abandonment of vernacular architecture? We will recall that his critique pointed to the feebleness of borrowings from commercial and industrial forms in the formalist vocabulary of architects. Such borrowings from industrial architecture, Venturi argued, came to resemble formal traits, thereby mitigating the conative dimension of inhabited areas of daily life. Yet it was permissible, in his view, to build head offices or even cultural spaces that incorporated certain motifs from industrial architecture of the twentieth or twenty-first century insofar as this continuity of motifs was compatible with a clearly identified patrimonial vocabulary. Indeed, industrial architecture, while not of "noble" origins, is respected today by architects who admire expressions of great formal ingenuity. From Chicago to Buffalo to Old Montreal, the unchanging features of this architecture have been a source of inspiration for many designers.

Writing about the sixties, Venturi dared to raise a fundamental question: What has happened to the commercial architecture universally scorned for conveying the preponderance of artificiality, consumerism, and speed in social exchanges? Was the Las Vegas extolled by Venturi an overlooked aspect of contemporary architectural thought? Venturi hoped that Las Vegas would become a *locus loci*. In his estimation, Las Vegas symbolized a new world patrimony of humanity. Although this assertion may seem amusing, Venturi recognized that our inherent references in the realms of culture and architecture are often conservative. Indeed, architects are interested in studying locations that represent, to use Michel de Certeau's expression, blank spaces. To them, these spaces are spheres of meaning that subscribe to the principle of private ownership of territory, to the need for a formal development plan that offers a renewed value to overlooked areas.

This conclusion brings us to another question: Who would have occupied this casino? Who would have peopled this prodigious spa? Who would have inhabited these premises destined for artists that Cirque du Soleil would have welcomed with open arms? As pointed out by RESO, it was decidedly difficult to construct an urban space from scratch, to keep it enclosed so as to protect the aforementioned fragile and disadvantaged populations in bordering neighbourhoods, and then profess to be open to the whole city. Moreover, the few architectural sketches made available to the public gave the impression of pedestrian creativity, for the project seemed to deny its immediate surroundings: the Peel Basin, an abandoned industrial zone which, despite its dilapidated appearance, is also a cultural heritage.

Is it necessary once more to emphasize the notion of colonization of territory? Here was a project initiated by Loto-Québec and Cirque du Soleil that purported to turn Montreal into a new Las Vegas. We have apprehended, however, that this concept of "à la Vegas" was outdated, that the Las Vegas of the 1950s and 1960s no longer exists. Thus, beginning in the late 1960s, Venturi made note of the disdain exhibited for the vernacular architecture of the Strip. At the time, urban planners in Las Vegas sought to mould their city into a tourist space in keeping with the current norms of grandiloquence. In summary, the Las Vegas to which we are referring is very often nothing more than fiction, case dismissed. The Hacienda Hotel and Casino is now the site of Mandalay Bay!

Montreal, a Vegas of the North? In my opinion, this endeavour was a case of deception, a specious marketing ploy based on a grievous misunderstanding. Each time Cirque du Soleil and Loto-Québec attempted to justify a permanent complex at the Peel Basin, the land would reclaim its rights! The brownfields of the Peel Basin embodied a certain value; community-based organizations, represented by the RESO, expressed their dissatisfaction with this tabula rasa that scorned the existence of working-class populations who for decades had called these neighbourhoods their home.

In an article entitled "Casino: Québec reporte sa décision à l'an prochain" (Casino: Quebec postpones its decision to next year), Lévesque (2005, A1) writes:

> Several aspects of the project require further explanation. Yesterday, *Le Devoir* revealed that the future casino would be built upon an archaeological site distinguished by the passage of Native Americans before the era of colonization and by the Canadian Industrial Revolution, whose backbone was the Lachine Canal. Loto-Québec will be forced to pay for and carry out several months of excavations that could amount to several hundreds of millions of dollars. "We do not believe there to be artifacts or relics anywhere on the land that we hope to use for the casino," Jean-Pierre Roy, a Loto-Québec spokesperson, stated yesterday. "But we will certainly make sure that everything is done by the book."[19]

What irony! It may seem hard to believe, but the Peel Basin casino project may well have allowed us to uncover that which is repressed with all architectural brutalism, the material pluralities of pre-existing forms: here, an original Montreal comes to the fore at the cost of a superficial discourse that would have staged a copy of Vegas at the Peel Basin.

CHAPTER 12

The Chinese Connection: The Transnational Origins of Québécois Circus Arts

Tracy Y. Zhang

Introduction

In the spring of 2005, a newly established Shanghai performance company (Shanghai Era Entertainment Ltd) recruited a group of Canadian circus producers and artists to create a multimedia acrobatic show, *Era: Intersection of Times*. Led by Érick Villeneuve, the visual director of the Montreal-based horse show *Cavalia*, the Canadian creative team was mostly composed of artists from Quebec. According to one of the participants from the Shanghai Acrobatic Troupe (SAT), this international recruitment was driven by local producers' aspirations to create a Chinese equivalent of a Cirque du Soleil show. From their perspective, *Era* would become the precursor of world-class "made-in-China" circus productions. Thus the recruiters were keen on Canadian artists, their management skills, and, especially, their experiences with Québécois circus arts that would contribute to making acrobatic spectacles in Shanghai.

I saw *Era* at the Shanghai Circus World in the summer of 2012, almost seven years after the show was launched in this theatre for acrobatics, now promoted as one of the city's key cultural destinations. Every night, busloads of American, European, and Japanese tourists crowd into this globe-shaped theatre (with 1,638 seats) to watch *Era*. While the show is marketed to international tourists as a Chinese production, its connection to Canada is no secret. However, few people are aware that the recent recruitment of Quebec artists has a historical dimension linked to China's socialist acrobatics and also to the emergence of Québécois circus arts. This chapter aims to shed light on the policies and events that activated the links between Chinese acrobatics and Québécois circus arts from a historical perspective. In both

12.1 *Era* at Shanghai Circus World

scholarly literature and the media, the emergence of Québécois circus arts has been frequently attributed to a few visionary circus pioneers and to financial support from the Quebec government (Babinski 2004; Leslie and Rantisi 2011). This research suggests that the ascendency of Québécois circus arts is not only a local phenomenon but has transnational entanglements linked to the People's Republic of China. In the recruitment of Chinese acrobats by Cirque du Soleil, I argue that Cirque's early uses of elite acrobatics relied on collaborations between the Chinese government and the Québécois circus company. This arrangement created problems for acrobats but also offered opportunities for empowerment.

Drawing on archival data and life history interviews with performers, this chapter focuses on policy developments in China's acrobatic sector from the 1950s to the 1980s and the ways in which such transformation has shaped Sino-Québécois cultural exchanges. Most of my research participants have won national or international awards and have extensive overseas performance experiences. Acrobats' narratives help enrich this analysis as their stories not only teach us about the complex effects of political forces on individual lives and careers but also illuminate these individuals' aspirations and creativity in their engagements with the Quebec circus world.

In the following pages, I first discuss the characteristics of socialist acrobatics. Using the example of Cirque du Soleil and the École nationale de cirque de Montréal, I reveal the early interactions between the socialist approach to acrobatics and Québécois circus arts. In the second section, I look at the transformation of the acrobatic sector amid China's economic liberalization reform, which opened spaces of encounter between Chinese acrobatic troupes and foreign entertainment companies. I describe the policy framework that the Chinese government created to facilitate movement of Chinese acrobats to North America, along with the policy implications for the Quebec circus industry. In the last section, I return to the case of *Era* to discuss the current policy discourse associated with acrobatics and the organizational changes shaping connections between the Chinese and Quebec circus worlds.

Prologue: The First Encounter

Guy Caron, who in the early 1980s was the head of the École nationale de cirque de Montréal and artistic director of Cirque du Soleil, described several sources of inspiration that shaped the emergence of Québécois circus arts. One of these was the introduction of Chinese acrobatics to Quebec in 1982 by a travelling troupe from the People's Republic of China (Babinski 2004, 62; Jacob and Vézina 2007, 38). Caron recalled,

> Their show was strong because the music was created from the beginning to the end, and was played by a band. The costumes were designed very specifically for the acts, and they were beautiful. The choreography was beautiful. I thought "Wow! This is a show!" We don't need horses, or animals, or any of that. It can be about physical performances linked together. (qtd in Babinski 2004, 62)

Due to an unexpected commercial success, the Chinese troupe extended its stay in Montreal from three weeks to two months. During this time, Caron invited Chinese acrobats to his newly established circus school, thus facilitating the earliest communications between Chinese and Quebec artists (Jacob and Vézina 2007, 38). The 1982 event also laid a foundation for future collaborations between Chinese troupes and Quebec's circus pioneers. With a grant from the Canada Council, Caron embarked on a research journey in 1986 to several Asian countries, including China, Japan, and Korea.[1] As a result, three Chinese acrobats who won the Silver Clown award at the International Circus Festival of Monte Carlo were invited by Cirque du Soleil to perform the "water meteor" act – spinning a rope with two bowls filled with water attached at each end – for the company's Vancouver tour.[2] The following year, Yin Yu Yun and Yang Feng Zheng from the Wuhan troupe spent two months training students at the École nationale de cirque de Montréal. Yin worked with jugglers while Yang supervised chair pyramid and cycling acts.[3] Cirque du Soleil's *Cirque Réinventé* (1987) and *Nouvelle Expérience* (1990) – the shows that placed the Quebec company on the international map – successfully incorporated Chinese acrobatics into a Quebec-styled production (Babinski 2004, 96). To achieve this outcome, Cirque's artistic directors had recruited Chinese acrobats in China and at international circus festivals. For example, Chinese bicycle acrobatics, performed by Zhao Yan Yan, Zhao Yan Ping, and Zhao Yan Yang, was incorporated into the 1987 production of *Cirque Réinventé*.[4] Caron came to know the Zhao brothers and sister when he saw them win a gold medal at the Festival Mondial du Cirque de Demain. Zhao Yan Yan, who worked for the Cirque in San Francisco for about a year, recalled in an interview that the audience loved the bicycle act; it was the closing act in the show.[5]

The seemingly accidental encounter between Chinese acrobatics and Québécois circus arts was not solely triggered by Québécois' interest in revolutionizing the circus. The arrival of the Chinese acrobatic troupe in 1982 and its unique performance style were embedded in the historical evolution of Chinese acrobatics in the twentieth century. Understanding this history can help illuminate the institutional challenges and opportunities facing both Chinese and Quebec artists in their early collaborative projects.

Socialist Entertainment and Cultural Diplomacy, 1950s–1970s

The premodern Chinese acrobatic culture has been associated with imperial armies, court entertainment, temple festivals, and harvest celebrations (Fu and Fu [2004] 2005; Jacob 2008). In the first half of the twentieth century, the rural acrobatic tradition, which was shaped by diverse regional cultures and had survived through complex family lineages, began to take form in small and medium-sized private theatres in major industrial cities, such as

Beijing, Shanghai, Tianjin, and Wuhan. Acrobats could make a living by performing in the open markets and also in sprawling urban entertainment spaces such as amusement parks and western-style shopping malls. For example, between 1912 and 1936, Shanghai was home to eleven amusement parks that accommodated several dozen acrobatic theatres (Wang et al. 1997, 18). Like folk operas and ballad singing (known in Chinese as ping tan), acrobatics was part of the popular performing arts that drew on Chinese urbanites' imaginations and aspirations. The success of an acrobatic theatre was dependent on an individual performer's charisma and exceptional acrobatic skills. At the same time, the familial or family-like social networks of acrobats mitigated the competition among these acrobatic theatres. Often, the economic stability of these theatres relied as well on connections to the underground criminal society that owned or controlled many of the local entertainment enterprises. Although the political elites in pre-socialist China had interactions with circus performers, state organizations overall did not have much involvement in acrobatic theatres' day-to-day operations. It was not until the Chinese Communist Party founded the government of the People's Republic of China in the fall of 1949 that systematic state planning drastically transformed the management and production of acrobatic shows.

One of the main institutional objectives of socialist cultural policy was to form government cultural institutions, aiming not only to entertain the proletariat but also to promote socialist values and morals (Galikowski 1998; Kraus 2004). Within a centralized, hierarchical political-economic system, fully subsidized arts and cultural organizations recruited writers, journalists, artists, and performers as government employees. The upper-level government agencies, such as municipal cultural bureaus, made policies and gave assignments to lower-level organizations, like acrobatic troupes. Under this system, acrobats were not allowed to perform for money. Instead, they gave free or affordable shows to peasants, workers, and even soldiers at the frontlines of the Korean War (Wang et al. 1997, 42–3).

Additionally, the socialist government quickly identified acrobatics as a national art of socialist China and an important tool of cultural diplomacy (Volland 2007).[6] The China National Acrobatic Troupe – the first state-run acrobatic troupe – was founded in October 1950, after a three-month-long recruitment effort by artist-officials who assembled acrobats from the cities and regions known for acrobatic excellence. One month later, the troupe boarded an airplane to the Soviet Union and then Poland. This first official tour lasted about five months and performed 105 shows for East European audiences (Wang et al. 1997, 401).

Thus, between 1950 and 1966, private acrobatic theatres across China were gradually merged into large state-owned troupes. Approximately twenty acrobatic troupes were formed and placed under various government jurisdictions, including municipal and provincial governments, the minister of transportation, and the People's Liberation Army. In general, the troupes' names reflect their association with various components of the government. For example, the Shanghai Acrobatic Troupe (SAT) is subject to the Shanghai municipal government, and the Chengdu Military District Battle Flag Acrobatic Troupe is administered by the People's Liberation Army's Chengdu branch. Despite their different affiliations, these acrobatic troupes followed in the footsteps of the China National Acrobatic Troupe. They travelled to perform in villages, factories, and army bases; many also entertained China's allies in Europe, Asia, and Africa. Statistical data suggest that before the People's Republic joined the United Nations in 1971, the Chinese acrobatic troupes had visited more than sixty countries promoting the "new China" (Wang et al. 1997, 63).

The reorganization of the acrobatic sector fostered a new occupational identity for performers; they became "revolutionary cultural workers" and as such enjoyed high status and privileges. According to retired members of the SAT, acrobats had a stable salary and welfare protection (e.g., housing, health care, and pension). Even when China staggered under food shortages in the 1960s, the acrobatic troupes still provided their members with meat, vegetables, and grains. Zhao Yan Yan's story exemplifies the employment security as well as the ideological incentives provided by the socialist cultural institutions. Raised in a family of acrobats, she joined the Beijing Acrobatic Troupe in 1970 when she was only nine. Even as a child, Zhao Yan Yan travelled to Africa and Europe, performing in front of high-level officials, including American ex-president Richard Nixon. When she was granted the title of China's first-class artist, she proudly told me, her salary was even higher than Chairman Mao's. In this work environment, acrobats developed a strong sense of professional identity, motivating them to perfect their techniques. This identity powerfully linked personal pride to a nationalist-socialist culture that emphasized personal sacrifice and celebrated collective glory. The retired acrobats believed that because of their upbringings under socialism, they could "eat more bitterness" than the younger generations, who nowadays are interested only in economic rewards.

Moreover, the socialist approach to acrobatics was expressed through performance style. The revised acts emphasized graceful movements, thus reducing the thrilling effects of physical actions. On stage, acrobats were dressed as peasants, workers, athletes, soldiers, and sometimes, martial artists. Their acts incorporated plain-looking bowls, plates, chairs, bicycles, and other objects that working-class people use in their daily lives. The body movements, costumes, and props were chosen with the intent to convince the audience that acrobats, too, are members of the proletariat. Thanks to preexisting tradition and political orientation, the early form of socialist acrobatics excluded animals and aerial acts. Not until the Soviet circus troupe visited China in 1956 did the Chinese begin to invest in animal circus and aerial acts.

Another new feature was the introduction of theatre elements into acrobatic show production. *Za ji wan hui* (literally meaning acrobatic evening gala) became popular in the 1950s. The show was usually composed of a series of acrobatic and magic acts centred on a revolutionary theme, for example "the Working Class People in Beijing." Between acts, an announcer introduced the name and content of the act to follow. Each act was created and performed by a group of acrobats whose costumes, stage sets, and handheld props were specially designed and made by the troupe's carpenters and tailors. The troupe musicians composed original scores (usually traditional Chinese music) for each act. This gala model was advanced throughout the 1960s and 1970s, especially when the animal circus and Russian acrobatics were criticized as examples of worshipping foreign culture and were banned amid the Cultural Revolution of 1966–76 (Wang et al. 1997, 77). During this time, most arts and cultural organizations were paralyzed by debates over what kinds of art and performances could best express revolutionary ideology (Clark 2008; Mittler 2010; Yung 1984). The acrobatics sector also experienced setbacks between 1966 and 1969, when state-run troupes across the country were shut down or dismantled. Nonetheless, in 1970, acrobatics was again identified by Beijing as a focal point for cultural innovation and diplomacy (Zhang 2014).

My interviewee Zhou Liang Tie, a retired acrobat from the Shanghai Acrobatic Troupe, remembered that in 1967 some radical performers requested that the government mobilize artists from outside the SAT to create an acrobatic play, aiming to "give acrobatics a new life" (Wang et al. 1991, 8). In collaboration with seven cultural and educational institutions, such as the Shanghai Theatre Academy and the Shanghai Conservatory of Music, the SAT produced a large acrobatic musical, *Long Live! The Cultural Revolution of the Proletariat*. After he told me this story, Zhou, who was vice-director of SAT during the production of *Era*, suddenly said, "We [the SAT] asked Canadians to help us make *Era* ... In fact, we [the SAT] were ahead of Cirque du Soleil for almost twenty years!"[7] thus implying that the Chinese acrobats were familiar with using acrobatics to tell stories.

Guy Caron's interpretation of the 1982 Chinese acrobatic performance reminds us of some key features of this gala model: for example, "the music was created from the beginning to the end, and was played by a band," "the costumes were designed very specifically for the acts," and "the physical performances linked together" (qtd in Babinski 2004, 62). This cultural legacy influenced Québécois circus arts in an unexpected way: the Chinese acrobatic plays inspired Quebec artists to formulate their own themed and story-driven circus shows.

Exporting Chinese Acrobatics for Money, 1980s–1990s

From 1950 to 1972, Chinese troupes left their footprints in numerous European, African, and Asian countries. Some had also toured in Argentina, Brazil, Uruguay, Chile, Cuba, and Mexico. However, not until US president Richard Nixon visited China in February 1972 did Chinese acrobatics begin to capture the attention of Canadian and American audiences. On the last night of his China trip, a special acrobatic show was staged for President and Mrs Nixon in Shanghai's International Exhibition Hall. The positive reception of this performance from the US diplomats led to a Chinese troupe's first North American tour. From November 1972 to March 1973, the China Shenyang Acrobatic Troupe performed a total of fifty-nine shows in Canada, the United States, Chili, Mexico, and Peru (Wang et al. 1997, 406). In Canada, the troupe stopped in Ottawa, Montreal, Toronto, and Quebec City. These acrobatic shows were so-called visiting shows, merely serving China's diplomatic objectives during the Cold War. Thus, the number of shows was strictly limited. In Montreal, the troupe performed in Salle Wilfrid-Pelletier for only two days.[8] Most Québécois had to wait another ten years before they could watch Chinese acrobatics performed by the Wuhan Acrobatic Troupe in Montreal's Maurice Richard Arena. China's economic liberalization reform was the main political force behind this troupe's 1982 visit.

"It all started in October 1980, when American magician Mark Wilson and his troupe came to China," said Zhou Liang Tie, who was describing his own participation in the revolutionary acrobatic play. Zhou had been practicing acrobatics since he was eleven and began studying magic after a serious leg injury. "Mark's show started like a fierce fire on a pile of dry wood," he said. "After my colleagues and I saw Mark's magic, we thought 'Wow. Now we were allowed [by the government] to put on a show with disco music and young women dressed in miniskirts in front of the audience.'" For Chinese acrobatic troupes, the arrival of the American magic show was a clear signal from the government that state censorship on performing arts was loosening and that commercial art was acceptable (Kraus 2004). The peasant-worker-soldier aesthetics no longer dominated the acrobatic stage. More significantly, the organizational model of Wilson's troupe inspired many Chinese artist-officials and acrobats to develop commercial shows that would enable them to gain some economic and administrative independence from the government. For instance, within the SAT, acrobats, musicians, and supporting staffs were reorganized into three groups. One group toured across China, and the other two groups pursued contracts overseas, mostly from the United States and Japan. Commercial acrobatic shows became the troupe's main source of income in the 1980s and 1990s (Wang et al. 1991, 100).

China's first contract for overseas acrobatic shows was jointly signed by the China Performing Arts Agency (incorporated in 2004 and renamed the China Arts and Entertainment Group), the Columbia Artists Management Inc., and the SAT. As a result, the Shanghai troupe, consisting of sixty members, launched fifty-four acrobatic shows in New York City, Washington, DC, Philadelphia, and Chicago between 18 March and 20 May 1980 (Wang et al. 1991, 80). This began China's cultural exportation of commercial acrobatic performances to North America, West Europe, and Japan. Canada was one of the few countries where Chinese troupes could make big profits.

According to a survey conducted by the Chinese Acrobatic Association, eleven different acrobatic troupes performed in Canada throughout the 1980s (see table 12.1). The Guangdong Acrobatic Troupe, followed by the Wuhan Acrobatic Troupe, was the first Chinese troup to make inroads into Canada's interior. The statistics in table 12.1 indicate the level of popularity in Canada of Chinese acrobatic shows. Excluding the US-Canada tours,

Table 12.1
Chinese acrobatic troupes' visits to Canada in the 1980s

Date	Troupe	Country	Artists & others	Number of shows per tour	Audience attendance
Aug–Dec 1980	Guangdong Acrobatic Troupe	Canada and the US	65	110	245,000
Dec 1981–Mar 1982	Wuhan Acrobatic Troupe	Canada	65	81	540,000
Apr–Aug 1983	Railway Acrobatic Troupe	Canada and the US	72	92	148,000
Mar–Jun 1984	Guangzhou Global Motorcycle Acrobatic Troupe	Canada	63	60	220,000
Apr–Sep 1986	Kaifeng Acrobatic Troupe	Canada	20	200	500,000
Aug–Sep 1987	Chongqing Acrobatic Troupe	Canada	33	78	85,775
Jan–May 1988	Qiqi Haer Acrobatic Troupe	Canada	18	105	650,000
Sep–Dec 1988	China Wuhan Acrobatic Troupe	Canada	63	92	250,000
Dec 1988–May 1989	Jiangxi Acrobatic Troupe	Canada and the US	26	150	200,000

Table 12.1 (*continued*)
Chinese acrobatic troupes' visits to Canada in the 1980s

Date	Troupe	Country	Artists & others	Number of shows per tour	Audience attendance
Apr–Jul 1989	Hei Longjiang Acrobatic Troupe	Canada and the US	18	85	100,000
May–Sep 1989	Shanghai Acrobatic Troupe	Canada and the US	12	372	120,000
Jun–Sep 1989	Shanghai Acrobatic Troupe	Canada	21	222	300,000

Source: Statistics are from "The Overview of China Acrobatic Art Overseas Performance in a Table 1949–1990" (Wang et al. 1997, 401).

total audience attendance reached 2.6 million. On average, more than seventy acrobatic shows were staged annually, and each show could sell approximately 3,000 seats.

Chinese archival materials suggest that these overseas commercial tours generated tremendous profits for the Chinese government and the troupes. In the case of the SAT, 30 per cent of the revenue from commercial tours went to the government. The troupe could keep close to 70 per cent of the profit, which was divided into a development fund (40 per cent) used to improve infrastructure and welfare facilities and a reward fund (30 per cent) distributed directly to employees (Wang et al. 1991, 101, 105). With the accumulated capital from overseas revenue, the SAT could renovate and expand the troupe's studio and theatre. In 1987, the income derived from overseas performances also enabled the SAT to fund the first circus school in China (Wang et al. 1991, 112). Working in North America helped individual acrobats enrich their lives at a time when most artists still lived on fixed salaries. Zhou Liang Tie and his colleague admitted that acrobats were among the first few people in Shanghai with enough money to buy imported appliances like colour television sets, refrigerators, and cassette players. Zhou said, "I first led the acrobatic team that performed for the domestic audience. Then, the overseas tours became very profitable. And they [the overseas teams] wanted more acrobats. Even our old janitors were recruited to perform lion dances in [North] America. So, eventually I left my team and started to work abroad."

The commercial success of Chinese acrobatic shows would not have been possible without the political-economic arrangements between the Chinese government and foreign entertainment companies. Such arrangements facilitated the movement of acrobats from China to the big top in Montreal and other North American cities. In the next few pages, I discuss two aspects of Sino-American relations that are especially important for understanding the challenges and opportunities that Chinese and Québécois confronted in their early collaborative work.

First, commercial agreements between Chinese troupes and North American companies were made on the basis of a particular contract model that was partially inherited from the institutional framework under Mao. Previously, the China Performing Arts Agency (CPAA) exclusively represented the central government and handled all diplomatic cultural exchange activities. When, in the early 1980s, the nonprofit cultural exchange endeavours turned into profitable cultural exports, the CPAA started to play a key role in matching Chinese troupes to different foreign contracts. The Chinese acrobatic troupes, which were still under the minister of culture, had to collaborate with the CPAA when they signed contracts with foreigners.[9] This three-party contractual model was first applied to group contracts. Then, around 1986, some foreign circus companies started to offer the CPAA contracts to "borrow" individual acrobats.

Cirque du Soleil was one of these circus production companies that wanted to hire only a few Chinese acrobats with exceptional skills. Again, according to the Chinese rule, the foreign companies could not negotiate a contract with either the acrobats or their troupes. Instead, each company had to formulate a labour contract with the CPAA stipulating the length of an acrobat's stay, the acrobat's stipend and welfare, and fees for the Chinese agency. Zhao Yan Yan and her brothers, for example, never saw their labour contracts with Cirque, but she was pleased by her new work in Montreal.

> Zhao Yan Yan: I received a US$25 food stipend per day from the Cirque. They also provided us with accommodation. The [Chinese]

> government gave us US$5 per day. In those days, I was very happy [about making this amount of money]. I thought I was a young rich woman.
>
> Tracy Zhang: I remember my father, who was an engineer in Shanghai, had a salary less than US$13 per month!

According to this contract, Zhao could work at Cirque du Soleil for sixteen months. The Québécois wanted to extend the contract for an additional year. However, the Chinese government decided to return Zhao to Beijing. Zhao Yan Yan states,

> After we went back to China, the government did not let us leave the country anymore. They said we were government artists. The Cirque worked very hard [to try to extend our contract]. Gilles [Ste-Croix] even went to Beijing to see some officials and looked for all kinds of methods that might help get us out of the country. But nothing worked out. The Chinese government was like this. So, we could not go [to Quebec] anymore.

It is unclear what rationale was behind the government's decision not to renew Zhao's contract. However, her comments demonstrate the unrelenting state power that imposed institutional constraints on working relationships between Chinese acrobats and the Québécois circus company.

Second, the state vis-à-vis company contract model caused tensions in Sino-Quebec employment relations at Cirque du Soleil. From the managers' perspective, Chinese artists were accustomed to a rigid organizational structure and had difficulty adjusting to a more flexible managerial style and work environment (Babinski 2004, 270). Yan recalls that when working for the Cirque in 1987, she and her brothers refused managers' requests to participate in other performances. "We said no. We said we would only perform our own act [according to the contract]. Later, they asked if they could use new music for our act. We said [the new music] was no good. We like *erhu* [Chinese instrument] and traditional music." Today, Zhao Yan Yan leads her own acrobatic troupe based in Las Vegas, and during the interview she commented on how difficult it is to manage her own employees from China. She used herself – the young Zhao Yan Yan from socialist China – to demonstrate the resistance of young acrobats trained under socialism.

To me, Zhao's story of refusing managers' demands demonstrates her strong sense of cultural identity and her desire to protect her work from managers' interventions. As I mentioned, Zhao Yan Yan and her brothers came from a family of acrobats. The team's award-winning bicycle act was created by their father, an acrobat who was forbidden to perform during the Cultural Revolution. This man put his imagination and hopes into the creation of the bicycle act for his children. Thus, the Zhaos' rejection of the managers' requests can be seen as evidence of the artists' interest in controlling their own work, which is connected not only to their professional identity but to their family history. These acrobats could say no to Cirque du Soleil because they were not subject to individual contracts with the company. Additionally, since they enjoyed secure employment back in China, they faced little risk confronting the managers.

These conflicts between the Chinese and Québécois articulated some fundamental differences between the two cultural institutions and ideologies. The Chinese socialist system places acrobats in the category of "revolutionary cultural workers" serving the Chinese state whereas the Quebec-style system is a profit-oriented cultural production subjecting artist-employees to managerial power and quality control. The tensions between the two systems – Chinese state socialism versus Québécois liberal capitalism – surfaced in the competition over who (the private company or the government) controlled performers' work. Although they received relatively small economic rewards and had limited mobility, Chinese acrobats found ways to obtain a certain degree of autonomy from both the state and the Québécois company.

As we have seen here, China's economic liberalization policy was the main political force shaping relationships between the Chinese troupes and foreign circus companies. Throughout the 1980s, China's connections to the Quebec circus world started to develop, along with loosened state censorship on the performing arts sector, the opening of China to foreign entertainment companies, and the increasing exportation of Chinese acrobatic shows to wealthy North American countries. Among these parallel policy developments, large circus companies such as the Big Apple Circus in New York City and the Ringling Brothers and Barnum & Bailey started to recruit Chinese acrobats. From 1983 to 1986, the Australian government even imported Chinese acrobats to train child performers (mostly members of Circus Oz and the Flying Fruit Fly Circus; Farrell 2008). In 1986, Cirque du

Soleil was still a small Quebec-based circus with an uncertain future. Nonetheless, like their American counterparts, the Québécois founders took advantage of China's open door policy to forge a partnership with the Chinese acrobatic troupes. The most striking example is *Dralion*. Created in 1999 in collaboration with the Battle Flag Acrobatic Troupe, this show about the meeting of Eastern and Western cultures employed more than thirty Chinese acrobats. This Chinese connection contributed to the transformation of Cirque du Soleil from a spectacle of jugglers and clowns on stilts to a global phenomenon of world-class acrobatics.

Two decades ago, Chinese acrobats were suspicious of Cirque's commercial shows. But in 2013, almost every acrobat I met in Shanghai spoke highly of Cirque du Soleil's approaches to multimedia acrobatic spectacles. At least in the circus world, the superiority of capitalist production and marketing is now taken for granted.

Coda: Acrobatics in the Era of Soft Power

Era, initially called "Magnificent Shanghai," was a multimedia show that used acrobatics to represent Shanghai's landscapes and history. The embryo of this show was created by the SAT after the completion of the Shanghai Circus World, a high-tech acrobatic theatre complex that provides the infrastructure for the SAT to invest in larger and more extravagant productions. As the *Era* project evolved, two more government enterprises got involved: Shanghai Media and Entertainment Group and the China Arts and Entertainment Group (CAEG). Altogether, the three companies put 30,000,000 yuan (approximately US$3,750,000) into the production and marketing of *Era* (He 2009, 37). The Shanghai Era Entertainment Ltd was formed to lead the project; in practice, each business partner plays a different role. The Shanghai Media and Entertainment Group, a government media conglomerate, covers marketing and public relations events for *Era*. The CAEG is responsible for recruiting Canadian artists, the SAT for managing artists and theatre space (He 2009, 43). In early January 2005, Érick Villeneuve, the leader of the Canadian creative team, signed a contract with the Chinese producer from the CAEG. On 27 September 2005, *Era* was launched. The director of the SAT, Yu Yigang, claims that most leaders of Chinese troupes lack understanding of the commodity aspects of acrobatics. He identified himself as a forward-looking manager, using *Era* to prove that the Chinese should use a business approach to analyzing acrobatics and searching for new development models (He 2009, 14). In May 2006, Shanghai Era Entertainment Ltd was designated by the government as China's "Cultural Industry Model Enterprise."

Director Yu's statement corresponds to an ongoing enterprise reform in China's arts and cultural sector. The infrastructural development of the SAT, the making of *Era*, and the recruitment of Quebec artists were part and parcel of this trend. The ideological base of this reform is largely constituted by an economic critique and a political discourse. The economic critique points to the problem of low "cultural productivity" and inefficiency in governmental cultural institutions. Since the 1980s, acrobatic troupes have undergone several organizational changes to tackle the "productivity problem." The most recent policy was to remove the troupes' nonprofit status, thus requiring each troupe to register with the Industry and Commerce Bureau as a business entity. In 2011, the SAT was reconfigured as a corporate structure and converted into the Shanghai Acrobatic Troupe Ltd. Under this business model, acrobats can no longer have cradle-to-grave job security but are required to sign labour contracts with the SAT. At the same time, Chinese acrobats have more freedom to choose their employers and join overseas companies.

In addition to the economic justification, the political rationale behind the cultural enterprise reform is premised on the assumption that China's fast economic growth must go hand in hand with the cultivation of the country's "soft power," a term that entered China's policy discourse in 2006 and has often been associated with national image-building, diplomacy, and cultural industries and trade (Kurlantzick 2007; Zhang 2010). For acrobats and their troupe leaders, the discourse of "soft power" is mobilized to address the questions of finding effective business models and international branding strategies (Chen 2009). The success of Cirque du Soleil has been frequently cited in discussions on how to build a Chinese acrobatic industry with a global outlook (Zhou 2009, 50). Thus, the hiring of Canadian circus producers was an effort by the Chinese to learn about the ingredients of Québécois circus arts and to test whether or not foreigners' creative energy could assist the local troupes in attracting international audiences.

On 27 September 2010, Shanghai Era Entertainment Ltd launched *Kaleido*, another high-tech, big budget circus show. The Québécois crew again participated in the creation process, including choreography, lighting, music, and costumes. Unfortunately, when I was doing fieldwork in Shanghai in the winter of 2012, the show, due to box office weakness, had already been cancelled. Meanwhile, Franco Dragone Entertainment Group recently signed a 2.5 billion RMB (approximately US$410,947,500) contract with the China Dalian Wanda Group, a Chinese conglomerate with major investments in real estate, tourism, hotels, and entertainment. Franco Dragone, the former artistic director of Cirque du Soleil, aimed to create at least five multimedia acrobatic shows in Mainland China (Sino-Belgian Trade and Investment Portal 2012). The first outcome of this collaborative work was the construction of a lantern-shaped theatre and the launch of *Han Show*, a mega water show (Wanda Group 2013). Despite some failures, the repeated attempts to produce large infrastructures and extravagant circus spectacles inside China point to intensified commercialization of performing arts, and also demonstrate a desire for building a nationwide circus industry for local consumption.

As this chapter shows, the emergence of Québécois circus arts was not simply part of the Quebec cultural renaissance subsidized by a sovereignist government in the aftermath of the Révolution tranquille. Through the lens of the Chinese connection, we can see that the formation of contemporary circus arts is linked to Cold War cultural diplomacy and entails complex transnational networks of government institutions, corporate actors, individual artists, and other professionals. Thus, global circus connections, activated by state-corporate arrangements, are made under multiple politico-economic regimes. The growth of Western European and North American circus economies is fuelled by labour markets in regions and areas, like Russia, Ukraine, Mongolia, and China, that had once established state-sponsored performing arts and sports sectors to entertain and educate the working-class citizen. Currently, the legacy of the socialist cultural institutions enables these countries to play a pivotal role in supplying global entertainment companies with skilled acrobats, contortionists, gymnasts, and other physical arts professionals.

Furthermore, for circus artists, career opportunities and challenges are often influenced by state-corporate interactions in various locales. As this chapter has revealed, the Chinese-Québécois connection took shape over a period of some thirty years, and continues to change in response to shifting state policies. In this process, Chinese government troupes, North American circus companies, and acrobats have negotiated the value and mobility of acrobatic bodies. In the early years of Sino-Québécois collaborations, the Chinese acrobats' agency was derived from guaranteed job security in China, and the acrobats could economically benefit from their overseas employment at least to some extent. Recent policy developments have instituted a contract model designed to reshape labour relations within the Chinese acrobatics sector. However, the state remains keenly interested in controlling acrobats' employment options. Further, new incarnations of government agencies, such as the China Arts and Entertainment Group and the Shanghai Circus World, are concerned not only with profits but also with national image. The recruitment of Québécois circus artists suggests the growing importance of acrobatics as a cultural medium for representing China's new affluence and power to both domestic and international audiences. The failure of *Kaleido* seen alongside Dragone's active engagement with Chinese investors reveals the tensions between Chinese nationalism, business interests, and artists' creative input. Understanding this latest phase in global circus history will help Chinese and Québécois artists navigate careers in this complex, often contradictory, work environment.

V.

Affecting Change

CHAPTER 13

Creativity and Place in the Evolution of a Cultural Industry: The Case of Cirque du Soleil

Deborah Leslie and Norma M. Rantisi

Introduction

Cirque du Soleil, based in Montreal, is a paradigm of creativity within the Canadian commercial performance sector. Despite a certain deterritorialization of Cirque from its original location of production that other chapters in this collection explore, we argue that Cirque's ability to innovate is underpinned by its historical and geographic situatedness in Montreal. Here we chart the place-specific and path-dependent trajectory that has informed the emergence of Cirque du Soleil, highlighting how the company has drawn upon local resources to solidify its competitive advantage. While a variety of local and historical characteristics of Montreal gave rise to Cirque, we highlight three local synergies that were particularly important to Cirque's evolution, threads interwoven into other chapters in this book: the vibrant tradition of street culture and festivals in Quebec, the lack of established circus conventions in the province, and the strength of related cultural sectors in Montreal such as dance, theatre, music, and television.

This chapter draws upon semi-structured interviews with Cirque employees involved in multiple aspects of the company's operations, including creative and artistic directors, labour recruiters, human resources personnel, production staff, writers, directors, performers, marketers, composers, and costume designers. Interviews were also conducted with a variety of officials involved in governing the circus arts in Quebec, such as representatives from the provincial and municipal governments, the École nationale de cirque de Montréal, the circus trade association En Piste, and TOHU (La Cité des arts du cirque).[1] Despite the focus on Cirque du Soleil, individuals working at other circus troupes in Montreal (such as Cirque Éloize and the 7 Fingers) were also interviewed.[2]

Interviews were conducted between 2008 and 2009, and ranged between one and two hours in length. Initial participants were identified through a review of trade publications, media coverage, and Cirque's website. A process of snowball sampling was used for subsequent interviews. Interviews were digitally recorded, transcribed, and coded according to theme. Information provided from interviews was considered in relation to an analysis of relevant policy documents, trade journals, newspapers, and websites.

The chapter is organized into three main sections. First, we discuss the literature on path dependency and the evolution of creative industries, highlighting the significance of fortuitous conditions, purposive action, and existing spatial structures in enabling the creation and institutionalization of a particular path of development. The second section outlines some of the latent historical and geographical synergies that gave rise to Cirque du Soleil, and the final section highlights the way in which government and institutional support has assisted in nurturing some of these latent synergies. The quotations included in this chapter reflect the prevalence of particular themes in the interviews, as well as their centrality in other materials such as newspaper articles and government policy documents.

Locating the Place-Based Dimensions of Creativity

Creativity as a place-based phenomenon

That Paris has reigned as the capital of fashion for so long is a testament to the fact that not all places are equally creative in all specializations. This begs the question of what allows particular places to excel in certain fields. Why is Paris synonymous with fashion, or Milan with design? Scholars such as Scott (1996, 1997, 2001) and Molotch (1996, 2003) lend insight into these matters by suggesting that there is a symbiotic relation between place and cultural products, be they goods or services. The producers of cultural commodities draw on place-specific resources (ranging from infrastructure to artists) and place-based images to imbue commodities with a distinct aesthetic quality, a feature that can serve as a basis for competitive advantage. Over time, the cultural commodities of a place can serve as its "emissaries," reinforcing its symbolic images and endowing it with a stamp of authenticity that precludes the entry of potential competitors (Scott 2001). Scott (2001) and Molotch (1996, 2003) further contend that such creative milieus are most likely to be found in urban settings due to the concentration of skilled personnel and a diverse set of specialized services. This concentration allows for a mix and match of competencies, promoting experimentation and exploration, on the one hand, and the capacity to design and develop new cultural creations, on the other. An agglomeration of economic activities also promotes shared understandings and conventions that underpin an open and fluid set of socioeconomic relations.

How creative milieus materialize

While Scott and Molotch highlight the features that distinguish a creative milieu, we are still left with the question of why certain creative milieus (e.g., Hollywood or Broadway) are only found in certain places. *How* do such milieus emerge?

Drawing on evolutionary economics,[3] geographers have recently accorded greater attention to the foundations of successful (and unsuccessful) regional economies (Cooke and Morgan 1998; Essletzbichler and Rigby 2007; Martin and Simmie 2008; Maskell and Malmberg 1999; Storper 1995). In particular, they have applied the concept of "path dependence" as the theoretical anchor on which to base their analyses. This concept, in contrast to the ahistorical approach of neoclassical economics, highlights the relevance of contextual specificities and historical factors. The basic tenets of this concept are that chance or historical accidents (e.g., the discovery of a new resource or the entry of a new firm/entrepreneur) can lead to more substantial consequences over time through spillover effects, locking a place into a particular path of development. The process can be illustrated as follows: a producer begins to specialize in charms after the discovery of a rare gemstone, then a market for the charms expands, attracting more producers. Training schools develop to supply the new producers with labourers, and new instruments are developed to facilitate the production process. In a path-dependent approach, such events are cumulative and serve to reinforce a specialization in a particular field. Initial advantages develop into more localized capabilities that are difficult for other regions to replicate. In some cases these capabilities establish a symbolic image and reputation for a region that lends a sense of authenticity to its products.

Within the path-dependence perspective, it is acknowledged that a path is not necessarily linear or fixed; ruptures may occur along the way, in the form of exogenous shocks or internal disturbances, which can alter the trajectory and set a locale onto a new course of development (Dosi 1997; Hodgson 1994). However, to date, much of the research has focused on how paths are reinforced (Storper 1995) or how they become rigidified (Grabher

1993). Less attention is paid to how a new course of development ensues. As indicated above, the origins or "creation" of a path are generally attributed to chance or historical accident, but as Martin and Sunley (2006) note, two important factors are neglected in such a view. The first is that a process of path creation is often related to purposive action on the part of agents to mobilize change (see also MacKinnon et al. 2009). The second is that change often depends on – and derives from – existing spatial attributes or structures, for example, industrial legacies or regional policies and institutions (Massey 1992). Accordingly, there is a need to view the evolutionary process as *place* – as well as path – dependent (Boschma and Martin 2007; MacKinnon et al. 2009; Martin and Sunley 2006, 409). To the extent that chance matters, it is the coming together of fortuitous conditions and of purposive or established activities within particular places that underlies the particular selection of a new course of development.

In his analysis of cultural production clusters more specifically, Mommaas (2004) echoes the contentions of path-dependent theorists by highlighting the circumstantial nature of the development of such locales. He further contends that the success of these locales as creative milieus depends on their ability to develop a "critical infrastructure" that can mediate the risks and uncertainty of cultural production, including a favourable climate for creative workers and wider symbolic and infrastructural spinoffs that can attract other creative workers and activities. In sum, Mommaas suggests that these places must deliver a mix of "spatial, professional and cultural qualities" that allow for "contexts of trust, socialisation, knowledge, inspiration, exchange and incremental innovation" (521).

Despite an emphasis on the organic nature of development, like recent evolutionary theorists, Mommaas (2004, 521–2) still sees a potential role for policy in enabling locales to chart an intended path. While public policies cannot organize creative milieus directly, they can create the conditions favourable for their development and subsequent institutionalization. Such policies can come in the form of financial support, the provision of resources (e.g., space, equipment), or the promotion of networks between potentially related actors. This view is corroborated by Scott (2004), who also emphasizes the significance of policy in the development of cultural products industries and in cultivating the latent cultural synergies that a locale may possess, that is, the linking of distinct but complementary skill sets.

In what follows, we examine how cultural legacies and government interventions have facilitated Cirque du Soleil's rise and its consequent evolution, as well as contributing to the rise of the circus arts milieu in which Cirque is embedded. By considering the role played by these factors in the creation *and* the institutionalization of a new brand of circus, we seek to contribute to recent theorizations on the evolution of cultural economies and the place-based possibilities for privileging certain paths of development. Our approach emphasizes the role of *purposive action* in the creation of new paths, and highlights the *place- and path-dependent nature* of innovation. We begin this examination with a review of latent (or emergent) attributes within Quebec and, more specifically, Montreal, that were instrumental to setting Cirque's path in motion.

Latent Synergies in the Formation of a Montreal Circus

A number of historical and geographical specificities were central to the rise of circus arts in Montreal in the 1980s. Cirque du Soleil, for example, grew out of a vibrant tradition of street performance, festivals, and café culture in Quebec.[4] In part, this tradition of street performance and the appeal of circus and clowning derives from Quebec's close ties to Europe – and in particular, France. In fact, one of Cirque's two founders toured Europe, learning the arts of busking, firebreathing, juggling, and walking on stilts (Babinsky 2004).

The company was founded by a series of marginal youths performing in public space. As one Cirque director puts it, it is significant "that [Cirque] was coming from street performers, people without education, without any kind of background ... people who were living and playing in the streets. A lot of them were on welfare, on unemployment or nothing. A lot of them were dropouts" (interview, December 2008). A distinct local ecology of street culture thus gave rise to the aesthetic mélange that became Cirque du Soleil. As a representative of the École nationale de cirque explains:

> Many of these people looking to become circus artists ... were working in the street ... The street in a certain way is a free space. There is no social class in the street. You can be classy or a beggar but you are at the same level ... This is why the people who started it [Cirque] were feeling free to do whatever they wanted. This is one of the explanations why, in the beginning of the circus arts in Quebec, that we were able to mix theatre, dance, music and circus. (interview, June 2008)

The street is the origin of the risk-taking entrepreneurialism that is Cirque's trademark: "In the street you take a lot of risks. You never know how people will react" (ibid.). An ability to tolerate inefficiency and uncertainty – to take risks – is important for adaptation and change and has helped the company to maintain a culture of continuous innovation.

Street culture is thus critical to the evolution of Cirque du Soleil. A creative director at the company, for example, suggests that his early experience working in the street provided him with the communication skills required to assemble a creative team and foster conditions conducive to artistic innovation: "I'm lucky because I improvised on the streets as a clown, so I learned a lot about people. I can read people. I know how to talk to them and stay open and listen ... I'm a pretty good judge of character. I think that is important because you want to be able to give everyone as much freedom as you can" (interview, December 2008). Thus, even when Cirque du Soleil moved indoors to a tent, the origins of the circus in the street – a place where people from all walks of life are forced to rub shoulders – continued to permeate its artistic trajectory.

While the origins of circus in Quebec lie in the European tradition of street performance, the lack of a long history of circus performance meant that performers were free to modify circus conventions. As Jan-Rok Achard, founder of the Montreal circus arts trade association En Piste, observed: "Cirque du Soleil started in a country where there was no tradition ... There was no circus. Once in a while ignorance can be a quality [an asset] ... We were in a certain way free to do something ... None of the ones who started around here had circus blood. They did not belong to a circus family ... So ... this gave them a lot of freedom ... They were coming to the circus ... because they believed there were less limits in terms of the expression" (interview, June 2008). A performer reiterates this sentiment: "We don't have a big history of circus. When you go to Europe, they have 250 years of family circus, of circus schools, of people, for us it's all new, so everything is merging right now ... We can still do what we want with it because it's only twenty-five years old" (interview, June 2009).

The lack of historical referents is significant because the literature on path dependency highlights the tendency among some industries and regions with established traditions toward "lock-in" (Grabher 1993). Strong ties can foster efficiency, but also have the potential to lock economic development into a narrow path that can become rigid and inefficient over time

(Grabher 2005, 64). In the case of the circus in Quebec, a lack of conventions fosters an openness to new ideas and influences.

Beyond the more general tradition of street performance and the lack of established conventions in Quebec, the strength of other cultural sectors in the city of Montreal – such as theatre, dance, and music – also helped to stimulate a process of cross-fertilization that contributed to Cirque du Soleil's unique style of circus production: "Theatre is very specific in Montreal ... because it is French," said Marc Lalonde, director of the École nationale de cirque (interview, May 2008).[5] "Historically, it supported the promotion of the Quebec identity ... so it is vibrant ... In contemporary music there is a lot in Montreal ... The leaders in contemporary dance have been – at least in the last twenty to thirty years – in Montreal ... So if you have this already, it helps a lot because most of the first circus performers in Montreal were street performers or actors." Montreal is home to the National Theatre School, the O Vertigo dance company, the world famous Jazz Festival, and a vibrant independent music scene. The city is the centre of fashion in Canada and is recognized for its strength in visual arts and design.[6]

In their discussion of creativity, Stolarick and Florida (2006) argue that knowledge transfers between industries – or what they refer to as "spillacross effects" – are even more important to innovation than spillovers within an industry. A diverse array of industries increases the likelihood of new ideas emerging through the incorporation of insights learned from other fields.

Grabher (2005) discusses this idea in relation to advertising agencies, which typically take on a variety of clients from different industries, affording opportunities to learn from creative practices, repertoires, and techniques in different product categories. In addition, many agencies have diversified into nonadvertising services such as public relations, architecture, new media, and design, again offering diverse sources of learning. As Grabher puts it, "The proliferation of a broad spectrum of different organizational forms and diverse practices – as opposed to the diffusion of a single 'best practice' – provides a richer 'selection environment' for regions, firms, and individual actors to co-evolve" (65). In the case of the circus, the presence of interrelated and complementary industries suggests the importance of path interdependence – situations where the path-dependent trajectories of different industries are mutually reinforcing (Martin and Sunley 2006).

Proximity and diversity are a central means for securing these spillacross effects (Stolarick and Florida 2006). Montreal is one of the densest cities in North America, and also the most diverse city in Canada in terms of number of industries (Beckstead and Brown 2003).[7] Density and diversity provide fertile opportunities for interesting connections and combinations to emerge.[8] A large reservoir of cultural talent, combined with sectoral diversity within the local economy, helps Cirque du Soleil to continually innovate. A representative of the circus arts community in Montreal sums it up this way: "The advantage of being in Montreal is the basin of creators that are in Montreal … in the performing arts – the artists, the conceptors … That is the strength of Cirque du Soleil."[9] It is this unique combination that helped set the scene for the evolution of a novel art form: "Cirque du Soleil is a hybrid. It is not only circus, and it's not only theatre and it's not only musical. It is like a hybrid of the two and gymnastics … Here [at Cirque] you work with actors, gymnasts, circus artists, musicians, dancers, clowns … acrobats. The paths of the melting pot are so different … There's a lot of energy finding ways to communicate with each other on stage and back stage."[10] Having to bridge the divide between these various art forms fosters a lively and dynamic corporate culture and a willingness to explore multiple paths.

Cirque du Soleil in turn has been able to draw on these established arts to strengthen and structure the creative dimensions of its shows. Jan-Rok Achard, founder of En Piste, comments on Cirque's influence on the contemporary Quebec circus:

> You cannot just juggle three balls. You have to move today. You have to have it to music … For years and years, circus people, circus artists were doing tricks, and they were in a certain way cutting or closing the doors to other arts influences. Now they see, they feel how much theatre can bring, how much music can bring, how much dance can bring. Not because they will become actors or dancers or musicians, but it is much more integrated [now]. (interview, June 2008)

Cirque du Soleil has thus derived multiple benefits from these local synergies, drawing both ideas and talent from these sources of inspiration. In terms of talent, for example, it has utilized local playwrights and directors from theatre and film (such as Robert Lepage), composers (such as René Dupéré and Benoit Jutras), and costume, textile, and fashion designers (such as Marie-Chantale Vaillancourt), as well as local riggers, choreographers, and other specialists.

Thus Cirque du Soleil owes its unique style and evolutionary path to the strength of related cultural industries in Montreal. It is clear that the ingredients for Cirque's success were present both in the Montreal setting and, more generally, in Quebec culture. An ability to benefit from these latent synergies, however, was bolstered by Cirque du Soleil's arrival on the scene at a time when the provincial government was growing more concerned with supporting cultural industries.

Government Support and the Development of Actualized Synergies

The evolution of provincial funding for cultural industries

In evolutionary economic geography, emphasis is placed on the context-specific and locally contingent nature of economic development and how purposive actions can mobilize place-based latent synergies. The success of Cirque du Soleil is in many ways a manifestation of the distinct historical moment in which it emerged, and the range of cultural and political currents that were circulating in Quebec.

Since the 1950s, provincial governments in Quebec have placed a strong emphasis on culture and the arts (Harvie and Hurley 1999; Paul 2004). This policy relates in part to the rise of Quebec nationalism and the widespread belief that the provincial government should support cultural sectors, which play an important role in identity formation. The Quebec government views art as a societal project; consequently, it has contributed significantly to the development of these fields through support from the Ministry of Cultural Affairs and the Society for the Development of Cultural Enterprises of Quebec (SODEC). Recognition of the need for strong government intervention in the cultural sector has parallels with France (McGuigan 2004; Québec. Ministère des affaires culturelles 1992). As one past director of the École nationale de cirque de Montréal asserts:

> We are a little nation, a French nation, and we are completely surrounded by English or American culture ... I am quite convinced that ... the Quebec government got involved ... [because] they took an example from France. We are speaking the same language ... France

> has made culture a societal project and for me this is one of the explanations that we can give for the fact that for Quebec, culture is very important ... So if the Quebec government ... is willing to invest, I believe for them it was, maybe still is, a question of the survival of our culture. (interview, June 2008)

Given the concentration of cultural industries in Montreal, the city has occupied a central place in cultural policy (Québec. Ministère des affaires culturelles 1992, 132). Since the 1950s, the city has been the site of massive investments in architecture, the arts, and special events, such as Expo 67 and the Summer Olympics of 1976 (Paul 2004).[11] These investments reflected an ideology of nationalism, but were also oriented toward garnering external validation for the city's unique cultural identity and world city status (Paul 2004).

In the 1970s and '80s, industrial decline, the rise of a francophone business class, and the growth of neoliberal governance regimes combined to force a reinterpretation of the world city project. New emphasis was placed on a consumerist cosmopolitanism oriented toward the construction of spectacle and an expanded symbolic economy to replace the eroding manufacturing base (Paul 2004, 58). Paul (2004) argues that under this new phase of investment, Quebec identity has been successfully linked with global neoliberal interests, and Québécois cultural identity "has become increasingly cosmopolitan and globalist rather than nationalist in any traditional sense" (590–1). In terms of cultural policy, this shift entailed a greater focus by the 1980s on the economic significance of culture and the support of cultural commodities – rather than traditional arts, per se – since those commodities can be exported and can thereby enhance economic competitiveness, as well as solidify foreign linkages (Conlogue 1994; Québec. Ministère des affaires culturelles 1992).

While the history of nationalism clearly contributed to the early evolution of Cirque du Soleil, today the company benefits equally from the socio-ethnic diversity of Montreal. In contrast to the hegemony of French language and culture in the province as a whole, Montreal projects a strongly multicultural and transnational identity, which contributes to the vibrancy of the cultural scene in the city. Cirque is able to draw artistic inspiration from these many influences.

History of provincial support for Cirque

Cirque du Soleil has been a major beneficiary of the broader policy orientation toward cultural industries, and the history of government support for Cirque can be traced back to the company's earliest days.[12] The company had its origins as an ad hoc troupe of street entertainers that took part in an annual street performance festival. Cirque du Soleil was formally launched in 1984 when the troupe, which was assembled by Guy Laliberté, received a contract from the Quebec Ministry of Cultural Affairs to tour Quebec and perform as part of the celebrations commemorating the 450th anniversary of Jacques Cartier's arrival to Canada. Initially, the ministry was hesitant to award the contract to this relatively unknown group of entertainers, but in a chance event, provincial premier René Lévesque had seen the troupe perform. He became a fan and took up their cause (David 2007; Dougherty 1990). The contract was significant – $1.3 million – for the group to show in eleven cities. To meet the demands of the tour, Cirque secured a tent and hired a tour manager, an artistic director, and a highly experienced technical operations manager.[13] Since government representatives were in attendance at the shows to ensure that the money was well spent, the company had to exhibit a level of organization and professionalism to which it was not previously accustomed.

The tours were met with a strong public reception and media coverage, heightening Cirque du Soleil's visibility throughout the province (David 2007). These trends prompted Cirque to plan another tour that would entail the performance of one big show and to apply for government grants as a nonprofit organization. By late 1985, Cirque was becoming a permanent showcase for circus arts. It had nearly eighty full-time employees and a hundred part-time employees, and a $3 million budget with more than half coming from government subsidies. The bulk of this support came from the Quebec Ministry of Culture (Chodan 1989).[14]

As Cirque du Soleil started expanding its geographic coverage and touring outside Quebec to cities across Canada, it faced the challenge of conveying a new brand of "circus" to an unfamiliar market. By the end of 1985, a plan was developed to "translate" Cirque's message to a nonfrancophone audience (David 2007). To ensure that the marketing was in sync with the company's overall vision, everything from the posters to the press releases were done in-house.[15] Accordingly, the costs for marketing were high and accounted for over 10 per cent of Cirque's budget. As Cirque ran a deficit in 1985, government funding was instrumental in enabling the company to launch this extensive promotional endeavour (Chodan 1989).

In 1986 Cirque's audience continued to grow across the country, and it was invited to perform at Expo 86 in Vancouver. According to a former vice-president of marketing and communications, "When we came back to Toronto, we sold out. We also achieved one of our goals, which was to be recognized as a national institution" (qtd in Dunn 1993, F3). Its status as a "national institution" enabled Cirque to begin leveraging support from corporate sponsors. Government subsidies were still significant in this period but now covered only one quarter of the budget, with Cirque's own ticket sales and modest private-sector contributions making up the balance (Enchin 1986).

A turning point for Cirque – and for its relations with the provincial government – came in 1987, when the company embarked on its first tour in the United States. Its foray into the US market began with an invitation to perform the opening show at the Los Angeles Arts Festival. The company took a risk in mounting this show because it only had the money to get to Los Angeles.[16] Cirque du Soleil was counting on its ability to raise the necessary funds to return home on its tour. In this case, an early critical decision reverberated throughout the firm's history, shifting it along a particular path. The show received positive reviews in the media and was followed by shows in other cities in California. While the risks of entering a foreign market were high, so were the opportunities. The company could extend its touring season since parts of the United States had a warmer climate than Canada.

Success in the United States also solidified Cirque du Soleil's reputation and credibility at home and abroad. As the former vice-president of marketing and communications explained: "The day we went to Los Angeles changed everything. We became international, an icon for part of the Canadian culture" (interview, December 2008). By this time, government subsidies constituted only 17 per cent of the budget (Enchin 1986, B1). Cirque had restructured its organization such that part of the company would remain nonprofit, while another part would become a "tax-sheltered investment instrument" (Enchin 1986, B1). Beyond the subsidies, however, Cirque benefited from its ability to access Quebec and Canadian government officials abroad in its expansion into foreign markets. These officials acted as intermediaries for the circus company by providing information on local market trends and business contacts (David 2007).

Overall, Cirque du Soleil had grown less reliant on direct government support by the late 1980s, and this path became self-reinforcing over time. Its private wing continued to grow as the company expanded into new markets, recruited new talent, and acquired technological innovations. The firm also developed its logistics division and entered into fields such as merchandising and music distribution. In terms of its relation with government, Cirque du Soleil was now claiming that, by the late 1980s, it was the government that wanted to retain a connection to the company. As the former vice-president of marketing and communications asserts: "We were a market for something very particular ... so they [the different levels of government] all wanted to be associated with us" (interview, December 2008). That the government increasingly viewed Cirque du Soleil as a means to extend government influence and appeal was also apparent in statements made by representatives from the provincial Ministry of Cultural Affairs. As the former minister Lise Bacon commented regarding Cirque's success abroad: "We – the Quebec government – have to maintain a link with them, if only to remind them of their responsibilities from time to time" (qtd in Drainie 1989, C3). For this reason, government continued to provide direct, yet modest, subsidies to Cirque du Soleil for several years after the company had became a global corporation.[17]

Provincial support for the Montreal circus arts milieu

While the story above highlights how Cirque's rise and evolution has benefited from direct government support, *indirect* government support, in the form of support given to the broader Montreal circus arts milieu and, most notably, the École nationale de cirque and the local circus arts trade association En Piste, also figures centrally in this narrative and illustrates the role of place-based institutions in shaping path creation *and* path development/institutionalization.

The École nationale de cirque had its origins in 1981, when it functioned as a training program for potential circus performers and operated out of a community centre (Chodan 1986). Over time, the program expanded its circus arts and academic training and became accredited as a school. It also attained nonprofit status through its association with the community centre and, due to the growth in popularity of the circus arts by the mid-1980s, was able to secure a grant from the Quebec Ministry of Cultural Affairs. This grant enabled the school to further develop its programs and leverage support from other levels of government to acquire a new space. The school eventually gain recognition as an accredited college specialized in circus arts training, which made it eligible for funding from the Quebec Ministry of Education.[18] Today, the school is the only one of its kind in North America and one of the few in existence worldwide. It is internationally renowned, with many of the school's students winning international competitions and several of its graduates establishing well-known circus troupes (Maser 1992).[19]

Since the official founding of Cirque du Soleil in 1984, the relations between the company and the École nationale de cirque have been close, and the school has contributed to Cirque's evolution in five distinct ways. First, the school has been an important source of skilled labour for the company. In Cirque's early years, when the founder of the school was also the artistic creator of Cirque, the vast majority (nearly 80 per cent) of Cirque performers came from the school (Morton 1988). Today, as Cirque has the means to recruit performers internationally, this number has declined significantly but it still remains a source. Cirque continues to conduct annual auditions of the graduating class at the school.[20]

The school has also helped to meet Cirque's labour market needs in two other ways. It mediates the risks for potential circus performers by providing them not only with circus training but also with a college diploma. The significance of this was expressed by a former director of the school in the following way: "The school is a place where you are coming to realize your dreams. And at the same time, I was looking to get a CEGEP diploma.[21] This was very important for me, morally speaking. Because if you don't have [a piece of] paper from a school, you don't have any value. Secondly, it is the fact that we are in the business where accidents can happen quite often and quite fast. So, if you are hurt and you aren't capable to keep on with your profession, you are stuck" (interview, June 2008). The school also provides special training programs for Cirque's employees. These programs function as a form of continuing education and allow existing employees to hone their skills or learn new ones (Fitterman 1989).[22]

Apart from its role in cultivating qualified circus arts performers, the school has benefited Cirque du Soleil in the past by providing it with a space to store equipment or hold practice sessions and rehearsals. The use of this space was particularly significant in the early years when this kind of infrastructure was cost-prohibitive for Cirque, since the company was only rehearsing in the winter and performing in the summer.[23]

In addition, Cirque occasionally tests out new productions at the school. One circus performer and graduate recalled: "In my third year at circus school, before they came out with the Beatles Love show, the creator of the show came to our school and did a one-week workshop with us. He tried out ideas" (interview, June 2009).

Finally, Cirque du Soleil has benefited from the cultural and institutional capital offered by the school. As mentioned above, by operating as an accredited training institution that awards a diploma, the school confers legitimacy on circus arts performers and on the circus arts field more generally as a professional discipline. It accords value to circus arts activities and, by extension, to Cirque as an artistic – as well as a commercial – enterprise.

Thus, government support has been critical to the school, and the school has played a central role in Cirque's evolution. However, it is also the case that the school has expanded in line with the growing needs of Cirque du Soleil and other circus troupes in the city, and therefore the school is a spillover effect as well. Although Cirque has become less dependent on the school over time, the relation continues to be a symbiotic one.

Another important element of the Montreal circus arts milieu that has contributed to a process of institutionalization is En Piste. This association was founded in 1996 as means to bring together members of the circus arts community to discuss the state of their milieu. At first it catered to individual performers, but over time it expanded its orientation to include creators, trainers, circus troupes, and learning institutions. This expansion was hastened by funding from SODEC, a para-public agency set up by the provincial government.[24] Today, En Piste provides members with news about the local milieu and the broader market through a catalogue, newsletter, and website. It also acts as a lobbying group for the circus field to leverage greater recognition and support from the different levels of government. Other services include an annual national arts forum, continuing education courses, workshops on relevant issues (e.g., security or marketing), and a calendar of circus events (www.enpiste.com). While Cirque du Soleil can now acquire many of these services on its own, the company still benefits from the networking and information exchange that is facilitated by the association. Cirque also profits from the wider acknowledgment and respect for the circus arts that the association has secured, such as the official designation of circus as an art form by the provincial Conseil des Arts et des lettres du Québec in 2001.[25]

Conclusion

Cirque du Soleil is one of Canada's best known exports. Its production system spans transnational space, with ownership, labour, funding, revenues, and production sites stretching across the globe. Despite its transnational networks, we argue that the company's evolution has been a *place*-dependent process and has relied on geographically and historically specific resources tied to the Montreal region. Specific spatial attributes and structures that have contributed to the company's rise include the high levels of urban density characteristic of Montreal and the diversity of the local economy, particularly in the arts and culture. Cirque du Soleil has benefited from a myriad of festivals and a vibrant street culture that further increase the temporary density of the city and foster an open, risk-taking environment. A lack of tradition in the circus arts also helped the firm to break free of traditional conventions, to experiment and recombine insights from different art forms.

These local synergies allow for the possibility of new cultural forms. However, following Martin and Sunley (2006), the case of Cirque du Soleil illustrates how the creation of a new path to development was related to the purposive action of agents who mobilized change by giving meaning to and enabling nascent synergies. Since its inception, Cirque has benefited from the support of a series of institutions that have helped to actualize novel ideas and impulses. Particularly important here is the strong historical support of the provincial government. Motivated by Quebec nationalism and more recently a desire to construct transnational, multicultural, and cosmopolitan connectivity for the city's business elite, government support has been critical to Cirque's success. Schools and trade associations have also played a key role in connecting actors and resources. As we've seen, these institutions have lent financial support, reinforcing positive spin-offs in the local economy. Institutional support has also offset some of the risks associated with creating novel products, genres, and processes. Moreover, educational programs and government support have served to validate the circus as an emergent art form. In this way, purposive action on the part of state actors has been central to Cirque's evolution and to facilitating the mobilization of local resources.

While ties to the local region are arguably less important today than in the past, they remain significant. Most of the creative direction is provided by local talent, and the company continues to draw on synergies with other cultural fields in Montreal. These ties, in turn, are a testament to the significance of place for the institutionalization of the company.

By demonstrating how a new brand of circus arts was created through the coming together (in time and place) of a number of place-based assets and highlighting the role of government in cultivating a cultural and political milieu in which Cirque du Soleil could mobilize such assets, our study substantiates recent evolutionary thinking on the need to integrate geography and agency into historical accounts of economic development (Martin and Sunley 2006), underscoring the need for a path- *and* place-dependent approach to better understand the evolution of firms and industries. The case of Cirque also corroborates the views of cultural economy scholars who see a role for policy in linking up localized cultural resources (Mommaas 2004; Scott 2004). Such policy must be informed by a thorough knowledge of existing localized assets and skill sets and must strive toward a creative recombination of such competencies. It requires an acknowledgment of how history and place matter for future prospects, and a view of history as "made" rather than simply "inherited." By adopting a historicized and spatialized account of economic evolution, we can read the story of Cirque du Soleil as having transpired from a mélange of local synergies, explaining why this global firm represents a place-based phenomenon.

CHAPTER 14

Introducing Decision Training into an Elite Circus Arts Training Program

Sylvain Lafortune, Jon Burtt, and Patrice Aubertin

The objective of this study was to introduce Decision Training on a trial basis into the elite circus arts training program at the École nationale de cirque de Montréal (National Circus School). We wanted to document qualitatively how the use of this approach, developed for sports, affected the work of teachers, particularly regarding goal setting, choice of teaching strategies, assessment of students' progress, and teacher/student rapport. The chapter begins by briefly presenting the motives behind this study, followed by an overview of the learning activities practised in circus art training, the characteristics of Decision Training as a sports training approach, and the methodology used to meet our research objectives. We then present the findings specific to each teacher/student team and summarize our interpretation of those findings as a whole.

Background

Since the emergence of new circus in the 1970s and contemporary circus in the 1990s, demands on circus artists have evolved in complexity. Circus artists are still expected to excel in one or several circus disciplines (e.g., trapeze, juggling, hand balance), but it has become customary for them to dance, act, sing, or play a musical instrument as well. For many circus performers, technical skills have become a means to serve a larger aesthetic goal (Cordier and Salaméro 2012). Today's circus artists are expected to be not only performers but creators, capable of proposing ideas as much as following directions. They should be able to create their own projects or join collective ones, adapt to different working contexts, embrace different creative methods, and express their opinions with eloquence while remaining open to hearing those of others. They should show initiative, autonomy, discipline, responsibility, and creativity (FEDEC 2009).

Therefore, the elite circus arts training programs must not only impart technical and artistic skills but also develop in students additional competencies that are essential in today's professional milieu. For us, the concept of self-regulation, used in the context of motor learning by Behncke (2002), Jonker, Elferink-Gemser, and Visscher (2010), and Kermarrec (2004), sums up the competencies now valued in a professional circus artist: the capacity to establish personal goals; to plan and implement the means to attain them (alone or with the help of external resources); to make a fair evaluation of the results; and to identify problems and apply solutions.

But what is involved in circus students becoming professional artists beyond the usual technical and artistic considerations? In general, circus training tends to replicate sports approaches, which are often characterized as behaviourist. As Vickers (2007) puts it in her description of behaviourist training approaches, "In order to become proficient in a motor skill, a close association must be fostered between a specific stimulus and response through extensive repetition" (163). In that sense, emphasis is usually placed on learning physical behaviours without much consideration of the mental processes that produce such behaviour. Traditional training often consists of blocked practice whereby skills are acquired separately through a progression, from the basic to the complex, under the strict control of a trainer who directs, evaluates, corrects, and motivates the student. In this context, feedback from the coach is given "as soon after performance as possible, as often as possible, and in such a way as to reduce performance errors as efficiently as possible" (Lee, Swinnen, and Serrien 1994, 332). In the process, the learner becomes dependent on such feedback.

For Chambers and Vickers (2006), this behaviourist training approach is often reinforced by studies that fail "to test a critical characteristic of learning, namely the relatively permanent change in athlete performance over time" (185). For athletes who followed a traditional training method (behaviour based, organized in block practices, heavily dependent on the trainer), performance tends to stagnate or even regress after some time. In contrast, athletes who train with variable practices and play a role in the analysis, evaluation, and correction of their own performance obtain better long-term results, which are attributable to the cognitive efforts of the athlete (Chambers and Vickers 2006). Ericsson (2008) argues that expertise does not automatically develop from extensive repetition or even experience;

rather, "superior performance requires the acquisition of complex integrated systems of representations for the execution, monitoring, planning, and analyses of performance" (993). Thus we see that the athlete must be mentally as well as physically engaged in deliberate practice during his or her training to fully benefit from the lessons provided (Ericsson 2008).

Taking a step closer to circus, research in dance confirms the importance of cognitive engagement while learning choreography, a factor often underestimated by practitioners who tend to value intuition (Lafortune 2010). Training in dance, as in circus, is primarily delivered by teachers from the field who rarely focus on the understanding of cognitive processes involved in performing or on the explicit development of cognitive skills required in practice.

It was this lack of focus on training the cognitive processes involved in practice and performance in the circus arts that prompted us to investigate Decision Training, a sports training approach developed by Dr Joan Vickers that is designed to develop athletes' cognitive skills along with their motor skills. Decision Training encourages students to take ownership of their learning process by asking them to make choices before, during, and after a performance, to form and share their insights, and to reflect on their processes through dialogue. Such skills promise long-term benefits for future circus artists not only by improving their performances but also by preparing students to take charge of their careers. Thus it seemed of interest to introduce Decision Training to a group of circus teachers at the École nationale de cirque and to invite them to integrate this approach into their practice. We wanted to study how its use affected their teaching and how they evaluated the pertinence of using this sports approach in the context of circus arts training.

Before we look at the components of Decision Training and how it was applied in this study, let us first review the circus training process itself. All École nationale de cirque students must demonstrate, through the periodical public presentation of an original circus number, the state of their artistic and technical progress. The purpose of this activity is to familiarize students with the presence of spectators and performance conditions, a goal that cannot be achieved any other way. The composition and presentation of a circus number is therefore an important pedagogical project around which most of a student's learning is centred. Here we introduce the different learning activities at the school according to their pedagogical goals to familiarize the reader with these practices.

Learning Activities in Circus Training

Activities in a circus discipline training class can be divided into two categories: activities oriented toward physical fitness, and activities oriented toward disciplinary skills. In the first category, exercises focus on developing the physical characteristics necessary to perform circus arts (e.g., upper body strength, flexibility, speed, endurance, balance). General fitness is required of all students, but there is also a fitness requirement specific to each discipline (e.g., aerials, acrobatics, juggling). A fair amount of class time is therefore spent on getting the students into the physical condition required by their chosen discipline, particularly at the beginning of their training but also throughout their program. The rest of the class time is dedicated to disciplinary skills, exercises that are further divided into three categories: acquisition of movement vocabulary, composition of a number, and interpretation of that number.

The acquisition of movement vocabulary constitutes the foundation of any circus discipline. Students must learn and memorize a growing number of known figures and master their execution. Additionally, part of the work consists of exploring and expanding this vocabulary, either by inventing new figures or by discovering variations on existing ones. It is these figures, known or invented, that become the material students will use to create their own compositions.

Compositional exercises entail selecting learned figures that will show off the student's strengths. Students must also order these figures in a sequence that will take into consideration technical constraints, endurance, and artistic choices. The student must then connect each figure by composing transitions that demand technical skill and artistic sensibility.

Finally, once the structure of the number is composed and its execution memorized and mastered, attention must be given to the exploration of its expressive potential: the interpretation of the number. At this stage, students have the opportunity to make qualitative choices in support of their artistic project. For example, the same sequence of movements can be executed either with a percussive quality (resulting in an energizing effect) or with a fluid quality (resulting in a soothing effect).

Learning how to choose what movements to perform, in what order, and with which quality are all part of the training at the École nationale de cirque and get dedicated class time. The exercises that serve this purpose require important cognitive skills. In regard to the present study, Decision

Training showed promise as a means for students to develop the cognitive skills needed for these activities as well as to evaluate and correct their own performances for better long-term results.

Decision Training: Three-Step Model

Vickers's Decision Training model for the development of cognitive skills in athletes occurs in three phases: the coach (1) determines which cognitive skill the athlete needs to develop in order to meet the challenges of competitive disciplinary performance; (2) designs specific exercises to develop that skill; and (3) employs specific Decision Training tools to further train the student's cognitive skill so as to gradually transfer the operations of analyzing, evaluating, and correcting the performance to the athlete.

Step 1: Determining cognitive skills. Based on observation and expertise in the disciplinary practices, the coach identifies one (or more) of seven cognitive skills an athlete needs to work on to improve his or her performance during competition:

- anticipation: to predict, from available information, what will occur during performance and to prepare for it
- attention: to select the most useful information before and during performance
- focus and concentration: to screen out irrelevant events and attend to salient ones for an extended period of time
- pattern recognition: to discern meaningful information, usually tactical, while moving in a complex environment
- memory retrieval: to choose, according to the changing needs of a situation, the best solution from those learned
- problem-solving: to reach the stated goal when no obvious solution is available
- decision-making: to make an effective choice among a set of alternatives

Step 2: Designing exercises. Once the cognitive skills to be trained are identified, the coach designs specific exercises to drill each one. For each exercise, the trainer and the athlete agree on a mental action that will act as a trigger to focus the attention while performing. Decision Training proposes the use of seven types of triggers, or cues, to ensure that the correct mental action is explicitly named and performed at the correct moment:

- object cues: to focus the attention on an object

- location cues: to focus the attention on a location or target area
- quiet-eye cues: a particular form of gaze behaviour that is located on a specific location or object in the visuomotor workspace within 3 degrees of visual angle (or less) for a minimum of 100 milliseconds
- memory cues: to retrieve on demand a specific solution learned from training
- reaction-time cues: to switch between skills under a time constraint, at the coach's command or any other external stimuli
- kinesthetic cues: to focus the attention on a sensation
- self-coaching cues: to make decisions on how to train based on the athlete's own assessment of the stated goal, the obstacles to overcome, and the plan needed to succeed

Step 3: Using Decision Training tools. The coach uses pedagogical tools that will stimulate the athlete's conscious and deliberate participation in the perception, analysis, evaluation, and correction of his or her own performance. Decision Training proposes seven such tools:

- variable practice: to change the context in which the same movement is performed. For example, it is possible to make a movement at a different speed or height, to make it precede or follow different moves or, in a more artistic context, to transform its quality.
- random practice: to destabilize the athlete with unexpected events that force quick adjustments. That may mean to change directives without warning, maybe even during performance, or to add or subtract constraints. Improvisation, widely use in performing arts, would fit into this category.
- bandwidth feedback: to give feedback only when necessary. The notion of bandwidth identifies a zone in which the athlete's performance is assessed as acceptable by the coach (Vickers 2003, 2007; Magill 2007). When this is the case, the coach should gradually diminish, delay, or even withhold feedback and give the athlete the opportunity to self-analyze, self-evaluate, and self-correct. The notion of bandwidth stretches with the athlete's progress: as the rate and range of success increases, the coach's feedback diminishes.
- questioning: to raise the athlete's own awareness through precisely directed questions and bring the athlete to share explicitly his or her perception, analysis, and evaluation of what happened while

performing. Questioning is designed to fill the sometimes uncomfortable silences that can occur when using bandwidth feedback.
- video feedback: to show the athlete images of his or her own performance. As with bandwidth feedback, the analysis and evaluation of the video images should gradually be transferred to the athlete. Questioning too can be useful while using video feedback.
- hard-first and modelling: to expose the athlete to the complexity of the disciplinary practice even if the athlete hasn't yet acquired basic skills. In circus training, for example, hard-first may mean to expose novices to the complexity of public presentations usually reserved for more advanced students. When safety is an issue, this exposure to complexity can be attained through modelling whereby the student observes live or videotaped high-level performances.
- external focus of instruction: to direct the attention of the athlete toward the outcome of actions instead of toward the production of the actions themselves. This last tool refers to a natural motor control system (Beilock et al. 2004; Duke, Davis Cash, and Allen 2011; McNevin, Shea, and Wulf 2003; Wulf 2007) that produces sequences of actions more fluidly and effectively when the athlete does not try to consciously control them.

Table 14.1 gives a schematic presentation of the three-step approach of Decision Training and of the elements that compose each step, as proposed by Vickers (2007). This approach formed the theoretical framework for our project.

The Research Methodology

The objective of this study was to introduce Decision Training on a trial basis in the elite circus arts training program at the École nationale de cirque de Montréal and to document its effects on teaching strategies over the course of a school year. Our approach was qualitative since we wanted to understand how a selected number of teachers were subjectively affected by the experience, as opposed to quantitatively measuring the outcome of their behaviour – for example, measuring how a certain intervention improved the speed or accuracy of a particular motor action of a trainee.

Because we wanted to implement changes in teachers' behaviour and understand how these changes affected their teaching experience, our methodology was inspired by an action research mode of inquiry. Contrary to more

Table 14.1
The three-step approach of Decision Training

Step 1	Determine cognitive skills to be trained	1. Anticipation 2. Attention 3. Focus and concentration 4. Pattern recognition 5. Memory retrieval 6. Problem-solving 7. Decision-making
Step 2	Design exercises to train the cognitive skill using cognitive triggers, or cues	1. Object cues 2. Location cues 3. Quiet-eye cues 4. Memory cues 5. Reaction-time cues 6. Kinesthetic cues 7. Self-coaching cues
Step 3	Use one or more Decision Training tools to train the cognitive skill	1. Variable practice 2. Random practice 3. Bandwidth feedback 4. Questioning 5. Video feedback 6. Hard-first and modelling 7. External focus of instruction

Source: Adapted from Vickers (2007), figure 9.2, 167.

traditional empirical studies that observe phenomena while trying not to disturb them, the essential aim of action research is to initiate changes in the modus operandi. For action research pioneers such as Lewin (1951) and Collier (1947), "major goals of action research were to create a change in practice and to develop or refine existing theory" (Holter and Schwartz-Barcott 1993, 299). Action research is used extensively in areas such as social advocacy, organizational change, and health services, and is also recognized as an effective tool in education (Noffke and Somekh 2009; Reason and Bradbury 2008).

Another aspect of action research that appealed to us is the collaboration of researchers and participants in the mutual understanding of the studied phenomena (Lavoie, Marquis, and Laurin 1996). Action research challenges traditional hierarchical relationships between the researchers and the researched. The relationships in action research are, in a sense, horizontal and take into account the human agency of the participants. As Bandura (2001) explains, "To be an agent is to intentionally make things happen by one's actions. Agency embodies the endowments, belief systems, self-regulatory capabilities and distributed structures and functions through which personal influence is exercised, rather than residing as a discrete entity in a particular place. The core features of agency enable people to play a part in their self-development, adaptation, and self-renewal with changing times" (2). There is a synergy between the idea of human agency prevalent in an action research methodology and the concepts of self-regulation and self-reflectiveness that Decision Training strives to develop in the trainee.

This kind of "co-operative inquiry," as Heron (1996) puts it, "is a form of participative, person-centered inquiry which does research *with* people not *on* them or *about* them. It breaks down the old paradigm separation between the roles of researcher and subject" (19). For his part, Stringer (2014) comments that action research is "phenomenological (focusing on people's actual lived experience or reality), interpretive (focusing on their interpretation of acts and activities), and hermeneutic (focusing on how people make meaning of events in their lives)" (37).

Action research methodology is iterative in that it consists of several cycles of data collection, analysis, and reflection, each cycle influencing how the next one is to be conducted (Lavoie, Marquis, and Laurin 1996). As Stringer (2014) explains, researchers and participants *collectively* ask, *What is happening now?* Then through a process of observation, interviews, and reflection, they ask, *How can we make what is happening now better?* This in turn prompts the planning of a new action.

Heron and Reason (2001) also talk about action research's "extended epistemology" in which "practical know-how" is of primary importance in "consummating" three forms of knowing – experiential, presentational, and propositional – that extend "beyond theory and academia" (183). Adopting the extended epistemology of action research in this project allowed the researchers to bring their extensive practical experience to bear. The research team's knowledge and understanding of the participants' needs and the inherent institutional constraints of the École nationale de cirque were based on prior knowledge combined with practical experience of working at the school and also in similar training environments. This practice-based body of knowledge encompasses dance, acrobatics, circus, learning and teaching, and sports science. In the action research model, having practice-based researchers doing the research creates the potential for real-world applications of research outcomes (Stringer 2014, 37). This means that research results may have transformative and practical potential. The researchers were therefore guided by a world view striving to balance agency with structure and informed by a specific body of practiced-based knowledge.

The Research Process

From the basis of action research as a mode of inquiry, we recruited three teacher/student teams to participate in this research. We used purposive sampling to provide an adequate representation of the varied student population at the École nationale de cirque (see table 14.2).

The inquiry occurred over the course of the 2011–12 school year at the École nationale de cirque de Montréal and was divided into cycles each lasting half a session (five to six weeks). In the first cycle, the participants were introduced to the basic principles behind Decision Training. During this preliminary period, the teachers first familiarized themselves with the seven Decision Training tools as described in step 3. At the end of this cycle, teachers assessed the strengths and weaknesses of their respective students and identified specific cognitive skills they wanted to train (step 1) in the context of this research. In subsequent cycles, their task was to design exercises (step 2) and choose those Decision Training tools most likely to contribute to the development of the chosen skill (step 3).

Both teachers and students were studied through observations, video recordings, interviews, and focus groups. Between cycles, a period of reflection and of theorization allowed the researchers and the teachers to acknowledge *what is happening now?* and to ask themselves *how can we make what is happening now better?* Together, the research team and the teachers planned a course of action for the following cycle, utilizing a dynamic relationship between the data collection and its analysis.

The data analysis of our observations and the verbatim transcripts of interviews (teachers and students) and focus groups (teachers only) provided

Table 14.2
Summary of the participants' profiles

	Teachers	Students
Team 1	Graduate studies in biomechanics and physiology of motor performance Completed teachers' training program at National Circus School Six years of experience as a circus arts teacher	Discipline: juggling with diabolo Previous training: self-taught plus other elite circus arts training programs Age: 19
Team 2	Trained in sports Master Learning Facilitator for Gymnastics Canada Forty years of experience as a sports trainer including 14 years as a circus arts teacher Familiar with Decision Training	Discipline: trampoline Previous training: community circus program Age: 19
Team 3	Trained in a professional circus school Extensive professional circus artist career Twenty years of experience as a circus arts teacher	Discipline: dance-trapeze Previous training: dance and rhythmic gymnastics Age: 19

some insights into how the use of Decision Training affected the work of teachers. It was clear early in the data collection that each teacher and student experienced the introduction of Decision Training from an individual perspective that was influenced by the personality and history of each person, by the work relationship that developed within each team, and by the context in which the teaching took place. Thus each team presented unique findings according to specific situations.

Findings

Team 1: Diabolo

14.1 Example of diabolo practice at the National Circus School

One element that distinguished the first team from the others was the high-level technical skill that the student demonstrated in his discipline, diabolo juggling, and the autonomy with which he worked and trained. In the first session, this organized student informed his teacher that he already had a comprehensive plan for his three years of training at the École nationale de cirque. His stated objective was not to improve on his technical skills (already excellent) but to use the resources of the school to develop an original artistic project. The teacher favoured a teaching philosophy that values autonomy and collaboration. He could not imagine imposing his objectives on a student by saying from the start, "I don't know you but by December, you have to do that that that." He added, "It's impossible for me to do that because [the students] have a certain [technical] level and they have also expectations." After discussions and negotiations, the two agreed on a plan: during class, the student would have some time to work on his own objectives, as stated in his three-year plan, but he would also work on technical skills and on movement quality, something his teacher wanted to explore with him.

After the first cycle, the teacher concluded that his student was working in a way that was too cerebral. In the number the student was composing, the teacher realized that "for each movement, he has a little story … If he turns the diabolo on the floor, he has a story: 'okay, it's like the fire and I observe and discover the fire.' And he's surprised and he's like an animal." The teacher felt that the student became so engrossed in his thoughts that it was difficult for him to consider additional information in the form of suggestions or feedback. At the public presentation of his number at the end of the first session, the student himself realized the limits of his approach: "On stage, I am still not alive. I am thinking about my things." The teacher wished that his student would focus more on the physical experience, on what was happening in the body, and stay connected to material references instead of conceptual ones. He wished his student had more spontaneity while working on composition and interpretation and wanted to make him understand, and feel, that movements can carry significance in and of themselves. For step 1, the teacher determined that *focus and concentration* were the cognitive skills he wanted to train in his student.

In step 2, to help his student stay focused on the movement experience and not be distracted by a cerebral approach, the teacher devised several exercises using object, location, or kinesthetic cues as triggers. For example, the teacher used improvisation to encourage more spontaneous reactions from the student and to make juggling a physical experience instead of a cerebral one. As the student reported, the goal of these exercises was "to put more consciousness on things we do not really think about. Because we are used to moving or doing things with the object by really disassociating the [object from] the body. [We now try] to incorporate the object to better understand what we can do with it." In step 3, the teacher was observed using multiple Decision Training tools including variable practice, random practice, bandwidth feedback, video feedback, and external focus of instruction.

Paradoxically, the high technical level and autonomy of the student appeared to prevent him from benefiting from certain learning experiences. The student's plan was so comprehensive that it left little room for other lessons the teacher felt necessary. The student himself reported his lack of open-mindedness: "We often have different points of view. I remember one time I was negative even before … Before he tells me something, I was already thinking 'Ah! What he's going to tell me is not right.' If I am able to say it now, it's that I realized it. When I realized it, [I told myself] 'Okay. Now, I am really going to listen to him and after, I am going to see how I react.' More often, the result at the end was the same. My point of view didn't change a lot with his."

This tension between the student's and the teacher's goals was exacerbated by the fact that the teacher, for the sake of this research, was experimenting with a pedagogical approach that was new to him. He reported, "Because it is a way of teaching I am not comfortable with, I think [my student] feels that. He feels I am not comfortable with some points, and maybe his confidence in me goes down." The student confirmed this impression: "I felt that [my teacher] was trying to figure out where we were going [with these exercises] at the same time as us. It didn't feel very efficient." One unintended consequence of this research seems to have been the negative impact on the teacher's performance and consequently on the student's confidence in him.

Despite these difficulties, the improvisation sessions left a strong impression on the student, who decided to include improvisation in his creative process and in his next public presentation. Indeed, improvisation became his new interest, as he admitted at the end of the study: "I would say that generally, I want to improvise more than people who are at school or the people who are in the world of circus on stage." This new approach is very different from the highly cerebral approach the student was using at the beginning of the school year, in which he tried to control every minute gesture by associating it with a mental image. Therefore, we can say the teacher succeeded in changing his student's working methods by bringing him closer to a more spontaneous process in the composition and interpretation of a circus number and by connecting his juggling to a more physical experience.

It is hard to determine which part of this change was specifically attributable to the use of Decision Training, but as the teacher declared in the last focus group, his participation in this research made him more aware of his teaching strategies and the rationale behind his choices. He discovered new pedagogical tools that would prove useful in the future, yet he also admitted having difficulties with changing some of his teaching habits. At ease with the idea of leaving his comfort zone, he felt that the introduction of new ways of teaching must be done in stages, in small doses, as to not lose all of his points of reference at once.

Team 2: Trampoline

In the second case study the student was learning trampoline, a discipline complementary to his disciplinary major of tumbling. This was particularly significant since the student didn't have the pressure to compose and present a trampoline number at the end of each session. Another particularity of team 2 was that the teacher was already familiar with Decision Training and had included some of its tools in his teaching before the start of this research.

After having spent some time working with his student, the teacher assessed that he had natural talent but that his progress would stall if he did not develop a better understanding of what his body was doing while performing and what actions must be done to perfect the more complex acrobatic figures. For his part, the student admitted that before arriving at the École nationale de cirque, he worked mostly intuitively, throwing himself into tricks without really knowing what he was doing. Therefore, in step 1, *attention* was the cognitive skill the teacher wanted him to develop. Specifically, he wanted his student to know which aspects of a figure were important to take into consideration: the push on the trampoline bed, the action sequence, the position of the head at certain key moments, and the body form.

To reach this goal, this teacher designed many step 2 exercises in which the student had to explicitly indicate when and where he was directing his

14.2 Example of trampoline practice at the National Circus School

attention with either location or kinesthetic cues. In other exercises, the student was deliberately placed in problematic situations that forced self-correction. For example, to augment the rotation of a salto (flip), the teacher asked the student to lower the height of his jump. With less airtime available, the student had to adjust by speeding up his rotation so as to land on his feet. Sometimes the teacher just let the student play on the trampoline, freely or under certain parameters, to encourage him to feel how the bed reacted to his push. For each exercise, the teacher trained the attention of the student by raising his awareness of the actions to do and his consciousness of those he actually did. In step 3, this teacher was observed using all the Decision Training tools.

Observations of team 2 revealed how well the teacher and the student understood each other. The teacher reported that as he broke down and analyzed the essential elements of acrobatic figures, the student became more able to do so himself: "He likes to have an extra point of view, but he likes to know how he feels and how he does it ... I kept saying 'remember the eyes' because he understands now where to look. I don't say when, now. I just say this [indicates two fingers to his eyes]." In many instances we observed the student describe to his teacher the objective of a new exercise and how he could apply lessons learned elsewhere. It became evident that the ability to describe the actions to be executed, to identify the mechanical principles at work, and to self-correct were natural strengths of this student. For the teacher, the use of bandwidth feedback was well suited to this student who demonstrated a genuine interest in analyzing and solving problems.

Through his use of Decision Training, the teacher therefore successfully developed his student's attention while performing. The student learned to break down complex figures into sequences of sub-objectives that, taken one at a time, could be more easily achieved – a method that he could apply to tackle any tricks. As the student explains, "You can do the trick because you know it and you know the small steps you need to do. Because you can think a lot and do a big trick or you cannot think as much and do a little trick. And every big trick is just several little tricks."

Concerning his participation in this research, the teacher welcomed the opportunity to review and deepen his understanding of Decision Training. In the past, he had used some of the tools informally, but in this context, he used them more systematically and deliberately. He now believes that there is an optimal order when using Decision Training tools. He proposes to start with variable practice and to follow with hard-first because human nature responds well to challenges if they are presented in the right progressive curve. Then, he would use modelling to build good references and to prevent bad habits from forming. Concerning feedback, he would start with questioning to show the student how to do analysis, and introduce bandwidth later to allow more space for reflection. Finally, he suggests using random practice only after the student has acquired basic coordination.

Team 3: Dance-trapeze

14.3 Example of trapeze practice at the National Circus School

Team 3, like the other pairs, possessed particularities that distinguished it from the other two. First, the student had been accepted into the École nationale de cirque in the Upgrade Program,[1] which required her to pass an audition in the middle of the second session to secure a place in the regular program the following year. This audition became the short-term priority for this student and her teacher. Another distinguishing characteristic of this team was the absence of a common language between them. The teacher spoke Russian and French; the student spoke English and understood some Russian, but couldn't speak it. Finally, this student had no previous experience in the circus discipline she had chosen, dance-trapeze, and while acquiring a movement vocabulary, she also had to develop a familiarity with the apparatus and the upper body strength necessary to perform an aerial discipline. For the teacher, these factors (upcoming audition, language problems, lack of experience) compounded the difficulties she had to deal with.

After a period of assessment, the teacher identified in her student a reluctance to take charge of her own learning process: "We have here a student who doesn't want to make decisions." This difficulty in making decisions manifested itself in many aspects of the student's work: at the start of a class, she waited for the teacher to arrive before beginning her warm-up (rather than taking the initiative to begin on her own); in her free time, she did not spend time on her trapeze to review what she had learned, to work on composition, or simply to develop familiarity with the apparatus; in analyzing her performance, she shared little information on what she perceived and how she felt about it; when facing problematic situations, she proposed few or no solutions. For step 1, the teacher identified *decision-making* as the most useful cognitive skill for this student to acquire at this point in her training.

In class, many exercises were dedicated to the acquisition of basic figures, to the creation of new ones, and to the composition of original movement sequences. To train her student in decision-making (step 2), the teacher often asked her to choose from a limited number of options such as "three different positions to be on the bar. You could be sitting, on the side, or lying." In another example, she directed her by saying: "You are standing, after that you are upside down and now, you play [between the two]." In these exercises, to make the student better understand how the trapeze and her body interacted, the teacher directed her attention using object and kinesthetic cues. In step 3, the Decision Training tools that were observed were variable practice, random practice (mostly improvisation exercises), questioning, video feedback, hard-first, and external focus of instruction. For the latter, the student's attention was directed toward musicality or interpretation, for example, away from the production of actions.

For the teacher, the difficulties her student was experiencing – when solving problems, when working on her own, or when sharing her opinion – were largely due to her lack of experience. "She's silent not because she's not independent or autonomous, but mostly because she doesn't have the movement vocabulary," the teacher reported. Later, concerning self-analysis, the teacher said, "She's not able to visualize her own body from the inside because she doesn't have experience."

For this teacher, the integration of Decision Training in her teaching practices was a challenging experience. Since she was asked to use pedagogical tools she was not familiar with, she felt her interventions were less sure and timely. Additionally, it was hard for her to discern whether her difficulties were due to her doubts and ineffectiveness or to this specific situation: teaching a student who showed little initiative in word and action, and mostly, working within a tight time frame with the audition imposing a short-term deadline. At the beginning of the second session, with the audition around the corner, the teacher chose to fall back on her usual strategies that had proven effective in the past.

Despite these difficulties, the teacher helped her student progress enough to pass the audition and to be accepted in the regular program of the École nationale de cirque the following year. In the last cycle of this research, the teacher noticed remarkable progress in her student's ability to solve problems, to train alone, and to make decisions concerning the composition and the interpretation of her number in preparation for the year-end presentation. However, she could not say if this progress can be attributed, principally or in part, to the use of Decision Training, to the relief of stress after a successful audition, or to the natural progression of this student at the École nationale de cirque.

From this teacher's perspective, Decision Training should not be used with novice students since one cannot expect a student who has no basic knowledge of her discipline and who comes from a very different environment (dance and rhythmic gymnastics in this case) to be able, from the start, to self-analyze her performance and to have opinions on the technical and artistic possibilities of her discipline. To her, Decision Training is "perfect for someone who already has an idea of what is possible with the apparatus ... But to use it in the first year caused delays [in the student's progression]." Nonetheless, the teacher still feels that she acquired new pedagogical tools during this research and foresees using them in the future with more advanced students.

Discussion

As previously stated, the introduction of Decision Training into the elite circus training program at the École nationale de cirque was not a uniform experience across the teacher/student teams. Nevertheless, our analysis identifies five factors affecting their experience: (1) the degree of familiarity of the teacher with Decision Training; (2) the technical level of the student; (3) the teaching and learning style of each individual; (4) the evaluation context; and (5) the support received by teachers for delivering Decision Training in their coaching.

1. *The degree of familiarity of the teacher with Decision Training* affected the ease of integrating this approach into teaching practices. One of the three teachers was more familiar with Decision Training than the others and had already used some of the proposed tools. For him, this experiment was less about discovering Decision Training and more about using it in a more systematic manner. This teacher didn't go through a period of discovery, adaptation, and appropriation, as did his colleagues, suggesting that it takes time to integrate a new teaching method and to become comfortable with its use.

2. *The technical level of the student* is another factor that seems relevant. One of the students was technically very advanced and arrived at the school with the intention of working on aspects of his discipline other than technique. This advanced student doubted the contributions his teacher could make to his training since the teacher was neither a diabolist nor a performer. This impression made him less open to his teacher's suggestions and proposed exercises. His skepticism makes it hard to evaluate the actual effectiveness of the teacher's interventions. For another student, it was the absence of basic disciplinary experience that seems to have been an obstacle since this lack of knowledge made it difficult for her to fully benefit from the pedagogical strategies her teacher was exploring.

3. *The learning style of each student* also affected how Decision Training was used, especially in the ability of students to self-analyze their per-

formance, a key element of this approach. For example, one student arrived at the school with a comprehensive work plan and preconceived ideas on how he wanted to work and what he wanted to work on. He did not participate in the bandwidth feedback sessions with an open mind, but rather mostly sought information that reinforced his beliefs. On the other end of the spectrum, another student who liked to analyze his performance tackled problem-solving with pleasure and used all the available feedback as an opportunity to deepen his understanding of his experience. And since this same student loved to talk, he gladly took part in bandwidth feedback and questioning sessions. Finally, a student who did not talk easily, for one reason or another, made bandwidth feedback sessions more problematic for her teacher because her silence was hard to decipher: was it due to a lack of opinion or to a difficulty with expressing her opinion?

The *teaching style* affected how the integration of new pedagogical tools happened in the classes. For example, one teacher who saw himself as a collaborator, open to the idea of pursuing goals stated by the student, easily adhered to a teaching paradigm promoting self-regulation. Moreover, because he perceived difficulties as welcomed opportunities to question his own practice, he willingly left his comfort zone to explore new pedagogical tools. Another teacher, for whom quality teaching is assessed by the long-term retention and transfer of information, had no problem adopting pedagogical tools that trained in his student abilities such as self-analysis, self-evaluation, and self-correction. Finally, a teacher who was rather directive during the training sessions felt a certain loss of control and found the use of a new approach to be a waste of time when it did not produce immediate results. Her reflex was then to fall back on old methods that had proven to be efficient in the past.

4. In each case study, the *context of the evaluation* had an important influence on how easily Decision Training was integrated in the training. Let us remember that public presentations play a big role in students' evaluations at the École nationale de cirque and create pressure to demonstrate short-term results. The two teachers whose students had to compose and present a circus number at the end of each session felt uneasy using a training approach that claimed to produce long-term results and with which they were not familiar. Changing one's teaching habits brings an inevitable period of uncertainties and adjustments during which the teacher feels less efficient than usual, an uncomfortable situation for one who is expected to deliver relatively quick results. In this study, one team didn't have to present a circus

number because the studied discipline was a complementary one for the student; this situation eliminated the pressure to show short-term results and gave freer opportunities to experiment.

5. *The support received by teachers* from the researchers also had an impact on their experience. It is important to note here that this list of factors affecting the experience of participants is based on data collected during our research, not on what should have happened according to Vickers's literature. It is possible that some of the challenges experienced by teachers and students alike were due in part to the researchers' lack of experience in testing an approach that was also new to them. During the study, the teachers were often puzzled by how to best integrate Decision Training in their teaching, how quickly and completely to change their teaching strategies, how to assess the adequacy of certain choices, how to read the reactions of the students, how to apply the researchers' directives, and how to transpose into the circus arts tools that were developed for sport. All these questions challenged the researchers as much as the participants. It was together, during individual meetings and focus groups, that solutions were proposed and discussed.

In the course of this study, we also realized that teachers at the École nationale de cirque already used many of the tools proposed in step 3 of Decision Training as a matter of course. For example, improvisation work is similar to the variable and random practices; frequent public presentations from the start of circus training are comparable to hard-first situations; modelling is omnipresent during the École nationale de cirque training, whether through observation of professional circus artists on stage or on video, or by the simple fact that students of all levels train together in the same room and often with the same teacher; and the importance of expressivity during presentations, beyond purely technical exposition, could be associated with the external focus of instruction. Through their participation in this study, the teachers were able, on the one hand, to examine the tools they were already using through the lens of Decision Training and, on the other hand, to identify and bring awareness to a range of cognitive skills that those tools were developing.

The teachers perceived this opportunity for reflection to be a major benefit of their participation in this research. They appreciated the occasion to examine their own practices, to become conscious of their habits, to share their doubts, to discuss the meaning of circus arts training, and to explore new approaches to teaching. One teacher said, "The fact I have to observe myself and my student and the relation between us ... and to put words on all of that, it's really stimulating for me." As for the students, they also appreciated sharing their experiences and reflections. One student mentioned how the interviews nourished his training by making him connect what happened in preceding classes with his work in subsequent classes. At the end of each interview, all participants showed continuing interest in this study.

Conclusions

The objective of this research was to document qualitatively how the introduction of Decision Training affected teaching practices in the context of an elite circus arts training program. The absence of quantitative measurements and a control group, and the small sample of participants made it impossible to assess the degree of success with which teachers employed Decision Training. With the data available, we cannot determine the exact contribution of this method to the students' progress. Is the apparent development in the students' cognitive skills attributable, in part or entirely, to the use of Decision Training, or does it follow the normal progression of first-year students at the École nationale de cirque? That question remains unanswered.

That said, the data collected does shed light on the personal experience of the teachers and students, and answers in part how they felt about changing their practice to include Decision Training. We found that adopting this new approach posed challenges for teachers who were inexperienced with it, reluctant to let go of personal teaching preferences, or working under time constraints. The appropriation of new teaching strategies was stimulating for them, but required a period of adjustment. Changing teaching habits produced doubts, hesitation, and awkwardness that lowered the quality of the teaching, at least temporarily, until new habits were developed. Teachers under pressure to deliver short-term results found it best not to radically change their teaching strategies but instead to improve on them with the gradual addition of new knowledge. At this point, because of the absence of a follow-up study, we cannot determine how permanent the changes in the teachers' practices were, despite their declared interest in using Decision Training in the future.

It is also clear from our study that the interpersonal dynamics of each teacher/student team was unique and that each learning situation evolved within its own parameters. It is essential to acknowledge the wide variation inherent in human relationships; in this case both teacher and student had to adapt to each other's teaching and learning style and use all means possible to maximize their working relationship. For both, this called upon the ability to question long-held beliefs and to reflect on the teaching and learning strategies usually employed. Considering the unique nature of each teaching situation, it may be inappropriate to recommend the systematic application of any training approach, as coherent and well-founded as it may seem.

We will also state that appropriate guidance is needed to support teachers through a harmonious transition from familiar teaching practices to new ones. If such changes in teaching practices were to be implemented, administrators need to consider the time it takes to change one's way of working. Professional development workshops, like the one-week, forty-hour course described by Vickers et al. (2004), could allow the necessary time and space for teachers to familiarize themselves with new training methods and to test them outside of the class framework, so as not to impede students' progress.

A benefit of the teachers' participation in this research was that they had access to new information. It is important to remember that most teachers at the École nationale de cirque come from the field, which tends to perpetuate traditional practices. Being introduced to an approach like Decision Training gave our participants access to rich theoretical content that opened new ways of considering teaching in general and their own practice in particular. This dialogue between theory and practice is still too rare in the circus field. With the emerging academic interest in circus practice, and vice versa, we can only wish to see this dialogue continue and expand.

Further, the teachers participating in this study enjoyed and welcomed the opportunity to discuss their work with colleagues and to share their reflections. Such exchanges should be encouraged and supervised in a formal setting to help teachers reflect not only on what to teach but on how to teach it – topics that they otherwise may not have the opportunity or inclination to discuss. This action research provided a forum for these important conversations.

As the founder of Decision Training, Joan Vickers (2007) admits that "during behavioural training, positive gains occur immediately" (163); hence its appeal to coaches. In a situation where short-term progress must be periodically demonstrated, a promising avenue may be a combination of approaches, one that is more direct and produces quicker results and one like Decision Training that reaches for long-term objectives. What proportion of interventions should be dedicated to one or the other approach? Should Decision Training be used only when students have acquired a basic understanding of their discipline? Is the use of Decision Training not appropriate when immediate results are required as when preparing for an audition or a show? All these questions were raised during this research and should be pursued in further investigations.

CHAPTER 15

Singular Bodies, Collective Dreams: Socially Engaged Circus Arts and the "Quebec Spring"

Jennifer Beth Spiegel

The spring of 2012 was a watershed moment in the social, political, and cultural history of Quebec, and it proved an unexpected time and venue for circus to emerge as a tool for social engagement – in a society that sees circus as a professionalized and high-performance art. Dubbed the "Quebec Spring,"[1] what began as a student movement against the provincial government's proposed 75 per cent tuition hikes rapidly transformed into a broad popular movement in defence of civil liberties[2] and against other proposed or realized cuts in social and public services.[3] The movement quickly reached historic proportions, with nightly marches and mass gatherings sometimes reaching up to 400,000 protestors (Cox 2012). Daily, for over a month, protests made front pages of nearly every provincial newspaper. The sounds of police sirens and media helicopters mixed with the banging of the protestors' pots and pans or "casseroles"[4] to create Montreal's nightly urban soundtrack. Throughout the six months of this student-strike-turned-popular-movement, street arts formed an integral component of the protests. Protestors were frequently seen stilt-walking during the demonstrations. Jugglers and clowns were particularly visible during the various daytime solidarity events in the parks, called "family days," as well as during the larger daytime marches, when parents brought children to join the protests. As we will see, these artistic activists drew from the growing circus culture of Quebec, seeking to offer a welcoming and festive sense to often heavily policed street protests, while a group of professional circus artists formed under the banner En Feu Contre La Hausse (On Fire against the Tuition Hike) with the intention of holding a fundraising show in early September.

The proliferation of circus-inspired, political street theatre during those 2012 street protests brought to the surface the questions of what role circus artists play in the changing sociopolitical landscape of Quebec, and what the implications are for cultures of artistic citizenship. My research suggests that these influential forms and impulses did not begin with the protests of 2012, and in fact drew from a little-known history of activist circus in Quebec. This chapter begins by pointing to that early contemporary activist circus, or what I call *cirque engagé*, highlighting the interrelated histories of professional, social, and alternative circus initiatives in the province. It then offers a more substantial genealogy of activist circus in both a global and local context, demonstrating that the performers' ways of "doing and making" (Rancière 2004, 13) directly related to the sociopolitical conditions in which they operated. This contextualization will enable us grasp more fully how the Quebec Spring became a scene for augmenting, rallying, and otherwise informing the various social currents within the circus community; that is, we will come to understand the significance of this sociopolitical moment for Quebec's circus scene. The final section of this chapter details some of the new ethical and aesthetic movements happening within socially engaged circus in Montreal following this heightened moment of civic engagement.

Cirque Engagé and the Changing Ethico-Aesthetics of Quebec's Circus Ecology

Quebec's Quiet Revolution throughout the 1960s famously sparked a popular, economic, and political commitment to the protection and expansion of Québécois culture and its expressions. In this mobilization for a strong, secular, francophone culture, the provincial government committed to funding the growth of local arts and promised affordable education to help the predominantly working-class francophone population rise from economic precarity to positions of leadership in society.[5] This was an era that coincided with growing antiwar demonstrations and other student-led mobilizations elsewhere in the world. It was also a period in which late avant-garde performance traditions found their way into protest politics in what has been dubbed by many as "new social movements" (Harding 2000; Kershaw 1997; Plant 1992; Sell 2011) with highly theatrical and media-savvy tactics.

Across North America and Europe, protests became punctuated by, and at times were indistinguishable from, a particular genre of street theatre led by such groups as the Yippies, the Bread and Puppet Theater, and the Living Theater, as well as the political "happenings" like those of Kaprow and Lebel (Brown et al. 1968; Kershaw 1997; Sell 2008). Such cultural and artistic transformations informed the development of a new physical, irreverent theatre, oriented toward collective creation and engaged with the sociopolitics of the day. This new sense of what theatre was and could do began to proliferate through groups in Quebec such as Théâtre Euh! and Grand Cirque Ordinaire, key players in the period immediately preceding the creation of the *nouveau cirque québécois*. Founded in 1970, Théâtre Euh! was known especially for its political clowning and commitment to professional-level performance while working closely with local communities (Sigouin 1982). Grand Cirque Ordinaire, formed in 1969, was known for shows that explored Quebec's new-found liberation from implicit and explicit forms of censorship (Cloutier 1979); this new company was deeply influenced by the US-based political street theatre collective Bread and Puppet Theater. A few years later, Quebec street performer Carmen Ruest met stilt-walker Gilles Ste-Croix while they were working with Bread and Puppet in Vermont. They would draw on their work there when they helped found Cirque du Soleil (Calamia 2013), which would soon flourish with the aid of the provincial support that had been promised during the Quiet Revolution (see Leslie and Rantisi, this volume).

This era of intense transformation in "artistic citizenship" (Campbell and Martin 2006) was thus marked by profound changes in the ethical and aesthetic configurations of global and local circus scenes. In the eighteenth and nineteenth centuries, at the height of traditional circus in the era of late-colonial industrialism, an ethic of the triumphant individual had exalted the ingenuity and capacities of the worldly human body, extolling the exceptional nature of the individual performer and individual performances (Stoddart 2000). The aesthetics of the *nouveau* or contemporary circus, however, formed in the later decades of the twentieth century, point not (only) to individual possibilities and capacities but (also) to the power and potential of the collective. In this era of change, circus performers began to be presented not as oddities, but as inspiring individuals whom spectators may wish to emulate. Even as the forms of contemporary circus, seen through the work of Cirque du Soleil and the contemporary practices it has inspired, hinge to a large extent on the exceptional body (Graver 2005;

Hurley 2008; Leroux 2012), the singular, expressive, and awe-inspiring bodies of the performers gesture toward a collective imaginary (Gagnon, qtd in Hurley 2008, 137). These new acts, which feature clowns, other-worldly aerialists, and even "ordinary" naive and childlike characters who wander into the world of dreams suggested by these circus productions, work to bring their audiences along to be transported and transformed by the possibilities opened on the onstage world (Hurley 2008).

A vibrant "alternative circus" (Hill 2004) scene also emerged alongside this developing international circuit of professional, contemporary circus companies. With roots that stretch back to at least the 1970s, this alternative circus grew in the 1990s as part of the popular, populist, street arts, "do it yourself" culture. As Hill (2004) points out, the alternative, ground-up, marginal circus arts may have more in common with the older tradition of travelling gypsy shows than with the contemporary commercial circus, which tends to draw on high-performance athletics and high-art aesthetic codes. Yet the growth of this alternative circus could only have occurred in tandem with a growing contemporary professional circus (Hill 2004, xii); indeed, this alternative circus could only be distinguished from the professionalized circus once a circus industry developed in which nouveau cirque shows could be sold to mass audiences. By 2001, many of Quebec's alternative circus artists (many of whom worked with Cirque du Soleil's Cirque du Monde on social circus models described later in this chapter), having assimilated the values of collective creation and committed to developing a nonhierarchical and inclusive model of circus arts, came together to create a nonprofit organization called Carmagnole Productions. The company, which organizes multiple cabarets throughout the year, is best known for Carnival Carmagnole held in August in rural Quebec. (Since 2012, the carnival has been held in an outdoor venue in Saint-Charles-sur-Richelieu.) Featuring over sixty volunteer artists, many of some renown, the festival continues to this day as a social experiment in collective creation, and has been the birth place of many other cabarets, collectives, and events, including Cirque Alkimic, Les Érotisseries, and the neighbourhood festival Fêtes du Parc.

Within the alternative circus scene, themes tend to be gritty, sometimes controversial, often plebian, dramatized by the raw energy emanating from the performers. The artists and acts developed here have not infrequently been recruited by larger circus companies or have led to the development of new major circus companies with significant commercial success. For instance, Cirque du Soleil, itself founded by street artists before it followed a more resolutely corporate route, has occasionally hired members of alternative circuses, such as San Francisco's Mystic Family Circus, to animate opening parties and even to perform in main-stage productions; some of the Family's temple dancers were featured, for example, in Cirque du Soleil's production of *Zumanity* (Hill 2004, 105). This professionalization of alternative circus initiatives can also be seen when the alternative collectives take on a professional status after years of experience, or their members pursue full-time careers in the circus. In Montreal, for example, self-trained artists frequently perform and train alongside formally educated circus artists at venues like La Caserne, a community centre specializing in circus. Heavily subsidized and located in Montreal's low-income neighbourhood Hochelaga, La Caserne provides affordable training space during the day for professional, semi-professional, and high-level amateur circus artists. In the evening, affordable, subsidized classes are offered at a recreational level, typically taught by some of those artists training during the day. Some of these artists are graduates of Montreal's elite École nationale de cirque, while others are active members of Montreal's alternative scene. Of the latter group, many received their own initial training in Quebec's social circus programs, largely offered by Cirque du Monde, one of Cirque du Soleil's major social action initiatives.

With a goal of fostering social inclusion, Cirque du Monde was founded in 1995 as a collaboration between Cirque du Soleil and Jeunesse du Monde. By 2014 it was functioning in over eighty communities in twenty-five countries worldwide and partnering with a range of organizations providing educational, social intervention services to youth living in precarious situations.[6] According to the social circus web page of Cirque du Soleil, the aim of Cirque du Monde is to "help these young people get their self-confidence back, make them realize their strengths and discover their hidden talents."[7] This educational arts model bears many similarities to that of Augusto Boal's famous "theatre of the oppressed," as the ideas and themes for shows are typically selected and shaped by the participant-performers (Spiegel 2013), and the choreography is derived largely from games played during social circus sessions.

Montreal was among the original sites of Cirque du Monde projects (along with Brazil). In 1995 La Caserne's then-dilapidated gym was repurposed for circus activities to become the first Montreal site for Cirque du Monde, when Paul Vachon of Cirque du Soleil rallied some youth in the streets and, in partnership with local social service organizations, created a space of creative expression through circus training.[8] Since 1995, social circus has expanded throughout Quebec with sites in Drummondville, Quebec City, Sherbooke, Manawan, Wemotaki, Victoriaville, and Baie St Paul. In 2011, Montreal's site became an autonomous NGO – the first such organization in Canada to be dedicated entirely to social circus – and took on the name Cirque Hors Piste. In addition to funds from Cirque du Soleil's Citizenship and Social Action Division (under which Cirque du Monde operates), Cirque Hors Piste receives support from the municipal government, Emploi Québec, and various social service organizations serving those living or working in the streets of downtown Montreal. Many of the alumni of these Cirque du Monde / Cirque Hors Piste programs have returned as social and recreational circus instructors at La Caserne and at social circus sites in Quebec and around the world.[9]

As with many community outreach initiatives, Cirque du Monde embodies the complexities of a program that seeks to cultivate social equity, solidarity, and alternative visions even as it is a product of the highly capitalized Cirque du Soleil (Leroux 2012)[10] although the majority of funding for the now independent Cirque Hors Piste's daily activities comes from social service and community nongovernmental organizations as well as government social service departments. Here, individual desires to excel and persevere, to attain professional-level skills, join – and occasionally clash with – the desire to work as a group for the success and integration of all (Spiegel et al. 2015). Whether aimed at street youth, recent immigrants, individuals with physical, mental, or health conditions, or others marginalized from the cultural mainstream who would not otherwise have access to much artistic training, such circus interventions aim to promote social change through creating a space where people can develop a set of creative skills, alter their own sense of what is individually and collectively possible, and experience a change in the way they are viewed by the wider society (Kekäläinen 2014).

While much of alternative circus avoids overtly political themes, in 1997 a collective headed by Norman Nawrocki formed as an artist-community collaboration to create a circus-inflected cabaret entitled Cirque en Cash, which explored questions of social and economic injustice faced by those living in Montreal's economically disadvantaged areas. Playing for only two nights, this "circus" took the form of a themed cabaret animated with jugglers, clowns, and acrobats. The ringmaster who introduced the performers set an ironic and political tone, screaming into the mic, for example, "The

Shriner Circus it ain't. It's the circus of life. It's the cash circus" (quoted and translated by Picard 1997, A2). A review in one of Canada's largest national newspapers, the *Globe and Mail*, described the performance in these terms: "While the show resembles a giant musical cartoon, the message is deadly serious, an examination of the roots of poverty and what people can do to fight back" (ibid.). The skills and aesthetic of circus were thus brought to the service of antipoverty work in a manner consistent with the broader explosion of activism seen in the late 1990s; the creators drew on the growth of circus to pursue both alternative aesthetics and political goals.

Playing on the tropes of the traditional circus brought into the contemporary era, the show offered a slideshow of "human curiosities," featuring those who have been left behind by the stock market boom and the wonders of globalization. As described by Nawrocki, this circus aimed to "popularize radical ideas that people don't have access to in the mainstream media" (qtd in Picard 1997, A2). On the second night, the community centre was surrounded by police officers who, due to the theme of the show, had mistakenly assumed a connection between the cast of Cirque en Cash and a group that earlier in the day had raided the all-you-can-eat buffet at the posh Queen Elizabeth Hotel, seeking to redistribute food to the poor. The police presence, however, did not deter audiences from attending the free show. The room was packed to capacity and people had to be turned away.

The concept-creation phase of the show had taken shape with a grant from the Canada Council for the Arts under the guidance of established artists working closely with community centres and people from Montreal's low-income neighbourhoods – people encountered in venues like food bank line-ups.[11] However, due to lack of ongoing funding, the actual production was mounted by artists and other community members who volunteered their time, including Nawrocki's internationally renowned Rhythm Activism band, various local actors and dancers, and circus performers from the École nationale de cirque, some of whom soon went on to perform with Cirque du Soleil. While the show was more of a thematized, multidisciplinary cabaret than a "real circus," the *Globe and Mail* reported that "Le Cirque [en Cash] was approached by the promoter of a real circus who said the show reminded him of the old days before TV, when the visit of the circus was the talk of the town" (Picard 1997, A2). Alternative, activist circus thus takes pride of place as a complement to, even a stand-in for, other commercial enterprises in the public's concept of what the nouveau cirque can do.

The movement between alternative circus, social circus, and political circus has inspired the trajectories of many Montreal-trained performers. Internationally renowned actor, musician, dancer, and circus performer Jerry Snell, for instance, has been exemplary in moving between these worlds. His Social Arts Network profile describes him as "committed to innovative theatre production and performance, and to left-field sociopolitical ideas."[12] Snell is known for creating shows infused with these values. A show that he created in 2004 while doing a residency at the École nationale de cirque reached 5,000 spectators in six days, and in 2008, inspired by the success of Cirque du Monde and other social circus initiatives, he founded Circus International Actions to network groups using circus and performing arts with youth in precarious situations in Asia.

Circus and the Quebec Spring of 2012: A Surfacing of Disparate Politics

The Quebec Spring with its revolutionary promise brought to the surface the disparate politics that have infused the ethical and aesthetic configurations of Quebec's circus scene for some time but that are rarely made explicit. In the streets of Quebec at this time, a return to the commitments, ethos, and aesthetics of the Quiet Revolution to maintain accessible education was repeatedly invoked,[13] often through the tools and shapes of the performing arts. Design students from the University of Quebec at Montreal (UQAM) formed the École de la Montagne Rouge, designing posters for the various protest events. Architecture students at the University of Montreal formed Archicontre (bringing together the French words for "architecture" and "against" to create the compound "very much against"), which staged multiple performance installations of students "crushed" under giant red squares. In trees throughout the city, the group hung small red squares in reference to the symbol of the student movement, denoting "squarely in the red."[14] The symbol was an invocation of the argument that young people were beginning their adult lives already deeply in debt and that education, like other public services, thus ought to be made more, not less, accessible. Theatre students at UQAM and Concordia University formed La Ligne Rouge and Theatre Struck, respectively, to generate a series of theatrical interventions in the streets and metro stations (Spiegel 2012, 2015). Calls for a "rêve general" – a collective dream – were put forth by artist-activists (Christoff 2013; Ferland 2012; Spiegel 2015). At its height, an estimated

300,000 students were on strike.[15] Among these were the vast majority of the province's university-level performing arts students (the Faculty of Fine Arts at both Concordia University and the University of Quebec at Montreal, for example, voted to join the protests), as well as a large cross-section of Montreal's francophone colleges or CEGEPS.

In spite of the fact that the École nationale de cirque did not organize a formal collective protest (a few students sported red squares on their bags and jackets), circus-inflected street arts peppered protests as the city's streets were filled by a popular outpouring of support that transformed the 2012 student strike into a broad movement. As such, these protests joined growing trends of global – and local – protest dramaturgies, playing with the relationship between "the symbolic" and "the real" in various ways (Kershaw 1997; Spiegel 2012b, 2015). During the international alter-globalization movements of the 1990s, for example, elements of street circus such as juggling and clowning became staples of activist protests (Gleason 2009; Graeber 2009). And it was during the alter-globalization protests of the early 2000s that Quebec-based groups like Artivistic, with its commitment to art in public space as a form of political "direct action" aimed at transforming social relations (Lamoureux 2013), began to form. Also new to the scene were Quebec-based "clown armies," mocking police practice through satiric street clowning during protests (Dupuis-Déri 2010). Participant-performers held a range of profiles from militant, nonartist activists to theatre students and social circus participants; circus artists typically participated as individual, concerned citizens and performed alongside amateur and professional practitioners of other art forms.

At the height of the 2012 student protests, however, a collective of artists from Quebec's alternative circus scene formed in support of the student movement and the spirit of contestation it had sparked. This collective of professional circus artists, dancers, and other performing artists (started by fire spinners based in the small city of Rimouski but populated mainly by those living and working in Montreal) established En Feu Contre la Hausse (On Fire against the Tuition Hike). Over seventy artists, including clowns, aerialists, and dancers – among them several graduates of the École nationale de cirque – as well as the original fire spinners, signed up as members of the collective.[16] They could be seen joining in protests as stilt-walkers, for example. In the solidarity "family days," more developed acts by circus professionals and semi-professionals could often also be seen, making these events stimulating ways for young families to show support for the movement. In these interventions, we saw a return of the circus artists to the street arts of their origins.

The fire featured in the name of the collective En Feu Contre la Hausse carries particular meaning for the group's members as a symbol for time-honoured traditions of collective visioning. As the collective writes on its website and Facebook pages, "Too often considered, in the era of social uprisings, as a dangerous weapon of revolt, fire is above and before all a gathering element around which to warm oneself, discuss, sing, and even create!"[17] The invocation of the image of fire was also reminiscent of the Greek figure Prometheus who stole the fire from the gods in order to offer it to the have-nots; this metonym for social justice and social change appeared in a few Québécois plays from the 1970s, including Victor-Lévy Beaulieu's *Cérémonial pour l'assassinat d'un ministre*.

This ethic of solidarity is further echoed by the group's proposal to create an event that would integrate artists' aesthetic, social, and economic contributions, with funds raised going to the organization Je donne à nous, which provided general support for students mobilizing during the 2012 student strike, including help with legal fees. The event was to be held at the Bain St Mathieu, a former swimming pool often leased to artists by the government for free or at low cost. This intention to do a benefit show in support of the student movement, however, encountered significant institutional barriers that eventually led to the demise of the project. Like all legal venues, the venue required special insurance for aerial and fire performance. While the artists from the small Pyro Del Arte fire-spinning group did indeed hold insurance that normally covered their shows, companies refused to insure any circus event related to the student movement.[18] Thus, all circus-related arts during the 2012 protests could take place only as street art, frequently driven by many of the same artists who had initially networked to offer the benefit show.

In a scene often repeated in the streets during those many marches of 2012, protestors donned bike helmets and clown wigs and noses, banged on plastic shields with little sticks, wrote tickets for ridiculous infractions, and yelled in exaggerated ways "bouge, bouge, bouge" ("move along, move along, move along"), mocking the riot police who would regularly charge the crowd, swinging their batons and clubbing anyone in their path, shortly after (and occasionally before) declaring the protest "illegal" (La Ligue des droits et libertés et al. 2013; Marcoux-Chabot 2013). This satirizing of police brutality was very much in keeping with global protest-clowning

15.1 Clowns Marie-France Bonenfant and François Genest enact an arrest using slapstick violence techniques at the satiric protest event "SouriFest '13: The people's kettle" against municipal antiprotest laws passed during the 2012 Quebec student movement.

traditions, in which clowning was used to de-escalate tensions. In 2003, for instance, the Clandestine Insurgent Rebel Clown Army (CIRCA) formed to celebrate George Bush's visit to the United Kingdom. Their invitation – "run away from the Circus: join the clandestine insurgent clown army" – explicitly courted skilled circus artists. In their mission statement, they took pains to articulate the rigour of their interventionist art and to develop an ethico-aesthetic of engagement on that basis: "CIRCA is not another excuse to dress up and bring colour and laughter to the grey ranks of protests. It isn't just a ragged bunch of activists sporting false noses, a smudge of grease paint, camouflage pants and bad wigs, but a highly disciplined army of immaculately trained clowns, a militia of authentic fools, a battalion of natural buffoons" (Klepto 2004).

CIRCA created shows and offered training that blended clowning skills with direct action training. For the troupe, this acquisition of skills has the double effect of inviting wider audiences and participants. Ultimately, the ethic here then becomes one of initiation: it invites onlookers to become initiated – and trained – participants. Interestingly, providing training that is required for safely and effectively engaging in direct action clowning produces a complex politics of collectivity. On the one hand, skills are democratized: anyone can come to the training session and learn to clown in tense situations. On the other hand, requesting a basic level of training before one joins a clown army means a hierarchy is established between those who have been trained and those who have not (yet) been trained (Klepto and Evil 2005).

As with such previous clown armies, during Montreal's student protests, clowns played a series of games and exploited their command of corporeal dynamics and physical expressivity to comment on social practices – including policing practices. While arguably more in keeping with an ethos of rebellion than systemic revolution, these clown troupes encouraged public participation in creative resistance to and re-explorations of rules and power dynamics of the regulated hierarchies they resist (Dupuis-Déri 2010). By ridiculing the forced control and displacement of bodies according to the terms of the state ("bouge, bouge, bouge"), they implicity exalted freedom of bodily movement of the collective.

Cirque Engagé in Quebec after 2012

It was in the aftermath of the Quebec Spring that the implications of what had, in fact, become an historical moment, inspired the formation of new politically conscious groups in Quebec's circus scene. As protestors and the province as a whole saw the tuition hike and the most repressive acts of new legislation repealed, circus arts continued to grow as an element of protest culture. New groups of slapstick clowning offered training on physical performance, including staged violence, as a means of satirizing police brutality. An activist collective called les Souris Fières (the Proud Mice, but also a homophonic pun on *souricière* or a "police kettle," the police tactic of surrounding the crowd on all sides, making any crowd movement dependent on police clearance) was formed by activists from virtually every walk of life, including professional circus artists who contributed their art to playfully oppose state repression and police brutality in collaboration with the clowns. SouriFest – a satiric event wherein clown police-activists trap and arrest other activists – staged a coming together of these groups wherein layers of skill sharing and inclusive celebration met activist culture. In the weeks leading up to the first event, the trained clown battalion offered open free training sessions in slapstick violence wherein participants learned how to appear to attack one another without risking injury; on the day of the event, there were more than a handful of newly trained clowns. Costumes and cardboard police shields were provided so that others could safely participate.[19] At the first SouriFest, just before the clown police enclosed the mock protestors, Justin Dale, a young circus student in the professional stream at the École nationale de cirque, performed a Cyr wheel solo while donning a police hat and yelling slogans against repressive legislation. As a budding young professional, Dale epitomized the potential of a skillfully trained and carefully disciplined human body to master its own movement; however, brought to this street level, in fluid relationship with and wearing the same costume police hats and mouse tails as all the others, including the amateurs, his performance points to the effacement of a strict hierarchy of bodies, much in keeping with the much written-about ethos of "carnivalesque" protest (Bakhtin 1984; Kershaw 1997; Schechner 1992). At SouriFest, those on the streets are singular in their potential but collective in their movement. As modeled by Dale, self-mastery of the body is not a practice of authoritative policing, but rather a force to attract more bodies into the streets, as passersby stop to ask questions and consider the unfolding spectacle. Similar events were repeated by the collective throughout the summer, though none with the same vigour as the first.

While police brutality is hardly a common theme in commercial circus, many artists in Montreal's social circus scene are intimately familiar with it. Moreover, during the 2012 protests, scores of college students who otherwise might never have experienced police violence came face-to-face with this reality. Since then, this theme has frequently been taken up in productions staged by the youth involved.[20] Police brutality, social justice, marginalized youth – these and other themes were taken up by social circus, alternative circus, and commercial circus in mutually influential critiques.

In March 2014, for example, ten youth participated in a three-week "creation intensive" conducted by the social circus organization Cirque Hors Piste that culminated in a performance presented as part of a youth-for-human-rights evening hosted by Equitas, a Montreal-based international centre for human rights education. In keeping with the focus of the soirée, the youth's show explored the theme of social prejudice, specifically the discrimination experienced by those living in the streets. Throughout the pro-

15.2 Opposite National Circus School student Justin Dale Furgala Krall performs on Cyr wheel wearing the emblematic red square of the Quebec student movement at the satiric protest event "SouriFest '13: The people's kettle" against municipal antiprotest laws passed in Montreal during the 2012 Quebec student movement.

duction, the language of circus became a vehicle for humorous critique of dominant social structures and policies. The piece began with a pyramid collapsing on itself as performers yelled "capitalism" – a literal critique of capitalist pyramid schemes. Soon after, a young man dressed as Waldo – the picture-book character famous for being forever lost in the crowd – is featured with a clipboard, suggesting the bureaucratic list-making of administrators; he eventually throws down his paper and clipboard in frustration with his own bureaucracy. In another scene two people drinking in the streets are confronted by a police officer who hands them a ticket and fine. A chase then ensues in which the young couple escapes and comes back to overpower the police officer, transforming the previously top-down power dynamic via teamwork, hula hooping, and partner acrobatics. While a fairly obvious, if humorous, critique of authority in the face of poverty, the scene could equally be read as a celebration of circus itself as a tool in "flipping the script," offering a language to explore the reality and talents of those typically judged, policed, and cast aside for not consuming in the "proper" places. Indeed, many of the performers identified with these communities and voiced a desire to awaken audiences to the prejudices often held against marginalized people.[21]

A number of smaller companies, collectives, and organizations had similarly emerged even shortly before the Quebec Spring, offering workshops and shows oriented toward social engagement, suggesting the bubbling up of a new cultural ethos. A small company called Poécirque, for example, cofounded by Nicolas Ottenheimer, a graduate of the instructor program at the École nationale de cirque, and Ashley Courtland, an artist and special educator trained in art and psychology, frames itself as a "cirque et théâtre engagé" collective, "engaged in the construction of the world now becoming."[22] Their pedagogical approach, in the language of their website, seeks to integrate participants into a supportive cooperative. In 2011 Ottenheimer worked to create a solidarity circus centre (Siag 2012). Although those plans did not come to fruition due to the high cost and architectural complexities of converting an industrial building into a functioning circus space, throughout 2012 Otterheimer hosted a series of improvisational evenings that brought together members of the alternative circus scene with other community-minded people in significant moments of creation.

The largest concentrated convergence of the social and alternative circus communities in Quebec, however, remains the Carnival Carmagnole, mounted by the above-described Carmagnole collective and NGO, which boasts a mission statement of "encouraging free creation and social engagement to inspire and eventually save the world."[23] Created in 2001 from the desire, largely on the part of social circus alumni from Cirque du Monde and joined by many others, "to emancipate and rally circus and multi-disciplinary artists,"[24] their well-known annual festival was extended from an evening and two days to a full three-day event for 2014's iteration, with large numbers of volunteers camping out for weeks before and after for set-up and strike. In a site in the Quebec countryside, alternative circus acts, shows, and workshops were offered by a range of artists: amateurs training at the recreational level, participants and recent alumni of social circus, recent graduates of the École nationale de cirque debuting a new number, and seasoned stars of the alternative circus scene. These moments of creation were complemented by a wide range of theatrical performances as well as alternative community-lifestyle workshops.

Over the course of the weekend, numerous circus shows played with many of the tropes that had been used in early Cirque du Soleil shows of the transmuting body, transforming, through the magic of circus, to become something more than it was, with clown-scientist emcees and performer audience-plants entering the scene (Harvie and Hurley 1999). Indeed, in the context of Carmagnole, the trope of the audience-turned-performer was particularly appropriate considering the dissolution of the amateur/professional divide enacted by the festival through its diverse and multiple training workshops and its overwhelming number of active festival-goers with widely variant backgrounds and statuses. While the reworking of these tropes may suggest a reprise of the American myth and apology of the "self-made man" (Leroux 2009a, 2012), their presence here suggests an ethos more in keeping with that of Boal's (1979) "theatre as a rehearsal for revolution." The coming together of this work in this particular context suggests the development of a distinct ethos celebrating at once singular bodies and a vision of nonhierarchical collectivity.

A number of acts and workshops further gestured toward the more overtly alternative politics that underscored the event. For instance L'infâme puppet crew, a multidisciplinary puppetry and performing arts collective formed in January 2013, performed a piece exploring themes of being "puppeted" and manipulated by a technologically driven "Control Society," and the effects of such manipulation on human relations and the human experience. Very much influenced by the giant puppet aesthetic of the Bread and Puppet Theater, the collective, which had emerged out of the political ethos of anarcho-collective governance that gained traction and visibility during the 2012 Quebec student protests, infused the festival with a renewed ethos of politically engaged collective creation. Other collectives, such as Théâtre de la Botte trouée, explored themes of solidarity, courage, and community engagement through fantastical mythological children's theatre. Finally, a number of representatives from permaculture farms operating outside of Montreal offered workshops, situating the alternative circus arts culture fostered by Carmagnole within a broader alternative community context. With its teams of volunteers, its large board of directors, its own productions and cabarets under the guidance of guest directors as well as the curated open venue it provides for artists at every stage of their development, Carmagnole suggests a vision of culture and cultural education that functions on a collective model from the grassroots up. While few of the key players were students in formal educational institutions during the Quebec Spring, many were active in the street protests. Above all, the ethos that this collective fosters through its cabarets and the carnival is one of an alternative model of accessibility and participation.

While the ethos of social and political engagement that surfaced during the 2012 student protests has most explicitly been felt in the social and alternative circus world, the pertinence of this cultural moment has not been entirely ignored by the professional or commercial circus world. During the summer of 2014, for example, during the Montreal Complètement Cirque festival, Les 7 doigts de la main (the 7 Fingers) began its production *Intersections* with a nod to the casserole protests that had taken place two summers earlier, as well as to the crowd-controlling municipal legislation that had been the target of SouriFest the previous spring, and that has continued to limit people and lead to arrests during public gatherings. Audience members were invited to mingle on the stage prior to the beginning of the show. The show began as cast members entered the stage banging on pots and pans, and the mingling of artists and audience members came to an end when one of the cast members announced through a megaphone that the gathering was illegal and that audience members were required to vacate the stage immediately and take their seats, enforcing the categorical separation between performer and audience member. People were ushered swiftly to their seats to the song "Intuition #1," recorded by Montreal-based folk band Avec pas d'casque (with no helmet). The song became anthemic during the 2012 student strike when it was used to create a music video of neighbourhood casserole protests that quickly went viral on social media.[25] The remainder of the show explored tensions in the personal lives of characters, and the sociopolitical context that had been used to seat audiences was never revisited. Nevertheless, the nod to this broader context served as a reminder of how all lives, and all art, function within a broader civic reality – one that artists, including Montreal's circus artists, could never completely ignore.

From its early growth following Quebec's Quiet Revolution, much has transformed in Quebec's circus scene. Beginning as an alternative, street-based art form rising to the cultural stage in the politically engaged era of the avant-garde, flavoured with its frequent street-level encounters with then-burgeoning new social movements, circus has since become a leading art form in Quebec's billion-dollar cultural industry. Nevertheless, beneath the sheen of the major commercial circus companies, and growing in part with their success, a vibrant socially engaged circus scene has emerged. Now, in the second decade of the twenty-first century, this activist, alternative circus scene can be said to take a certain pride of place.

The heightening of social and political discourse in Quebec during the spring of 2012 challenged the various players of this diverse cultural scene to define themselves, not only in terms of their widely recognized artistic excellence, but as transformers of artistic engagement. These events perhaps tested their bohemian rhetoric (see Leroux 2012) as they were called to take a stand against austerity measures in spite of the usual apolitical stance associated with Quebec's circus scene. At the same time, this cultural milieu raised the profile of traditionally marginalized artists. The Quebec Spring had raised the question of who would have access to what educational opportunities. In the artistic arena this translated into the question of who would have access to which cultural opportunities and to what end. As we have seen, responses to this call have been varied and have been met with a number of institutional, infrastructural, and legal barriers. In the context of the 2012 protest movement itself, involvement ranged from clowning in the streets, to fundraising efforts, to the dramatization of politicized themes in commercial productions. Previous and ongoing approaches have further included everything from community-professional show development to free productions exploring social justice concerns, social circus as intervention allowing youth living in precarious situations to explore and express their world view, and the development of alternative circus communities through accessible participatory festivals. In Quebec these varied approaches have formed a mutually informing ecology – with the professional circus helping to fund social circus initiatives, the social circus feeding the alternative circus scene, and the alternative circus reminding artists of the relationship between their art and the broader sociopolitical context in which they create. If the arts have a role to play in expanding visions of the possible and in shaping collective dreams, the dynamics of who is able to contribute to and enjoy such explorations are surely of consequence to the future of our shared society. As we have seen with this study of Quebec's various cirques engagés, the time, energy, and resources allocated to the socially engaged arts and the recognition of the interdependence among the multiple dimensions of our expanding circus scenes have had, and will continue to have, lasting impacts on the cultural tenor of our era.

Epilogue: Circus Reinvested

Louis Patrick Leroux

We opened this voluminous collection with a sense of physical, political, and national boundaries pulling at the seams of a nascent discourse on contemporary Quebec circus. Our understanding of this circus scene keeps widening and complexifying. As I write this epilogue, Cirque du Soleil, Cirque Éloize, 7 Fingers, and Cavalia shows are touring the world, present on every continent at one time or another. Smaller companies, such as Quebec City's energetic FlipFabriQue, played Berlin's Chamäleon Theatre for several months, and Cirque Alfonse is extensively touring American and European venues. In Sochi, Russia, the 7 Fingers created portions of the opening ceremonies for the Olympic Games, and the Daniele Finzi Pasca–Julie Hamelin duo worked on the opening and closing ceremonies for the Paralympic Games. Cirque du Soleil has opened its Broadway production company, exploring new possible venues for live entertainment, inaugurating their theatrical presence with a reworked version of the Los Angeles production *Iris* under the new title *Paramour*. Meanwhile, the 7 Fingers has two New York Broadway and off-Broadway collaborations with the revival of the musical *Pippin* and the bacchanalian food and circus event *Queen of the Night*. The company has also ventured into the dance world with an exciting production with London's Saddlers' Wells that features three collaborations with international choreographers Marie Chouinard, Victor Quijada, and Marco Morau working closely with hand-balancing artists in particular.

Montréal Complètement Cirque's annual selection of contemporary circus from Europe, Australia, and North America is more diverse than ever with productions exploring the boundaries between artistic genres and audience expectations of what constitutes "circus." Younger companies such

16.1 *Timber!*, Cirque Alfonse

as Cirque Alfonse (and their hirsute neotraditional folk-singing and acrobatic lumberjack tricks reposing on an aesthetic and ethos of the rural clan) and Bande artistique (with their show *Sometimes in Life, Things Change*, a self-described "idiotic alliance between juggling, opera, and clowns") offer high-skill acrobatics combined with unexpected and uncannily spectacular comedy.

Decades after Cirque Éloize, another circus company has emerged from the Magdalene Islands by way of the École nationale de cirque. Vague de cirque produces shows that follow traditional act-based circus dramaturgy with contemporary numbers, tracing an arc of slow, incremental build-up following technical difficulty and accomplishment, all of this under a big top meant to tour Quebec beyond its urban theatre spaces. Meanwhile, one of the original Cirque du Soleil clowns, Rodrigue "Chocolat" Tremblay, has decided to sell off Cirque Akya's big top and its distinctive Streamline trailers, after a decade of offering a family-friendly show by a family-driven company (his wife, tightrope walker Nicolette Hazewinkel, and their children also performed for years) as an alternative to the large, narrative-driven multimedia offerings from the "big three."[1]

Former students of the École nationale de cirque, after having worked and toured with the larger companies, have started creating companies resolutely steeped in a Quebec "tradition" of dynamic, virtuosic performances of athletics and acrobatics brought together by an inquisitive exploration of technology or other arts and disciplines. For instance, Throw2Catch explores technology with rare efficacy by relying on a do-it-yourself, low-tech approach, while the established companies such as Cirque du Soleil, 7 Fingers, and Cirque Éloize pursue their forays into ever-present and more immersive technology, not infrequently with artists who are graduates of the École.

Machine de cirque, bringing two Quebec circus cultures together, those of artists trained alternately in Montreal and in Quebec City circus schools, offers a spectacle of acrobatic inventiveness and audacity presented as an unveiling – or a poetics – of circus mechanics. These early- to mid-career circus artists show the mastery of their craft and bodies at a level that might prove difficult to sustain during constant touring, but that could have a similar impact to the one that 7 Fingers' *Traces* had ten years ago on a generation of young spectators and their sense of the possibilities in contemporary circus.

Circus directors (*metteurs en piste*, as distinct from their theatrical equivalents, *metteurs en scène*) are emerging who have a keen understanding of the specificity of circus combined with a strong sense of theatre conventions and dance vocabulary, including Alain Francoeur,[2] Anthony Venisse, and Estelle Clareton, to name but a few of these artists with distinctive signatures. Andréane Leclerc and Anna Ward, two École nationale de cirque–trained performers who have had rich careers working with many companies in North America and in Europe, have challenged circus conventions by purposefully confronting their art, training, and disciplines with a clearly postdramatic reading of dance-theatre, flirting with performance art and pulling farther and farther away from what the audience and the contemporary

16.2 *RESET*, Throw2Catch

16.3 Andréane Leclerc, *Cherepaka*, Nadère Arts Vivants

cirque milieu has come to expect from them. Andréane Leclerc is a contortionist with a vast experience of putting her distended body on display in the contexts of circus, burlesque, alternative music (she worked alongside the Tiger Lilies and developed *Whore of Babylon* currently touring internationally), and feminist performance (she toured with Annie Sprinkle). Her experiences creating full-length solo contortion pieces (most notably *Cherepaka*) welcome the audience's gaze in order to challenge it and sit interestingly alongside the most provocative pieces of contemporary dance and performance art. Anna Ward's collaboration with theatre artist Benoît Landry has produced a multidisciplinary company, Nord Nord Est. Its inaugural production, *Le voyage d'hiver*, inspired by Schubert's twenty-four lieder-suite *Winterreise*, proposed its own twenty-four deconstructed tableaux held together by the logic of postdramatic juxtaposition (parataxical jump cuts, stretching of time and action, etc.). The production presented at the 2013 Montréal Complètement Cirque festival seemed to baffle the audience, but a reprise one year later in the Théâtre Prospéro, a well-funded alternative

16.4 *Le voyage d'hiver*, Compagnie Nord Nord Est

theatre space, was much better understood and received and suggests further exploration into the blurring of artistic borders. Paradoxically, Quebec circus, even as it retains its strong commercial appeal at home and abroad, is nevertheless seeping from the mainstream into alternative, experimental spaces. It is following a movement inverse to that of most contemporary circus scenes, which tend to emerge on the fringes and eventually find some measure of commercial success with a broader appeal.

The most successful crossovers are self-consciously assumed as such, as we have seen, where clowning, opera, and a chainsaw meet, or where contortion and dance join each other, or when postdramatic fragments make their own circus. Some of these hybrid experiences have, however, retained marks of not being completely developed experiments, including, for example, Éloize's combination of music-hall vaudeville and circus arts, *La Baronesse*, which opened the 2013 Montréal Complètement Cirque festival, and the 7 Fingers' 2013 *Le murmure du coquelicot*, which was included as part of the regular theatrical season of Montreal's establishment venue, the Théâtre du Nouveau Monde. Certain productions seem to have gotten lost along the way due to untenable, production-driven concessions, as can be surmised with the ever-fluctuating steampunk light operetta circus

Zarkana, which Cirque du Soleil moved from New York to Moscow to Madrid then back to New York, and which was retired in Vegas in 2016. Samuel Tétreault's collaboration in 2015 with three choreographers of international reputation – Marie Chouinard, Victor Quijada, and Marcos Morau – on their new tryptich, simply titled *Triptyque*, of hand-balancing and dance pieces promises to bring the 7 Fingers to new audiences and, especially, to develop new artistic dialogues and affinities that echo their history of groundbreaking explorations, which Batson examines in this collection's pages.

Even so, new formal boundaries are being stretched: those traditionally separating the disciplines, as well as those separating traditional from nouveau and contemporary circuses. The circus emerging from Quebec today is anything but formulaic and homogenous, in spite of recurring criticism from other performing arts disciplines and other circus nations that seems to reduce Quebec circus to a commercial offering of virtuosic and impeccable technique in a well-honed but rather superficial aesthetic. Some elements of this critique may be applicable to a number of productions, of course, but it would be a gross and ill-informed generalization to reduce all of Quebec circus – or indeed even a single company – to this notion. If Quebec "reinvented" circus from its keen but young understanding of a centuries-old tradition, drawing from each epoch and each circus nation what they had to offer, one can argue that it continues to pursue an original contemporary path, constantly confronting codes and expectations, engaging with interarts cross-pollination, flirting at times with immersive technology, music video, performance art, theatre, dance, and burlesque, all the while constantly striving for doxa and a legitimacy that – we hope – will be late in coming, as such institutional legitimacy might prove stifling.

This first major collection of scholarly writing on contemporary Quebec circus has covered much ground and has uncovered many future fields of inquiry. The Sisyphean task of offering an authoritative book on current research trends has revealed that much of the work on Quebec circus is yet to come. We see a need, and put forth a call, for further examinations of the aesthetics and discourse of small Quebec companies, for even more in-depth exploration in the fields of circus dramaturgy and narrative, for a greater understanding of models of social circus emerging from Quebec and promoted here and abroad by the likes of Cirque du Monde (and its own new reconfigured position internationally), and for increasingly deep readings of circus history. Circus history, we have noted through our own research and the editing of this book, is not only nostalgic and archival; it

16.5 “C’est assez pour aujourd’hui,” research-creation workshop at ’École nationale de cirque, 2008

is also made up of the living archive that needs to be recorded, transcribed, perpetuated, and shared with practitioners and scholars alike.

Practitioners of traditional circus did not ask, What discipline or role should a child take on? Circus children simply followed in their parents' footsteps. In that traditional world, the specialty, discipline, and method of training were generative. By contrast, contemporary Quebec circus is marked by unexpected feats, inventiveness, and uncanny entrepreneurship. The history of Quebec circus – which emerged out of a few signal occasions staggered over three centuries – is constantly in the making. This creative world allowed for a distinctive approach to combining performance styles, codes, and training circus creators. Audiences, teachers, performers, and scholars need to engage with the circus, not only to challenge their assumptions but also to recognize its value in a small nation only just emerging and starting to achieve its potential.

I alluded, in the introduction, to the recent sale of Cirque du Soleil to equity investment firms from Texas and Shanghai. While the company seems to be pursuing "business as usual" as this book goes to press, one can certainly expect profound changes in the Montreal circus ecology over the next few years. Will Cirque du Soleil keep its headquarters in Montreal, tied into a unique creative and business environment? Only the future will tell, but it does not make business or creative sense to uproot Cirque du Soleil from its generative milieu. And yet one can already anticipate a certain distancing between the corporate entity, owned and controlled from afar by investors, and the community that grew from Cirque du Soleil and allowed it to thrive. The company will most likely grow, like Éloize and the 7 Fingers, at a more measured pace; smaller companies, artistically driven collectives that have been consistently emerging over the past few years, might have more space to grow out of the shadow of such illustrious founding figures. I expect that Cirque du Soleil's clear corporate stance will feed a certain sense of artistic and moral urgency in the Quebec circus scene: What is this scene about? What does it have to say? How can it engage with peers internationally rather than compete with or, indeed, crush "competitors" in other "markets"? None of the smaller companies are interested in copyrighting the word *cirque*, for example, nor are they particularly secretive about what they are developing; they seek only to practice contemporary circus at the best of their artists' abilities.

Circus in Quebec, as we have seen throughout this book, is a site of audacity, creativity, and commerce. Its strengths – technical innovation and acrobatic achievement – are feats that nevertheless seem to cross over to the audience and inspire wonder and engagement. Until very recently, this circus has not proven to be the most aesthetically or politically driven, if one compares it to the multiplicity and range of practices in European nouveau and contemporary circus, for instance, but a shift is occurring. Cirque du Monde, for one, has developed circus arts as a tool for social change, though the most recent cuts to Cirque du Soleil's Citizenship Division in October 2015 will have an impact on Cirque du Monde's pivotal and instrumental role and will impose a reconsideration of its philanthropic and social roles. Also, over the past decade, a community and recreational circus scene has developed, offering sites for pursuits of physical health, artistic expression, and community outside a professionalizing setting. In Quebec, paradoxically, the trail-blazing and innovative multinational corporation came first, then a more complex and varied circus and creative ecosystem emerged.

Circus's exceptionalism has been, interestingly, normalized to a certain extent. It has been integrated into Quebec culture and society as a given, as a "symbolic resource" of its cultural national wealth, to use Bandejl and Wherry's (2011) language. These theorists posit, in their development of a new field of economic sociology drawing on both Adam Smith and Pierre Bourdieu, that "evidence has begun to accumulate. Economic success results from the symbolic resources – collective narratives, reputations, status, and ideas – that nations, regions, and communities have at their disposal" (1). The cultural narrative of circus in Quebec is one of creativity, adaptability, and collective know-how in a field most Québécois had never considered until very recently. For a small emerging nation, the international impact of one of its art forms – and the economic weight it has wielded – cannot be underestimated. Bandejl and Werry insist that "a nation's cultural wealth derives from the reputational attributes and cultural products of that nation" (7). This particular nation's cultural wealth, in spite of its linguistic awareness and historical logocentric discursive predilection, has been bolstered by circus: its projections of possibilities and its marriage of art, sport, and commerce.

We close this collection satisfied with the scope of research we were able to bring into dialogue in these pages. And yet we remain keenly aware of the work to be done and look forward to joining the continued and expanding conversations with colleagues, students, and practitioners in Quebec and abroad.

Glossary of Circus Terms

Anna-Karyna Barlati
Translated by Susan Kelly

Acrobatic chair (Chaise acrobatique)
Circus discipline in which the acrobat accomplishes various balancing and acrobatic moves using a straight and sturdy chair. The balancing artist may use only one acrobatic chair or may stack multiple chairs. The *chair pyramid* is a circus discipline wherein the artist uses a large number of chairs stacked one upon the other and then performs balancing moves at the top of the structure.

Aerial cradle (Cadre aérien)
Fixed aerial apparatus that consists of a rectangular metal framework, often affixed under the cupola of a circus tent, to which the catcher attaches him- or herself by a bend in the knees as s/he assists the flyer in performing various aerial acrobatics.

Aerial hoop (Cerceau aérien)
Metal circular aerial apparatus of varying diameters, affixed by one or two points, in which the artist performs acrobatic movements. The aerial hoop may be stationary or swinging and may be used at great height or close to the ground. Used close to the ground, the hoop allows the acrobat to use the feet for thrust, variations of speed, and various choreographic moves.

Aerial rings (Anneaux aériens)
Aerial apparatus used by gymnasts composed of two suspended metal circles. The ring artist may use them to perform turns, swivels, drops, and balances, from a stationary position or while swinging.

17.1 Aerial hoop

Antipodism (Antipodisme)
Sometimes called Foot Juggling, this ancient juggling discipline was once practiced by the Aztecs. The juggler lies on a trinka (a low sloping armchair) while juggling various items with the feet, such as cylinders, barrels, carpets, and other objects.

Banquine (Banquine)
Acrobatic discipline executed at ground level by two bases who, using their arms, catapult a flyer to land upright, often back onto the interlaced hands of the bases, a position called banquette. The toss also allows the flyer to perform acrobatic leaps and return to the starting point, the ground, or the banquette of a second team of bases.

Bicycle (Bicyclette)
Discipline in which the acrobat executes acrobatic balances or tricks using a bicycle in a way that is quite removed from – or is an exaggerated form of – its usual function. In the nouveau cirque, the bicycle often serves as an allegory for the horse.

17.2 Chinese hoops

17.3 Chinese pole

Chair pyramide (Pyramid de chaises)
Circus discipline in which balancing artists use a significant number of stacked chairs and perform balancing moves at the top of the pile or stack. The chairs are both straight and durable, and may also be used for the acrobatic chair discipline.

Chinese diving hoops (Cerceaux chinois)
Specialty originating in China, consisting of a set of wooden or metal hoops of varying diameters that are balanced on the ground, one on top of the other, through which the acrobats propel themselves while performing various acrobatics.

Chinese pole (Mât chinois)
Apparatus of Asian origin consisting of one or several vertical metal posts fixed into the ground and generally 3 to 9 m in height, along which acrobats move as they climb and perform various movements and acrobatic jumps.

An offshoot of the Chinese pole is the swinging pole; rather than being fixed into the ground, however, the swinging pole is suspended by cables to hang roughly 60 cm from the ground. Due to its oscillations, the swinging pole allows the acrobat to put more dynamic and diverse moves into the number.

Cloud swing (Corde volante)
Aerial discipline consisting of a slack rope attached at both ends to form a swing roughly 6 m long. As it swings, the acrobat performs holds, turns, and other aerial acrobatics. Used in the seventeenth century by tightrope walkers, this discipline predates the invention of the trapeze.

Clowning (Art clownesque)
Clowning can be traced back to the English comedies of the pre-Shakespearian era. Originally a comic country buffoon character, a kind of equestrian and acrobatic burlesque artist, the clown later became the generalized comic grotesque character that appears in pantomime and circus shows. Clowning employs dramatic arts, mime, farce, and burlesque to create sketches intended to make audiences laugh. The first famous pantomime clown was Joey Grimaldi (1778–1837).

Contortion (Contorsion)
The practice of extreme physical flexibility, thousands of years old, which allows the contortionist to accomplish positions of extreme stretching, flexing, and bending of the arms and legs. The practice of contortion can be divided into three categories: backbending, frontbending, and dislocation. Backbending has its origins in European travelling shows while frontbending originated in Asia. A contortionist may practice more than one type.

Corde lisse (Corde lisse)
Aerial apparatus consisting of a cotton rope, hanging vertically and stranded or braided to have a 3 to 5 cm diameter, on which the acrobat executes various acrobatic tricks and moves. The corde lisse may be used with a web into which the acrobat can insert either the hand or foot to perform various feats while spinning with the help of rotational push provided by an assistant on the ground.

17.4 Corde lisse

17.5 Cyr wheel

17.6 Diabolos

17.7 German wheel

Cyr wheel (Roue Cyr)
Acrobatic discipline derived from the German wheel invented by the Québécois Daniel Cyr, cofounder of Cirque Éloize, and composed of a simple metal circle in which the acrobat moves. Using his or her own forward thrust, the acrobat is able to make constant turns while performing acrobatics. As opposed to the German wheel, the Cyr wheel's structure allows more fluidity in the rotations, which accentuates the dynamics of the discipline.

Dance trapeze (Trapèze danse)
Discipline evolving from the aerial hoop using a simple trapeze attached at only one end, and on which the acrobat performs choreographic and acrobatic movements. The dance trapeze may be static or swinging, and may be elevated or low to the ground. Used close to the ground, the dance trapeze allows the acrobat to use his or her feet for thrust, variations of speed, and various choreographic moves.

Devil sticks (Bâtons du diable)
Juggling specialty made popular in the early nineteenth century by Indian artists Medua and Mooty Samme. It consists of using two sticks to manipulate a baton roughly 80 cm in length, usually tapered in the middle.

Diabolo (Diabolo)
Juggling discipline with Chinese origins, derived from a spinning top, that is performed with two sticks connected by a taut wire on which glide the diablo(s). The diablos themselves resemble double-isoceles spools that the juggler spins along the wire, throwing them in the air and giving them various aerial trajectories. The discipline's name refers to the sound that the air makes as it is sucked into the spinning spools, a sound known as the "devil's sound" in the eighteenth century.

German wheel (Roue allemande)
Of German origin, this apparatus comprises two large metal circles joined along the perimeter by a series of short bars, inside which the acrobat stands and uses his or her own thrust to propel the wheel while whirling and performing acrobatics.

17.8 Hand to hand

17.9 Handstand

Hand to hand (Main à main)
Demanding acrobatic discipline performed by two or more acrobats on the ground in which the base executes various moves involving strength, balance, elevation, and flexibility by carrying the flyer on the hands or sometimes the head. There are two forms: dynamic hand to hand and static hand to hand.

Static hand to hand often is executed in a smaller space, because the base and flyer perform only moves involving strength and balance with no great need to move through space. The feats of balancing and strength are presented in slow movements, so that the audience can fully appreciate the skill and endurance of the acrobats.

Dynamic hand to hand makes use of the entire performance space with much larger movements and a faster rhythm to some moves, since the bass provides propulsion, via a push of the arms, to the flyer, who is then able to perform different acrobatic jumps, land on the shoulders of the partner, another base, or the ground. Several individual types of acrobatics, synchronized or not, are often added to the number. Because of certain movement qualities and the performance by two acrobats, dynamic hand to hand is similar to banquine.

Handstand (Équilibre)
Ancient acrobatic discipline predating the classical period that requires the balancing acrobat to execute various moves and acrobatics while balancing on the hands or head, either on the ground or on virtually any type of apparatus. The principal apparatus used in balancing is called canes, two metal bars set at varying heights with small blocks on the top where the balancing acrobat places the hands to perform the balancing moves.

Icarian Games (Jeux icariens)
Discipline evolving from acrobatics and antipodism in which a juggler lying on a trinka (a low sloping armchair) propels a flyer into the air. The flyer then executes various balancing moves and risky jumps. A second team of bases and flyers may join the number to perform various hazardous jumps and to allow for an exchange of flyers.

Juggling (Jonglerie)
Art requiring dexterity and agility dating to the most ancient of times. Juggling may be practiced individually or in a group, in the air or on the ground, and consists of throwing various objects in the air that may be of almost any type: rings, balls, pins, etc. The goal is to keep them in motion at all times, with the juggler relaunching each object as it falls. Juggling is frequently performed in combination with other circus disciplines such as the unicycle, tight wire, rola bola, etc. There are subcategories of juggling: balancing juggling, which consists of balancing objects such as bowls, glasses, and balloons, often stacked on the head, chin, or feet; and manipulation, which consists of keeping various items like hats, sticks, and balls moving across different parts of the body.

Korean board (Planche coréenne)
Discipline similar to the teeterboard that was invented by artists from North Korea. It consists of a rocking board upon which two acrobats stand and then are catapulted, continuously performing vaults, spins, and other acrobatic jumps.

17.10 Korean board

Ladder (Échelle libre)
A simple ladder that the acrobat climbs and maintains in an upright position through constant movement of the hips that creates a perpetual side-to-side motion. The acrobat then performs mounts, balances, and other acrobatics at the top. A ladder number may be combined with certain hand to hand or juggling moves in order to increase the level of difficulty.

Perch (Perche)
Acrobatic accessory from Asia consisting of a metal or wooden bar that is carried by a base or is fixed on the ground, up which an acrobat climbs to perform balances and acrobatics at the top. The perch may also be combined with other circus disciplines such as tight wire, hand to hand, and teeterboard.

Rola bola (Rola bola)
Invented in 1898 by Vasque, a Frenchman, this discipline consists of standing and balancing on an unstable assembly of boards supported by cylinders roughly 25 cm in diameter. Rola bola may be combined with other circus disciplines such as juggling and hand to hand.

17.11 Russian bar

Rolling globe (Boule d'équilibre)
Wood or plastic sphere with a large diameter (up to 1.5 m) upon which the performer walks while executing acrobatic feats. Some jugglers also use the rolling globe in their numbers to increase the level of difficulty.

Russian bar (Barre russe)
First used by Boris Isaevy in 1958, this acrobatic discipline is performed on the ground by two bases who carry on the shoulder or arms a flexible bar upon which a flyer stands upright and performs a variety of precarious moves.

Russian cradle (Cadre russe)
Apparatus composed of one or two gantries equipped with platforms facing each other and fastened to the ground at variable heights. One or more bases stand with their waists attached to the platforms, a position that allows them to propel one or more flyers, who then execute various aerial acrobatics. This apparatus is often added to installations along with flying trapeze numbers.

17.12 Russian cradle

17.13 Silks

Russian swing (Balançoire russe)
Discipline originating in Eastern Europe consisting of a large oblong-shaped swing that is propelled using the natural movement of the mechanism and the weight of two or three spotters who push it. The flyer standing at the end of the swing launches into the air and performs acrobatic leaps or vaults as high as 20 m or more over the ring, landing either on the ground or on the shoulders of bases.

Silks (Tissu)
Aerial discipline invented by the French circus artist Gérard Fasoli. Derived from the corde lisse, silks consist of a large length of fabric folded in half to form two fabric panels hanging vertically from a hooking device and inside which the acrobat rolls and contorts to perform various acrobatic moves and tricks. Like the straps, silks allow the acrobat to perform large rotations above the ring, giving the artist a certain grace while in flight.

17.14 Straps

Slack wire (Fil mou)
Apparatus related to the tight wire, the difference being the slack tension to the cable or rope that creates a curved line between the two mounts. The acrobat moves along the wire and, while rocking, executes a series of moves, balances, jumps, and dance steps.

Static trapeze (Trapèze fixe)
Discipline using a simple trapeze hung at various heights upon which one or two acrobats execute moves and acrobatics without using the trapeze's swinging movement. When used by two acrobats, the static trapeze strongly resembles the aerial cradle, as the base attaches him- or herself to the trapeze by a bend of the knees, enabling the flyer to perform various aerial acrobatics.

Straps (Sangles)
Acrobatic specialty of Asian origin, consisting of two thin parallel straps several metres in length, along which the acrobat rolls and twists, using

the wrists and arms to perform lifts, drops, and acrobatics while suspended in the air. Like silks, the straps allow the acrobat to perform large rotations above the ring, giving the artist a certain grace while in flight.

Swinging trapeze (Trapèze ballant)
Discipline using a simple trapeze hung at a great height upon which the acrobat balances and performs various moves and acrobatics.

Teeterboard (Planche sautoir)
Group number involving several acrobats in which one or two spotters leap onto one end of a rocking board from atop a pedestal and catapult flyers into the air. The flyers perform acrobatic feats before returning either to the ground, to the shoulders of a team of bases, or to a perch or chair. For some time this discipline was a specialty in Eastern European countries.

Tight wire (Fil de fer)
Apparatus consisting of a metal cable suspended horizontally between two mounts upon which the acrobat executes a series of moves, balances, dance steps, leaps, and acrobatics. Tight wire is generally performed at a low height, often just metres from the ground, distinguishing it from another tightrope walking form, the high wire, which is performed at a great height.

Trampoline (Trampoline)
Discipline evolving from gymnastics that first made an appearance in circus shows at the beginning of the twentieth century. It consists of an elastic tarp of varying sizes stretched between springs on a footed frame, on which acrobats perform various moves and jumps. The trampoline is often used with other acrobatic disciplines to increase the height of the flyers' leaps.

Trapeze (Trapèze)
Aerial acrobatic apparatus consisting of a round horizontal bar suspended from both ends by two vertical cords to which it is attached. Several versions of the trapeze exist: flying trapeze, swinging trapeze, dance trapeze, static trapeze, Washington trapeze, double or triple trapeze, etc.

17.15 Trampoline

Unicycle (Monocycle)
Derived from the bicycle, this apparatus, invented circa 1880 by the Italian Alessandro Scuri, is composed of a single wheel with pedal and seat, on which the acrobat performs various acrobatic moves, balances, or jumps. Frequently, the unicyle is performed in combination with juggling.

Notes

PROLOGUE

1 Louis Allen, interview by Charles Batson, 11 December 2014, Albany, New York.

INTRODUCTION

1 Precise operation budgets have always been contentious and complicated when reporting Cirque du Soleil's activities, and the information is mostly privately held, so one has to filter through whatever information one can get from press releases and interviews. The numbers have been rather consistent whether given in a crisis situation (as in January 2013), in public relations exercises, or during its recent sale in April 2015. Some interesting coverage in English about the 2013 crisis can be found in the work of Nestruck (2013) and Marotte and Barber (2013). Cirque du Soleil's public relations staff proved to be refreshingly frank and open about numbers, new orientations, and challenges in the months preceding its sale; for instance, see the dossier in *Le Devoir* (Baillargeon 2014; Paré 2014a, 2014b), which included a front-page feature on the current state of flux of the multinational corporation, and especially the *Wall Street Journal* article in 2014 (Berzon 2014). The media flurry of April 2015 revealed many fascinating aspects of Cirque du Soleil operations, its holding companies, the capital gains taxes founder Guy Laliberté could expect to pay on the sale of his company, and many other formerly little investigated angles. In addition to relatively focused international coverage by CNN, the *New York Times* (Austen 2015), and London's *Financial Times* (Hill 2015), Toronto's *Globe and Mail* followed the story closely, as did the *Wall Street Journal* (Berzon 2014; Berzon and Tan 2015). Montreal media closely and passionately covered the anticipated transaction and ultimately confirmed sale. Eventually, a detailed social, political, and corporate discursive study focusing on the intense two weeks of media coverage will be of interest. One example, among many: the Montreal daily *La Presse* had three business journalists working on various angles of the story, Francis Vailles (2015), Jean-Philippe Décarie (2015), and Vincent Brousseau-Pouliot (2015a, 2015b, 2015c; Brousseau-Pouliot and Lessard 2015a, 2015b), as well as editorialists, including Alain Dubuc (2015) and arts columnists Nathalie Petrowski

(2015) and Marc Cassivi (2015), not wanting to be outdone by their business section colleagues. This unprecedented coverage of Cirque du Soleil seems to have had a positive effect on its media relations, as Guy Laliberté addressed the media without complacency in a press conference covered by live telecast on RDI (I was invited to be a live commentator for this event; for a summary, see Radio-Canada 2015). What's more, the new chairman of the board, Mitch Garber – already a highly mediatized figure in Quebec – quickly made himself available to the media, for the most part to reassure people that the new ownership would not move Cirque du Soleil away from Montreal.

2 Permanent productions in Las Vegas, all running ten performances a week, roughly year round, include *Mystère*, directed by Franco Dragone (running continuously since 1993); *O*, directed by Dragone (since 1998); *Zumanity*, directed by Dominique Champagne and René-Richard Cyr (since 2003); *KÀ*, directed by Robert Lepage (since 2005); *The Beatles Love*, directed by Dominic Champagne (since 2006); and *Criss Angel Believe*, directed by Serge Denoncourt (since 2008). *Viva Elvis* closed after two years and was replaced in 2012 with *Zarkana* (which then closed in 2016), directed by François Girard, and *Michael Jackson ONE* opened in 2013. *La Nouba* has been running at Orlando's Walt Disney World since 1999. *Iris* in Hollywood, directed by French choreographer Philippe Decouflé, closed prematurely in January 2013 after an eighteen-month run. At the time this chapter was written, Cirque du Soleil had ten productions touring internationally (excluding the permanent productions in Vegas and Orlando), and a new production, *Kurios*, opening in the spring of 2014. Some of their productions are relatively recent "big top" shows, while a growing number are older big top productions that were converted into arena shows, accessing a new market and decreasing the set-up and travel time between cities.

3 After the initial shock and media frenzy surrounding the 400 employees laid off between January and March 2013, Cirque du Soleil discreetly pursued its re-engineering. Cirque spokespeople admit that there are but 1,500 employees left in Montreal (down from 2,000 in 2012) and 4,000 worldwide, down 1,000 (Paré 2014a). However, the staff reductions are also due to the closing of a number of permanent productions and to a rationalization of technical and production resources.

4 Both these companies have not-for-profit and commercial entities. While the not-for-profit numbers can be verified, the commercial ones cannot readily be. I have relied, for these numbers, on confidential conversations with administrators and industry insiders, and they remain an educated guess.

5 The Quebec provincial arts funding agency, Conseil des arts et des lettres du Québec, established a circus arts program with a distinct budget from other performing arts in 2001. The Canada Council for the Arts integrated contemporary circus into its interdisciplinary Inter-Arts Office. Most recent organizational and policy changes at the Canada Council will in theory make circus funding more largely available through a number of different programs. However, the lack of peer assessment by circus specialists and peers has proven to be a sore point with the professional contemporary circus community.

6 Much has been written about the animal-free origins of Qubec circus, but Cirque du Soleil has made it clear that the initial decision was not ethical but economical. For instance, when presented with the opportunity to work with animals, Guy Caron and Guy Laliberté did not hesitate to cocreate a show with their Swiss counterparts, Cirque Knie, in 1985. Cirque du Soleil alumni and cofounders Normand Latourelle and Gilles Ste-Croix each created their own horse-based circuses. Latourelle's Cavalia has become an important producer of equestrian spectacle, touring shows around the world. Ste-Croix's Cheval-Théâtre and later Saka have not attained the same level of success. There is also a smaller regional equestrian circus, near Montmagny, La Centaurée. While Quebec contemporary circus is first and foremost acrobatic and artistic, it does include a few interesting examples of equestrian practice.

7 Andréane Leclerc (2012), a circus-trained, high-level practitioner, has written a particularly strong and lucid master's thesis in theatre at Université du Québec à Montréal on the dramaturgy of contortion. I also cosupervised a master's thesis on social clowning written by long-time clown Sue Proctor (2013) and am currently supervising one on circus education by aerialist and educator Alisan Funk. There seems to be a growing number of scholar-practitioners, scholars who also seriously practice circus part-time.

8 The Research Chair is managed by the Social Sciences and Humanities Research Council of Canada. The Chair holder, Patrice Aubertin, a former director of training programs at Cirque du Soleil, is also director of research and of the teacher-training program at Montreal's National Circus School.

9 These figures were compiled from in-house statistics at the École nationale de cirque de Montréal. The programs, in addition to the extracurricular high school preparatory program, are as follows: (1) Circus and High School, intensive training with circus professionals for Grades 7–11); (2) Diploma of College Studies in Circus Arts (DEC), a three-year program leading to a professional career; (3) Diploma of National Circus School Studies, intended exclusively for foreign students as a parallel to the DEC; and three specialized programs in circus training: (4) Assistant Instructor, (5) Instructor, and (6) Trainer in Circus Arts Attestations of College Studies (AEC). The school also runs summer camps and a recreational program.

10 Various research initiatives are under the umbrella of the École nationale de cirque, others at Concordia, others at Université de Montréal or McGill. The Montreal Working Group on Circus Research, while independent from the national school's own research initiatives and agreements with industry partners, remains in constant conversation with all concerned. A growing number of graduate students and postdoctoral fellows are drawn to Montreal's circus scene, and the universities have only begun to tap into this rich and varied field.

11 The Montreal Working Group on Circus Research documents these on its website: http://resonance.hexagram.ca. Most of the talks and round table discussions are now recorded (video or audio) and are available for consultation, on site, at the library of the École nationale de cirque.

CHAPTER 2

1 Jean-Pierre Dion, interview by Louis Patrick Leroux, 8 May 2014, New York City.

2 A strong amateur and semi-professional circus tradition extends to extracurricular activity on college campuses such as Illinois State University (Gamma Phi Circus, since 1929), Florida State University (The FSU Flying High Circus, since 1947), and University of Chicago (Le Vorris & Vox Circus, since 2002).

3 Massicotte's use of the term *race* in the title and throughout his book must be read in the context of late nineteenth- and early twentieth-century usage in Quebec. The politically charged term *race* has since been replaced by *nation* in political discourse in Quebec.

4 The 2013 film *Louis Cyr* casts Barré in a subservient role and ultimately uses his lower status to signify a weak character in a strong body. This interpretation contradicts Paul Ohl's biography but makes for a fascinating narrative of unfulfilled possibilities in the film. In a sense, Louis Cyr is portrayed as the Québécois superman, the focused and never satisfied overachiever, the one who *could* and *did*, and Horace Barré is portrayed as a realistic, disappointing metonymic representation of the Quebec that *could have been*, but lacked the moral strength to assume its destiny.

5 A small Quebec circus community developed around Cirque Gatini. While most Gatini performers were American, Quebec artists such as Claude Bordez, Giovanni Iuliani, Pierre Jean, and dog trainer Robert Cimse found steady employment with various circuses in Quebec and in the United States, and made appearances on television and in amusement parks. Giovanni Iuliani's August clown was immortalized by Canada Post in 2001 on two commemorative stamps honouring the Shrine Circus with which he was associated for many years. Bordez and Iuliani evoke the details of the Cirque Gatini tours and organization in their 2002 book. Pierre Jean also recounts some of his experiences in circus and its fusion with televised entertainment in his own 1987 work, *Le monde fascinant du cirque*. Many feel that this circus tradition has been essentially ignored by circus history in Quebec in order for the nouveau cirque to emerge as the success story.

6 From the 1920s into the 1940s there were two performances a day of "World Renowned" acts represented by the New York agent Wirth and Hamid. George Hamid, a Lebanese-born circus performer before becoming an agent, had been a successful gymnast with Buffalo Bill's Wild West Show. He cofounded the Hamid-Morton Circus in 1932, which often performed at the Montreal Forum over the years (Proulx 2005, 87, 93–4).

7 National Circus School founder and Cirque du Soleil cofounder Guy Caron trained in Hungary's National Circus School, as did fellow clowns Rodrigue "Chocolat" Tremblay and Sonia "Chatouille" Côté from 1974 to 1976. This simultaneous training in both artistic and acrobatic streams, as well as the experience of learning disciplines anchored in generations-old traditions seemed to

have revelatory impact on the trio, who returned to Canada convinced of the importance of their pioneering work in establishing modern circus here. Caron was especially motivated to adapt the Hungarian school to the North American context where modern circus had yet to emerge beyond a handful of companies and individual artists, but where a well-developed clowning practice was established. Many Eastern and Central European trainers and coaches have joined the École nationale de cirque (ENC) since the 1980s, bringing with them their traditions and work ethic. For instance, the Slovakian director of studies, Daniela Arendasova, came to the ENC from a high-performance rhythmic gymnastics tradition. With the explosion of circus opportunities internationally in the late 1980s and into the 1990s, the market demanded higher technical skills of circus graduates. It should also be noted that the ENC, while it did act as a feeder school for Cirque du Soleil for its first few years, has since become independent and distinct from Cirque du Soleil's aesthetics and expectations, and its well-trained graduates are sought out internationally.

CHAPTER 3

1 In 1793, he introduced it to Russia.
2 Another directing duo that left its mark was Page and Wells, respectively a circus director and a man of theatre. For twelve months beginning in the summer of 1830, they worked as a tag team: one worked when the other took time off, and vice versa. A person named J.F. Schinotti was a star of Page's circus while also acting in Wells's troupe. I have yet to discover the nationality of Page and can therefore not confirm whether he was British.
3 In *La Gazette de Québec*, 9 August 1798, and *La Gazette de Montréal*, 12 February 1798.
4 The original French reads: "les cirques faisaient partie des théâtres de l'époque." Translator's note: all translations are mine unless specifically noted otherwise.
5 The original French reads: "Depuis la bonne société jusqu'au gamin du plus bas étage, tout le monde [voulait les] voir."
6 The original French reads: "Nous regrettons que cette compagnie [on parle ici du Cirque de John H. Murray] nous arrive dans un temps où l'argent est absolument rare, où les gens ont peine à se procurer l'absolu nécessaire. Il est inouï de voir qu'à Montréal et à Québec, où la misère se fait vivement sentir, pas moins de 40,000 personnes aient assisté aux quatre représentations d'un cirque qui a eu lieu récemment."
7 The original French reads: "jusqu'à lui offrir trois mille piastres par année pour remplir les fonctions de bête curieuse."
8 To learn more about what I elsewhere call "métacirques," those companies that explicitly think about their art and whose shows point to specific elements borrowed or reworked from other circus vocabularies, please see my doctoral dissertation, "Les nouveaux cirques: rupture ou continuité" (Boudreault 1999), in particular the discussion on Cirque du Soleil, 202–4.

CHAPTER 4

1 PR Newswire, 18 October 2010.

CHAPTER 5

1 It is uncertain if Cirque du Soleil still shines as brightly, and it is obvious – this book is proof – that critical discourse has since broadened greatly.
2 Translations here are by the translator of the full article, unless otherwise noted.
3 As he was receiving an honorary doctorate from Université Laval in 2008, Guy Laliberté thanked the Université de Montréal.

CHAPTER 6

1 Five of those shows were eventually cancelled, including *Iris* discussed here. The company's layoffs, announced in January 2013, received extended media coverage. See CBC News (2013) for more details. www.cbc.ca/news/canada/montreal/cirque-du-soleil-to-lay-off-400-employees-1.1355468.
2 This plan as well as the RiverPlace case study can be downloaded from the "Downtown Waterfront URA [Urban Renewal Area]: Overview" web page of the Portland Development Commission, www.pdc.us/our-work/urban-renewal-areas/downtown-waterfront/overview.aspx.
3 Cirque du Soleil offers a search tool on its website, "Help, have we ever visited your area?" (www.cirquedusoleil.com/en/help/history-shows.aspx, accessed 20 November 2013), that allows users to find the shows and performance dates for every city where the Cirque has travelled.
4 Portland's enthusiasm for Cirque du Soleil shows has also been tapped by a two-night stop (18–19 November 2011) for *Michael Jackson: The Immortal World Tour*. This show was staged at the Rose Garden Arena, home to the city's NBA team.
5 Cirque also visited Vancouver with arena shows in 2006 (*Delirium*) and 2011 (*Quidam*); the Michael Jackson show had dates at Rogers Arena in both 2011 and 2012.
6 When *Iris* first opened, Dolby Theater was still known as Kodak Theater; Eastman Kodak Company had paid $75 million for the naming rights. After Eastman Kodak sought bankruptcy protection early in 2012, the theatre was temporarily referred to as the Hollywood and Highland Theater before a twenty-year contract was signed with Dolby Laboratories for naming rights and for the theatre to act as a showcase for the company's latest sound technology (Crowe 2012).
7 In 2013 the theatre was renamed the TCL Chinese Theater, following a deal with TCL ("The Creative Life"), a Chinese electronics manufacturer, for ten-year naming rights. This information as well as a history of Chinese theatre is available at www.tclchinesetheatres.com/history/ (accessed 2 January 2014).

CHAPTER 7

1 "Le Cirque du Soleil y occupe bien entendu une place centrale, mais son seul rayonnement interdit en quelque sorte un portrait complet de la situation." For

this and other French-language sources, I have provided translations, unless otherwise noted.

2 *Psy* program notes, http://7doigts.com/en/shows/3-psy.

3 An announcement reported on 2 February 2015 (Corbo 2015) that Cirque du Soleil would be creating a show for July 2015 in Trois-Rivières based on the music of the famed Québécois folk-rock group Beau Dommage offers an interesting intertext to this discussion: after some thirty years and shows based on non-Québécois musical artists such as the Beatles and Michael Jackson, the multinational enterprise here explores, for an announced run of twenty performances, musical textures from the company's home province. The production, *Le monde est fou*, is part of a series of shows the company is calling "homages."

4 "s'écarte[r] des standards du cirque fantastique"; Les 7 doigts de la main, le Collectif, 2010 press kit.

5 Les 7 doigts de la main website, accessed 21 December 2013, http://7doigts.com/.

6 Ibid.; *Loft* program notes, http://7doigts.com/en/shows/4-loft.

7 Ibid.

8 See my "'Bêtes de scène'" (Batson 2012a) for an analysis of Grosz in the context of the 2010 Cirque du Soleil show *Totem*. That article also examines the role of the Montreal press in the perceptions of the lovebird couple mentioned below.

9 Shana Carroll, interview by Charles Batson, 6 November 2012, Montreal.

10 In a sign of this company's contributions to the global presence and reputation of Quebec's circuses, the Paris premiere of *Cuisine & Confessions* in December 2014 made it the troupe's third show (along with *Traces* and *Patinoire*) then running concurrently in France.

11 *Queen of the Night* program notes, http://7doigts.com/en/shows/21-queen-of-the-night.

12 Two independent short films featuring the 7 Fingers – *Corps* (https://www.youtube.com/watch?v=9soJSbLObow) and *Freestyle Bowling* (https://www.youtube.com/watch?v=r3L_TrVeCU4) – are available on Youtube, with one of them, *Corps*, produced by the acclaimed Bravofact.

13 "un 'late night show' un peu dans la lignée du film *Moulin Rouge*, avec de gros costumes flamboyants et affriolants. Mais c'est pas nous les gros costumes flamboyants. On s'est donc battus pour raconter une histoire … pour démontrer que ce n'est pas nécessaire d'être nus pour être sexy."

14 *Psy* program, 2010; "les profondeurs denses et surréalistes de la psyché humaine"

15 Ibid.; "en plus de leur rôle d'interprête … [les artistes] ont offert jusqu'à leur âme"

16 Ibid.; "un homme entend des voix lui ordonner de se suspendre à un trapèze par les orteils dans le paisible bureau de son *psy* … Un patient atteint de troubles obsessionnels compulsifs pris dans la cohue tente de s'échapper par une série d'acrobaties au travers de la marée humaine; une femme surmonte son agoraphobie en se balançant dans les airs; un homme recherche son identité parmi une foule de visages masqués en équilibre." Ellipses in the original.

17 Ibid.

18 "Depuis *Loft*, leur premier spectacle, les 7 doigts ont toujours misé sur la proximité avec le public, laissant les personnalités de leurs membres s'exprimer."
19 "A travers une interaction avec le public et quelques pointes d'ironie, *Séquence 8* investit à nouveau l'émotion du spectateur."
20 "versions édulcorées"; "créer une intimité avec le public"
21 "tisse le fil entre eux et le public"
22 "une communion réussie"
23 As a sign of this troupe's continued international presence, in April 2015 *Séquence 8* opened in the 2,750-seat New York City Center. The influential *New York Times* critic Ben Brantley (2015) noted the artists' perceived authenticities in his review of this intimist show in this arguably cavernous theatre: "What sets the Fingers ... apart is the relative plainness of their presentation and their insistence that there's nothing exotic about them. They're just ordinary folks in street clothes, hanging out on a naked stage (no nets!) and listening to a mixtape. They just happen to have really great, supremely bendable bodies and are able to fly."
24 "On a essayé d'être vrais."
25 "Le spectacle se targue d'en être un sur l'intime – l'intimité du sexe, le dévoilement de ses désirs, de ses perversions et de ses préférences. En réalité, c'est le Cirque qui s'exhibe."
26 "la volonté et la capacité du Cirque du Soleil de révéler ses atouts sans gêne ni honte"
27 "Le documentaire laisse entrevoir des individus dignes d'intérêt et d'empathie plutôt que des types d'un bestiaire sexuel, tels qu'ils sont présentés dans le cabaret."
28 "La confiance entière que le cinéaste, Lewis Cohen, réussit à établir entre ses sujets et lui."
29 "Le théâtre des années 1980 semble prendre du recul par rapport au modèle dominant d'un théâtre de la *québécité* et insiste plutôt sur l'image visuelle."
30 "Les arts de la scène abandonnent en quelque sorte le regard sociocritique et le mode réaliste afin d'embrasser de nouvelles formes d'expression et de renouveler le langage scénique."
31 Perhaps most influentially in Maranca's (1996) texts on Robert Wilson.
32 Dario's original 2012 French-language interview, for the *Journal des Nuits de Fourvière*, included references to "images de marque" and "danse et théâtralité." https://www.youtube.com/watch?v=cONukJCI4pQ.
33 "laiss[e] une grande place à la danse et aux chorégraphies entre les différents numéros acrobatiques"
34 William Smith, interview by Charles Batson, 9 December 2012, Montreal.
35 "Merci à Montréal cette ville chaleureuse et cosmopolite pour nous avoir influencés, nous le collectif"; *Séquence 8* program, 2012.
36 Floch's original French-language communication included references to "la part du lion" for those companies who "ont du mal à percer."
37 Marie-Josee Gauthier, conversation at meeting of the Working Group on Circus Research, 12 June 2011, Montreal. "les références, sinon *la* référence, auprès des finissants de l'Ecole [nationale de cirque]"

38 Nassib El-Hussieni, conversation with members of the Working Group on Circus Research, 13 January 2012, Montreal.

39 See my "Dis/locating Dominion" (Batson 2012b) for an analysis of Barthes's essay that reveals this same Montreal as a vibrantly queer city.

40 See, for example, *Journal de Deuil* 2009 (Paris: Seuil).

CHAPTER 8

1 "lorsque la technique d'un numéro est avancée et qu'il y a du danger"; all translations from the French are mine.

2 "Les artistes du Cirque du Soleil ne sont pas des trompe-la-mort. [...] Le Cirque du Soleil exploite l'imaginaire du public, son goût du rêve [...] et non pas un attrait morbide pour le danger."

3 "Et avec la croissance phénoménale du Cirque, il a fallu très tôt prévoir les remplacements et la relève [...] il faut constamment des artistes de qualité pour suffire à la demande ou aussi pour remplacer les athlètes malades, blessés, à la retraite ou parvenus à la fin d'un contrat non renouvelé."

4 Some Cirque du Soleil productions boast more "scenery" or architectural elements than others, of course. *Varekai* (2002) featured a forest of Chinese poles filling the upstage area and *Quidam*'s (1996) *téléférique* – its elaborate grid and rigging system that arched over the ¾ thrust ring – practically upstaged the show's human elements. All shows have needed to house the band in architectural elements; *Alegría* (1994) used simple elevated platforms, while *Dralion* (1999) masked them behind a tall bamboo-like wall structure that covered the upstage wall. Despite these variations, and even with KOOZÅ's ornate and imposing three-storey tower dubbed the "Bataclan," the scenic environment tends to fade into the background when acts are being performed, courtesy of strong spotlights on the performers and a softer light-wash bathing the rest of the stage area.

5 The most complete investigation into the question of circus and theatricality can be found in *L'Annuaire théâtral: revue québécoise d'études théâtrales*, no. 32, 2002. To be clear, however, traditional circus also had a narrative of sorts, as finely detailed by Paul Bouissac in *Circus and Culture: A Semiotic Approach*. In this book, Bouissac (1976) maintains that circus "language" – its visual, oral, and kinesthetic clues – constructs a meta-narrative pitting constraint against freedom.

6 "l'expressivité du corps, la voix (des soupirs et des cris) et les expressions du visage"

7 "entièrement créés par le Cirque du Soleil qui choisit les artistes, engage les formateurs et voit à toutes les étapes de leur élaboration"

8 Skidmore goes on to recuperate the corps performers' individuality through their occasional virtuosic acts and their varying interpretations of their shared characteristics. A contrasting effect that also stresses the corps' synchronicity occurs during *Quidam*'s curtain call when the performers remove their head-coverings (hats, wigs, and hoods). The increased visibility of their faces and the revelation of their own hair seem to suddenly individualize them.

9 "deviennent des outils, des moyens pour communiquer"

10 As Helen Stoddart (2000) in her lucid discussion of the craft-art tension in traditional circus performance points out, the notion that "art" is not subject to commodification in the same way as the circus is an illusion (709–83).

11 Upon leaving the Cirque du Soleil, Chassé founded Les 7 doigts de la main with Shana Carroll, Patrick Léonard, Faon Shane, Gypsy Snider, Sébastien Soldevila, and Samuel Tétreault.

12 "Ce que j'entends par nouveau cirque américain est un courant constitué d'un ensemble de jeunes troupes ayant pour objectif commun de réinventer le cirque en vue de le faire reconnaître comme une véritable forme d'art au même titre que la musique, la danse et le théâtre."

13 "Dès sa fondation, [le Cirque du Soleil] souhaita que ses acrobates et tous ceux qui se joignaient à eux soient considérés comme des artistes à part entière."

14 "On cherche à toucher le public autant par la beauté des mouvements, par la théâtralité et la mise en scène que par les prouesses acrobatiques."

15 The first performance I attended was a preview on 26 April 2007. The second, a regular performance, was on 10 May 2007.

16 "Ce pseudo-événement [...] communique au public une information que celui-ci ne percevait pas nécessairement dans la routine habituelle du numéro : la difficulté qui fait que l'exercice est une prouesse." "Le ratage permet au numéro de quitter le strict domaine de la technique pour prendre une dimension humaine. L'artiste indique lui-même sa propre limite et témoigne de sa propre incertitude quant à sa réussite [...] Il cesse d'être la mécanique que l'on admire pour, un instant, retrouver la faiblesse de l'être humain qu'il n'a jamais cessé d'être, malgré les apparences."

17 Here *KOOZÅ*'s costume designer, Marie-Chantale Vaillancourt, references the circus's beginnings when, according to circus historian and circus costume designer, Pascal Jacob, "the first circus costumes were military uniforms" [les premiers costumes de cirque sont des uniformes militaires] (Jacob 2002, 109).

18 Note that *KÀ*, Cirque du Soleil's permanent installation at the MGM Casino in Las Vegas directed by Robert Lepage, is furnished with a net, erected out of sight underneath the hydraulic stage. Remember too the tragic death of *KÀ* aerial performer, Sarah Guillot-Guyard, in July 2013.

19 Other Québécois "new circuses" like Cirque Éloize and Cirque Eos also mix ring and stage, even abandoning the ring configuration altogether. Boudreault attributes this combination space to a number of factors, including historical precedents (hippodrome, nautical presentations), aesthetic drivers (looking for new performance spaces), and economic factors (it is cheaper to rent theatres for performance than to have one's own tent; J. Boudreault 2002a, 26–30).

CHAPTER 9

1 I saw the production twice during in its run in Montreal in the summer of 2010, and again in London, UK, in January 2011.

2 *Totem*, 2010 press kit, 2, http://static01.cirquedusoleil.com/en/~/media/press/PDF/totem/totem-press-kit.pdf.

3 "Totem," accessed 12 December 2013, http://www.cirquedusoleil.com/en/shows/totem/default.aspx.
4 "Je trouve ça incroyable qu'un pays comme les États-Unis permette d'enseigner le créationnisme. Je trouve que ça les fait reculer. Et je pensais à ça en créant le spectacle ... Si Darwin avait raison!" Translation mine.
5 *Totem*, 2010 press kit, 3.
6 Since approximately 2008, Lepage has become particularly engaged with the Huron-Wendat nation, whose reserve is near Quebec City where he lives and works. In 2009 he created an on-water performance in canoes, as part of the Festival de canotgraphie near Quebec City, exploring the intertwined histories of French, Irish, and Huron-Wendat peoples in the area (see CBC News 2012). He directed a French-language production of Shakespeare's *The Tempest* on the Wendake reserve in the summer of 2011, featuring some Wendat performers; and his outdoor sound-and-light spectacle *The Image Mill*, which played in Quebec City each summer from 2008 to 2013, includes depictions of the relationship between native peoples and white settlers in Quebec. See lacaserne.net.
7 *Totem*, 2010 press kit, 2.
8 *Oxford Dictionaries*, s.v. "totem," accessed 12 December 2013, http://www.oxforddictionaries.com/definition/english/totemsch.
9 *Totem*, 2010 press kit, 33.
10 Ibid., 5.
11 *Totem*, 2010 souvenir program.
12 Ibid., 13.
13 *Totem*, 2010 press kit, 6.
14 Ibid., 3.
15 Ibid., 4.
16 The production's relative lack of engagement in the representational potential of these Western-focused acts is suggested by the fact that the clowns are mentioned only once in its seven-page press kit.
17 *Totem*, 2010 press kit, 10.
18 The representation of characters who long to fly or are fascinated with flying, and the image of the human body in flight, are ongoing preoccupations for Lepage. Many of his productions, such as *Needles and Opium* (originally produced in 1991, remounted in 2013), *Geometry of Miracles* (1998), and *Zulu Time* (1999), feature images of bodies suspended in space. The solo piece *The Far Side of the Moon* (2000, made into a film in 2003) has as its subject matter the Soviet-American space race.
19 "Le spectacle laisse croire qu'il serait possible pour les Terriens de tous les règnes (humain, animal, végétal, et minéral) de vivre un jour en harmonie, toutes couleurs unies, dans un seul et même monde." Translation mine.
20 Larance and Laveau were the only two Aboriginal performers in *Totem* when it premiered. Larance's sister Shandien joined the production as an understudy when the show was touring, and was added into the show's second hoop dance, previously a solo. Nakotah Larance left the production in 2012, replaced by Eric

Hernandez, who is of Lumbee and Mexican-American descent. At the time of writing, Hernandez, Shandien Larance, and Laveau continue in the production (see Diamond 2013; Kennedy 2012).

21 According to Laveau's personal website and press reports, Lepage saw Laveau perform in *Kiugwe*, a production celebrating First Nations culture staged on the Wendake reserve during Quebec City's 400th anniversary celebrations in 2008, and invited him to participate in the Cirque du Soleil production. See Boisvert (2009); http://www.christianlaveau.ca.

22 *Totem*, 2010 press kit, 5.

23 See ondinnok.org; http://www.christianlaveau.ca.

CHAPTER 10

1 Guy Laliberté is the street artist – accordionist, stilt-walker, and fire-eater – who founded Cirque du Soleil.

2 C2-MTL is an example of such gatherings. The aim of this event is "all about finding creative answers to commercial questions." The registration costs were $3,600 for the 2013 conference. http://www.c2mtl.com/.

3 Cirque du Soleil, "Creative Approach," https://www.cirquedusoleil.com/en/home/about-us/creative-approach.aspx.

4 In an address to the Montreal business community on 9 April 2002, Guy Laliberté presented the Complexe Cirque project as part of a larger initiative that would have leveraged Montreal as a worldwide cultural destination. His speech can be found here: http://www.btmm.qc.ca/en/news/speech—guest-speaker mr-guy-laliberte-founding-president-cirque-du-soleilmontreal-as-an-international-culture-metropolis/.

5 Tcherkessy or "Circassie" in French refers to a formerly independent country located in the north of the Caucasus region, now part of the Russian Federation, and to its homonym which means the land of circus and its inhabitants, the Circassians. Western orientalism was fuelled by several influential writers like Voltaire who spoke of Circassian women as the ideal of feminine beauty.

6 To get an idea of the "Happy Few" lifestyle, consult the luxury and ultra-luxury trends on www.trendhunter.com.

7 "La belle Essayade" is the narrative presented in Mahy (2008a), chapter 3.

8 The next phase was to be the construction phase, starting after the ideation and the design phases were completed. As mentioned previously, the project was stopped right before construction.

9 See http://letroisiemeoeil.weebly.com/3rd-eye-description.html.

CHAPTER 11

1 A revised edition of *Learning from Las Vegas,* entitled *Learning from Las Vegas: The Forgotten Symbolism of Architectural Form,* was published in 1977. The quotations that appear in this chapter are taken from the revised publication (Venturi, Brown, and Izenour 1977).

2 "L'essence même de notre projet était liée à la présence dynamique du Cirque du

Soleil, à sa signature distincte, au cachet particulier dont il allait doter toutes les composantes du complexe, à sa créativité remarquable ainsi qu'à sa capacité d'attirer des partenaires privés." Translator's note: All excerpts and titles from newspaper articles are my own translations.

3 "d'un formidable outil de développement"

4 "l'apport de son attrait international"

5 "Montréal, non. Mais l'Asie, peut-être. Quelques jours après avoir annoncé son retrait du projet du casino au bassin Peel, le Cirque du Soleil s'associe à l'entreprise MGM Mirage pour tenter de décrocher un lucratif contrat de casino à Singapour. Quatre équipes se battent pour la construction d'un immense complexe à Marina Bay, à Singapour. Le projet, évalué à 3 milliards de dollars américains, comprendra un casino, un hôtel, plusieurs restaurants, une ou deux discothèques et un centre de congrès ... Quatre spectacles du Cirque du Soleil sont actuellement présentés dans des casinos exploités par MGM Mirage : *KÀ* au Grand à Las Vegas, O au Bellagio, *Zumanity* au New York-New York, et *Mystère* au Treasure Island. Un cinquième, mettant en vedette la musique des Beatles, sera aussi présenté à l'été au Mirage Resort, toujours à Las Vegas."

6 "Question d'identité"

7 "Le Cirque du Soleil a habitué ses admirateurs à des projets audacieux. Mais, en 2006, l'entreprise dirigée par Guy Laliberté a atteint de nouveaux sommets. Que ce soit la présentation de Love, un spectacle inspiré de l'univers des Beatles – une collaboration rare avec un groupe qui gère soigneusement son héritage –, le succès de ses spectacles itinérants, de nouveaux projets à New York, en Asie et en Amérique du Sud, tous les événements se sont conjugués pour que le Cirque réalise une année record [...] La vision de Guy Laliberté, qui se voit toujours comme le 'guide créatif' du Cirque du Soleil, est acclamée sur toute la planète."

8 "Guy se souvient toujours que c'est le Québec qui a lancé le Cirque du Soleil, et il s'efforce de renvoyer l'ascenseur. L'une de ses grandes contributions est d'avoir permis à des Québécois de rayonner dans le monde entier ... Il a également contribué à faire de Montréal une capitale internationale des arts du cirque et inspiré la création de compagnies comme le Cirque Éloize et Les 7 doigts de la main."

9 "Le Cirque, [qui] reçoit annuellement plus de 50 000 curriculum vitae, est d'ailleurs à l'étroit à son siège social qui fait présentement les frais d'un agrandissement majeur, le troisième depuis son établissement dans le quartier Saint-Michel en 1997."

10 "Selon des calculs de la CCMM (Chambre de commerce du Montréal métropolitain), la région de Toronto compte au total plus de trois millions de pieds carrés en centres de foires, alors que la région montréalaise est limitée à quelque 600 000 pieds carrés. 'Il faut qu'Ottawa comprenne que Montréal doit augmenter son offre,' estime Madame Hudon. Le contexte de divertissement est le bon projet pour y arriver."

11 "Ça y est, la locomotive est en marche, et le Casino est dans le train. Ainsi donc, un projet qui associera l'image de Montréal à celle du jeu, qui nous donnera un

centre de foires et de spectacles qui risque de faire double emploi avec les équipements existants, et dont nul ne sait s'il ne s'agira pas d'une aventure encore plus ruineuse que le Stade olympique, Mirabel ou le métro de Laval, vient de recevoir les bénédictions de nos élites, et le peuple n'a plus qu'à embarquer."

12 "On ne le dira jamais assez, les métropoles intéressantes n'ont pas de casino. New York n'en a pas, ni Paris, ni même Toronto. Là où on les tolère, il s'agit de petits établissements discrets qui ne font pas partie de l'image de la ville. En règle générale, ce sont dans de petites localités touristiques que l'on implante des casinos, pas dans les grandes villes qui ont d'autres choses à offrir. Veut-on vraiment que Montréal devienne 'La Vegas du Nord'?"

13 "Loto-Québec préfère passer à l'attaque avec un complexe intégré de 1,175 milliard au bassin Peel, comprenant un hôtel de 300 chambres, un spa spectaculaire, une salle de spectacles de 2,500 places, une scène extérieure pouvant accueillir 10,000 personnes, une marina, des parkings sous-terrains et de surface et, bien sûr, un casino. Enfin 'l'âme de ce complexe sera le Cirque du Soleil,' explique Monsieur Cousineau."

14 "Nulle part ailleurs dans le monde le Cirque n'a-t-il investi dans une salle de spectacles. Pourquoi aurait-il fallu qu'il en soit autrement à Montréal? Le droit d'utiliser le logo, la signature et les marques de commerce du Cirque du Soleil représentent des sommes importantes qu'il est difficile de quantifier mais qui ont une valeur considérable qui doit être prise en compte autant que la brique et le mortier. En agissant comme concepteur et directeur artistique du projet, le Cirque lui aurait donné une remarquable force d'attraction qui lui aurait permis de se démarquer."

15 "Si on s'associe au casino, c'est pour augmenter le marketing du projet. Si on augmente le marketing du projet, c'est pour attirer plus de monde. Et si ça attire plus de monde, ça va créer plus de problèmes de jeu. Cette association avec le Cirque du Soleil visant une plus grande visibilité, une plus grande acceptabilité sociale, va créer plus de problèmes. Dis autrement, ce serait un excellent projet s'il n'y avait pas de casino."

16 "Une nouvelle rallonge de huit étages avec, en son coeur, un collecteur d'eau de pluie de la taille d'une piscine. C'est comme si un géant en goguette avait déposé sa gigantesque coupe de champagne à travers le toit du nouvel immeuble. Seulement, ce cristal ne retient pas les liquides : il les évacue vers un drain placé à la base de l'immense cône transparent, haut d'environ sept mètres, large de six et fort de quelques tonnes. Ce collecteur liant l'éthique et l'esthétique amassera assez d'eau pluie et de neige fondue pour rendre autonome une partie du complexe du Cirque du Soleil à Montréal, où travaillent 1,700 employés."

17 "verre chauffé, enrichi d'effets lumineux, traverse et embellit les deux derniers locaux fusionnés de la nouvelle construction, avec un foyer à l'éthanol pour l'ambiance des soirées d'hiver, un grand écran de projection et des cuisines"

18 "Le promoteur fait valoir l'accessibilité du site et ses liens avec le centre-ville tout en soulignant qu'il sera enclavé, ce qui permettrait de limiter les impacts négatifs sur la population environnante. Ou bien le projet est centré sur lui-même et vise

à s'autosuffire en offrant "aux visiteurs une expérience unique qui les retiennent le plus longtemps sur place et qui, d'une certaine façon, tourne le dos à la ville," ou bien il est intégré au quartier et, plus largement, à toute la ville. De plus, "le design architectural, qui ressemble à un vaisseau intersidéral [...], n'a rien avoir avec l'historicité du lieu et son environnement."'

19 "Plusieurs aspects du projet doivent être approfondis. Hier, *Le Devoir* révélait que le futur casino serait construit sur un site archéologique marqué par le passage des Amérindiens d'avant la colonisation ainsi que par la révolution industrielle canadienne dont le canal de Lachine a été l'épine dorsale. Loto-Québec sera obligée de faire des fouilles pendant plusieurs mois et d'en payer la note, laquelle pourrait s'élever à plusieurs centaines de milliers de dollars. 'On ne croit pas qu'il y ait des artefacts et des vestiges sur l'ensemble du terrain qu'on aimerait utiliser pour le casino. Mais c'est sûr qu'on va s'assurer que tout se déroule selon les règles de l'art,' a affirmé hier le porte-parole de Loto-Québec, Jean-Pierre Roy."

CHAPTER 12

1 Cirque du Soleil Tour, 1986 official program.
2 Ibid.
3 Cirque du Soleil Quebec/California Tour, 1987 official program, 32.
4 Ibid., 63–4.
5 Zhao Yan Yan, interview by Tracy Zhang, 4 October 2011, Montreal.
6 Nicolai Volland (2007) has shown that the socialist Chinese government was eager to establish the People's Republic of China as a modern nation-state in the world. Cultural exchange activities, such as mutual visits of orchestras, writers, and drama troupes, and the participation of Chinese artists in international competitions and festivals, are crucial means of promoting new China. My research suggests that acrobats were also active participants in such diplomatic activities.
7 Zhou Liang Tie, interview by Tracy Zhang, 10 August 2012, Shanghai.
8 Shenyang Acrobatic Art Troupe of China, 1972 official program.
9 From 1986 to 1990, Shanghai was an exception. The Shanghai Acrobatic Troupe could sign contracts with overseas performance agencies directly. This policy ended in the 1990s.

CHAPTER 13

1 The authors would like to thank all the participants in this study and Mia Hunt and Carla Klassen for their research assistance. This study was funded in part by the Canadian Research Chair and the Social Science and Humanities Research Council – Major Collaborative Research Initiative (award number 412-2005-1001).
2 Cirque du Soleil is the dominant circus company in Montreal, but there are a number of other smaller troupes in the city. Many of these have emerged out of the Cirque.
3 See for example Arthur (1989), David (1985), Dosi (1997), Hodgson (1994), and Nelson (1994).

4 Montreal is known as the "city of festivals." There are over seventy festivals each year, many of which are outdoors (http://www.montreal.com/tourism/festivals/index.html).
5 Lalonde left the École nationale de cirque in October 2015.
6 While Toronto is the dominant location for cultural industries in Canada, Montreal is the second-largest centre and the most significant for Quebec (Coish 2004).
7 This finding was derived by measuring both the number of industries in a city, and how employment is shared across these industries (see Beckstead and Brown 2003).
8 Stolarick and Florida (2006) cite Cirque du Soleil as a prominent example of cross-fertilization not only between different cultural industries but also between culture and technology sectors.
9 Interview with a former employee/TOHO manager, August 2008.
10 Interview with the artistic director of Cirque du Soleil, December 2008.
11 It is important to note, however, that many of these projects ended in financial disaster.
12 A number of initiatives, mainly government funded, have emerged in Quebec to support artists and designers. For further discussion of these initiatives, see Leslie and Rantisi (2006).
13 Interview with a former vice-president of marketing and communications for Cirque du Soleil, December 2008.
14 Ibid.
15 Ibid.
16 Interview with a Cirque official, December 2008.
17 Interview with a former vice-president of marketing and communications.
18 Interview with a former director of École nationale de Cirque de Montréal, June 2008.
19 Ibid.
20 Interview with a circus performer and graduate of École nationale de cirque de Montréal, June 2009.
21 A CEGEP is a unique educational institute in Quebec. Students who complete high school must complete two years at a CEGEP before going to university.
22 Interview, former director of École nationale de cirque de Montréal, June 2008.
23 Ibid.
24 Jan-Rok Achard, interview by authors, June 2008.
25 En Piste, "Achievements," http://www.enpiste.qc.ca/en/pages/achievements.

CHAPTER 14

1 "The Upgrade Program is aimed at the candidate who demonstrates the potential to undertake advanced training but lacks the required physical or artistic skills. The Upgrade Program consists of skills and courses in basic circus techniques and disciplines. The student is able to participate in general training as well as the various courses specific to the higher education program. Conditional

admission is granted for the period of one year, after which the student must retake the Entrance Exam for final admission to the program." École nationale de cirque website, http://ecolenationaledecirque.ca/en.

CHAPTER 15

1 Media outlets initially dubbed the movement the "Maple Spring," in somewhat ironic and homophonic reference (*printemps érable*) to the previous uprisings called the *printemps arabe*. While the label was initially embraced by activist groups, it has since been rejected by many, including prominent student spokesperson Gabriel Nadeau-Dubois, due to the asymmetry in scale and the nature of what those involved in the "Arab" uprisings had confronted.

2 On 18 May 2012, the government of Quebec passed a "special law," Bill 78 (Quebec National Assembly 2012), outlawing the picketing of classes, as well as the refusal to teach during the strike (section 13). It further prohibited public gatherings of more than fifty people without eight hours' prior notice given to the police (section 16), and also prohibited acts of civil disobedience against the above legislation (section 15). Denounced as an infraction of human rights by Amnesty International (Zúñiga 2012) and as unconstitutional by the Quebec Bar Association (Le Barreau du Québec 2012), concern about this law is thought to have prompted an increase in support for the movement. After the election the following September, the new government repealed the law.

3 For an indication of student association responses to the proposed budget, see Condordia University's Geography, Planning and Environment Graduate Students Association (Geograds), http://geograds.wordpress.com/geogradsnewsletter/funding-plan/719-2/ (accessed 22 October 2014). For an overview and analysis of various positions among students and supporters involved in the protests, see Ancelovici and Dupuis-Déri (2013).

4 Throughout the month of May 2012, supporters of the student movement across the island of Montreal stood on balconies and street corners nightly at eight o'clock and banged on pots and pans as a form of symbolic protest. This adaptation of the Latin America protest tradition of "cazzeroles" was known in Montreal as "les casseroles." For a discussion of the role and significance of this tactic during the 2012 Quebec student protests, see Drapeau-Bisson, Dupuis-Déri, and Ancelovici (2013) and Rosen (2012).

5 Original promises made by Liberal government officials of eventually free tuition were covered in the 1960s by the Canadian Broadcasting Corporation. See for instance Radio-Canada (1960).

6 For an analysis of Cirque du Monde's social intervention model, see Rivard (2007); for an example of how Cirque du Soleil's social circus training has been appropriated and transformed by a government program in South America, see Spiegel et al. (2015).

7 "What Is Cirque du Monde?" http://www.unitipercrescereinsieme.it/studi-e-ricerche/cirque-du-monde.

8 Guided tour of La Caserne offered to Circus Now in July 2014.

9 Cirque Hors Piste, *Rapport d'activité 2013*.
10 On 14 October 2013, Nicolas Bérubé and Marc Thibodeau published an editorial in *La Presse,* one of Quebec's most prominent newspapers, entitled "Cirque du Soleil: divertir au Kazakhstan, un pays totalitaire," in which they raised the question as to whether the show performed as a benefit concert for orphans in Kazakhstan, paid for by what the authors argue is a totalitarian government with a brutal record of human rights abuses including recent killings of minors on strike, was really to the benefit of the underprivileged as Cirque du Soleil claimed, or whether Cirque was actually complicit with, and financially benefiting from, a public relations effort launched by this dictatorship.
11 Norman Nawrocki, interview, December 2012.
12 http://www.artsnetworkasia.org/directory_detail.php?id=118.
13 The significance of such promises and other historical factores in shaping the 2012 student movement are discussed in Theurillat-Cloutier, Leduc, and Lacoursière (2013).
14 For a genealogy of the "red square" symbol and its meaning during the Quebec student movement, see Asselin (2012).
15 For the numbers of students on strike during various periods, see Ancelovici and Dupuis-Déri (2012).
16 The original website was taken down in 2013. The original Facebook event can be found at https://www.facebook.com/events/422275694475942/ (accessed 18 December 2014).
17 My translation from the French found on the former website and Facebook group En Feu Contre La Hausse: "Trop souvent considéré, à l'époque des grandes luttes sociales, comme un outil de révolte dangereux, le feu est d'abord et avant tout l'élément rassembleur autour duquel il est bon se réchauffer, discuter, chanter et même … créer!" (accessed 2 October 2013).
18 Interview with En Feu Contre La Hausse spokesperson Louve, September 2012.
19 The event invitation as well as documentation can be found at https://www.facebook.com/events/513701932021864 (accessed 19 December 2014). Video documentation by the Montreal-based photographer and videographer Madoc can be found at http://printempsquebecois.com/sourifest-auto-souriciere-du-peuple/.
20 Interview with Cirque Hors Piste participant, May 2014.
21 Interviews with Cirque Hors Piste participants, May 2014.
22 http://www.poecirque.org/Poecirque/Acceuil.html, my translation.
23 http://www.carmagnole.net/productions/a-propos-de-nous/, my translation.
24 http://www.carmagnole.net/productions/a-propos-de-nous/, my translation.
25 http://vimeo.com/42848523 (accessed 13 December 2014).

EPILOGUE

1 Rodrigue Tremblay, interview by Louis Patrick Leroux, 17 December 2014, Longueuil, Quebec.
2 Alain Francoeur, interview by Louis Patrick Leroux, 11 September 2014, Montreal.

References

Achard, Jan Rok, with Patrick Léonard, Catherine Léger, and Magali Marcheschi. 2013. "Le respect de l'intégrité morale et physique dans les arts du cirque." Position papers delivered at Concordia University, 11 February.

Adams, Rachel. 2001. *Sideshow U.S.A.: Freaks and the American Cultural Imagination*. Chicago: University of Chicago Press.

Albrecht, Ernest. 2002. "Le nouveau cirque américain." *L'Annuaire théâtral: revue québécoise d'études théâtrales* 32: 37–46.

Ancelovici, Marcos, and Francis Dupuis-Déri, eds. 2013. *Un Printemps rouge et noir: Regards croisés sur la grève étudiante de 2012*. Montreal: Les Éditions Écosociété.

Arthur, Brian. 1989. "Competing Technologies, Increasing Returns, and Lock-In by Historical Events." *The Economic Journal* 99: 116–31.

Asakawa, Kiyoshi. 2004. "Flow Experience and Autotelic Personality in Japanese College Students: How Do They Experience Challenges in Daily Life?" *Journal of Happiness Studies* 5: 123–54.

Asselin, Olivier. 2012. "Red Square: A Colored Form's Political Destiny." Translated by Laura Balladur. *Theory & Event* 15 (3). Accessed 5 January 2015. http://muse.jhu.edu/login?auth=0&type=summary&url=/journals/theory_and_event/v015/15.3S.asselin_sub01.html.

Attleo, Shawnæ A-in-chut. 2013. "Special Chiefs Assembly Opening Address." 10 December. Accessed 28 December 2013. http://www.afn.ca/index.php/en/news-media/latest-news/special-chiefs-assembly-opening-address-national-chief-shawn-a-in-chut.

Aubin, Benoit. 2006. "The Disney of the New Age." *Maclean's*, 26 June.

Austen, Ian. 2015. "Sale of Cirque du Soleil Aims to Open Doors in China." *New York Times*, 20 April. Accessed 23 July 2015. http://www.nytimes.com/2015/04/21/business/dealbook/cirque-de-soleil-deal.html?_r=0.

Babinski, Tony. 2004. *Cirque du Soleil: 20 Years under the Sun*. New York: Harry N. Abrams.

Baillargeon, Stéphane. 2007. "Le Cirque du Soleil s'agrandit (encore!)." *Le Devoir*, 24 May, B6.

– 2014. "En avant, comme avant! Diversification et dilution à la mode Cirque du Soleil, qui est en redefinition." *Le Devoir*, 18 January, A6.

Bakhtin, Mikhail. 1984. *Rabelais and His World*. Translated by Hélène Iswolsky. Bloomington: Indiana University Press.

Bandelj, Nina, and Frederick F. Wherry. 2011. "Introduction: An Inquiry into the Cultural Wealth of Nations." In *The Cultural Wealth of Nations*, edited by Nina Banjelj and Frederick F. Wherry, 1–20. Stanford: Stanford University Press.

Bandura, Albert. 2001. "Social Cognitive Theory: An Agentic Perspective." *Annual Review of Psychology* 52: 1–26.

Barlati, Anna-Karyna, and Stéphane Zummo. 2014. "Les archives du cirque: quoi, comment, pour qui, pourquoi?" Working Group on Circus Research talk at National Circus School, 31 January.

Barthes, Roland. 1977. "The Grain of the Voice." Translated by Stephen Heath. In *Image, Music, Text*, 179–89. New York: Hill and Wang.

– 1980. *La chambre claire: note sur la photographie*. Paris: Gallimard.

– 1997. "Semiology and the Urban." In *Rethinking Architecture: A Reader in Cultural Theory*, edited by Neil Leach, 166–71. London: Routledge.

Batson, Charles. 2005. *Dance, Desire, and Anxiety in Early Twentieth-Century French Theater*. Aldershot and Burlington: Ashgate Publishing.

– 2012a. '"Bêtes de scène': Robert Lepage's *Totem*, Circus, and the Freakish Human Animal." *Contemporary French and Francophone Studies* 16 (5): 615–23.

– 2012b. "Dis/locating Dominion: Being at Home with Claude and Re-Membering a Queer Montreal." *Contemporary French Civilization* 37 (2–3): 159–75.

– 2014. "Pink, Cirque, and the *Québécisation de l'industrie*." *Québec Studies* 58: 25–44.

Beauchamp, Hélène, and Bernard Lavoie. 2003. *DynamO Théâtre. Théâtre de mouvement acrobatique*. Outremont: Duchesne éditeur.

Beaudet, Véronique. 2011. "Les 7 doigts de la main acclamés." *Canoe*, 24 November. http://fr.canoe.ca/divertissement/arts-scene/nouvelles/2011/11/24/19017051-qmi.html.

Beaunoyer, Jean. 2004. *Dans les coulisses du Cirque du Soleil*. Montreal: Québec Amérique.

Beckstead, Desmond, and Mark Brown. 2003. *From Labrador City to Toronto: The Industrial Diversity of Canadian Cities, 1992–2002*. Catalogue 11-624-MIE. No. 003. Ottawa: Statistics Canada.

Behncke, Luke. 2002. "Self-Regulation: A Brief Review." *Athletic Insight: The Online Journal of Sport Psychology*. http://www.athleticinsight.com/Vol4Iss1/SelfRegulation.htm.

Beilock, Sian L., Bennett I. Bertenthal, Annette M. McCoy, and Thomas H. Carr. 2004. "Haste Does Not Always Make Waste: Expertise, Direction of Attention, and Speed versus Accuracy in Performing Sensorimotor Skills." *Psychonomic Bulletin & Review* 11 (2): 373–9.

Bennett, Susan. 2005. "Theatre/Tourism." *Theatre Journal* 57 (3): 407–28.

Benston, Liz. 2004. "Judge Rejects Claim for 'Cirque' Name." *Las Vegas Sun*, 23 April. http://www.lasvegassun.com/news/2004/apr/23/.

Bergeron, Maxime. 2015a. "Cirque du Soleil: cap sur la Chine." *La Presse*, 29 July. Accessed 29 July 2015. http://affaires.lapresse.ca/economie/international/201507/28/01-4888834-cirque-du-soleil-cap-sur-la-chine.php.

– 2015b. "Cirque du Soleil: une filiale de contenus 'sur mesure.'" *La Presse*, 29 July. Accessed 29 July 2015. http://affaires.lapresse.ca/economie/é/201507/29/01-4888846-cirque-du-soleil-une-filiale-de-contenus-sur-mesure.php.

Berkery, Sheri. 2013. "Hoop Dancing with *Totem*'s Eric Hernandez." *Courier-Post*. Accessed 23 December. http://www.courierpostonline.com/VideoNetwork/2424119928001/Hoop-Dancing-with-Cirque-du-Soleil-s-Eric-Hernandez.

Berlant, Lauren. *Cruel Optimism*. Durham: Duke University Press.

Bérubé, Nicolas. 2005. "Des gens d'affaires appuient le déménagement du casino." *La Presse*, 13 October, A5.

Bérubé, Nicolas, and Marc Thibodeau. 2013. "Cirque du Soleil: divertir au Kazakhstan, un pays totalitaire." *La Presse*, 14 October.

Berzon, Alexandra. 2014. "Cirque du Soleil's Next Act: Rebalancing the Business." *Wall Street Journal*, 1 December.

Berzon, Alexandra, and Gillian Tan. 2015. "Cirque du Soleil Nears Sale to TPG Group. Founder in Talks to Sell Stake in Deal that Values Circus Company at 1.5 Billion." *Wall Street Journal*, 16 April. Accessed 23 July 2015. http://www.wsj.com/articles/cirque-du-soleil-nears-sale-to-tpg-group-1429220100.

Beyard, Michael D., Raymond E. Braun, Herbert McLaughlin, Patrick L. Phillips, and Michael S. Rubin. 2001. *Developing Retail Entertainment Destinations*. Washington: Urban Land Institute.

Blais, Marie-Christine. 2008. "Les 7 doigts de la main: la vie avant *La vie*." *La Presse,* 20 September. http://www.lapresse.ca/arts/spectacles-et-theatre/humour-et-varietes/200809/20/01-21831-les-7-doigts-de-la-main-la-vie-avant-la-vie.php.

Boal, Augusto. 1979. *Theatre of the Oppressed*. Translated by Charles A. McBride and Maria-Odilia Leal McBride. New York: Urizen Books.

Boisvert, Richard. 2009. "L'aventure de *Kiugwe* se poursuit cet été." *Le Soleil*, 21 May. http://www.lapresse.ca/le-soleil/arts-et-spectacles/sur-scene/200905/21/01-858588-laventure-de-kiugwe-se-poursuit-cet-ete.php.

Bordez, Claude, and Giovanni Iuliani. 2002. *Dernier tour de piste*. Chicoutimi: Éditions JCL.

Boschma, Ron, and Ron Martin. 2007. "Constructing an Evolutionary Economic Geography." *Journal of Economic Geography* 7 (5): 537–48.

Boudreault, Françoise. 2002. "Acrobatie aérienne et théâtralité." *L'Annuaire théâtral: revue québécoise d'études théâtrales* 32: 75–92.

– 2009. "Visite sur l'histoire du cirque au Québec." Briefing document for TOHU walking tour. Consulted at National Circus School Library.

– 2012. "Le cirque parlant des 7 doigts de la main." *Jeu* 145 (4): 125–33.

Boudreault, Julie. 1996. *Le Cirque du Soleil. La création d'un spectacle : Saltimbanco*. Quebec City: Nuit blanche.

– 1999. "Les nouveaux cirques: rupture ou continuité?" PhD diss., Université Laval.

– ed. 2002a. "Cirque et théâtralité: nouvelles pistes." Special issue. *L'Annuaire théâtral* 32 (Fall).

– 2002b. "Le Cirque au Québec: Une pratique culturelle méconnue." In *Traité de la culture*, edited by Denise Lemieux, Gilles Bibeau Michelle Comeau, François-Marc Gagnon, Fernand Harvey, Marc-André Lessard, and Gilles Marcotte, 787–98. Sainte-Foy: Presses de l'Université Laval.
– 2002c. "Quelques rapports entre le théâtre et le cirque au Québec." *L'Annuaire théâtral: revue québécoise d'études théâtrales* 32: 22–36.
– 2012. "Le Cirque au Québec est-il de souche étrangère?" Paper presented at The State of Circus Research in Quebec: Workshop Session on the Models and Conditions of Possibility, held at Concordia University, McGill University, National Circus School, and TOHU, September 2012.
Bouissac, Paul. 1976. *Circus and Culture: A Semiotic Approach*. Bloomington: Indiana University Press.
Bourassa, André-Gilles. 2004. "Entrée des artistes." *L'Annuaire théâtral: revue québécoise d'études théâtrales* 35: 177–203.
Brantley, Ben. 2015. "In 'Séquence 8' Acrobats Defy Gravity and Constrictive Words." *New York Times*, 20 April. http://www.nytimes.com/2015/04/21/theater/review-in-sequence-8-acrobats-defy-gravity-and-constrictive-words.html?_r=0.
Brousseau-Pouliot, Vincent. 2009. "Guy Laliberté acquiert 10% du Massif." *La Presse*, 4 May. http://affaires.lapresse.ca/economie/quebec/200905/04/01-853096-guy-laliberte-acquiert-10-du-massif.php.
– 2015a. "TPG Capital remporte les enchères." *La Presse*, 16 April.
– 2015b. "TPG: 'Le Québec est un atout pour le Cirque.'" *La Presse*, 21 April.
– 2015c. "Les coulisses de la vente du Cirque." *La Presse*, 21 April.
Brousseau-Pouliot, Vincent, and Denis Lessard. 2015a. "Le siège social reste à Montréal." *La Presse*, 20 April.
– 2015b. "La Caisse a discuté d'un consortium québécois." *La Presse*, 22 April.
Brown, Helen, Jane Seitz, Peter Schumann, Kelly Morris, and Richard Schechner. 1968. "Puppet Theatre: An Interview with Peter Schumann." *TDR: The Drama Review* 12 (2): 62–73.
Burger, Baudoin. 1974. *L'activité théâtrale au Québec (1765–1825)*. Montreal: Parti Pris.
Butler, Grant. 2013. "Cirque du Soleil Returns to Portland in 2014 with 'Totem.'" *The Oregonian*, 3 October. www.oregonlive.com/performance/index.ssf/2013/10/cirque_du_soleil_returns_to_po_2.html.
Calamia, Donald V. 2013. "Cirque du Soleil Explores the Hustle and Bustle of Urban Life." *Encore Michigan*. http://www.encoremichigan.com/article.html?article=23.
Campbell, Mary Schmidt, and Randy Martin, eds. 2006. *Artistic Citizenship: A Public Voice for the Arts*. New York: Routledge.
Cardinal, François. 2009. "Guy Laliberté: riche, philanthrope et écolo." *La Presse*, 2 May. http://www.lapresse.ca/environnement/200905/01/01-852493-guy-laliberte-riche-philanthrope-et-ecolo.php.
Cassivi, Marc. 2009. "Le Cirque de Montréal." *La Presse*, 30 April. http://www.lapresse.ca/arts/spectacles-et-theatre/humour-et-varietes/200904/30/01-851740-le-cirque-de-montreal.php.

– 2015. "Le facteur 'cool.'" *La Presse*, 21 April.
"Causerie." 1883. *Le Canard* 42. 21 July.
CBC News. 2012. "Lepage Choreographs Canoe Performance." 14 August. http://www.cbc.ca/news/canada/montreal/lepage-choreographs-canoe-performance-1.812062.
– 2013. "Cirque du Soleil to Lay Off 400 Employees." 15 January. www.cbc.ca/news/canada/montreal/cirque-du-soleil-to-lay-off-400-employees-1.1355468.
Chambers, Kristine L., and Joan N. Vickers. 2006. "Effects of Bandwidth Feedback and Questioning on the Performance of Competitive Swimmers." *The Sport Psychologist* 20 (2): 184–97.
Chaudhuri, Una, and Shonni Enelow. 2006. "Animalizing Performance, Becoming-Theatre: Inside Zooësis with *The Animal Project* at NYU." *Theatre Topics* 16 (1): 1–17.
Chen, Lung Hung, Yun-Ci Ye, Mei-Yen Chen, and I-Wu Tung. 2010. "Alegría! Flow in Leisure and Life Satisfaction: The Mediating Role of Event Satisfaction Using Data from an Acrobatics Show." *Social Indicators Research* 99: 301–13.
Chen Runhua, ed. 2009. 杂技产业发展论坛, 北京论坛集萃 [The forum of the acrobatic industry: The collections of articles from the Beijing forum]. Beijing: China Association of Arts and Culture Publishing House.
Chodan, Lucinda. 1986. "Clowning Around Gets Marks at Montréal's Circus School." *The Gazette (Montréal)*, 17 January, C1.
– 1989. "Balancing Act." *The Gazette (Montréal)*, 2 May, M13.
Christoff, Stefan. 2013. "'Rêve général illimité' in Quebec." In *Le fond de l'air est rouge*, edited by Stefan Christoff, 29–31. Montreal: Howl Arts Collective.
"Le Cirque de M. John H. Murray." 1876. *Gazette des campagnes* 39.
Cirque du Soleil. 2010. "*Mystère* by Cirque du Soleil Celebrates Record-Breaking 8,000 Performances." News release, 18 October. http://www.cirquedusoleil.com/en/press/news/2010/mystere-8000.aspx.
– 2011. "The Creation Process at Cirque du Soleil." News release, 17 May. https://www.cirquedusoleil.com/en/press/news/2011/creation-process.aspx.
– 2013. "Cirque du Soleil at a Glance." static01.cirquedusoleil.com/en/~/media/press/PDF/cds/cirque-du-soleil-at-glance.pdf#page=1&zoom=auto,0,800.
City of Portland. 2004. *River Renaissance Strategy*. December. www.portlandoregon.gov/bps/article/86274.
Clairoux, Jacques. 1988. "Du spectacle de la force à l'athlétisme théâtral: Louis Cyr et le cirque au Québec." *L'Annuaire théâtral: revue québécoise d'études théâtrales* 4: 107–23.
– 1993. "Le théâtre ambulant et ses amuseurs publics." *Cap-aux-Diamants: la revue d'histoire du Québec* 35: 46–9.
– 2009. "Des hommes forts aux artistes de la piste: l'invention du cirque québécois." *Cap-aux-Diamants: la revue d'histoire du Québec* 97: 16–19.
Clark, Paul. 2008. *Chinese Cultural Revolution: A History*. New York: Cambridge University Press.

Cloutier, Mario. 2009. "Le Cirque du Soleil se moque de la crise économique." *La Presse*, 18 March. http://www.lapresse.ca/arts/200903/18/01-837594-le-cirque-du-soleil-se-moque-de-la-crise-economique.php.

Cloutier, Raymond. 1979. "Le grand cirque ordinaire: réflexions sur une expérience." *Etudes françaises* 15 (1–2): 187–93.

Coish, David. 2004. *Census Metropolitan Areas as Culture Clusters*. Catalogue no. 89-613-MWE2004004. Ottawa: Ministry of Industry.

Collier, John. 1947. *Indians of the Americas*. New York: Mentor Books.

Collins, Glenn. 2009. "Run Away to the Circus? No Need. It's Staying Here." *New York Times*, 28 April. http://www.nytimes.com/2009/04/29/theater/29circ.html?pagewanted=all&_r=0.

Colman, Andrew M. 2012. "Totem." In *A Dictionary of Psychology*. 3rd ed. Accessed 12 December 2014. http://www.oxfordreference.com/view/10.1093/acref/9780199534067.001.0001/acref-9780199534067-e-8485?rskey=V2Drbh&result=2.

Conlogue, R. 1994. "State of the Arts: Even the Old Reliables Stumbled." *Globe and Mail*, 31 December.

Conrad, Margaret, Alvin Finkel, and Cornelius J. Jaenen. 1998. *History of the Canadian Peoples: Beginnings to 1867*. 2nd ed. Toronto: Copp Clark.

Cooke, Phil, and Kevin Morgan. 1998. *The Associational Economy: Firms, Regions and Innovation*. Oxford: Oxford University Press.

Corbo, Linda. 2015. "Le Cirque du Soleil va rendre hommage à Beau Dommage." *La Presse*, 2 February. http://www.lapresse.ca/le-nouvelliste/arts-spectacles/201502/02/01-4840634-le-cirque-du-soleil-va-rendre-hommage-a-beau-dommage.php.

Cordier, Marine, and Émilie Salaméro. 2012. *Être artiste de cirque*. Lyon: Lieux dits.

Cousineau, Alain. 2006. "Projet bassin Peel: une réflexion en profondeur pour la réussite des grands projets s'impose." *Le Devoir*, 22 June, A7.

Cox, Ethan. 2012. "400 000+ in the Streets? Quebec's Students Are Winning …" rabble.ca, 24 May. Accessed 22 October 2014. http://rabble.ca/blogs/bloggers/ethan-cox/2012/05/500000-streets-quebecs-students-arewinning.

Crowe, Deborah. 2012. "Kodak Theater Now Dolby Theater; Oscars to Remain." *Los Angeles Business Journal*, 1 May. www.labusinessjournal.com/news/2012/may/01/dolby-signs-kodak-theatre-renaming-deal-oscars-rem/.

Cruz, Carlos Alexis, ed. 2014. "Circus Dramaturgy, an Interview with Louis Patrick Leroux." *Theatre Topics. Journal of the Association for Theatre in Higher Education* 24 (3): 269–73.

Csikszentmihalyi, Mihaly. 1996. *Creativity: Flow and the Psychology of Discovery and Invention*. New York: HarperCollins Publishers.

– 1990. *Flow: The Psychology of Optimal Experience*. New York: Harper Perennial.

Cyr, Céline. 2003. "Mailhot, Nicolas-François." *Dictionnaire biographique du Canada*. Vol. 6. Université Laval/University of Toronto. Accessed 15 July 2014. http://www.biographi.ca/fr/bio/mailhot_nicolas_francois_6F.html.

"Dansant cirkusterapi." 2009. *Svenska dagbladet*, 30 December.

David, Gilbert. 2009. "Quelques metteurs en scène québécois bercés par le chant des Sirènes." *Spirale* 227: 16–8.

David, Jean. 2007. "What a Cirque!" Unpublished manuscript available from author.
David, Paul. 1985. "Clio and the Economics of QWERTY." *American Economic Review* 75: 332–7.
Dawkins, Richard. 1976. *The Selfish Gene*. Oxford: Oxford University Press.
de Briant, Vincent, and Yves Palau. 1999. *La médiation: Définition, pratiques et perspectives*. Paris: Nathan.
Décarie, Jean-Philippe. 2015. "Orchestrer la reliance du Cirque." *La Presse*, 25 April.
de Certeau, Michel. 1990. *L'invention du quotidien*. Paris: Gallimard.
Denzin, Norman K. 2013. *Indians on Display. Global Commodification of Native America in Performance, Art, and Museums*. Walnut Creek: Left Coast Press.
Diamond, Elin. 1996. *Performance and Cultural Politics*. London: Routledge.
Diamond, Sarah. 2013. "Meet One of L.A.'s Top Native American Hoop Dancers, Now Performing in Cirque du Soleil." *LA Weekly Blogs*, 28 October. http://blogs.laweekly.com/arts/2013/10/cirque_de_soleil_totem_native.php.
Donnelly, Pat. 2010. "First Nations Performers." *The Gazette*, 16 April.
Dosi, Giovanni. 1997. "Opportunities, Incentives and Collective Patterns of Technological Change." *Economic Journal* 107: 1530–47.
Dougherty, Kevin. 1990. "Cirque du Soleil Succeeds Juggling Business with Art." *Financial Post*, 30 April, 1.
Drainie, Bronwyn. 1989. "Can Masse Navigate a New Course for Canadian Culture?" *Globe and Mail*, 8 April, C3.
Drapeau-Bisson, Marie-Lise, Francis Dupuis-Déri, and Marcos Ancelovici. 2013. "'La grève est étudiante, la lutte est populaire!' Manifestation de casseroles et assemblée de quartier." In *Un Printemps rouge et noir: Regards croisés sur la grève étudiante de 2012*, edited by Marcos Ancelovici and Francis Dupuis-Déri, 150–84. Montreal: Les Éditions Écosociété.
Dubuc, Alain. 2015. "Faire quelque chose, mais quoi?" *La Presse*, 18 April.
Duke, Robert A., Carla Davis Cash, and Sarah E. Allen. 2011. "Focus of Attention Affects Performance of Motor Skills in Music." *Journal of Research in Music Education* 20 (10): 1–12.
Dunn, Brian. 1993. "Filling the Big Top." *The Gazette (Montreal)*, 8 February, F3.
Dupuis-Déri, Francis. 2010. "Nouvelles du front altermondialiste: l'armée de clowns rebelles tient bon." *Les Cahiers de l'idiotie*, no. 3.
Durang, John. 1966. *The Memoir of John Durang. American Actor 1785–1816*. Edited by Alan Seymour Downer. Pittsburg: University of Pittsburg Press for the Historical Society of York County and the American Society for Theatre Research.
DynamO Théâtre. 2012. *30 ans: 30 mouvements*. Written for the artistic collective by members Pierre-Etienne Locas, Jacqueline Gosselin, and Yves Simard. Montreal: Dramaturges Éditeurs, collection "Didascalies."
Enchin, Harvey. 1986. "Cirque du Soleil." *Globe and Mail*, 8 December, B1.
Ericsson, K. Anders. 2008. "Deliberate Practice and Acquisition of Expert Performance: A General Overview." *Academic Emergency Medicine* 15: 988–94.
Ermine, Willie. 1995. "Aboriginal Epistemology." In *First Nations Education in Canada: The Circle Unfolds*, edited by Marie Ann Battiste and Jean Barman, 101–12. Vancouver: University of British Columbia Press.

Essletzbichler, Jurgen, and David Rigby. 2007. "Exploring Evolutionary Economic Geographies." *Journal of Economic Geography* 7 (5): 549–71.

Fagot, Sylvain. 2006. "Le cirque québécois: 'Les enjeux de la performance.'" In *Énonciation artistique et socialité*, edited by Sylvain Fagot and Jean-Philippe Uzel, 231–42. Paris: L'Harmattan.

Farrell, Rosemary. 2008. "Nanjing Project: Chinese Acrobatics, Australian New Circus and Hybrid Intercultural Performance." *Australasian Drama Studies* 53: 186–202.

FEDEC. 2009. *Analyse des compétences clés des jeunes artistes de cirque professionnel*. Brussels: Fédération européenne des écoles de cirque professionnelles. http://www.fedec.eu/datas/files/fedec_miroir_fr_web.pdf.

Ferland, Raphaël Dallaire. 2012. "Premier Rêve général illimité." *Le Devoir*, 6 June.

Fitterman, Lisa. 1989. "Ringleaders: Expect the Unexpected in the Topsy-Turvy World of National Circus School." *The Gazette (Montreal)*, 17 December, F1.

Floch, Yohann. 2011. "Les politiques publiques en faveur du cirque en Europe." Paper presented at the conference A Week of Circus, Montpellier, November.

Florida, Richard. 2002. *The Rise of the Creative Class. And How It's Transforming Work, Leisure and Everyday Life*. New York: Basic Books.

Fricker, Karen. 2004. "Tourism, The Festival Marketplace, and Robert Lepage's *The Seven Streams of the River Ota*." *Contemporary Theatre Review* 13 (4): 79–93.

– 2008. "Cultural Specificity or Cultural Blankness? The Paradox of Québec in Vegas." *Revista mexicana estudias canadiense* 16: 127–32.

Fricker, Karen, Françoise Boudreault, Louis Patrick Leroux, and Duncan Wall. 2013. "Writing for the Circus." Paper presented to the Working Group on Circus Research, Montreal, 3 April.

Fu Qifeng, and Fu Tenglong. [2004] 2005. 中国杂技史 [The history of Chinese acrobatics]. 2nd ed. Shanghai: Shanghai People's Publishing House.

Gagnon, Lysiane. 2005. "Las Vegas du Nord." *La Presse*, 15 October, A28.

Galikowski, Maria. 1998. *Art and Politics in China, 1949–1984*. Hong Kong: Chinese University Press.

Gardner, Lyn. 2010. "Can Circus Really Tackle 9/11?" *Guardian*, 10 March. http://www.theguardian.com/stage/2010/mar/10/circus-les-7-doigts-circa.

Gaudet, Sylvain. 2009. "Un haut lieu de la culture populaire à Montréal au XIXe siècle: le Jardin Guilbault." *Cap-aux-Diamants: la revue d'histoire du Québec* 97: 25–9.

Gleason, Susan. 2009. "Behind the Scenes of Seattle's 1999 WTO Protests: Interview with Alli Starr." *Yes! Magazine*. http://www.yesmagazine.org/people-power/behind-the-scenes-of-seattle.

Goodall, Jane R. 2002. *Performance and Evolution in the Age of Darwin. Out of the Natural Order*. London and New York: Routledge.

Grabher, Gernot. 1993. "The Weakness of Strong Ties: The Lock-In of Regional Development in the Ruhr Area." In *The Embedded Firm: On the Socioeconomics of Industrial Networks*, edited by Gernot Grabher, 255–77. New York: Routledge.

– 2005. "Switching Ties, Recombining Teams: Avoiding Lock-In through Project Organization?" In *Rethinking Regional Innovation and Change: Path-Dependency or Regional Breakthrough?*, edited by Gerhard Fuchs and Philip Shapira, 63–83. New York: Springer.

Graeber, David. 2009. *Direct Action: An Ethnography*. Oakland: AK Press.

Graver, David. 1997. "The Actor's Bodies." *Text and Performance Quarterly* 17 (3): 221–35.

– 2005. "The Actor's Bodies." In *Performance: Critical Concepts in Literary and Cultural Studies*, edited by Philip Auslander, 157–74. New York: Routledge.

Griffin, Kevin, and Matthew Robinson. 2013. "Concord Pacific Unveils Massive New Development Near BC Place." *Vancouver Sun*, 3 October. http://www.vancouversun.com/Concord+Pacific+unveils+massive+Vancouver+development+near+Place/8989658/story.html?__lsa=cb3f-4ad8.

Grosz, Elizabeth. 1996. "Intolerable Ambiguity: Freaks as/at the Limit." In *Freakery: Cultural Spectacles of the Extraordinary Body*, edited by Rosemarie Garland Thomson, 55–66. New York: New York University Press.

Harding, James Martin. 2000. *Contours of the Theatrical Avant-Garde: Performance and Textuality*. Ann Arbor: University of Michigan Press.

Hardt, Michael. 1999. "Affective Labor." *Boundary 2* 26 (2): 89–100.

Hardt, Michael, and Antonio Negri. 2000. *Empire*. Cambridge, MA: Harvard University Press.

– 2004. *Multitude: War and Democracy in the Age of Empire*. New York: Penguin Books.

Harvie, Jennifer, and Erin Hurley. 1999. "States of Play: Locating Québec in the Performances of Robert Lepage, Ex Machina and the Cirque du Soleil." *Theatre Journal* 51 (3): 299–315.

He Zhen. 2009. 时空战略：时空之旅带给中国文化产业的启示 [The strategy of "Era": The inspirations that "Era" offers to China's cultural industries]. Shanghai: Shanghai People's Publishing House.

Heinich, Nathalie. 2005. *L'élite artiste. Excellence et singularité en régime démocratique*. Paris: Gallimard.

Heron, John. 1996. *Co-operative Inquiry: Research into the Human Condition*. Thousand Oaks, CA: Sage Publications.

Heron, John, and Peter Reason. 2001. "The Practice of Co-operative Inquiry: Research with Rather Than on People." In *Handbook of Action Research: Participative Inquiry and Practice,* edited by P. Reason and H. Bradbury, 179–88. London: Sage.

Hill, Andrew. 2015. "Contortions Are Required for Cirque du Soleil to Keep Its Magic. The Steps to Take to Prevent Innovative Businesses Turning into Bland Production Lines." *Financial Times* (UK), 27 April. Accessed 23 July 2015. http://www.ft.com/intl/cms/s/0/581f73a2-e9d4-11e4-ae1c00144feab7de.html#axzz3grPeBqWt.

Hill, J. Dee. 2004. *Freaks and Fire: The Underground Reinvention of Circus*. Brooklyn: Soft Skull Press.

Hochschild, Arlie. 1983. *The Managed Heart: Commercialization of Human Feeling*. Berkeley: University of California Press.

Hodgins, Paul. 2012. "New Offbeat Circus Combines Acrobats, Break Dancing, Basketball." *The Orange County Register*, 23 February. http://www.ocregister.com/articles/traces-341740-carroll-register.html.

Hodgson, Geoffrey. 1994. "The Return of Institutional Economics." In *The Handbook of Economic Sociology*, edited by Neil J. Smelser and Richard Swedberg, 58–76. Princeton: Princeton University Press.

Hoh, LaVahn G., and William H. Rough. 1990. *Step Right Up! The Adventure of Circus in America*. White Hall: Betterway Publications.

Holter, Inger M., and Donna Schwartz-Barcott. 1993. "Action Research: What Is It? How Has It Been Used and How Can It Be Used in Nursing?" *Journal of Advanced Medicine* 18 (2): 298–304.

Human, Katy. 2006. *Biological Evolution: An Anthology of Current Thought*. New York: Rosen Publishing.

Hurley, Erin. 2008. "Les corps multiples du Cirque du Soleil." Translated by Isabelle Léger. *Globe: Revue internationale d'études québécoises* 11 (2): 135–57. Chapter 8 of this volume is a revised version of this article.

– 2009. "Le cirque: de la différence à la ressemblance." *Spirale* 227: 24–7.

– 2010. *Theatre & Feeling*. New York: Palgrave Macmillan.

– 2011. *National Performance: Representing Quebec from Expo 67 to Céline Dion*. Toronto: University of Toronto Press.

Jacob, Pascal. 2002. "L'adieu aux armes. Repères pour une analyse du vestiaire circassien." *L'Annuaire théâtral: revue québécoise d'études théâtrales* 32: 109–23.

– 2006. "Les arts du cirque en France: une exception culturelle à la croisée des chemins." In *Énonciation artistique et socialité*, edited by Sylvain Fagot and Jean-Philippe Uzel, 221–30. Paris: L'Harmattan.

– 2008. *La Souplesse du Dragon*. Paris: Magellan & Cie.

– 2012. "Le Québec sur la planète cirque." Keynote address at The State of Circus Research in Quebec, a workshop held at Concordia, McGill, and the National Circus School, 21 September.

Jacob, Pascal, and Michel Vézina. 2007. *Désir(s) de vertige (25 ans d'audace)*. Montreal: École nationale de cirque de Montréal & Les 400 coups.

Jando, Dominique. n.d. "The First Circus in America." In *Circopedia: The Free Encyclopedia of the International Circus*. http://www.circopedia.org/John_Bill_Ricketts.

Jean, Pierre. 1987. *Le monde fascinant du cirque*. Montreal: Les Éditions de l'Époque.

Johnson, Allen W., and Timothy Earle. 2000. *The Evolution of Human Societies: From Foraging Group to Agrarian State*. Stanford: Stanford University Press.

Johnson, Reed. 2011. "Cirque du Soleil Has a Kodak (Theatre) Moment during Sneak Preview of New Show, *Iris*." *Los Angeles Times*, 18 June. articles.latimes.com/2011/jun/18/entertainment/la-et-0618-cirque-du-soleil-20110618.

Joli-Coeur, Sophie. 2007. *Définition des termes et des concepts, Lexique et bibliographie*. Groupe de recherche sur la médiation culturelle. http://montreal.mediationculturelle.org/wp-content/uploads/2010/04/Lexique_biblio_2007.pdf.

Jonker, Laura, Marije Elferink-Gemser, and Chris Visscher. 2010. "Differences in

Self-Regulatory Skills among Talented Athletes: The Significance of Competitive Level and Type of Sport." *Journal of Sports Sciences* 28 (8): 901–8.

Keel, Jefferson. "President's Address – 2013 Executive Council Winter Session." National Congress of American Indians, 5 March.

Kekäläinen, Katri, ed. 2014. *Studying Social Circus: Openings and Perspectives*. Tampere: University of Tampere.

Kennedy, Shana. 2012. "*Totem* Artist Profile: Shandien Larance." *Running Away with the Circus* (blog), 24 June. http://withthecircus.blogspot.com/2012/06/totem-artist-profile-shandien-larance.html.

Kermarrec, Gilles. 2004. "Stratégies d'apprentissage et autorégulation. Revue de question dans le domaine des habiletés sportives." *Science et motricité* 53: 9–38.

Kershaw, Baz. 1997. "Fighting in the Streets: Dramaturgies of Popular Protest 1968–1989." *New Theatre Quarterly* 13 (51): 255–76.

Kidd, Kenneth. 2012. "World's Largest Touring Tent Prepared for Odysseo." *Toronto Star*, 30 April. Accessed May 2013. http://www.thestar.com/entertainment/2012/04/30/worlds_largest_touring_tent_prepared_for_odysseo.html.

Kirschenblatt-Gimblett, Barbara. 1998. *Destination Culture: Tourism, Museums, and Heritage*. Berkeley: University of California Press.

Klepto, Kolonel. 2004. "Making War with Love: The Clandestine Insurgent Rebel Clown Army." *City: Analysis of Urbana Trends, Culture, Theory, Policy, Action* 8.

Klepto, Kolonel, and Major Up Evil. 2005. "The Clandestine Insurgent Rebel Clown Army Goes to Scotland via Few Other Places." In *Shut Them Down!*, edited by David Harvie, Keir Milburn, Ben Trott, and David Watts, 243–54. Leeds: Dissent! and Autonomedia.

Klingmann, Anna. 2007. *Brandscapes: Architecture in the Experience Economy*. Cambridge, MA: MIT Press.

Kovach, Margaret. 2009. *Indigenous Methodologies: Characteristics, Conversations, and Contexts*. Toronto: University of Toronto Press.

Kraus, Richard Curt. 2004. *The Party and the Arty in China: The New Politics of Culture*. Lanham: Rowman and Littlefield.

Kriellaars, Dean. 2013. "Physical Literacy and the Circus." Paper presented to the Working Group on Circus Research, National Circus School, 1 November.

Kurlantzick, Joshua. 2007. *Charm Offensive: How China's Soft Power Is Transforming the World*. New York: Vail-Ballou Press.

Lachance, Julie, and Pierrette Venne. 2004. "L'École Internationale de Cirque de Montréal : une approche pluridisciplinaire." In *Les nouvelles formations de l'interprète. Théâtre, danse, cirque, marionnettes*, edited by Anne-Marie Gourdon, 243–52. Paris: CNRS Éditions.

Lafortune, Sylvain. 2010. "L'apprentissage du duo chez les danseurs experts: De l'intuition à la négociation des savoirs." PhD diss., Université du Québec à Montréal.

Lafortune, Sylvain, Jon Burtt, and Patrice Aubertin. 2014. "L'introduction de l'entraînement à la prise de décision dans la formation supérieure en arts du cirque et ses effets sur les strategies d'enseignement sur l'apprentissage et sur la performance." Research report, National Circus School of Montreal.

La Ligue des droits et libertés, Association des juristes progressistes, and Association pour une solidarité syndicale étudiante. 2013. *Répression, discrimination et grève étudiante: analyse et témoignages*. Montreal, April.

Lamonde, Yvan, and Raymond Montpetit. 1986. *Le parc Sohmer de Montréal 1889–1919. Un lieu populaire de culture urbaine*. Quebec City: Institut québécois de recherche sur la culture.

Lamoureux, E. 2013. "L'art de la manif réinventé? Analyse de l'importance actuelle des pratiques culturelles et artistiques." *Bulletin d'histoire politique* 21 (2): 70–81.

Lapointe, Josée. 2012. "*Séquence 8*: la magie des 7 doigts." *La Presse,* 6 July. http://www.lapresse.ca/arts/festivals/montreal-completement-cirque/critiques/201207/06/01-4541302-sequence-8-la-magie-des-7-doigts.php.

Larrue, Jean-Marc. 1988–89. "Mémoire et appropriation: essai sur la mémoire théâtrale au Québec." *L'Annuaire théâtral: revue québécoise d'études théâtrales* 5–6: 61–72.

Lavers, Katrina. 2012. "The Political Body – Embodied Protest in Contemporary Circus: Archaos, Circus Oz, 7 doigts de la main." Paper presented to the Working Group on Circus Research, National Circus School, 3 February.

– 2014. "Sighting Circus: Perceptions of Circus Phenomena Investigated through Diverse Bodies." PhD diss., Western Australia Academy of Performing Arts, Edith Cowan University, Perth.

Lavoie, Louisette, Danielle Marquis, and Paul Laurin. 1996. *La recherche-action. Théorie et pratique*. Sainte-Foy: Presse de l'Université du Québec.

Lavoie, Sylvain, ed. 2009a. "Le dernier homme, entre cirque et religion." *Spirale* 227: 31–33.

– 2009b. "Rayonnement du cirque québécois." Special issue, *Spirale* 227 (Summer).

– 2009c. "Rayonnement du cirque québécois." *Spirale* 227: 11.

Le Barreau du Québec. 2012. PL 78: Loi permettant aux étudiants de recevoir l'enseignement dispensé par les établissements de niveau postsecondaire qu'ils fréquentent: Le Barreau du Québec formule de sérieuses inquiétudes. Activités Médias et Positions, 18 May. Accessed 26 July 2014. http://www.barreau.qc.ca/fr/actualites-medias/ communiques/2012/05/18-etudiants.

Lebergott, Stanley. 1960. "Wage Trends, 1800–1900." In *Trends in the American Economy in the Nineteenth Century*, edited by The Conference on Research in Income and Wealth, 449–500. National Bureau of Economic Research (NBER) Book Series Studies in Income and Wealth. Princeton: Princeton University Press. http://www.nber.org/chapters/c2486.

Leclerc, Andréane. 2012. "Entre contorsion et écriture scénique : la prouesse comme technique évocatrice de sens, mémoire-création." Master's thesis, École supérieure de théâtre, Université du Québec à Montréal.

Leclerc, Andréane, Paloma Holmes, and Patrice Aubertin. 2013. "On Pain and Circus in Training and Practice." Paper presented to the Working Group on Circus Research, Montreal, 25 January.

Lee, Timothy D., Stephan Swinnen, and Deborah Serrien. 1994. "Cognitive Effort and Motor Learning." *Quest* 46 (3): 328–44.

Leroux, Louis Patrick. 2009a. "Cohérence esthétique, anémie dramaturgique." *Spirale* 227: 28–30.
– 2009b. "Le Québec à Las Vegas: pérégrinations postidentitaires dans l'hyper-Amérique." *L'Annuaire théâtral: revue québécoise d'études théâtrales* 45: 9–20.
– ed. 2009c. "Le Québec à Las Vegas." Special issue, *L'Annuaire théâtral: revue québécoise d'études théâtrales* 45 (Spring).
– 2009d. "*Zumanity*: la spectacularisation de l'intime ou le pari impossible d'authenticité au Cirque." *L'Annuaire théâtral: revue québécoise d'études théâtrales* 45: 69–91.
– 2012. "Cirque in Space! The Ethos, Ethics, and Aesthetics of Staging and Branding the Individual of Exception." Paper presented at the Centre for Canadian Studies, Duke University, Durham, North Carolina, 11 April.
– 2013. "Que raconte le cirque québécois, quel sens y donner? Quelques pistes pour une dramaturgie circassienne." École nationale de cirque de Montréal, 10 May.
– 2014a. "Contemporary Circus Research in Québec: Building and Negotiating an Emerging Interdisciplinary Field." *Theatre Research in Canada* 34 (2): 263–70.
– 2014b. "Le Cirque du Soleil et Hollywood: *Iris*." *Québec Studies* 58: 45–64.
– ed. 2014c. "North-South Circus Circulations between Québec and the U.S." Special issue, *Québec Studies*.
– 2014d. "What Is Circus Dramaturgy?" Position paper, panel discussion at Chicago Contemporary Circus Festival and Circus Now, 11 January.
Leroux, Louis Patrick, and Jane Moss, ed. 2014. "Cross-Border Circus: Americans in Montreal." With Amy Cohen, Francisco Cruz, Kyle Driggs, Louis Patrick Leroux, Sarah Poole, and Duncan Wall. *Québec Studies* 58 (Fall-Winter): 65–86.
Lesage, Valérie. 2010. "Robert Lepage et *Totem*: pour l'amour des défis casse-gueule." *Le Soleil*, 22 July.
Leslie, Deborah, and Norma M. Rantisi. 2006. "Governing the Design Economy in Montréal, Canada." *Urban Affairs Review* 40 (5): 1–29.
– 2010. "Creativity and Urban Regeneration: The Role of La Tohu and the Cirque du Soleil in the Saint-Michel Neighbourhood in Montreal." Paper presented to the Working Group on Circus Research, Concordia University, 16 November.
– 2011. "Creativity and Place in the Evolution of a Cultural Industry: The Case of Cirque du Soleil." *Urban Studies* 48 (9): 1771–87.
Lévesque, Kathleen. 2005. "Casino: Québec reporte sa décision à l'an prochain." *Le Devoir*, 28 October, A1.
– 2006a. "Le RESO émet des réserves au sujet du projet de casino." *Le Devoir*, 26 January, A2.
– 2006b. "Le bassin Peel, le pire endroit pour un casino: l'analyse de la Direction de la santé publique est sans équivoque." *Le Devoir*, 22 February, A1.
Lewin, Kurt. 1951. *Field Theory in Social Science*. New York: Harper and Row.
Ley, David. 1996. *The New Middle Class and the Remaking of the Central City*. Oxford: Clarendon.
Little Bear, Leroy. 2000. "Jagged Worldviews Colliding." In *Reclaiming Indigenous Voice and Vision*, edited by Marie Battiste, 77–85. Vancouver: University of British Columbia Press.

Lonergan, Patrick. 2009. *Theatre and Globalization: Irish Drama in the Celtic Tiger Era*. London: Palgrave Macmillan.
Lyons, Harriet. 2008. Review of *The Secret of the Totem: Religion and Society from McLennan to Freud*, by Robert Alun Jones. *Journal of the History of Sexuality* 17 (3): 483–6.
MacKinnon, Danny, Andrew Cumbers, Andy Pike, Kean Birch, and Robert McMaster. 2009. "Evolution in Economic Geography: Institutions, Political Economy and Adaptation." *Economic Geography* 85 (2): 129–50.
Magill, Richard A. 2007. *Motor Learning and Control: Concept and Applications*. Boston: McGraw-Hill.
Maheu, Gilles. 1978. "Les Enfants du paradis." *Cahiers de théâtre Jeu* 8: 79–82.
Mahy, Isabelle. 2008a. *Les coulisses de l'innovation, création et gestion au Cirque du Soleil*. Quebec City: Presses de l'Université Laval.
– 2008b. "Il était une fois ... Ou la force du récit dans la conduite du changement." *Revue Communication & Organisation*, numéro thématique: Conduire le changement organisationnel? Entre émergence et instrumentalisation 33 (10): 50–60.
Maranca, Bonnie, ed. 1996. *The Theater of Images: Robert Wilson, Richard Foreman, Lee Breuer*. Baltimore: John Hopkins University Press.
Marcoux-Chabot, Moïse, dir. 2013. *Bouge!* Montreal: Ceci N'est Pas Un Film.
Marotte, Bertrand, and John Barber. 2013. "The Show Won't Go On for 400 Cirque du Soleil Employees." *Globe and Mail*, 16 January.
Martel, Frédéric. 2011. *Mainstream. Enquête sur la guerre globale de la culture et des médias*. Paris: Flammarion, Champs Actuel.
Martin, Ron, and James Simmie. 2008. "Path Dependence and Local Innovation Systems in City-Regions." *Innovation: Management, Policy & Practice* 10: 183–96.
Martin, Ron, and Peter Sunley. 2006. "Path Dependence and Regional Economic Evolution." *Journal of Economic Geography* 6 (4): 395–438.
Maser, Peter. 1992. "School for Clowns Is All Fun and Games for 200 Lucky Students." *Edmonton Journal*, 26 November, A3.
Maskell, Peter, and Anders Malmberg. 1999. "Localized Learning and Industrial Competitiveness." *Cambridge Journal of Economics* 23 (2): 167–86.
Massey, Doreen. 1992. "Politics and Space/Time." *New Left Review*, no. 196, 65–84.
Massicotte, Édouard-Zotique. 1909. *Athlètes canadiens-français. Recueil des exploits de force, d'endurance, d'agilité des athlètes et des sportsmen de notre race, depuis le XVIIIe siècle. Biographies-Portraits-Anecdotes-Records*. Montreal: Librairie Beauchemin.
– 1923–24. "Noms de rues et de localités dans la région de Montréal: le Jardin Guilbault." *Bulletin de recherches historiques* 29–30: 245–6.
– 1937. "Coins historiques du Montréal d'autrefois: le Jardin Guilbault." *Cahier des Dix* 2: 142–6.
McGuigan, J. 2004. *Rethinking Cultural Policy*. Maidenhead: Open University Press.
McKenzie, Jon. 2001. *Perform, Or Else*. New York: Routledge.
McNevin, Nancy H., Charles H. Shea, and Gabriele Wulf. 2003. "Increasing the Distance of an External Focus of Attention Enhances Learning." *Psychological Research* 67: 22–9.

Mercure, Philippe. 2006. "Le Cirque du Soleil mise sur Singapour." *La Presse*, 16 March, A1.
Métais-Chastanier, Barbara. 2012. "Écriture(s) du cirque: une dramaturgie?" *Agôn, revue des arts de la scène*. Accessed 12 December 2012. http://w7.ens-lsh.fr/agon.
Millard, N. 2006. "Learning from the 'Wow' Factor – How to Engage Customers through the Design of Effective Affective Customer Experiences." *BT Technology Journal* 24 (1): 11–16.
Miller, Debra. 2012. "3 Letters for 7 Fingers' SEQUENCE 8: OMG!!!" *Stage Magazine*, 22 September. Website discontinued.
Mittler, Barbara. 2010. '"Eight Stage Works for 800 Million People': The Great Cultural Revolution in Music – a View from Revolutionary Opera." *Opera Quarterly* 26 (2–3): 377–401.
Molotch, Harvey. 1996. "L.A. as a Design Product. How Art Works in a Regional Economy." In *The City: Los Angeles and Urban Theory at the End of the 20th Century*, edited by Allen J. Scott and Edward W. Soja, 223–75. Berkeley: University of California Press.
– 2003. *Where Stuff Comes From: How Toasters, Toilets, Cars, Computers, and Many Other Things Come to Be as They Are*. New York: Routledge.
Mommaas, Hans. 2004. "Cultural Clusters and the Post-Industrial City: Towards the Remapping of Urban Cultural Policy." *Urban Studies* 41 (3): 507–32.
Morton, Lawrence. 1988. "That Daring Woman on Her Flying Trapeze." *The Whig* (Kingston), 31 December, 1.
Moses, L.G. 1996. *Wild West Shows and the Images of American Indians, 1883–1933*. Albuquerque: University of New Mexico Press.
Moy, James S. 1980. "The First Circus in Eastern Canada." *Theatre Research in Canada* 1(1). http://journals.hil.unb.ca/index.php/tric/article/view/7538/8597.
Nadeau, Pierre O. 2009. "Le rêve pour un Amérindien de Québec." *Le Journal de Québec*, 20 July.
National Aboriginal Health Organization. 2010. "Drug Abuse Major Concern among First Nations and Inuit." 27 June. http://www.naho.ca/blog/2011/06/27/drug-abuse-major-concern-among-first-nations-and-inuit/.
Nelson, Richard. 1994. "Evolutionary Theorizing about Economic Change." In *The Handbook of Economic Sociology*, edited by Neil J. Smelser and Richard Swedberg, 108–36. Princeton: Princeton University Press.
Nestruck, J. Kelly. 2012. "Cirque du Soleil Hits Hollywood – and It's Pretty Good." *Globe and Mail*, 21 November. www.theglobeandmail.com/arts/theatre-and-performance/theatre-reviews/cirque-du-soleil-hits-hollywood-and-its-pretty-good/article5538284/.
– 2013. "Massive Layoffs and Mediocrity: Has Cirque du Soleil Lost Its Way?" *Globe and Mail*, 16 January.
Ng, David. 2013. "Cirque du Soleil's 'Iris' says 'au revoir' to Hollywood." *Los Angeles Times*, 20 January. articles.latimes.com/2013/jan/20/entertainment/la-et-cm-cirque-du-soleil-iris-20130119.
Ng, David, and David Zahniser. 2012. "Cirque du Soleil's Extravagant 'Iris' Will Close Jan 19." *Los Angeles Times*, 30 November. articles.latimes.com/2012/nov/30/entertainment/la-et-1201-cirque-closes-iris-20121201.

Nightingale, Benedict. 2011. "'The Circus Can Be Spicy Too.'" *The Times* (London), 5 January.
Noffke, Susan, and Bridget Somekh, eds. 2009. *The Sage Handbook of Educational Action Research*. Thousand Oaks, CA: Sage Publications.
Ohl, Paul. 2013. *Louis Cyr, biographie*. Rev. ed. Montreal: Libre expression.
Ooi, Can-Seng. 2002. *Cultural Tourism and Tourism Cultures*. Copenhagen: Copenhagen Business School Press.
Paré, François. 1992. *Les littératures de l'exiguïté*. Ottawa: Le Nordir.
Paré, Isabelle. 2014a. "Le Cirque du Soleil cherche un nouvel élan." *Le Devoir*, 18 January, A1, A12.
– 2014b. "Les retombées de la 'comète' Cirque du Soleil." *Le Devoir*, 18 January, A7.
Paul, Darel E. 2004. "World Cities as Hegemonic Projects: The Politics of Global Imagineering in Montreal." *Political Geography* 23 (5): 571–96.
Pépin, Elsa. 2012. "Le cirque souverain." *Voir*, 5 July. http://voir.ca/scene/2012/07/05/sebastien-soldevila-et-shana-carroll-le-cirque-souverain/.
Petrowski, Nathalie. 2015. "Circus interruptus." *La Presse*, 18 April.
Picard, André. 1997. "Staging an Attack on Social Injustice: The Radical Cabaret That May Have Inspired Activists to Raid a Hotel's Grand Buffet." *Globe and Mail*, 9 December, A2.
Pincus-Roth, Zachary. 2011. "A Circus That Lets Its Freak Flag Fly." *New York Times*, 9 February. http://www.nytimes.com/2011/02/13/theater/13seven.html?_r=0/.
Pine, Joseph, and James H. Gilmore. 1999. *The Experience Economy: Work Is Theatre and Every Business Is a Stage*. Boston: Harvard Business School Press.
Plant, Sadie. 1992. *The Most Radical Gesture*. Abingdon, UK: Taylor & Francis.
Portland Development Commission. 1977. *Downtown Waterfront Urban Renewal Plan and Amendments*. www.pdc.us/our-work/urban-renewal-areas/downtown-waterfront/overview.aspx.
Portland Expo Center. 2012. "The Expo Story." www.expocenter.org/about-expo/the-expo-story.
Proctor, Sue. 2013. "The Archetypal Role of the Clown as a Catalyst for Individual and Societal Transformation." Master's thesis, Concordia University, Montreal.
Proulx, Steve. 2005. *Les saisons du Parc Belmont 1923–1983*. Montreal: Libre expression.
Québec. Ministère des affaires culturelles. 1992. *La politique culturelle du Québec: Notre culture, notre avenir*. Quebec City: Gouvernement du Québec.
Quebec National Assembly. 2012. Bill 78: An Act to Enable Students to Receive Instruction from the Postsecondary Institutions They Attend. Quebec City: Quebec National Assembly.
Radio-Canada. 1960. "Les Élections du Québec." 22 June.
– 2015. "Guy Laliberté 'serein' après la vente de la majorité du Cirque du Soleil." Radio-Canada summary with links to video interviews, 20 April. Accessed 23 July 2015. http://ici.radio-canada.ca/nouvelles/economie/2015/04/20/001-cirque-soleil-montreal-vente-laliberte.shtml.

Rancière, Jacques. 2004. *The Politics of Aesthetics: The Distribution of the Sensible.* Translated by Gabriel Rockhill. London and New York: Continuum.
Reason, Peter, and Hilary Bradbury, eds. 2008. *The Sage Handbook of Action Research: Participative Inquiry and Practice.* Thousand Oaks, CA: Sage Publications.
Rebellato, Dan. 2009. *Theatre and Globalization.* London: Palgrave Macmillan.
Rivard, J. 2007. *Le mouvement paradigmatique autour du phénomène des jeunes qui vivent des difficultés: l'exemple du programme Cirque du Monde* [The new paradigm for youth who live with difficulties: The example of the Cirque du Monde program]. Montreal: Université de Montréal.
Robert-Macaire. 1846. "Chronique des Salons." *La Revue canadienne* 3 (53): 215.
Roby, Daniel, dir. 2013. *Louis Cyr.* Producer Christian Larouche. Feature film, 130 min.
Rosen, Joseph. 2012. "Multigenerational Casserole Orchestras: The New Face of Anarchist Insurgency." *Wi: Journal of Mobile Media* 6 (2). Accessed 24 October 2014. http://wi.mobilities.ca/multigenerational-casserole-orchestras-the-new-face-of-anarchist-insurgency/.
Roy, Pierre-Georges. 1936. "Le Cirque royal ou Théâtre royal." *Bulletin des recherches historiques* 42 (11): 641–66.
Ruse, Michael. 1997. *From Monad to Man: The Concept of Progress in Evolutionary Biology.* Cambridge, MA: Harvard University Press.
Saint-Pierre, Christian. 2010. "Couleurs unies." *Voir*, 6 May.
Schechner, Richard. 1992. "Invasions Friendly and Unfriendly: The Dramaturgy of Direct Theatre." *South African Theatre Journal* 6 (1): 4–24.
Scott, Allen J. 1996. "The Craft, Fashion and Cultural-Products Industries of Los Angeles: Competitive Dynamics and Policy Dimensions in a Multisectoral Image-Producing Complex." *Annals of the Association of American Geographers* 86 (2): 306–23.
– 1997. "The Cultural Economy of Cities." *International Journal of Urban and Regional Research* 21 (2): 323–39.
– 2001. *The Cultural Economy of Cities: Essays on the Geography of Image-Producing Industries.* London: Sage.
– 2004. "Cultural-Products Industries and Urban Economic Development: Prospects for Growth and Market Contestation in Global Context." *Urban Affairs Review* 39 (4): 461–90.
Sell, Mike. 2008. *Avant-Garde Performance and the Limits of Criticism: Approaching the Living Theatre, Happenings/Fluxus, and the Black Arts Movement.* Ann Arbor: University of Michigan Press.
– 2011. *Avant-Garde Performance and Material Exchange.* New York: Palgrave Macmillan.
Shields, Alexandre. 2006. "Loto-Québec jette l'éponge: le retrait du Cirque du Soleil enterre le projet." *Le Devoir*, 11 March, A1.
Siag, Jean. 2012. "Cirque: nouveau lieu de formation et de diffusion." *La Presse*, 7 September.
Sigouin, Gerald. 1982. *Théâtre en lutte: Le Theatre Euh!* Montreal: VLB Editeur.

Sino-Belgian Trade and Investment Portal. 2012. "Belgian Franco Dragone Signs 2.5 Billion RMB Contract with Dalian Wanda Group." Last modified 1 November. http://www.belgiuminchina.org/en/news/item/257.html.

Skidmore, Jamie. 2002. "A Critical Analysis of Cirque du Soleil, 1987–2001." PhD diss., University of Toronto.

Spiegel, Jennifer. 2012a. "Singular Bodies, Collective Dreams and the Making of a Mass Movement: How Street Circus Helped Create the 'Maple Spring.'" Paper presented at The State of Circus Research in Quebec workshop, Montreal, September.

– 2012b. "Quebec's Noisy Revolution: Social Dramaturgies of the "Maple Spring." *Out of the Mouths of "Casseroles."* Textes qui bougent au rythme du carré rouge. Special issue, *Wi: Journal of Mobile Media.*

– 2013. "Social Circus as an Art for Social Change: Promoting Social Inclusion, Social Engagement and Cultural Democracy in Studying Social Circus." In *Studying Social Circus: Openings and Perspectives*, edited by Katri Kekäläinen, 70–5. Tampere: University of Tampere.

– 2014. "Evaluating the Socio-Cultural Impact of Social Circus in Quebec." Paper presented to the Working Group on Circus Research, McGill University, 28 February.

– 2015. "*Rêve Général Illimité*? The Role of Creative Protest in Transforming the Dynamics of Space and Time during the 2012 Quebec Student Strike." *Antipode* 47 (3): 770–91.

Spiegel, Jennifer Beth, Maria-Christina Breilh, Arturo Campaña, Judith Marcuse, and Annalee Yassi. 2015. "Social Circus and Health Equity: Exploring the National Social Circus Program in Ecuador." *Arts & Health: An International Journal for Research, Policy and Practice* 7 (1): 65–74.

Stewart-Harawira, Makere. 2005. *The New Imperial Order. Indigenous Responses to Globalization.* New York: Zed Books.

Stoddart, Helen. 2000. *Rings of Desire: Circus History and Representation.* Manchester: Manchester University Press.

Stolarick, Kevin, and Richard Florida. 2006. "Creativity, Connections and Innovation: A Study of Linkages in the Montreal Region." *Environment and Planning A* 38 (10): 1799–1817.

Storper, Michael. 1995. "The Resurgence of Regional Economies, Ten Years Later: The Region as a Nexus of Untraded Interdependencies." *European Urban and Regional Studies* 2 (3): 191–221.

Stringer, Ernest T. 2014. *Action Research.* 4th ed. Thousand Oaks, CA: Sage Publications.

Tait, Peta. 2005. *Circus Bodies: Cultural Identity in Aerial Performance.* London and New York: Routledge.

Tardif, Mélanie. 2009. "Déserts." *Spirale* 227: 12–15.

Tembeck, Iro. 1994. *Dancing in Montreal: Seeds of a Choreographic History.* Madison: Society of Dance History Scholars.

Thai, Ian. 2012. "Fuse Theater Review: Les 7 doigts de la main Return to Boston with the Innovative Artistry of 'Sequence 8.'" *The Arts Fuse*, 30 September.

http://artsfuse.org/70017/fuse-theater-review-les-7-doigts-de-la-main-return-to-boston-with-the-innovative-artistry-of-sequence-8/.

Therborn, Goran. 2000. "Globalizations: Dimensions, Historical Waves, Regional Effects, Normative Governance." *International Sociology* 15 (2): 151–79.

Théroux, Pierre. 2006. "Aujourd'hui Las Vegas, demain le monde." *Les Affaires*, 23 December, 4.

Theurillat-Cloutier, Arnaud, Alexandre Leduc, and Benoît Lacoursière. 2013. "Les racines historiques du Printemps érable." In *Un Printemps rouge et noir: Regards croisés sur la grève étudiante de 2012*, edited by M. Ancelovici and F. Dupuis-Déri, 37–58. Montreal: Les Éditions Écosociété.

Thomson, Rosemarie Garland. 1992. "Introduction: From Wonder to Error – A Genealogy of Freak Discourse in Modernity." In *Freakery: Cultural Spectacles of the Extraordinary Body*, edited by Rosemarie Garland Thomson, 1–19. New York: New York University Press.

Todorov, Tzvetan. 1968. *Qu'est-ce que le structuralisme? Tome 2, Poétique*. Paris: Éditions du Seuil.

Toepfer, Karl. 1999. "Twisted Bodies: Aspects of Female Contortionism in the Letters of a Connoisseur." *The Drama Review* 43 (1): 104–36.

Turcotte, Claude. 2005. "Loto-Québec veut 'prendre de l'avance' dans son projet du bassin Peel." *Le Devoir*, 29 September, B1.

Turenne, Martine. 2011. "Le Top 10 des 150 sociétés les plus admirées." *Les Affaires*, 18 February. http://www.lesaffaires.com/secteurs-d-activite/general/le-top-10-des-150-societes-les-plus-admirees/524900.

United States Census Bureau. 2015. "Portland (City), Oregon." Last modified 3 September. quickfacts.census.gov/qfd/states/41/4159000.html.

Vailles, Francis. 2015. "Les impôts de Guy Laliberté." *La Presse*, 17 April.

Venturi, Robert, Denise S. Brown, and Steven Izenour. 1977. *Learning from Las Vegas: The Forgotten Symbolism of Architectural Form*. Cambridge, MA: MIT Press.

Vickers, Joan N. 2003. "Decision Training: An Innovative Approach to Coaching." *Canadian Journal for Women Coaches* 3 (3). http://www.coach.ca/print-version-p132841.

– 2007. *Perception, Cognition and Decision Training, the Quiet Eye in Action*. Champaign, IL: Human Kinetics.

Vickers, Joan N., Mary-Ann Reeves, Kristine L. Chambers, and Steve Martell. 2004. "Decision Training: Cognitive Strategies for Enhancing Motor Performance." In *Skill Acquisition in Sport: Research, Theory and Practice*, edited by A. Mark Williams and Nicola J. Hodges, 103–20. New York: Routledge.

Volland, Nicolai. 2007. "Translating the Socialist State: Cultural Exchange, National Identity, and the Socialist World in the Early PRC." *Twentieth-Century China* 33 (2): 51–72.

Von Hendy, Andrew. 2006. Review of *The Secret of the Totem: Religion and Society from McLennan to Freud*, by Robert Alun Jones. *Victorian Studies* 48 (3): 520–2.

Wall, Duncan. 2014. "Circus as Community Building." Paper presented to the Working Group on Circus Research, McGill University, 28 February.

Wanda Group. 2013. "Wuhan Han Xiu Official Trailer." Last modified 27 July. http://www.wanda.cn/2013/advert_0727/57.html.

Wang Feng, Fu Qifeng, Fu Tenglong, Li Zhijuan, and Huang Jienong. 1997. 中国当代杂技 [The contemporary Chinese acrobatics]. Beijing: Contemporary China Publishing House.

Wang Feng, Zong Zhengwen, Zhou Shixi, Zhou Qiufan, and Dai Shucheng. 1991. 上海杂技团团史 [The history of Shanghai Acrobatic Troupe], *1951–1990*. Shanghai: Shanghai Acrobatic Troupe.

Weider, Ben, and E.Z. Massicotte. 1999. *Les Hommes forts du Québec. De Jos. Montferrand à Louis Cyr*. Trois-Pistoles: Éditions Trois-Pistoles.

Wilson, Ame. 2002. "Cirque du Soleil Reimagines the Circus: The Evolution of an Aesthetic." PhD diss., University of Oregon.

Wittmann, Matthew. 2012. *Circus and the City: New York, 1793–2010*. New York: Bard Graduate Center.

Wright, Jordan. 2012. "Keeping to His Roots – Interview with Christian Laveau, Lead Singer of Cirque du Soleil's Totem and Artistic Director Tim Smith." *Indian Country Today Media Network*, 2 July. http://whiskandquill.com/?p=4739.

Wulf, Gabriele. 2007. "Attentional Focus and Motor Learning: A Review of Ten Years of Research." *Bewegung und Training* (ejournal) 1: 4–14. http://sportwissenschaft.de/fileadmin/img/publikationen/BuT/aktuelles/Wulf_target_article_2007.pdf.

Yung, Bell. 1984. "Model Opera as Model: From Shajiabang to Sagabong." In *Popular Chinese Literature and Performing Arts in the People's Republic of China, 1949–1979*, edited by Bonne McDougall, 144–64. Berkeley: University of California Press.

Zhang, Tracy. 2011. "A Preliminary Study: International Recruitment and Chinese Artists at Cirque du Soleil." Paper presented to the Working Group on Circus Training, Concordia University, 9 December.

– 2014. "Bending the Body for China: The Uses of Acrobatics in Sino-US Diplomacy during the Cold War." *International Journal of Cultural Policy* (October). http://www.tandfonline.com/doi/abs/10.1080/10286632.2014.956665#.VHH-AodetMY.

Zhang Weihong. 2010. "China's Cultural Future: From Soft Power to Comprehensive Power." *International Journal of Cultural Policy* 16 (4): 383–402.

Zhou Hong. 2009. "太阳马戏团, 产业链， 中国杂技" [Cirque du Soleil, the industry chains, Chinese acrobatics]. In 杂技产业发展论坛, 北京论坛集萃 [The forum of the acrobatic industry: The collections of articles from the Beijing forum], edited by Chen Runhua, 50–67. Beijing: China Association of Arts and Culture Publishing House.

Zoglin, Richard. 2011. "*Traces*." *Time*, 9 December. Accessed 10 November 2015. http://content.time.com/time/specials/packages/article/0,28804,2101344_2100961_2100959,00.html.

Zúñiga, Javier. 2012. "Quebec Law Breaches Canada's International Human Rights Obligations." *Amnesty International News*, 25 May. Accessed 24 October 2014. https://www.amnesty.org/en/latest/news/2012/05/quebec-law-breaches-canada-s-international-human-rights-obligations/.

Contributors

PATRICE AUBERTIN is the director of research and teacher training programs at the National Circus School in Montreal, Canada, and holds the Social Sciences and Humanities Research Council of Canada Industrial Research Chair for Colleges in Circus Arts. Through the Chair, he has developed over twenty industrial, institutional, and associative partnerships. Prior to joining the National Circus School in 2008, he was director of research and development–new creation projects at Cirque du Soleil.

ANNA-KARYNA BARLATI is the library manager at the National Circus School in Montreal, where she manages the school's collections related to the circus arts, among the largest in the Americas: http://ecolenationaledecirque.ca/en/school/library. She also regularly teaches circus arts history, research methodology, and artistic approaches at the school. Previously, she worked for the Daniel Langlois Foundation and Special Collections at Université de Montréal.

CHARLES R. BATSON is associate professor at Union College, Schenectady, New York, where he teaches and writes on French and Francophone literature, culture, and performance, and where he received the Stillman Award for Excellence in Teaching. His work has appeared in such journals as *Québec Studies*, *Contemporary French and Francophone Studies*, *French Politics, Culture & Society*, *Contemporary French Civilization*, *Dance Chronicle*, and *Gradiva*. His book, *Dance, Desire, and Anxiety in Early Twentieth-Century French Theater*, was published by Ashgate in 2005. Current projects include a series of coedited issues of *Québec Studies* on Queer Québec.

SUSAN BENNETT is professor of English at the University of Calgary. Her most recent books are *Performing Environments: Site-Specificity in Medieval and Early Modern Drama* (coedited with Mary Polito and published by Palgrave in 2014), *Theatre & Museums* (Palgrave, 2013) and *Shakespeare beyond English* (coedited with Christie Carson, Cambridge, 2014). Among her current projects is a new series coedited with Kim Solga, Theory for Theatre Studies (eight books to be published by Methuen Bloomsbury in 2017 and 2018 – one of which she will author, a volume on "sound").

JULIE BOUDREAULT has conducted research on the circus for over twenty-five years, first as a graduate student at Université Laval, where she taught circus history and devoted both her MA and PhD to circus topics. She was a pioneering force in circus research in Quebec and has continued writing as an independent scholar. After charting and documenting the creation of Cirque du Soleil's *Saltimbanco*, she published *Le Cirque du Soleil. La création d'un spectacle: Saltimbanco* (Nota Bene, 1996). In 2002, she edited a special theme issue for *L'Annuaire théâtral* on circus and theatricality. She was also a consultant on the *Circus Magicus* exhibition at the Musée de la civilisation in Quebec City.

JON BURTT is lecturer in dance and performance studies in the Department of Media, Music, Communication, and Cultural Studies at Macquarie University in Sydney, Australia. His research interests include interdisciplinary research collaborations, social intervention through social circus practice, and the development of expertise in physical art forms. He worked for three years as a Cirque du Monde–trained social circus instructor in the Inuit community in Nunavik, Quebec. He was, for two years, researcher-in-residence at the National Circus School in Montreal.

KAREN FRICKER is assistant professor in the Department of Dramatic Arts at Brock University, where her research focuses on contemporary Quebec theatre and performance (particularly the work of Robert Lepage), the intersections of performance and national identity, contemporary circus, and theatre criticism. Her coedited volume, with Milija Gluhovic, *Performing the 'New' Europe: Identities, Feelings, and Politics in the*

Eurovision Song Contest, was published in 2013 by Palgrave Macmillan, and she is completing a monograph, *Making Theatre Global: Robert Lepage's Original Stage Productions*, for Manchester University Press.

SIMON HAREL is a full professor at the Université de Montréal, where he is co-chair of the Départment de littératures et de langues du monde. Prior to joining Université de Montréal in 2011, he was the director of the Centre for the Study of Arts, Letters and Traditions at the Université du Québec à Montréal, where he taught literature and conducted research for over twenty-five years. His 1989 book, *Voleur de parcours*, is recognized as a beacon in Quebec cultural studies. He is the author or editor of over thirty books. In 2009, he was elected both Trudeau fellow and a member of the Royal Society of Canada.

ERIN HURLEY, professor of English at McGill University, is the author of *National Performance: Representing Quebec from Expo 67 to Céline Dion* and *Theatre and Feeling* and the editor of *Theatres of Affect*. Her circus-related publications have appeared in *Theatre Journal* ("States of Play," coauthored with Jen Harvie), *Globe: Revue internationale d'études québécoises*, and *Spirale*. She is currently publishing on the use of objects in women's solo performance in Montreal and researching the history of English-language theatre in Quebec, for which she has received a Fulbright Award.

PASCAL JACOB is a circus historian and devoted collector (part of his collection is housed at the National Circus School in Montreal and TOHU). The artistic director of Cirque Phénix and of the Festival Mondial du Cirque de Demain in Paris, he also works for the Franco Dragone Entertainment Group as a talent scout. Pascal regularly lectures on circus history at professional schools in Montreal, Brussels, and Châlons-en-Champagne. He is the author of seventeen books on traditional, modern, and contemporary circuses, from *La Grande Parade du Cirque* (Gallimard, 1992) and *Le Cirque: Regards sur les arts de la piste du XVIe siècle à nos jours* (Plume, 1996) to *Bêtes de cirque* (Magellan & Cie, 2004) and *La Souplesse du dragon: Repères et references pour une histoire du théâtre acrobatique en Chine* (Magellan & Cie, 2008).

SYLVAIN LAFORTUNE is pursuing an international career as a professional dancer and also teaches both dance and circus arts. His postgraduate studies on dance partnering (MA and PhD at Université du Québec à Montréal) and ongoing teaching and writing on the subject have established him as a leading expert. He is an ongoing artistic adviser, director, and choreographer for circus students at the National Circus School in Montreal.

SYLVAIN LAVOIE is a PhD candidate in the humanities program at Concordia University, working on representations of nature in Canadian drama. He has also studied popular theatrical culture in Europe and Quebec, which led him to guest edit the "Rayonnement du cirque Québécois" special issue for *Spirale*, a magazine where he also writes theatre criticism. He coedited Pierre L'Hérault's writings on theatre, *L'assemblée pensante* (Nota bene, 2009) with Ginette Michaud and Élisabeth Nardout-Lafarge.

LOUIS PATRICK LEROUX is an associate professor at Concordia University and an associate researcher at the National Circus School in Montreal where he also guest teaches performance history and aesthetics. He is the founding director of the Montreal Working Group on Circus Research. He has conducted funded research on Cirque du Soleil's impact on Las Vegas and North American cultural industries, the state and conditions of circus research in Quebec and North America, and circus dramaturgy and creative process. Recent scholarly collections include circus-themed edited issues of *L'Annuaire théâtral* (2009), *Québec Studies* (2014), and a coedited book, *Le jeu des positions: Discours du théâtre québécois* (Nota Bene, 2014).

DEBORAH LESLIE is a professor in the Department of Geography at the University of Toronto. Her research focuses on the role of cultural industries in urban economic development. She has published in a wide variety of journals and has coedited a book for Routledge Press on *Spaces of Vernacular Creativity* (2009). She has done research on a variety of sectors such as fashion, art, and design. Most recently, she has been involved in a study of the Montreal circus with Norma Rantisi.

ISABELLE MAHY is an associate professor in Social and Public Communication at the Université du Québec à Montréal. Prior to academic life, she worked in the corporate sector in research and development as a change management consultant for twenty-five years, mostly in innovation, organizational transformation, and leadership development. After spending a year at Cirque du Soleil with a creative and management team, she wrote *Les coulisses de l'innovation, création et gestion au Cirque du Soleil* (Presses de l'Université de Laval, 2008). She also co-edited *Théorie U – Changement emergent et innovation: Modèles, applications et critique* (Presses de l'Université du Québec, 2012).

NORMA M. RANTISI is a professor in the Department of Geography, Planning and Environment at Concordia University in Montreal. Her research has centred on the social and geographical foundations of creativity for cultural industries, with a focus on apparel. She has published widely in geography and urban studies journals and coedited a book for Routledge titled *Spaces of Vernacular Creativity* (2009). She is completing a research study on the place-based dimensions of creativity and learning in Montreal circus arts with Deborah Leslie.

JENNIFER BETH SPIEGEL holds a PhD in cultural studies from Goldsmiths College, University of London, and is a part-time faculty member at Concordia University in Montreal. She is also a research associate in the International Centre for Arts for Social Change at Simon Fraser University, where she is currently pursuing research on critical theories of art for social change as well as coleading an international, interdisciplinary research project on social circus in Ecuador.

TRACY ZHANG is a Bader postdoctoral fellow in the Department of Film and Media at Queen's University in Kingston, Ontario. She holds a doctorate in communications studies from Simon Fraser University. Her ongoing project examines Chinese acrobatics as an institution and a cultural medium that has evolved from a popular form of entertainment to a socialist performing art, and finally to one of China's most profitable cultural exports. Her most recent publication is "Bending the Body for China: The Uses of Acrobatics in Sino-US Diplomacy," *International Journal of Cultural Policy* (2014). This article won the 2015 award from the Fonds de recherche du Québec for best original research paper.

Index